ANNUAL EDITIONS

Management

Fourteenth Edition

EDITOR

Fred H. Maidment

Western Connecticut State University

Dr. Fred Maidment is Professor of Management at Western Connecticut State University in Danbury, Connecticut. He received his bachelor's degree from New York University and his master's degree from the Bernard M. Baruch College of the City University of New York. In 1983 Dr. Maidment received his doctorate from the University of South Carolina. He resides in Connecticut with his wife.

2460 Kerper Blvd., Dubuque, IA 52001

Visit us on the Internet
http://www.mhcls.com

Credits

1. **Managers, Performance, and the Environment**
   Unit photo—Artville/Getty Images
2. **Planning**
   Unit photo—Royalty-Free/CORBIS
3. **Organizing**
   Unit photo—Ryan McVay/Getty Images
4. **Directing**
   Unit photo—Ryan McVay/Getty Images
5. **Controlling**
   Unit photo—Walter Hodges/Getty Images
6. **Staffing and Human Resources**
   Unit photo—Digital Vision
7. **Perspectives and Trends**
   Unit photo—Image Source/Getty Images

Copyright

Cataloging in Publication Data
Main entry under title: Annual Editions: Management. 14th Edition.
1. Management—Periodicals. I. Maidment, Fred, *comp.* II. Title: Management.
ISBN-13: 978–0–07–352844–1 ISBN-10: 0–07–352844–7 658'.05 ISSN 1092–4876

Fourteenth Edition

Cover images Photos.com
Printed in the United States of America 1234567890QPDQPD9876 Printed on Recycled Paper

Editors/Advisory Board

Members of the Advisory Board are instrumental in the final selection of articles for each edition of ANNUAL EDITIONS. Their review of articles for content, level, currentness, and appropriateness provides critical direction to the editor and staff. We think that you will find their careful consideration well reflected in this volume.

Preface

In publishing ANNUAL EDITIONS we recognize the enormous role played by the magazines, newspapers, and journals of the public press in providing current, first-rate educational information in a broad spectrum of interest areas. Many of these articles are appropriate for students, researchers, and professionals seeking accurate, current material to help bridge the gap between principles and theories and the real world. These articles, however, become more useful for study when those of lasting value are carefully collected, organized, indexed, and reproduced in a low-cost format, which provides easy and permanent access when the material is needed. That is the role played by ANNUAL EDITIONS.

Management is evolving into a highly exciting and diverse profession. Managers are the people charged with getting things done in today's society—a society that has been molded by the success of the management profession. The world faces many new challenges, and those challenges will be met, at least in part, by managers.

Some of those challenges will include dealing with the new environment that began when the United States was attacked by terrorists on September 11, 2001. This attack ushered in a new era for western society, as well as for the businesses and corporations that have flourished in the capitalist environment provided by the democracies. Things are going to change both in the United States and abroad and managers are going to be involved in those changes.

Managers must respond to a changing environment by keeping informed on the developments in the field. The articles that have been chosen for *Annual Editions: Management 14/e* represent a cross section of the current writings on the subject with a few selected classics. This collection addresses the various components of management with emphasis on the functions of planning, organizing, directing, controlling, and staffing. Readings have been chosen from a wide variety of publications, including *The Harvard Business Review, Vital Speeches of the Day, Across the Board,* and *Business Horizons.*

This publication contains a number of features designed to make it useful for people interested in management. These features include a *topic guide* for locating articles on a specific subject and a *table of contents* with *abstracts* that summarize each article, highlighting key ideas in bold italics. Also, there are selected Internet Reference sites that can be used to further explore the topics. These sites are cross-referenced by number in the topic guide.

This volume is organized into seven units, each dealing with specific interrelated topics in management. Each unit begins with an overview that provides the necessary background information that allows the reader to place the selections in the context of the book. Important topics are emphasized, and *key points to consider* address major themes.

This is the fourteenth edition of *Annual Editions: Management,* and we hope that it will be one of a long line of books addressing the evolution of management. This collection, we believe, provides the reader with the most complete and current selection of readings available on the subject. We would like to know what you think. Please take a few minutes to complete and return the postage-paid article rating form at the back of the volume. Any book can be improved, and we need your help to improve *Annual Editions: Management.*

Fred H. Maidment

Contents

UNIT 1
Managers, Performance, and the Environment

The concepts in bold italics are developed in the article. For further expansion, please refer to the Topic Guide and the Index.

UNIT 2
Planning

UNIT 3
Organizing

The concepts in bold italics are developed in the article. For further expansion, please refer to the Topic Guide and the Index.

UNIT 4
Directing

The concepts in bold italics are developed in the article. For further expansion, please refer to the Topic Guide and the Index.

UNIT 5
Controlling

UNIT 6
Staffing and Human Resources

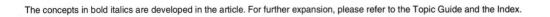

The concepts in bold italics are developed in the article. For further expansion, please refer to the Topic Guide and the Index.

UNIT 7
Perspectives and Trends

The concepts in bold italics are developed in the article. For further expansion, please refer to the Topic Guide and the Index.

The concepts in bold italics are developed in the article. For further expansion, please refer to the Topic Guide and the Index.

The concepts in bold italics are developed in the article. For further expansion, please refer to the Topic Guide and the Index.

Topic Guide

This topic guide suggests how the selections in this book relate to the subjects covered in your course. You may want to use the topics listed on these pages to search the Web more easily.

On the following pages a number of Web sites have been gathered specifically for this book. They are arranged to reflect the units of this *Annual Edition*. You can link to these sites by going to the student online support site at *http://www.mhcls.com/online/*.

ALL THE ARTICLES THAT RELATE TO EACH TOPIC ARE LISTED BELOW THE BOLD-FACED TERM.

Accounting

6. Choose the Right Tools for Internal Control Reporting
13. The Change-Capable Organization
21. Zero In on the Numbers
26. The Health-Care Tussle

Balanced scorecard

2. Success in Management
12. The Dark Side of Change
16. The True Measure of a CEO
19. Disaster's Future
41. In Fourth Year of 'War on Terror': Successes, Failures, Blowback from Iraq.

Benefits

4. It's a Flat World, After All
5. Globalization and the American Labor Force
13. The Change-Capable Organization
20. An Uneasy Look at Performance Appraisal
25. Management Women and the New Facts of Life
26. The Health-Care Tussle
29. Turning Boomers Into Boomerangs
35. The Real Reason You're Working So Hard...and What You Can Do About It.

Blue-collar jobs

4. It's a Flat World, After All
5. Globalization and the American Labor Force
16. The True Measure of a CEO
18. Can One Man Save GM?

Business environment

2. Success in Management
3. The New Organisation
4. It's a Flat World, After All
5. Globalization and the American Labor Force
7. Let's Be Friends
8. Embracing Confusion: What Leaders Do When They Don't Know What to Do
9. Why Environmental Scanning Works Except When You Need It
12. The Dark Side of Change
13. The Change-Capable Organization
14. Build Your Own Change Model
16. The True Measure of a CEO
17. The Myth of Charismatic Leaders
18. Can One Man Save GM?
22. Corporate Security Management: What's Common? What Works?
23. Quality Is Easy
25. Management Women and the New Facts of Life
26. The Health-Care Tussle
29. Turning Boomers Into Boomerangs
30. Do Americans Work Too Hard?
32. Thinking Locally, Succeeding Globally
33. The Great Wal-Mart of China
35. The Real Reason You're Working So Hard...and What You Can Do About It.
36. For New "Old Boys" Only
37. The Tone at the Top and Ethical Conduct Connection
38. The Road to Stronger Corporate Governance
39. Up to the Challenge

Business ethics

2. Success in Management
7. Let's Be Friends
12. The Dark Side of Change
16. The True Measure of a CEO
20. An Uneasy Look at Performance Appraisal
22. Corporate Security Management: What's Common? What Works?
25. Management Women and the New Facts of Life
27. Who Are You Really Hiring?
35. The Real Reason You're Working So Hard...and What You Can Do About It.
37. The Tone at the Top and Ethical Conduct Connection
38. The Road to Stronger Corporate Governance

Business leadership

2. Success in Management
3. The New Organisation
4. It's a Flat World, After All
7. Let's Be Friends
8. Embracing Confusion: What Leaders Do When They Don't Know What to Do
9. Why Environmental Scanning Works Except When You Need It
12. The Dark Side of Change
13. The Change-Capable Organization
14. Build Your Own Change Model
16. The True Measure of a CEO
17. The Myth of Charismatic Leaders
18. Can One Man Save GM?
19. Disaster's Future
23. Quality Is Easy
32. Thinking Locally, Succeeding Globally
33. The Great Wal-Mart of China
34. American Corporations: The New Sovereigns
35. The Real Reason You're Working So Hard...and What You Can Do About It.
36. For New "Old Boys" Only
37. The Tone at the Top and Ethical Conduct Connection
38. The Road to Stronger Corporate Governance
39. Up to the Challenge

Codes of conduct

16. The True Measure of a CEO
22. Corporate Security Management: What's Common? What Works?
23. Quality Is Easy
35. The Real Reason You're Working So Hard...and What You Can Do About It.
37. The Tone at the Top and Ethical Conduct Connection
38. The Road to Stronger Corporate Governance

Communication

1. The Manager's Job: Folklore and Fact
2. Success in Management
3. The New Organisation
4. It's a Flat World, After All
5. Globalization and the American Labor Force
6. Choose the Right Tools for Internal Control Reporting
7. Let's Be Friends
8. Embracing Confusion: What Leaders Do When They Don't Know What to Do

Competitive advantage

Consumer power

Consumer protection

Corporate leadership

Corporate strategy

Discipline

Entrepreneurship

Feedback

Internet References

The following Internet sites have been carefully researched and selected to support the articles found in this reader. The easiest way to access these selected sites is to go to our student online support site at *http://www.mhcls.com/online/*.

AE: Management

The following sites were available at the time of publication. Visit our Web site—we update our student online support site regularly to reflect any changes.

General Sources

The New York Times

http://www.nytimes.com

Browsing through the extensive archives of the *New York Times* will provide you with a vast array of articles and information related to management issues.

STAT-USA

http://www.stat-usa.gov/stat-usa.html

This site, a service of the U.S. Department of Commerce, contains daily economic news, frequently requested statistical releases, information on export and international trade, domestic economic news, statistical series, and databases. Also try *http://www.fedstats.gov* for statistics produced by more than 70 U.S. federal government agencies.

The Wall Street Journal

http://interactive.wsj.com

This is an Internet edition of the *Wall Street Journal,* a newspaper that is used by managers the world over to put their business environments in context.

Workforce Online

http://www.workforceonline.com

This site, sponsored by *Workforce* magazine, discusses trends and resources, legal information, and fluctuating pay methods data, and it also offers a research center.

UNIT 1: Managers, Performance, and the Environment

Krislyn's Favorite Advertising & Marketing Sites

http://www.krislyn.com/sites/adv.htm

This extensive list of Web sites includes information on marketing research, marketing on the Internet, demographic sources, organizations, and associations. The site also features current books on business management and marketing.

Two Scenarios for 21st Century Organizations

http://ccs.mit.edu/21c/21CWP001.html

The MIT Scenario Working Group here presents "Shifting Networks of Small Firms" and "All-Encompassing 'Virtual Countries'" that will be of interest to any company involved in organizing and structuring to meet the demands of the new business environment.

UNIT 2: Planning

Benchmarking Network

http://www.well.com/user/benchmar/tbnhome.html

This Web site is an international resource guide to benchmarking as a method of corporate planning.

UNIT 3: Organizing

From Foosball to Flextime: Dotcommers Are Growing Up

http://www.fastcompany.com/articles/2000/12/act_childcare.html

This article by Cecilia Rothenberger explains how dot.com companies are maturing and providing flextime, on-site day care, and other benefits that "grown-up" companies have provided for years.

Sympatico: Careers

http://www.ntl.sympatico.ca/Contents/Careers/

This Canadian media site provides an electronic network with a "GripeVine" for complaining about work and finding solutions to everyday career problems.

U.S. Department of Labor (DOL)

http://www.dol.gov

Browsing through this DOL site will lead you to a vast array of labor-related data and discussions of issues affecting managers, such as the minimum wage. It presents statutory and regulatory information, and more.

Work and Organizational Psychology, Stockholm University

http://www.psychology.su.se/units/ao/ao.html

Explore topics related to job design and other management organizational concerns through this site presented by Stockholm University's Department of Psychology, Division of Work and Organizational Psychology.

UNIT 4: Directing

ADR (Alternative Dispute Resolution): General

http://www.opm.gov/er/adrguide/

Essays on the subject of alternative dispute resolution can be found at this page, which includes an ADR glossary, a definition, techniques and evaluations, issues and problems facing judges, evaluation of ADR procedures, and much more information important to the area of conflict management.

Equity Compensation, Employee Ownership & Stock Options

http://www.fed.org

The Foundation for Enterprise Development is a nonprofit organization that suggests strategies to those who are making critical decisions to improve their companies' bottom lines. This site includes interactive resources and case studies.

UNIT 5: Controlling

Bill Lindsay's Home Page

http://www.nku.edu/~lindsay/

Professor William M. Lindsay's home page points to a variety of interesting Internet sources to aid in the study and application of Total Quality Management principles.

Computer and Network Security

http://www.vtcif.telstra.com.au/info/security.html

Telstra provides this index for those interested in technology/security issues. It provides links to Web sources, including commercial, educational, and government materials.

Internal Auditing World Wide Web

http://www.bitwise.net/iawww/

Valuable news, resources, events, and associations related to business auditing topics are provided here.

Office of Financial Management

http://www.doi.gov/

This site of the Office of Financial Management, in the U.S. Department of the Interior, describes its financial policy and procedures, financial reporting, management control program, accounting policy and systems, and auditing follow-up.

Total Quality Leadership (TQL) vs. Management by Results

http://deming.eng.clemson.edu/pub/den/files/tql.txt

Brian L. Joiner and Peter R. Scholtes describe the reasons why the TQL system of management should replace management by results for most companies, whether small or large. It addresses such concerns as how TQL can improve customer service and return on investment, lead to higher productivity and more jobs, and affect utilization of information technology.

Workplace Violence

http://www.osha-slc.gov/SLTC/workplaceviolence/

The Occupational Safety & Health Administration (OSHA) maintains this site, which provides information and resources on workplace violence. OSHA has developed guidelines and recommendations to reduce worker exposure to this hazard.

UNIT 6: Staffing and Human Resources

Electronic Frontier Foundation "Privacy" Archive

http://www.eff.org

This civil liberties organization site provides links to articles, FAQs, and databases having to do with protection of privacy and free expression in the workplace. Drug testing and electronic communications privacy are explored.

School of Labor and Industrial Relations Hot Links

http://www.lir.msu.edu/hotlinks

This page links to government statistics, newspapers, libraries, and international intergovernmental organizations.

U.S. Equal Employment Opportunity Commission

http://www.eeoc.gov

Consult this site for small-business information, facts about employment discrimination, and enforcement and litigation.

UNIT 7: Perspective and Trends

Institute for International Economics

http://www.iie.com

The site of this nonpartisan research institution, devoted to the study of international economics, contains views, reviews, working papers, publications, and press releases.

Small Business Management

http://management.tqn.com/msubs.htm

Information on how to start and effectively manage a small business is available on this site.

Terrorism Research Center

http://www.terrorism.com

The Terrorism Research Center features original research, counterterrorism documents, a comprehensive list of Web links, and monthly profiles of terrorist and counterterrorist groups.

World Trade Organization (WTO) Web Site

http://www.wto.org/index.htm

The home page of the WTO contains a wealth of information: click on About the WTO, Site Map, Search, and Links to Related Organizations.

We highly recommend that you review our Web site for expanded information and our other product lines. We are continually updating and adding links to our Web site in order to offer you the most usable and useful information that will support and expand the value of your Annual Editions. You can reach us at: *http://www.mhcls.com/annualeditions/.*

UNIT 1

Managers, Performance, and the Environment

Unit Selections

1. **The Manager's Job: Folklore and Fact**, Henry Mintzberg
2. **Success in Management**, Anne M. Mulcahy
3. **The New Organisation**, The Economist
4. **It's a Flat World, After All**, Thomas L. Friedman
5. **Globalization and the American Labor Force**, Fred Maidment

Key Points to Consider

- What do you think of the manager's job? Do you think it is only to plan, direct, organize, control, and staff, or does he or she do other things? Explain.
- Do you think the manager's job is likely to change in the 21st century? In what ways?
- How do you think the environment is going to change for business and other organizations in the coming years? Do you think that change will increase or decrease in speed? Explain your answer.
- How do you think conditions will change for American industry and American workers in the 21st century? What do you think American workers can do about it? What can government policymakers do about it?

Student Website

www.mhcls.com/online

Internet References

Further information regarding these websites may be found in this book's preface or online.

Krislyn's Favorite Advertising & Marketing Sites
http://www.krislyn.com/sites/adv.htm

Two Scenarios for 21st Century Organizations
http://ccs.mit.edu/21c/21CWP001.html

The need for management has been recognized since the early days of civilization and the concepts of leadership, administration, and management have existed since at least before the time of Plato. Some of the early modern writers in management include Frederick W. Taylor, Elton Mayo, and Mary Parker Follett. These people helped to establish the basis of modern management theory during the first part of the twentieth century.

Management has come a long way since the days of Taylor, Mayo, and Follett. The techniques and theories that they and their successors helped to develop have contributed to the establishment of industrialized countries as major forces in the world. These ideas helped American culture dominate the better part of the twentieth century and the success of western concepts is even now being seen in Eastern Europe and the republics of the former Soviet Union. Management—the way people arrange their lives and businesses—is a major part of the success that capitalism is currently enjoying. The failure that the communist system experienced in the former Soviet bloc was not a failure of industrialism, rather it was a failure of a system that unsuccessfully attempted to use that industrial base. This was not a failure of the machines or the workers that comprised the system but of the way the system operated and managed the equipment and people. It was a situation that people of those countries would no longer tolerate as they rushed to embrace capitalism, democracy, pluralism, and finally management as keys to their future in the twenty-first century.

As a discipline, management faces new challenges. These challenges are mostly the result of management's success. They include the transformation of the American economy from one based upon industrialization to one based upon knowledge, and the challenge of other economies—in particular, the newly integrated Europe and the developing economies of Asia. Another challenge is the new role of managers and management as more women, African Americans, Hispanic Americans, and other minorities, as well as more demanding groups of workers with different expectations, enter the workforce. This will be true not only in the United States but in the rest of the world as discussed in "It's a Flat World, After All," and "Globalization and the American Labor Force."

Management is responding to these challenges in various ways. New ideas are constantly being projected in the midst of the chaos that is the legacy of the post–cold war world. Times have indeed changed, and the tools necessary to meet those changes are only now being developed. Some of these tools and techniques will have a lasting impact on the way managers perform their jobs, but others will be merely passing fads.

The new economy and the forms it will support will be very different from the environment of the past. "Success in Management" must be analyzed to determine the reasons many organizations crashed during the burst in the stock market bubble and what can be done to make strong organizations again. The dominating strength of corporations will be based on brains, not brawn; the economic system will be international, not national, in scope; and competition will be even more fierce while an organization's competitive advantage in the marketplace will be even more fleeting. Only those organizations and managers that are strong will be able to meet the challenges of the future as seen in "The New Organisation."

Organizations will need managers who can think clearly, and are capable of dealing with the changes in all kinds of environments. But first, it will be necessary to restore the confidence that has been lost by Americans as a result of the recent scandals in industry. Future organizations that think, create, and adapt to the changing conditions of an increasingly fluid environment are the ones that will survive and be successful.

America's new economy and the managers who plan, direct, organize, control, and staff its businesses must provide new, different, and creative approaches to meet the new competitive global environment. This will require better products and services, produced and marketed with improved, more efficient methods. Organizations no longer compete only domestically, as they did in the 1950s when General Motors, Ford, and Chrysler dominated an American auto industry that also included such names as Studebaker-Packard, Hudson, Desoto, and Nash. Today, Ford and GM must compete on an international basis with Diamler Chrysler and names like Nissan, Toyota, Honda, Volkswagen, and BMW, while Plymouth and Oldsmobile are now gone. Corporations the world over must meet these new conditions or accept the fate of past organizations and follow Studebaker on the road to oblivion.

The Manager's Job: Folklore and Fact

The classical view says that the manager organizes, coordinates, plans, and controls; the facts suggest otherwise.

Henry Mintzberg

Henry Mintzberg is the Bronfman Professor of Management at McGill University. His latest book is Mintzberg on Management: Inside Our Strange World of Organizations *(Free Press, 1989). This article appeared originally in HBR July–August 1975. It won the McKinsey Award for excellence.*

If you ask managers what they do, they will most likely tell you that they plan, organize, coordinate, and control. Then watch what they do. Don't be surprised if you can't relate what you see to these words.

When a manager is told that a factory has just burned down and then advises the caller to see whether temporary arrangements can be made to supply customers through a foreign subsidiary, is that manager planning, organizing, coordinating, or controlling? How about when he or she presents a gold watch to a retiring employee? Or attends a conference to meet people in the trade and returns with an interesting new product idea for employees to consider?

What do managers do? Even managers themselves don't always know.

These four words, which have dominated management vocabulary since the French industrialist Henri Fayol first introduced them in 1916, tell us little about what managers actually do. At best, they indicate some vague objectives managers have when they work.

The field of management, so devoted to progress and change, has for more than half a century not seriously addressed *the* basic question: What do managers do? Without a proper answer, how can we teach management? How can we design planning or information systems for managers? How can we improve the practice of management at all?

Our ignorance of the nature of managerial work shows up in various ways in the modern organization—in boasts by successful managers who never spent a single day in a management training program; in the turnover of corporate planners who never quite understood what it was the manager wanted; in the computer consoles gathering dust in the back room because the managers never used the fancy on-line MIS some analyst thought they needed. Perhaps most important, our ignorance shows up in the inability of our large public organizations to come to grips with some of their most serious policy problems.

Somehow, in the rush to automate production, to use management science in the functional areas of marketing and finance, and to apply the skills of the behavioral scientist to the problem of worker motivation, the manager—the person in charge of the organization or one of its subunits—has been forgotten.

I intend to break the reader away from Fayol's words and introduce a more supportable and useful description of managerial work. This description derives from my review and synthesis of research on how various managers have spent their time.

In some studies, managers were observed intensively; in a number of others, they kept detailed diaries; in a few studies, their records were analyzed. All kinds of managers were studied—foreman, factory supervisors, staff managers, field sales managers, hospital administrators, presidents of companies and nations, and even street gang leaders. These "managers" worked in the United States, Canada, Sweden, and Great Britain.

A synthesis of these findings paints an interesting picture, one as different from Fayol's classical view as a cubist abstract is from a Renaissance painting. In a sense, this picture will be obvious to anyone who has ever spent a day in a manager's office, either in front of the desk or behind it. Yet, at the same time, this picture throws into doubt much of the folklore that we have accepted about the manager's work.

Folklore and Facts About Managerial Work

There are four myths about the manager's job that do not bear up under careful scrutiny of the facts.

Folklore: The manager is a reflective, systematic planner. The evidence of this issue is overwhelming, but not a shred of it supports this statement.

Fact: Study after study has shown that managers work at a unrelenting pace, that their activities are characterized by brevity, variety, and discontinuity, and that they are strongly oriented to action and dislike reflective activities. Consider this evidence:

Half the activities engaged in by the five chief executives of my study lasted less than nine minutes, and only 10% exceeded one hour.[1] A study of 56 U.S. foremen found that they averaged 583 activities per eight-hour shift, an average of 1 every 48 seconds.[2] The work pace for both chief executives and foremen was unrelenting. The chief executives met a steady stream of callers and mail from the moment they arrived in the morning until they left in the evening. Coffee breaks and lunches were inevitably work related, and ever-present subordinates seemed to usurp any free moment.

How often can you work for a half an hour without interruption?

A diary study of 160 British middle and top managers found that they worked without interruption for a half hour or more only about once every two days.[3]

Of the verbal contacts the chief executives in my study engaged in, 93% were arranged on an ad hoc basis. Only 1% of the executives' time was spent in open-ended observational tours. Only 1 out of 368 verbal contacts was unrelated to a specific issue and could therefore be called general planning. Another researcher found that "in *not one single case* did a manager report obtaining important external information from a general conversation or other undirected personal communication."[4]

Is this the planner that the classical view describes? Hardly. The manager is simply responding to the pressures of the job. I found that my chief executives terminated many of their own activities, often leaving meetings before the end, and interrupted their desk work to call in subordinates. One president not only placed his desk so that he could look down a long hallway but also left his door open when he was alone—an invitation for subordinates to come in and interrupt him.

Clearly, these managers wanted to encourage the flow of current information. But more significantly, they seemed to be conditioned by their own work loads. They appreciated the opportunity cost of their own time, and they were continually aware of their ever-present obligations—mail to be answered, callers to attend to, and so on. It seems that a manager is always plagued by the possibilities of what might be done and what must be done.

When managers must plan, they seem to do so implicitly in the context of daily actions, not in some abstract process reserved for two weeks in the organization's mountain retreat. The plans of the chief executives I studied seemed to exist only in their heads—as flexible, but often specific, intentions. The traditional literature notwithstanding, the job of managing does not breed reflective planners; managers respond to stimuli, they are conditioned by their jobs to prefer live to delayed action.

Folklore: The effective manager has no regular duties to perform. Managers are constantly being told to spend more time planning and delegating and less time seeing customers and engaging in negotiations. These are not, after all, the true tasks of the manager. To use the popular analogy, the good manager, like the good conductor, carefully orchestrates everything in advance, then sits back, responding occasionally to an unforeseeable exception. But here again the pleasant abstraction just does not seem to hold up.

Fact: Managerial work involves performing a number of regular duties, including ritual and ceremony, negotiations, and processing of soft information that links the organization with its environment. Consider some evidence from the research:

A study of the work of the presidents of small companies found that they engaged in routine activities because their companies could not afford staff specialists and were so thin on operating personnel that a single absence often required the president to substitute.[5]

One study of field sales managers and another of chief executives suggest that it is a natural part of both jobs to see important customers, assuming the managers wish to keep those customers.[6]

Someone, only half in jest, once described the manager as the person who sees visitors so that other people can get their work done. In my study, I found that certain ceremonial duties—meeting visiting dignitaries, giving out gold watches, presiding at Christmas dinners—were an intrinsic part of the chief executive's job.

Studies of managers' information flow suggest that managers play a key role in securing "soft" external information (much of it available only to them because of their status) and in passing it along to their subordinates.

Folklore: The senior manager needs aggregated information, which a formal management information system best provides. Not too long ago, the words *total information system* were everywhere in the management literature. In keeping with the classical view of the manager as that individual perched on the apex of a regulated, hierarchical system, the literature's manager was to receive all important information from a giant, comprehensive MIS.

But lately, these giant MIS systems are not working—managers are simply not using them. The enthusiasm has waned. A look at how managers actually process information makes it clear why.

Fact: Managers strongly favor verbal media, telephone calls and meetings, over documents. Consider the following:

In two British studies, managers spent an average of 66% and 80% of their time in verbal (oral) communication.[7] In my study of five American chief executives, the figure was 78%.

These five chief executives treated mail processing as a burden to be dispensed with. One came in Saturday morning to process 142 pieces of mail in just over three hours, to "get rid of all the stuff." This same manager looked at the first piece of "hard" mail he had received all week, a standard cost report, and put it aside with the comment, "I never look at this."

Today's gossip may be tomorrow's fact—that's why managers cherish hearsay.

These same five chief executives responded immediately to 2 of the 40 routine reports they received during the five weeks of my study and to 4 items in the 104 periodicals. They skimmed most of these periodicals in seconds, almost ritualistically. In all, these chief executives of good-sized organizations initiated on their

Research on Managerial Work

In seeking to describe managerial work, I conducted my own research and also scanned the literature to integrate the findings of studies from many diverse sources with my own. These studies focused on two different aspects of managerial work. Some were concerned with the characteristics of work—how long managers work, where, at what pace, with what interruptions, with whom they work, and through what media they communicate. Other studies were concerned with the content of work—what activities the managers actually carry out, and why. Thus, after a meeting, one researcher might note that the manager spent 45 minutes with three government officials in their Washington office, while another might record that the manager presented the company's stand on some proposed legislation in order to change a regulation.

A few of the studies of managerial work are widely known, but most have remained buried as single journal articles or isolated books. Among the more important ones I cite are:

- Sune Carlson developed the diary method to study the work characteristics of nine Swedish managing directors. Each kept a detailed log of his activities. Carlson's results are reported in his book *Executive Behaviour*. A number of British researchers, notably Rosemary Stewart, have subsequently used Carlson's method. In *Managers and Their Jobs*, she describes the study of 160 top and middle managers of British companies.
- Leonard Sayles's book *Managerial Behavior* is another important reference. Using a method he refers to as "anthropological," Sayles studied the work content of middle and lower level managers in a large U.S. corporation. Sayles moved freely in the company, collecting whatever information struck him as important.
- Perhaps the best-known source is *Presidential Power,* in which Richard Neustadt analyzes the power and managerial behavior of Presidents Roosevelt, Truman, and Eisenhower. Neustadt used secondary sources—documents and interviews with other parties.
- Robert H. Guest, in *Personnel,* reports on a study of the foreman's working day. Fifty-six U.S. foremen were observed and each of their activities recorded during one eight-hour shift.
- Richard C. Hodgson, Daniel J. Levinson, and Abraham Zaleznik studied a team of three top executives of a U.S. hospital. From that study they wrote *The Executive Role Constellation.* They addressed the way in which work and socioemotional roles were divided among the three managers.
- William F. Whyte, from his study of a street gang during the Depression, wrote *Street Corner Society*. His findings about the gang's workings and leadership, which George C. Homans analyzed in *The Human Group,* suggest interesting similarities of job content between street gang leaders and corporate managers.

My own study involved five American CEOs of middle- to large-sized organizations—a consulting firm, a technology company, a hospital, a consumer goods company, and a school system. Using a method called "structural observation," during one intensive week of observation for each executive, I recorded various aspects of every piece of mail and every verbal contact. In all, I analyzed 890 pieces of incoming and outgoing mail and 368 verbal contacts.

own—that is, not in response to something else—a grand total of 25 pieces of mail during the 25 days I observed them.

An analysis of the mail the executives received reveals an interesting picture—only 13% was of specific and immediate use. So now we have another piece in the puzzle: not much of the mail provides live, current information—the action of a competitor, the mood of a government legislator, or the rating of last night's television show. Yet this is the information that drove the managers, interrupting their meetings and rescheduling their workdays.

Consider another interesting finding. Managers seem to cherish "soft" information, especially gossip, hearsay, and speculation. Why? The reason is its timeliness; today's gossip may be tomorrow's fact. The manager who misses the telephone call revealing that the company's biggest customer was seen golfing with a main competitor may read about a dramatic drop in sales in the next quarterly report. But then it's too late.

To assess the value of historical, aggregated, "hard" MIS information, consider two of the managers's prime uses for information—to identify problems and opportunities[8] and to build mental models (e.g., how the organization's budget system works, how customers buy products, how changes in the economy affect the organization). The evidence suggests that the manager identifies decision situations and builds models not with the aggregated abstractions an MIS provides but with specific tidbits of data.

Consider the words of Richard Neustadt, who studied the information-collecting habits of Presidents Roosevelt, Truman, and Eisenhower: "It is not information of a general sort that helps a President see personal stakes; not summaries, not surveys, not the *bland amalgams*. Rather… it is the odds and ends of *tangible detail* that pieced together in his mind illuminate the underside of issues put before him. To help himself he must reach out as widely as he can for every scrap of fact, opinion, gossip, bearing on his interests and relationships as President. He must become his own director of his own central intelligence."[9]

The manager's emphasis on this verbal media raises two important points. First, verbal information is stored in the brains of people. Only when people write this information down can it be stored in the files of the organization—whether in metal cabinets or on magnetic tape—and managers apparently do not write down much of what they hear. Thus the strategic data bank of the organization is not in the memory of its computers but in the minds of its managers.

Second, managers' extensive use of verbal media helps to explain why they are reluctant to delegate tasks. It is not as if they can hand a dossier over to subordinates; they must take the time to "dump memory"—to tell subordinates all about the subject. But this could take so long that managers may find it easier to do the task themselves. Thus they are damned by their own information system to a "dilemma of delegation"—to do too much or to delegate to subordinates with inadequate briefing.

Folklore: Management is, or at least is quickly becoming, a science and a profession. By almost any definition of *science* and *profession*, this statement is false. Brief observation of any manager will quickly lay to rest the notion that managers practice a science. A science involves the enaction of systematic, analytically determined procedures or programs. If we do not even know what procedures managers use, how can we prescribe them by scientific analysis? And how can we call management a profession if we cannot specify what managers are to learn? For after all, a profession involves "knowledge of some department of learning or science" (*Random House Dictionary*).[10]

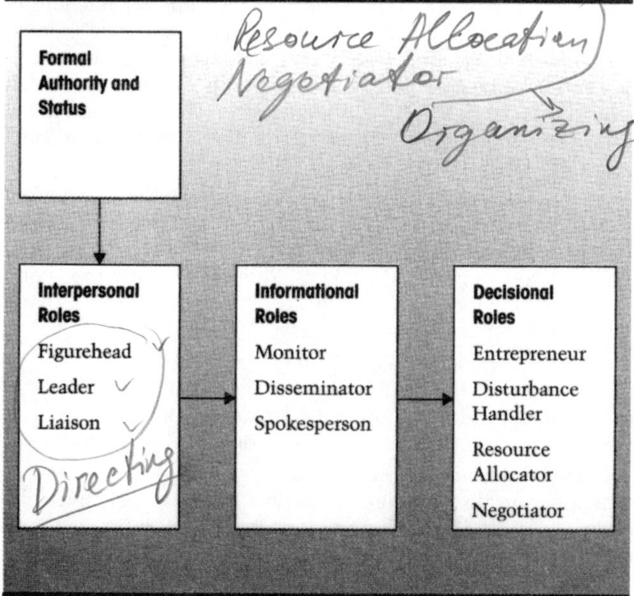

Fact: The managers' programs—to schedule time, process information, make decisions, and so on—remain locked deep inside their brains. Thus, to describe these programs, we rely on words like *judgment* and *intuition*, seldom stopping to realize that they are merely labels for our ignorance.

I was struck during my study by the fact that the executives I was observing—all very competent—are fundamentally indistinguishable from their counterparts of a hundred years ago (or a thousand years ago). The information they need differs, but they seek it in the same way—by word of mouth. Their decisions concern modern technology, but the procedures they use to make those decisions are the same as the procedures used by nineteenth century managers. Even the computer, so important for the specialized work of the organization, has apparently had no influence on the work procedures of general managers. In fact, the manager is in a kind of loop, with increasingly heavy work pressures but no aid forthcoming from management science.

Considering the facts about managerial work, we can see that the manager's job is enormously complicated and difficult. Managers are overburdened with obligations yet cannot easily delegate their tasks. As a result, they are driven to overwork and forced to do many tasks superficially. Brevity, fragmentation, and verbal communication characterize their work. Yet these are the very characteristics of managerial work that have impeded scientific attempts to improve it. As a result, management scientists have concentrated on the specialized functions of the organization, where it is easier to analyze the procedures and quantify the relevant information.[11]

But the pressures of a manager's job are becoming worse. Where before managers needed to respond only to owners and directors, now they find that subordinates with democratic norms continually reduce their freedom to issue unexplained orders, and a growing number of outside influences (consumer groups, government agencies, and so on) demand attention. Managers have had nowhere to turn for help. The first step in providing such help is to find out what the manager's job really is.

Back to a Basic Description of Managerial Work

Earlier, I defined the manager as that person in charge of an organization or subunit. Besides CEOs, this definition would include vice presidents, bishops, foremen, hockey coaches, and prime ministers. All these "managers" are vested with formal authority over an organizational unit. From formal authority comes status, which leads to various interpersonal relations, and from these comes access to information. Information, in turn, enables the manager to make decisions and strategies for the unit.

The manager's job can be described in terms of various "roles," or organized sets of behaviors identified with a position. My description, shown in "The Manager's Roles," comprises ten roles. As we shall see, formal authority gives rise to the three interpersonal roles, which in turn give rise to the three informational roles; these two sets of roles enable the manager to play the four decisional roles.

Interpersonal Roles

Three of the manager's roles arise directly from formal authority and involve basic interpersonal relationships. First is the *figurehead* role. As the head of an organizational unit, every manager must perform some ceremonial duties. The president greets the touring dignitaries. The foreman attends the wedding of a lathe operator. The sales manager takes an important customer to lunch.

The chief executives of my study spent 12% of their contact time on ceremonial duties; 17% of their incoming mail dealt with acknowledgments and requests related to their status. For example, a letter to a company president requested free merchandise for a crippled schoolchild; diplomas that needed to be signed were put on the desk of the school superintendent.

Duties that involve interpersonal roles may sometimes be routine, involving little serious communication and no important decision making. Nevertheless, they are important to the smooth functioning of an organization and cannot be ignored.

Managers are responsible for the work of the people of their unit. Their actions in this regard constitute the *leader* role. Some of these actions involve leadership directly—for example, in most organizations the managers are normally responsible for hiring and training their own staff.

In addition, there is the indirect exercise of the leader role. For example, every manager must motivate and encourage employees, somehow reconciling their individual needs with the goals of the organization. In virtually every contact with the manager, subordinates seeking leadership clues ask: "Does she approve?" "How would she like the report to turn out?" "Is she more interested in market share than high profits?"

The influence of managers is most clearly seen in the leader role. Formal authority vests them with great potential power; leadership determines in large part how much of it they will realize.

The literature of management has always recognized the leader role, particularly those aspects of it related to motivation. In comparison, until recently it has hardly mentioned the *liaison* role, in which the manager makes contacts outside the vertical chain of command. This is remarkable in light of the finding of virtually every study of managerial work that managers spend as much time with peers and other people outside their units as they do with their own subordinates—and, surprisingly, very little time with their own superiors.

In Rosemary Stewart's diary study, the 160 British middle and top managers spent 47% of their time with peers, 41% of their time with people inside their unit, and only 12% of their time with their superiors. For Robert H. Guest's study of U.S. foremen, the figures were 44%, 46%, and 10%. The chief executives of my study averaged 44% of their contact time with people outside their organizations, 48% with subordinates, and 7% with directors and trustees.

The contacts the five CEOs made were with an incredibly wide range of people: subordinates; clients, business associates, and

The Chief Executive's Contacts

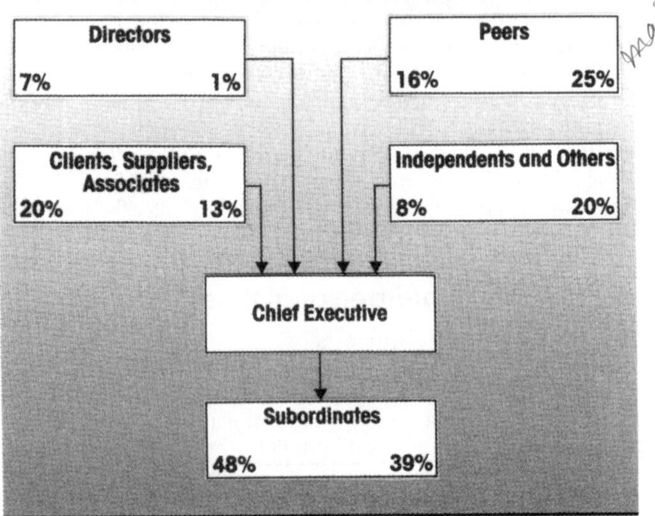

Note: The first figure indicates the proportion of total contact time spent with each group and the second figure, the proportion of mail from each group.

suppliers; and peers—managers of similar organizations, government and trade organization officials, fellow directors on outside boards, and independents with no relevant organizational affiliations. The chief executives' time with and mail from these groups is shown in "The Chief Executive's Contacts." Guest's study of foremen shows, likewise, that their contacts were numerous and wide-ranging, seldom involving fewer than 25 individuals, and often more than 50.

Informational Roles

By virtue of interpersonal contacts, both with subordinates and with a network of contacts, the manager emerges as the nerve center of the organizational unit. The manager may not know everything but typically knows more than subordinates do.

Studies have shown this relationship to hold for all managers, from street gang leaders to U.S. presidents. In *The Human Group*, George C. Homans explains how, because they were at the center of the information flow in their own gangs and were also in close touch with other gang leaders, street gang leaders were better informed than any of their followers.[12] As for presidents, Richard Neustadt observes: "The essence of [Franklin] Roosevelt's technique for information-gathering was competition. 'He would call you in,' one of his aides once told me, 'and he'd ask you to get the story on some complicated business, and you'd come back after a couple of days of hard labor and present the juicy morsel you'd uncovered under a stone somewhere, and *then* you'd find out he knew all about it, along with something else you *didn't* know. Where he got this information from he wouldn't mention, usually, but after he had done this to you once or twice you got damn careful about *your* information.'"[13]

We can see where Roosevelt "got this information" when we consider the relationship between the interpersonal and informational roles. As leader, the manager has formal and easy access to every staff member. In addition, liaison contacts expose the manager to external information to which subordinates often lack access. Many of these contacts are with other managers of equal status, who are themselves nerve centers in their own organization. In this way, the manager develops a powerful database of information.

Processing information is a key part of the manager's job. In my study, the CEOs spent 40% of their contact time on activities devoted exclusively to the transmission of information; 70% of their incoming mail was purely informational (as opposed to requests for action). Managers don't leave meetings or hang up the telephone to get back to work. In large part, communication *is* their work. Three roles describe these informational aspects of managerial work.

As *monitor*, the manager is perpetually scanning the environment for information, interrogating liaison contacts and subordinates, and receiving unsolicited information, much of it as a result of the network of personal contacts. Remember that a good part of the information the manager collects in the monitor role arrives in verbal form, often as gossip, hearsay, and speculation.

In the *disseminator* role, the manager passes some privileged information directly to subordinates, who would otherwise have no access to it. When subordinates lack easy contact with one another, the manager may pass information from one to another.

In the *spokesperson* role, the manager sends some information to people outside the unit—a president makes a speech to lobby for an organization cause, or a foreman suggests a product modification to a supplier. In addition, as a spokesperson, every manager must inform and satisfy the influential people who control the organizational unit. For the foreman, this may simply involve keeping the plant manager informed about the flow of work through the shop.

The president of a large corporation, however, may spend a great amount of time dealing with a host of influences. Directors and shareholders must be advised about finances; consumer groups must be assured that the organization is fulfilling its social responsibilities; and government officials must be satisfied that the organization is abiding by the law.

Decisional Roles

Information is not, of course, an end in itself; it is the basic input to decision making. One thing is clear in the study of managerial work: the manager plays the major role in the unit's decision-making system. As its formal authority, only the manager can commit the unit to important new courses of action; and as its nerve center, only the manager has full and current information to make the set of decisions that determines the unit's strategy. Four roles describe the manager as decision maker.

As *entrepreneur*, the manager seeks to improve the unit, to adapt it to changing conditions in the environment. In the monitor role, a president is constantly on the lookout for new ideas. When a good one appears, he initiates a development project that he may supervise himself or delegate to an employee (perhaps with the stipulation that he must approve the final proposal).

The scarcest resource managers have to allocate is their own time.

There are two interesting features about these development projects at the CEO level. First, these projects do not involve single decisions or even unified clusters of decisions. Rather, they emerge as a series of small decisions and actions sequenced over time. Apparently, chief executives prolong each project both to fit

Retrospective Commentary

Henry Mintzberg

Over the years, one reaction has dominated the comments I have received from managers who read "The Manager's Job: Folklore and Fact": "You make me feel so good. I thought all those other managers were planning, organizing, coordinating, and controlling, while I was busy being interrupted, jumping from one issue to another, and trying to keep the lid on the chaos." Yet everything in this article must have been patently obvious to these people. Why such a reaction to reading what they already knew?

Conversely, how to explain the very different reaction of two media people who called to line up interviews after an article based on this one appeared in the *New York Times*. "Are we glad someone finally let managers have it," both said in passing, a comment that still takes me aback. True, they had read only the account in the *Times*, but that no more let managers have it than did this article. Why that reaction?

One explanation grows out of the way I now see this article—as proposing not so much another view of management as another face of it. I like to call it the insightful face, in contrast to the long-dominant professional or cerebral face. One stresses commitment, the other calculation; one sees the world with integrated perspective, the other figures it as the components of a portfolio. The cerebral face operates with the words and numbers of rationality; the insightful face is rooted in the images and feel of a manager's integrity.

Each of these faces implies a different kind of "knowing," and that, I believe, explains many managers' reaction to this article. Rationally, they "knew" what managers did—planned, organized, coordinated, and controlled. But deep down that did not feel quite right. The description in this article may have come closer to what they really "knew." As for those media people, they weren't railing against management as such but against the cerebral form of management, so pervasive, that they saw impersonalizing the world around them.

In practice, management has to be two-faced—there has to be a balance between the cerebral and the insightful. So, for example, I realized originally that managerial communication was largely oral and that the advent of the computer had not changed anything fundamental in the executive suite—a conclusion I continue to hold. (The greatest threat the personal computer poses is that managers will take it seriously and come to believe that they can manage by remaining in their offices and looking at displays of digital characters.) But I also thought that the dilemma of delegating could be dealt with by periodic debriefings—disseminating words. Now, however, I believe that managers need more ways to convey the images and impressions they carry inside of them. This explains the renewed interest in strategic vision, in culture, and in the roles of intuition and insight in management.

The ten roles I used to describe the manager's job also reflect management's cerebral face, in that they decompose the job more than capture the integration. Indeed, my effort to show a sequence among these roles now seems more consistent with the traditional face of management work than an insightful one. Might we not just as well say that people throughout the organization take actions that inform managers who, by making sense of those actions, develop images and visions that inspire people to subsequent efforts?

Perhaps my greatest disappointment about the research reported here is that it did not stimulate new efforts. In a world so concerned with management, much of the popular literature is superficial and the academic research pedestrian. Certainly, many studies have been carried out over the last 15 years, but the vast majority sought to replicate earlier research. In particular, we remain grossly ignorant about the fundamental content of the manager's job and have barely addressed the major issues and dilemmas in its practice.

But superficiality is not only a problem of the literature. It is also an occupational hazard of the manager's job. Originally, I believed this problem could be dealt with; now I see it as inherent in the job. This is because managing insightfully depends on the direct experience and personal knowledge that come from intimate contact. But in organizations grown larger and more diversified, that becomes difficult to achieve. And so managers turn increasingly to the cerebral face, and the delicate balance between the two faces is lost.

Certainly, some organizations manage to sustain their humanity despite their large size—as Tom Peters and Robert Waterman show in their book *In Search of Excellence*. But that book attained its outstanding success precisely because it is about the exceptions, about the organizations so many of us long to be a part of—not the organization in which we actually work.

Fifteen years ago, I stated that "No job is more vital to our society than that of the manager. It is the manager who determines whether our social institutions serve us well or whether they squander our talents and resources." Now, more than ever, we must strip away the folklore of the manager's job and begin to face its difficult facts.

---

it into a busy, disjointed schedule, and so that they can comprehend complex issues gradually.

Second, the chief executives I studied supervised as many as 50 of these projects at the same time. Some projects entailed new products or processes; others involved public relations campaigns, improvement of the cash position, reorganization of a weak department, resolution of a morale problem in a foreign division, integration of computer operations, various acquisitions at different stages of development, and so on.

Chief executives appear to maintain a kind of inventory of the development projects in various stages of development. Like jugglers, they keep a number of projects in the air; periodically, one comes down, is given a new burst of energy, and sent back into orbit. At various intervals, they put new projects on-stream and discard old ones.

While the entrepreneur role describes the manager as the voluntary initiator of change, the *disturbance handler* role depicts the manager involuntarily responding to pressures. Here change is beyond the manager's control. The pressures of a situation are too severe to be ignored—a strike looms, a major customer has gone bankrupt, or a supplier reneges on a contract—so the manager must act.

Leonard R. Sayles, who has carried out appropriate research on the manager's job, likens the manager to a symphony orchestra conductor who must "maintain a melodious performance,"[14] while handling musicians' problems and other external distur-

Self-Study Questions for Managers

1. Where do I get my information, and how? Can I make greater use of my contacts? Can other people do some of my scanning? In what areas is my knowledge weakest, and how can I get others to provide me with the information I need? Do I have sufficiently powerful mental models of those things I must understand within the organization and in its environment?

2. What information do I disseminate? How important is that information to my subordinates? Do I keep too much information to myself because disseminating it is time consuming or inconvenient? How can I get more information to others so they can make better decisions?

3. Do I tend to act before information is in? Or do I wait so long for all the information that opportunities pass me by?

4. What pace of change am I asking my organization to tolerate? Is this change balanced so that our operations are neither excessively static nor overly disrupted? Have we sufficiently analyzed the impact of this change on the future of our organization?

5. Am I sufficiently well-informed to pass judgment on subordinates' proposals? Can I leave final authorization for more of the proposals with subordinates? Do we have problems of coordination because subordinates already make too many decisions independently?

6. What is my vision for this organization? Are these plans primarily in my own mind in loose form? Should I make them explicit to guide the decisions of others better? Or do I need flexibility to change them at will?

7. How do my subordinates react to my managerial style? Am I sufficiently sensitive to the powerful influence of my actions? Do I fully understand their reactions to my actions? Do I find an appropriate balance between encouragement and pressure? Do I stifle their initiative?

8. What kind of external relationships do I maintain, and how? Do I spend too much of my time maintaining them? Are there certain people whom I should get to know better?

9. Is there any system to my time scheduling, or am I just reacting to the pressures of the moment? Do I find the appropriate mix of activities or concentrate on one particular function or problem just because I find it interesting? Am I more efficient with particular kinds of work, at special times of the day or week? Does my schedule reflect this? Can someone else schedule my time (besides my secretary)?

10. Do I overwork? What effect does my work load have on my efficiency? Should I force myself to take breaks or to reduce the pace of my activity?

11. Am I too superficial in what I do? Can I really shift moods as quickly and frequently as my work requires? Should I decrease the amount of fragmentation and interruption in my work?

12. Do I spend too much time on current, tangible activities? Am I a slave to the action and excitement of my work, so that I am no longer able to concentrate on issues? Do key problems receive the attention they deserve? Should I spend more time reading and probing deeply into certain issues? Could I be more reflective? Should I be?

13. Do I use the different media appropriately? Do I know how to make the most of written communication? Do I rely excessively on face-to-face communication, thereby putting all but a few of my subordinates at an informational disadvantage? Do I schedule enough of my meetings on a regular basis? Do I spend enough time observing activities firsthand, or am I detached from the heart of my organization's activities?

14. How do I blend my personal rights and duties? Do my obligations consume all my time? How can I free myself from obligations to ensure that I am taking this organization where I want it to go? How can I turn my obligations to my advantage?

---

bances. Indeed, every manager must spend a considerable amount of time responding to high-pressure disturbances. No organization can be so well run, so standardized, that it has considered every contingency in the uncertain environment in advance. Disturbances arise not only because poor managers ignore situations until they reach crisis proportions but also because good managers cannot possibly anticipate all the consequences of the actions they take.

The third decisional role is that of *resource allocator*. The manager is responsible for deciding who will get what. Perhaps the most important resource the manager allocates is his or her own time. Access to the manager constitutes exposure to the unit's nerve center and decision maker. The manager is also charged with designing the unit's structure, that pattern of formal relationships that determines how work is to be divided and coordinated.

Also, as resource allocator, the manager authorizes the important decisions of the unit before they are implemented. By retaining this power, the manager can ensure that decisions are interrelated. To fragment this power encourages discontinuous decision making and a disjointed strategy.

There are a number of interesting features about the manager's authorization of others' decisions. First, despite the widespread use of capital budgeting procedures—a means of authorizing various capital expenditures at one time—executives in my study made a great many authorization decisions on an ad hoc basis. Apparently, many projects cannot wait or simply do not have the quantifiable costs and benefits that capital budgeting requires.

Second, I found that the chief executives faced incredibly complex choices. They had to consider the impact of each decision on other decisions and on the organization's strategy. They had to ensure that the decision would be acceptable to those who influence the organization, as well as ensure that resources would not be overextended. They had to understand the various costs and benefits as well as the feasibility of the proposal. They also had to consider questions of timing. All this was necessary for the simple approval of someone else's proposal. At the same time, however, the delay could lose time, while quick approval could be ill-considered and quick rejection might discourage the subordinate who had spent months developing a pet project.

One common solution to approving projects is to pick the person instead of the proposal. That is, the manager authorizes those projects presented by people whose judgment he or she trusts. But the manager cannot always use this simple dodge.

The final decisional role is that of *negotiator*. Managers spend considerable time in negotiations: the president of the football team works out a contract with the holdout superstar; the corporation president leads the company's contingent to negotiate a new strike issue; the foreman argues a grievance problem to its conclusion with the shop steward.

These negotiations are an integral part of the manager's job, for only he or she has the authority to commit organizational resources in "real time" and the nerve-center information that important negotiations require.

The Integrated Job

It should be clear by now that these ten roles are not easily separable. In the terminology of the psychologist, they form a gestalt, an integrated whole. No role can be pulled out of the framework and the job be left intact. For example, a manager without liaison contacts lacks external information. As a result, that manager can neither disseminate the information that employees need nor make decisions that adequately reflect external conditions. (This is a problem for the new person in a managerial position, since he or she has to build up a network of contacts before making effective decisions.)

Here lies a clue to the problems of team management.[15] Two or three people cannot share a single managerial position unless they can act as one entity. This means that they cannot divide up the ten roles unless they can very carefully reintegrate them. The real difficulty lies with the informational roles. Unless there can be full sharing of managerial information—and, as I pointed out earlier, it is primarily verbal—team management breaks down. A single managerial job cannot be arbitrarily split, for example, into internal and external roles, for information from both sources must be brought to bear on the same decisions.

To say that the ten roles form a gestalt is not to say that all managers give equal attention to each role. In fact, I found in my review of the various research studies that sales managers seem to spend relatively more of their time in the interpersonal roles, presumably a reflection of the extrovert nature of the marketing activity. Production managers, on the other hand, give relatively more attention to the decisional roles, presumably a reflection of their concern with efficient work flow. And staff managers spend the most time in the informational roles, since they are experts who manage departments that advise other parts of the organization. Nevertheless, in all cases, the interpersonal, informational, and decisional roles remain inseparable.

Toward More Effective Management

This description of managerial work should prove more important to managers than any prescription they might derive from it. That is to say, *the managers' effectiveness is significantly influenced by their insight into their own work*. Performance depends on how well a manager understands and responds to the pressures and dilemmas of the job. Thus managers who can be introspective about their work are likely to be effective at their jobs. The questions in "Self-Study Questions for Managers" may sound rhetorical; none is meant to be. Even though the questions cannot be answered simply, the manager should address them.

Let us take a look at three specific areas of concern. For the most part, the managerial logjams—the dilemma of delegation, the database centralized in one brain, the problems of working with the management scientist—revolve around the verbal nature of the manager's information. There are great dangers in centralizing the organization's data bank in the minds of its managers. When they leave, they take their memory with them. And when subordinates are out of convenient verbal reach of the manager, they are at an informational disadvantage.

The manager is challenged to find systematic ways to share privileged information. A regular debriefing session with key subordinates, a weekly memory dump on the dictating machine, maintaining a diary for limited circulation, or other similar methods may ease the logjam of work considerably. The time spent disseminating this information will be more than regained when decisions must be made. Of course, some will undoubtedly raise the question of confidentiality. But managers would be well advised to weigh the risks of exposing privileged information against having subordinates who can make effective decisions.

If there is a single theme that runs through this article, it is that the pressures of the job drive the manager to take on too much work, encourage interruption, respond quickly to every stimulus, seek the tangible and avoid the abstract, make decisions in small increments, and do everything abruptly.

Here again, the manager is challenged to deal consciously with the pressures of superficiality by giving serious attention to the issues that require it, by stepping back in order to see a broad picture, and by making use of analytical inputs. Although effective managers have to be adept at responding quickly to numerous and varying problems, the danger in managerial work is that they will respond to every issue equally (and that means abruptly) and that they will never work the tangible bits and pieces of information into a comprehensive picture of their world.

To create this comprehensive picture, managers can supplement their own models with those of specialists. Economists describe the functioning of markets, operations researchers simulate financial flow processes, and behavioral scientists explain the needs and goals of people. The best of these models can be searched out and learned.

In dealing with complex issues, the senior manager has much to gain from a close relationship with the organization's own management scientists. They have something important that the manager lacks—time to probe complex issues. An effective working relationship hinges on the resolution of what a colleague and I have called "the planning dilemma."[16] Managers have the information and the authority; analysts have the time and the technology. A successful working relationship between the two will be effected when the manager learns to share information and the analyst learns to adapt to the manager's needs. For the analyst, adaptation means worrying less about the elegance of the method and more about its speed and flexibility.

Analysts can help the top manager schedule time, feed in analytical information, monitor projects, develop models to aid in making choices, design contingency plans for disturbances that can be anticipated, and conduct "quick and dirty" analyses for those that cannot. But there can be no cooperation if the analysts are out of the mainstream of the manager's information flow.

The manager is challenged to gain control of his or her own time by turning obligations into advantages and by turning those things he or she wishes to do into obligations. The chief executives of my study initiated only 32% of their own contacts (and another 5% by mutual agreement). And yet to a considerable extent they seemed to control their time. There were two key factors that enabled them to do so.

First, managers have to spend so much time discharging obligations that if they were to view them as just that, they would leave no mark on the organization. Unsuccessful managers blame failure on the obligations. Effective managers turn obligations to advantages. A speech is a chance to lobby for a cause; a meeting is a chance to reorganize a weak department; a visit to an important customer is a chance to extract trade information.

Second, the manager frees some time to do the things that he or she—perhaps no one else—thinks important by turning them into obligations. Free time is made, not found. Hoping to leave some time open for contemplation or general planning is tantamount to hoping that the pressures of the job will go away. Managers who want to innovate initiate projects and obligate others to report back to them. Managers who need certain environmental information establish channels that will automatically keep them informed. Managers who have to tour facilities commit themselves publicly.

The Educator's Job

Finally, a word about the training of managers. Our management schools have done an admirable job of training the organization's specialists—management scientists, marketing researchers, accountants, and organizational development specialists. But for the most part, they have not trained managers.[17]

Management schools will begin the serious training of managers when skill training takes a serious place next to cognitive learning. Cognitive learning is detached and informational, like reading a book or listening to a lecture. No doubt much important cognitive material must be assimilated by the manager-to-be. But cognitive learning no more makes a manager than it does a swimmer. The latter will drown the first time she jumps into the water if her coach never takes her out of the lecture hall, gets her wet, and gives her feedback on her performance.

In other words, we are taught a skill through practice plus feedback, whether in a real or a simulated situation. Our management schools need to identify the skills managers use, select students who show potential in these skills, put the students into situations where these skills can be practiced and developed, and then give them systematic feedback on their performance.

My description of managerial work suggests a number of important managerial skills—developing peer relationships, carrying out negotiations, motivating subordinates, resolving conflicts, establishing information networks and subsequently disseminating information, making decisions in conditions of extreme ambiguity, and allocating resources. Above all, the manager needs to be introspective in order to continue to learn on the job.

No job is more vital to our society than that of the manager. The manager determines whether our social institutions will serve us well or whether they will squander our talents and resources. It is time to strip away the folklore about managerial work and study it realistically so that we can begin the difficult task of making significant improvements in its performance.

References

1. All the data from my study can be found in Henry Mintzberg, *The Nature of Managerial Work* (New York: Harper & Row, 1973).
2. Robert H. Guest, "Of Time and the Foreman," *Personnel*, May 1956, p. [illegible]
3. [illegible] *nd Their Jobs* (London: Macmillan, [illegible] *ecutive Behaviour* (Stockholm: Strom- [illegible]
4. [illegible] *usiness Environment* (New York: Mac- [illegible]
5. [illegible] oran, reported in Mintzberg, *The Na-* [illegible]
6. [illegible] *d Development of Field Sales Manag-* [illegible] h, Harvard Business School, 1957); [illegible] *of the Managing Director* (London: [illegible]
7. [illegible]; Tom Burns, "The Directions of Ac- [illegible] Departmental Executive Group," *Hu-* [illegible].
8. H. Edward Wrapp, "Good Managers Don't Make Policy Decisions," HBR September–October 1967, p. 91. Wrapp refers to this as spotting opportunities and relationships in the stream of operating problems and decisions; in his article, Wrapp raises a number of excellent points related to this analysis.
9. Richard E. Neustadt, *Presidential Power* (New York: John Wiley, 1960), pp. 153–154; italics added.
10. For a more thorough, though rather different, discussion of this issue, see Kenneth R. Andrews, "Toward Professionalism in Business Management," HBR March–April 1969, p. 49.
11. C. Jackson Grayson, Jr., in "Management Science and Business Practice," HBR July–August 1973, p. 41, explains in similar terms why, as chairman of the Price Commission, he did not use those very techniques that he himself promoted in his earlier career as management scientist.
12. George C. Homans, *The Human Group* (New York: Harcourt, Brace & World, 1950), based on the study by William F. Whyte entitled *Street Corner Society*, rev. ed. (Chicago: University of Chicago Press, 1955).
13. Neustadt, *Presidential Power*, p. 157.
14. Leonard R. Sayles, *Managerial Behavior* (New York: McGraw-Hill, 1964), p. 162.
15. See Richard C. Hodgson, Daniel J. Levinson, and Abraham Zaleznik, *The Executive Role Constellation* (Boston: Division of Research, Harvard Business School, 1965), for a discussion of the sharing of roles.
16. James S. Hekimian and Henry Mintzberg, "The Planning Dilemma," *The Management Review*, May 1968, p. 4.
17. See J. Sterling Livingston, "Myth of the Well-Educated Manager," HBR January–February 1971, p. 79.

Success In Management

CEO'S TAKING RESPONSIBILITY

Address by ANNE M. MULCAHY, *Chairman and Chief Executive Officer, Xerox Corporation*
Delivered to the Economic Club of Detroit, Detroit, Michigan, September 30, 2002

Thank you, Dr. Price, for your wonderful introduction. It's the first time an educator has ever spoken so kindly about me. I only wish my mother could have heard it!

And thanks to all of you for your warm reception. It's always great to be in Detroit—a city that's been a very good place for Xerox to do business over the years.

I had a chance over lunch to chat with some of our customers and I see a lot more of you in the audience. At the outset, I'd like to thank you for your business and your loyalty. It's something all of us at Xerox deeply appreciate... never take for granted... and always work hard to nurture.

There's an old Chinese proverb that can be used as either a curse or a blessing depending on the circumstance: "May you live in interesting times!"

Given our experience at Xerox the past two years, I'd like to try living for a while in less interesting times. Unless you've been living on another planet, you undoubtedly know that Xerox has been through a period of enormous crisis, challenge and change. But I'm pleased to say that we're back. We're getting stronger every day. And we firmly believe that our best days are ahead of us.

As a relatively new CEO, I realize I'm the new kid on the block. Many of you have been through your own "interesting times" and I'm sure you have learned a great deal from them. So at the risk of being presumptuous what I'd like to do with my time today is describe briefly how Xerox got into so much trouble so quickly... what we've done to get ourselves back on course... and what we've learned along the way.

A few months ago, I had a breakfast meeting with some of our customers in Dallas. One of them was both a prominent businessman and also a real mover and shaker in the civic and political life of Dallas. He's a self-made man who prides himself on speaking plain English—on telling it like it is. He delighted in telling me that I reminded him of the farmer whose cow got stuck in the ditch.

I've been told a lot of stories the past few years, but this was clearly a new one. So I took the bait and asked him what he meant. He said: "You've got to do three things. First, get the cow out of the ditch. Second, find out how the cow got in the ditch. Third, make sure you do whatever it takes so the cow doesn't go in the ditch again."

That struck me then as good advice and now as a good outline for my talk. So let me begin by telling you very briefly how the cow got in the ditch and how we got it out. Then I'll spend the bulk of my time on what we learned about making sure the cow never goes back in the ditch.

In 1998, Xerox was doing very, very well. Our market share was improving. Competition was faltering. Our financials were sound. The growth in our stock was outpacing the market by a fair amount. A change in leadership had apparently gone well. We were setting our sights on a bright future.

Or so we thought. With alarming speed, things unraveled in the latter part of 1999 and early 2000. We attempted too much change too fast. Competition stiffened while economies here at home and around the world weakened. We uncovered accounting improprieties in Mexico that led to the S.E.C. investigation that sucked up precious management time. And we took some actions that in the broad daylight of hindsight were dumb.

All these and other forces hit us simultaneously in what we came to call "The Perfect Storm." We probably could have managed our way through a few of these issues. But the cumulative impact overwhelmed us, and set us back on our heels.

By May of 2000, we were in deep trouble. Revenue and profits were declining. Cash on hand was shrinking. Debt was mounting. Customers were irate. Employees were defecting. Shareholders saw the value of their stock cut in half and continuing to head south. On May 11, 2000, it hit \$25 per share—down from more than \$60 a year earlier.

That was the day I was named President and Chief Operating Officer and typically the point in a talk like this when I would say that it fulfilled a life-long dream. In truth, it did not. This was clearly a case of the responsibility being thrust upon me. And I accepted it with equal parts of pride and dread, confidence and doubt, conviction and uncertainty.

Fortunately, I had not one but two aces in the hole. The first was a loyal customer base that wanted Xerox to survive. And the second was an incredibly talented and committed workforce who love Xerox and would do anything to help save the company. They remind me of a quote from no less an icon of Detroit than Henry Ford. More than a century ago he said he would be successful by attracting a workforce with "an infinite capacity to not know what can't be done."

At Xerox, we're blessed with a wonderful group of people a lot like that. And so we went to work. The management team spent lots of time with customers, industry experts and employees, and most of that time was spent listening. Customers told us we had great technology, but our response to them had slipped badly. Industry experts told us our technology was leading edge, but we had to focus on doing a few things extremely well. And employees told us they would do whatever it took to save the company, but they needed clear direction.

We laid out a bold and ambitious plan that had three major planks—focus on cash generation to improve liquidity... take $1 billion out of the cost base to improve competitiveness... and strengthen our core businesses to ensure growth in the future. The results have been stunning in both their magnitude and their swiftness.

On the liquidity front, we sold more than $2.5 billion worth of non-core assets... outsourced office manufacturing... exited our small office-home office business... and focused on operational cash generation through disciplined management of inventory, receivables and fixed capital. We also entered into a series of framework agreements—primarily with GE Capital—to outsource the financing of our customer receivables. This move alone is expected to erase more than $8 billion in debt from our balance sheet over time.

On the cost front, we exceeded our $1 billion goal. We're now at $1.3 billion and have set our sights on further savings. We reduced inventory by about $600 million last year, a year-over-year improvement of 30 percent. We reduced our selling, general and administrative costs by 15 percent. We cut our capital spending in half. And we reduced worldwide employment levels by about 15 percent.

As a result of these and other actions, we dramatically reduced our debt... improved our cash situation... and returned to profitability.

As proud as I am of the financial turnaround, what gives me the greatest satisfaction is the progress we made on the third leg of our strategy—strengthening our core business to ensure future growth. As we were righting our ship, we were preparing it for a very exciting and promising voyage. All the cost cutting and cash generation have been done with a purpose beyond mere survival. We have been investing in—and preparing for—a future of growth for Xerox and opportunity for Xerox shareholders, customers and employees.

Even as we dramatically reduced our cost base, we maintained research and development spending in our core businesses. Together with our partner Fuji, we invested about $1.6 billion in R&D last year with a similar amount planned for this year.

This year is our biggest new product year in recent history. We are bringing to market our third generation color digital production publisher... new color and black-and-white office multi-function devices... and an impressive set of solutions and services in such areas as knowledge management, one-to-one marketing, book publishing and print-on-demand.

Although we have a few remaining pieces of the puzzle to put in place, we feel very good about our progress. It's been quite a couple of years. And although I yearn for a period of "less interesting times," I'm thrilled to have had the opportunity to lead Xerox through this turnaround. It's been the experience of a lifetime.

And in what may be the understatement of all time, I've learned a lot along the way. That's what I'd like to turn to now. When I reflect on the past year and a half, and ask what we've learned, I come up with ten items.

First, look before you leap. I've been at Xerox for 25 years—most of my business career. I know the place. I feel like I've grown up in the company. And so there's a tendency to think you know all the answers. Combine that with a strong desire to make quick decisions in a time of crisis and you have a recipe for potential failure.

Fortunately, I was slowed down. I spent three months settling the troops and understanding the problems. It was essential that I did. What I found out was that the more obvious problems were masking more fundamental problems. It was as if everyone was trying to put out a fire that was obviously burning, but not fixing the fuel leak that was causing the fire.

Taking the precious time needed to truly understand the problems was critical. Had we not addressed all the issues, I believe I would be giving a very different speech this afternoon!

Second, you can't communicate too much in a time of crisis. Someone told me soon after I was named president that when times are good you should talk about what needs improvement and when things are bad you should assure people they will get better.

I took that advice to heart. I worried constantly. I had doubts. There were times when the challenges seemed insurmountable. But in public—especially with employees—I was always both candid about our problems and confident we could overcome them.

Someone just counted up the amount of time I devoted to communicating internally the past two years. It surprised even me. I've done a dozen live television broadcasts for employees, held more than 80 town meetings, sent out more than 40 letters to the troops, did hundreds of roundtables and logged about 200 thousand miles visiting employees in more than a dozen countries.

My message was always consistent:

"Here's the problem. Here's the strategy. Here's what you can do to help. You have a choice to make: Leave Xerox... or roll up your sleeves and get to work saving the company we all love."

The response was overwhelming. Defections slowed to a trickle. Hope rekindled. Energy returned. When people ask me now how we made so much progress in so short a period of time, I don't have to think about the answer. I tell them that you have to have a good strategy, but it can be roughly right. The critical component is the alignment of your people around a common set of objectives.

The third lesson learned is that crisis is a powerful motivator. It enables you to do things you should have been doing all along. Whoever said that nothing focuses the mind like the sight of the gallows had it right.

Let me give you one example. If I had taken over Xerox in good times, I probably wouldn't have immediately set a goal of taking $1 billion out of the cost base my first year. Even if I had, the idea would have been met with resistance, foot-dragging and outright opposition.

But given the crisis we were in, no one could argue. It was either the $1 billion or the gallows for Xerox. And now we're making good progress on the next $1 billion.

Here's the point. We are taking that cost out without harming the core business. We may even be strengthening it by eliminating waste and increasing clock speed. And it's the type of restructuring we should have been doing without a crisis to motivate us. The challenge now is to maintain that same type of intensity and focus as we return to sustained profitability—when there is no perceived crisis.

Fourth, the way out of trouble is sometimes back to basics—the things that made you great in the first place. When things are unraveling fast, it's tempting to look for quick fixes and new answers. In our own experience at Xerox, the real answers lay in getting back to some things we had always done well, but had abandoned.

Simple things—like rejuvenating our rich quality tradition... putting discipline back into our sales process... aligning our organizations and people around a common set of objectives... regular and tough-minded operations reviews... strict management of all the usual metrics like cash and inventory and gross margins and capital spending.

Frankly, I was aghast at how many of our internal processes were broken and how fast it had happened. For four out of five quarters, we issued early earnings—not because we had given rosy forecasts we couldn't meet, but because we had simply lost the ability to forecast with any precision.

Processes that had taken years to develop and refine broke down after only months of neglect. The good news is that they can be built back quickly.

Fifth, use good times to change. I believe there's a tendency to take your foot off the pedal when things are going well—to bask in the glory a little too much and too long.

And yet that's precisely the time when the organization can tolerate the most change and needs some energy. It's also the time when management has the luxury of time—time to devote to strategy. There are two cautions here. First, don't change for the sake of change. Second, understand how much change the organization can assimilate.

I know there are at least a few business professors here so I'd like to register a request. I've seen virtually no research that helps determine how much change organizations can go through and at what pace. We talk constantly about the pace of change and the need to change and even how to change. But precious little on how much our organizations—and our people—can tolerate.

Sixth, follow your instincts. Get the data. Solicit opinions. Listen carefully. Be open-minded. But at the end of the day, trust your own instincts. Plays that look good on the chalkboard don't always work on the field.

For example, we had lots of consulting projects that resulted in organizational changes to enable managing the business by product, industry and geography. My instincts told me that complex organizational matrices create complexity and lack of accountability. Despite the "academic views," we made clear choices, eliminated the matrix organization and created clear accountability. It has been critical to our operational success.

Seventh, not all corporate culture is bad, nor good. I recall meeting with a large customer—the CEO of a major bank—soon after I became president.

He gave me a rather forceful lecture on the need to change the Xerox culture and to shake things up.

On the surface, it made great sense. But the more I reflected on it, the more I came to realize it was nonsense. Our corporate culture was one of our major strengths during the decade of the nineties. Did we need to adapt it to an ever-changing world? Sure. Did we have to add things? Absolutely. Greater speed for one. But throw the baby out with the bath water? I didn't think so and I'm glad I didn't.

Our culture puts a premium on quality... empowerment... results... diversity... fairness... putting the customer first... corporate responsibility. They're the reasons a lot of us came to Xerox and why we stayed. And they're the reasons we achieved greatness in the nineties and can again this decade.

Eighth, never, never forget the reason the company exists—to provide value to customers. When bankers are calling and shareholders are yelling and the press is having a field day, it's so easy to forget the most important constituency of all—the customer.

Fortunately, we didn't. That's testimony to how ingrained the customer is in our culture. I've met personally over the past year with close to a hundred CEOs with whom we do business. Everyone on my senior team maintains an equally aggressive customer engagement schedule.

And we launched a program called Focus 500. Our 500 major accounts around the world are assigned to our top executives. Each executive is responsible for communicating with the customer... understanding their concerns and requirements... and making sure the appropriate Xerox resources are marshaled to fix problems and address issues.

And I've got to tell you that our customers have been wonderful. They've asked us the tough questions you would expect. They've been as demanding as ever as we would want. And their loyalty has been a source of strength to the entire Xerox community.

Ninth is what I call a "vision thing." Even while Rome was burning, people wanted to know what the city of the future would look like. I plead guilty that I didn't immediately get the importance of giving people—particularly employees—a clear picture of where we were heading. I believe it was the single most often asked question—not whether or not we would survive, but what we would look like after we came through the crisis. I attribute that to the remarkable optimism of Xerox people even in the face of extreme adversity. And I took it as a very good sign.

But I must tell you that I'm not very patient with things like vision statements that are exercises in grandiose thinking and round words and not rooted in reality.

So we tried something a little different—not a vision statement per se but a fictitious *Wall Street Journal* article written in 2005 about where Xerox was and how we had gotten there. It forced us to express our vision in simple English to put numbers on paper for revenue, profit, the stock price… to make up quotes of how we would like to be seen by various constituencies.

For us the *Wall Street Journal* article was a useful vehicle, but the important thing was to paint a picture of the future… to give people a sense of optimism based on reality… to provide a roadmap to a future of opportunity.

Tenth, surround yourself with at least a few good critics. I like to think of myself as open and approachable. And I like to think of the Xerox culture as non-hierarchical and free. But the reality is that once you step across the threshold to the corner office, things change—subtly perhaps—but they change nonetheless.

People around you want to please. They are more respectful and more easily intimidated. If you're not careful, you can begin to delude yourself and lose touch. That's where the honest critics can play an important role. Encourage them to tell it like it is. Schedule time for this express purpose. Don't leave it to chance.

Although it's not on my "top ten" list, I also learned a lot about leadership this past year—particularly that the power of leadership can't be overemphasized. We all know it. Library shelves are packed with books about it. Consultants have made reputations teaching it. Yet until you come face-to-face with the impact of leadership, I don't think you can fully appreciate it.

Poor leadership can do serious damage virtually overnight. Good leadership leadership that is consistent, honest and forceful—can move mountains over a longer period of time. To be honest with you, I don't do a lot of reading on the subject. But I have been struck by the work of Jim Collins—a former Professor at Stanford and now a consultant and author.

He looked at companies with great results which he defines as cumulative stock returns at least three times better than the general market over a fifteen-year period. That's a very tough standard. Only a handful of companies meet it. And then he looked at what made these companies great. The not-so-surprising answer was the quality of the company's leadership.

But here's what is surprising. The difference between good leaders—even really good leaders—and great leaders is a paradoxical blend of personal humility and professional will. Great leaders are self-effacing. They deflect adulation. They give credit to others. Yet they have a stoic resolve to do whatever it takes to make their company great. Their ambition is first and foremost about the company, not about themselves.

That makes a great deal of sense to me—and it's a style of leadership I'm trying to emulate. If you focus on the institution, your contributions are much more likely to be lasting ones. Let me give you one example I'm close to—Fannie Mae where I serve on the board.

David Maxwell was CEO through the decade of the eighties and into the early nineties. He took over a bureaucratic, quasi-governmental entity losing $1 million every business day and turned it into one of the smartest, best run financial institutions in the world, $4 million every business day. Under his leadership, Fannie Mae stock returns beat the general stock market by four times. Even more impressive to me is that he set the stage for the next generation to continue the momentum—eventually outperforming the market by seven times.

When David Maxwell's $20 million retirement package became a point of controversy, he became concerned it might damage the company's reputation. So he insisted that the last third of his package be donated to the Fannie Mae Foundation for low-income housing.

Even at the height of this success, David Maxwell was not a household name. The same can be said of leaders like Darium Smith at Kimberly Clark or Kristine McDivitt at Patagonia. They built great companies—companies that outpaced the market by a factor of three over the long haul—because they focused on the success of the institution, not personal celebrity. If personal fame was a byproduct, so be it. But it's never the point.

At Xerox, we still have a long way to go, but we have little doubt that we will be successful. Our management team has been tested. We've learned from our mistakes. We feel no task is too large if we stay together and stay focused… remember how the cow got in the ditch… and vow never to let it happen again.

And now I'd be pleased to take a few questions.

From *Vital Speeches of the Day*, Vol. LXIX, No. 2, November 1, 2002, pp. 43-48. Reprinted by permission of Anne M. Mulcahy.

Article 3

The new organisation

The Economist

FIFTY years ago William Whyte, an editor at *Fortune* magazine, wrote a book called "The Organisation Man" that defined the nature of corporate life for a generation. The book described how America (whose people, he said, had "led in the public worship of individualism") had recently turned into a nation of employees who "take the vows of organisation life" and who had become "the dominant members of our society".

Foremost among the organisations that Whyte had in mind was the corporation, which he thought rewarded long service, obedience and loyalty quite as faithfully as did any monastery or battalion. "Blood brother to the business trainee off to join DuPont is the seminary student who will end up in the church hierarchy," he wrote. The *New York Times* praised Whyte for recognising that "the entrepreneurial scramble to success has been largely replaced by the organisational crawl."

Half a century on, organisation man seems almost extinct, though occasionally he can still be spotted in Hollywood. In "The Hours", a 2002 Oscar-winning film, the actor John Reilly plays a character who lives in a 1950s Los Angeles suburban bungalow, just as Whyte's organisation man lived in "the new suburbia, the packaged villages that have become the dormitory of the new generation of organisation men". Mr Reilly is waved off to work every morning by his young son and his faithful wife, played by Julianne Moore. His shirt is white and his suit and tie are dark, broken only by the line of a white handkerchief in his breast pocket. He spends all day in an office with the same small group of people and returns home each evening at the same time. "This is perfect," he says of his life over dinner one evening.

The company that used to be most closely identified with this way of life was IBM. For many years its managers wore only dark blue suits, white shirts and dark ties, symbols of their lifetime allegiance to Big Blue. It is some measure of the change that has taken place since Whyte's day that today 50% of IBM's employees have worked for the company for under five years; 40% of its 320,000 employees are "mobile", meaning that they do not report daily to an IBM site; and about 30% are women. An organisation that was once dominated by lifetime employees selling computer products has been transformed into a conglomeration of transient suppliers of services. Organisation man has been replaced by a set of managers much more given to entrepreneurial scramble than to organisational crawl.

This transformation has been brought about by a variety of changes in the environment in which businesses operate, particularly in communications technology, in the globalisation of production and sales, and in the large-scale shift of responsibility to outsiders for what were once considered a company's core functions—via outsourcing, joint-ventures and other sorts of alliances that involve a loosening of control over vital inputs.

Whyte, who died in 1999, would have enjoyed witnessing organisation man's metamorphosis into "networked person", a species that can now be observed in airport lounges, on fast inter-city trains and at motorway service stations. Networked person is always on the move, juggling with a laptop computer, a mobile phone and a BlackBerry for e-mails, keeping in electronic touch with people he (and increasingly she) no longer regularly bumps into in a corridor. Indeed, there may be no corridor. These days, many employees besides IBMers no longer have a physical home base in a building provided by their employer.

Organisation man did bump into people in corridors, but he was cautious about networking. In his world, knowledge was power, and he needed to be careful about sharing out his particular store of it. He found comfort in hierarchy, which obviated the need to be self-motivating and take risks. He lived in a highly structured world where lines of authority were clearly drawn on charts, decisions were made on high, and knowledge resided in manuals.

Networked person, by contrast, takes decisions all the time, guided by the knowledge base she has access to, the corporate culture she has embraced, and the colleagues with whom she is constantly communicating. She interacts with a far greater number of people than her father did. A famous 1967 study by Stanley Milgram (which later became the basis for a film) suggested that there were at most "six degrees of separation" between any two people in America, meaning that the chain of acquaintances between them never had more than six links. According to more recent work along similar lines, that number has now fallen to 4.6, despite the growth in America's population since Milgram's study. Being able to keep in touch with a much wider range of people through technologies such as e-mail has brought everyone closer.

And yet despite the dramatic changes in the way people work, the organisations in which they carry out that work have changed much less than might be expected. In an article in the *McKinsey Quarterly* last year, Lowell Bryan and Claudia Joyce, two of the firm's consultants, argued that "today's big companies do very little to enhance the productivity of their professionals. In fact, their vertically oriented organisational structures, retrofitted with ad hoc and matrix overlays, nearly always make professional work more complex and inefficient." In other words, 21st-century organisations are not fit for 21st-century workers.

Mercer Delta, a consulting firm that specialises in "organisational architecture", recently observed that "the models and frameworks that shaped our leading organisations from the end of the second world war through the conclusion of the cold war are clearly obsolete in this new era of e-business, perpetual innovation and global competition." The design of today's complex enterprises, says Mercer Delta, requires an entirely new way of thinking about organisations.

The classic structure in which organisation man felt comfortable consisted of a number of business units that operated similarly but separately. They were controlled by a head office that determined strategy and watched over its implementation. It was a system of command and control in which everybody knew his place, made visible in the organisation charts that laid down the corporate hierarchy.

A surprising number of companies today still have much the same command-and-control structure that they had 50 years ago. According to the Boston Consulting Group, what it calls "the imperialist corporate centre" is still the most common type of headquarters. And companies that do decentralise decision-making and accountability often recentralise it again when they run into trouble.

Twenty years ago, Motorola, a co-inventor of the mobile phone, was a tightly centralised business. Three men in its headquarters at Schaumburg, Illinois (including Bob Galvin, the founder's son), were in control of almost everything that went on. As the company grew, they decided to decentralise. But by the mid-1990s the company's mobile-phone business was growing so fast that decentralisation made it impossible to control. "While the numbers are getting better, an organisation can be falling apart," says Pat Canavan, Motorola's chief governance officer. In 1998 the company laid off 25,000 people and repatriated control to the Schaumburg headquarters.

The trouble with silos

The main failing of the classic structure was that it impeded the spread of knowledge and limited the economies of scale that could be reaped. Ideas and commands moved up and down from headquarters to the units, leading to the creation of vertical "silos" with very little communication between them. Financial-service institutions were notorious for not knowing whether customers who signed up for one service were already customers for other services being provided by the same institution.

As firms became more global, they added what McKinsey called a "matrix overlay" to this structure. Most famously associated with Philips, a Dutch electrical and electronics giant, this attempted to take more account of the different national markets in which a company was operating by superimposing geographical silos that cut across the traditional business units.

Such organisations have not commanded universal admiration. In 1990, in a paper published by the *Harvard Business Review*, Sumantra Ghoshal and Christopher Bartlett, two academics, reported that matrix structures "led to conflict and confusion; the proliferation of channels created informational logjams as a proliferation of committees and reports bogged down the organisation; and overlapping responsibilities produced turf battles and a loss of accountability." Nigel Nicholson, a professor of organisational behaviour at the London Business School, called the matrix structure "one of the most difficult and least successful organisational forms."

Messrs Ghoshal and Bartlett wrote in the past tense, suggesting that companies had escaped from the matrix corset. But 15 years after the article was published, many are still trying to struggle free.

Gerard Fairtlough, a former CEO of Shell Chemicals and the founder of Celltech, a British biotechnology company, also suggests that companies are still being held back by their addiction to hierarchy. In a recent book, "The Three Ways of Getting Things Done", he points to alternatives to the hierarchical structure that many companies see as their only option.

"You can't have a bunch of hippies running a plant full of explosive hydrocarbons," he says. "But would you rather have the plant operated by trained professionals, for whom pride in safe working is part of their personal identity, or by people who only work safely because they are afraid of the boss? The identification of discipline with hierarchy is a dangerous mistake." Mr Fairtlough's preferred alternative is something he calls "responsible autonomy", a form of organisation in which groups of workers decide for themselves what to do, but are accountable for the outcome.

Clearly there is a need for new kinds of organisation that are more appropriate to modern working methods. But there are many reasons why companies are not in a hurry to adopt them.

Article 4

It's a Flat World, After All

Thomas L. Friedman

In 1492 Christopher Columbus set sail for India, going west. He had the Nina, the Pinta and the Santa Maria. He never did find India, but he called the people he met "Indians" and came home and reported to his king and queen: "The world is round." I set off for India 512 years later. I knew just which direction I was going. I went east. I had Lufthansa business class, and I came home and reported only to my wife and only in a whisper: "The world is flat."

And therein lies a tale of technology and geoeconomics that is fundamentally reshaping our lives—much, much more quickly than many people realize. It all happened while we were sleeping, or rather while we were focused on 9/11, the dot-com bust and Enron—which even prompted some to wonder whether globalization was over. Actually, just the opposite was true, which is why it's time to wake up and prepare ourselves for this flat world, because others already are, and there is no time to waste.

I wish I could say I saw it all coming. Alas, I encountered the flattening of the world quite by accident. It was in late February of last year, and I was visiting the Indian high-tech capital, Bangalore, working on a documentary for the Discovery Times channel about outsourcing. In short order, I interviewed Indian entrepreneurs who wanted to prepare my taxes from Bangalore, read my X-rays from Bangalore, trace my lost luggage from Bangalore and write my new software from Bangalore. The longer I was there, the more upset I became—upset at the realization that while I had been off covering the 9/11 wars, globalization had entered a whole new phase, and I had missed it. I guess the eureka moment came on a visit to the campus of Infosys Technologies, one of the crown jewels of the Indian outsourcing and software industry. Nandan Nilekani, the Infosys C.E.O., was showing me his global video-conference room, pointing with pride to a wall-size flat-screen TV, which he said was the biggest in Asia. Infosys, he explained, could hold a virtual meeting of the key players from its entire global supply chain for any project at any time on that supersize screen. So its American designers could be on the screen speaking with their Indian software writers and their Asian manufacturers all at once. That's what globalization is all about today, Nilekani said. Above the screen there were eight clocks that pretty well summed up the Infosys workday: 24/7/365. The clocks were labeled U.S. West, U.S. East, G.M.T., India, Singapore, Hong Kong, Japan, Australia.

"Outsourcing is just one dimension of a much more fundamental thing happening today in the world," Nilekani explained. "What happened over the last years is that there was a massive investment in technology, especially in the bubble era, when hundreds of millions of dollars were invested in putting broadband connectivity around the world, undersea cables, all those things." At the same time, he added, computers became cheaper and dispersed all over the world, and there was an explosion of e-mail software, search engines like Google and proprietary software that can chop up any piece of work and send one part to Boston, one part to Bangalore and one part to Beijing, making it easy for anyone to do remote development. When all of these things suddenly came together around 2000, Nilekani said, they "created a platform where intellectual work, intellectual capital, could be delivered from anywhere. It could be disaggregated, delivered, distributed, produced and put back together again—and this gave a whole new degree of freedom to the way we do work, especially work of an intellectual nature. And what you are seeing in Bangalore today is really the culmination of all these things coming together."

At one point, summing up the implications of all this, Nilekani uttered a phrase that rang in my ear. He said to me, "Tom, the playing field is being leveled." He meant that countries like India were now able to compete equally for global knowledge work as never before—and that America had better get ready for this. As I left the Infosys campus that evening and bounced along the pot-holed road back to Bangalore, I kept chewing on that phrase: "The playing field is being leveled."

"What Nandan is saying," I thought, "is that the playing field is being flattened. Flattened? Flattened? My God, he's telling me the world is flat!"

Here I was in Bangalore—more than 500 years after Columbus sailed over the horizon, looking for a shorter route to India using the rudimentary navigational technologies of his day, and returned safely to prove definitively that the world was round—and one of India's smartest engineers, trained at his country's top technical institute and backed by the most modern technologies of his day, was telling me that the world was flat, as flat as that screen on which he can host a meeting of his whole global supply chain. Even more interesting, he was citing this development as a new milestone in human progress and a great opportunity for India and the world—the fact that we had made our world flat!

This has been building for a long time. Globalization 1.0 (1492 to 1800) shrank the world from a size large to a size medium, and the dynamic force in that era was countries globalizing for resources and imperial conquest. Globalization 2.0 (1800 to 2000) shrank the world from a size medium to a size small, and it was spearheaded by companies globalizing for markets and labor. Globalization 3.0 (which started around 2000) is shrinking the world from a size small to a size tiny and flattening the playing field at the same time. And while the dynamic force in Globalization 1.0 was countries globalizing and the dynamic force in Globalization 2.0 was companies globalizing, the dynamic force in Globalization 3.0—the thing that gives it its unique character—is individuals and small groups globalizing. Individuals must, and can, now ask: where do I fit into the global competition and opportunities of the day, and how can I, on my own, collaborate with others globally? But Globalization 3.0 not only differs from the previous eras in how it is shrinking and flattening the world and in how it is empowering individuals. It is also different in that Globalization 1.0 and 2.0 were driven primarily by European and American companies and countries. But going forward, this will be less and less true. Globalization 3.0 is not only going to be driven more by individuals but also by a much more diverse—non-Western, nonwhite—group of individuals. In Globalization 3.0, you are going to see every color of the human rainbow take part.

"Today, the most profound thing to me is the fact that a 14-year-old in Romania or Bangalore or the Soviet Union or Vietnam has all the information, all the tools, all the software easily available to apply knowledge however they want," said Marc Andreessen, a co-founder of Netscape and creator of the first commercial Internet browser. "That is why I am sure the next Napster is going to come out of left field. As bioscience becomes more computational and less about wet labs and as all the genomic data becomes easily available on the Internet, at some point you will be able to design vaccines on your laptop."

Andreessen is touching on the most exciting part of Globalization 3.0 and the flattening of the world: the fact that we are now in the process of connecting all the knowledge pools in the world together. We've tasted some of the downsides of that in the way that Osama bin Laden has connected terrorist knowledge pools together through his Qaeda network, not to mention the work of teenage hackers spinning off more and more lethal computer viruses that affect us all. But the upside is that by connecting all these knowledge pools we are on the cusp of an incredible new era of innovation, an era that will be driven from left field and right field, from West and East and from North and South. Only 30 years ago, if you had a choice of being born a B student in Boston or a genius in Bangalore or Beijing, you probably would have chosen Boston, because a genius in Beijing or Bangalore could not really take advantage of his or her talent. They could not plug and play globally. Not anymore. Not when the world is flat, and anyone with smarts, access to Google and a cheap wireless laptop can join the innovation fray.

When the world is flat, you can innovate without having to emigrate. This is going to get interesting. We are about to see creative destruction on steroids.

How did the world get flattened, and how did it happen so fast?

It was a result of 10 events and forces that all came together during the 1990's and converged right around the year 2000. Let me go through them briefly. The first event was 11/9. That's right—not 9/11, but 11/9. Nov. 9, 1989, is the day the Berlin Wall came down, which was critically important because it allowed us to think of the world as a single space. "The Berlin Wall was not only a symbol of keeping people inside Germany; it was a way of preventing a kind of global view of our future," the Nobel Prize-winning economist Amartya Sen said. And the wall went down just as the windows went up—the breakthrough Microsoft Windows 3.0 operating system, which helped to flatten the playing field even more by creating a global computer interface, shipped six months after the wall fell.

The second key date was 8/9. Aug. 9, 1995, is the day Netscape went public, which did two important things. First, it brought the Internet alive by giving us the browser to display images and data stored on Web sites. Second, the Netscape stock offering triggered the dot-com boom, which triggered the dot-com bubble, which triggered the massive overinvestment of billions of dollars in fiber-optic telecommunications cable. That overinvestment, by companies like Global Crossing, resulted in the willy-nilly creation of a global undersea-underground fiber network, which in turn drove down the cost of transmitting voices, data and images to practically zero, which in turn accidentally made Boston, Bangalore and Beijing next-door neighbors overnight. In sum, what the Netscape revolution did was bring people-to-people connectivity to a whole new level. Suddenly more people could connect with more other people from more different places in more different ways than ever before.

No country accidentally benefited more from the Netscape moment than India. "India had no resources and no infrastructure," said Dinakar Singh, one of the most respected hedge-fund managers on Wall Street, whose parents earned doctoral degrees in biochemistry from the University of Delhi before emigrating to America. "It produced people with quality and by quantity. But many of them rotted on the docks of India like vegetables. Only a relative few could get on ships and get out. Not anymore, because we built this ocean crosser, called fiber-optic cable. For decades you had to leave India to be a professional. Now you can plug into the world from India. You don't have to go to Yale and go to work for Goldman Sachs." India could never have afforded to pay for the bandwidth to connect brainy India with high-tech America, so American shareholders paid for it. Yes, crazy overinvestment can be good. The overinvestment in railroads turned out to be a great boon for the American economy. "But the railroad overinvestment was confined to your own country and so, too, were the benefits," Singh said. In the case of the digital railroads, "it was the foreigners who benefited." India got a free ride.

The first time this became apparent was when thousands of Indian engineers were enlisted to fix the Y2K—the year 2000—computer bugs for companies from all over the world. (Y2K should be a national holiday in India. Call it "Indian Interdependence Day," says Michael Mandelbaum, a foreign-policy analyst at Johns Hopkins.) The fact that the Y2K work could be outsourced to Indians was made possible by the first two flatteners, along with a third, which I call "workflow." Workflow is shorthand for all the software applications, standards and electronic transmission pipes, like middleware, that connected all those computers and fiber-optic cable. To put it another way, if the Netscape moment connected people to people like never before, what the workflow revolution did was connect applications to applications so that people all over the world could work together in manipulating and shaping words, data and images on computers like never before.

Indeed, this breakthrough in people-to-people and application-to-application connectivity produced, in short order, six more flatteners—six new ways in which individuals and companies could collaborate on work and share knowledge. One was "outsourcing." When my software applications could connect seamlessly with all of your applications, it meant that all kinds of work—from accounting to software-writing—could be digitized, disaggregated and shifted to any place in the world where it could be done better and cheaper. The second was "offshoring." I send my whole factory from Canton, Ohio, to Canton, China. The third was "open-sourcing." I write the next operating system, Linux, using engineers collaborating together online and working for free. The fourth was "insourcing." I let a company like UPS come inside my company and take over my whole logistics operation—everything from filling my orders online to delivering my goods to repairing them for customers when they break. (People have no idea what UPS really does today. You'd be amazed!). The fifth was "supply-chaining." This is Wal-Mart's specialty. I create a global supply chain down to the last atom of efficiency so that if I sell an item in Arkansas, another is immediately made in China. (If Wal-Mart were a country, it would be China's eighth-largest trading partner.) The last new form of collaboration I call "informing"—this is Google, Yahoo and MSN Search, which now allow anyone to collaborate with, and mine, unlimited data all by themselves.

So the first three flatteners created the new platform for collaboration, and the next six are the new forms of collaboration that flattened the world even more. The 10th flattener I call "the steroids," and these are wireless access and voice over Internet protocol (VoIP). What the steroids do is turbocharge all these new forms of collaboration, so you can now do any one of them, from anywhere, with any device.

The world got flat when all 10 of these flatteners converged around the year 2000. This created a global, Web-enabled playing field that allows for multiple forms of collaboration on research and work in real time, without regard to geography, distance or, in the near future, even language. "It is the creation of this platform, with these unique attributes, that is the truly important sustainable breakthrough that made what you call the flattening of the world possible," said Craig Mundie, the chief technical officer of Microsoft.

No, not everyone has access yet to this platform, but it is open now to more people in more places on more days in more ways than anything like it in history. Wherever you look today—whether it is the world of journalism, with bloggers bringing down Dan Rather; the world of software, with the Linux code writers working in online forums for free to challenge Microsoft; or the world of business, where Indian and Chinese innovators are competing against and working with some of the most advanced Western multinationals—hierarchies are being flattened and value is being created less and less within vertical silos and more and more through horizontal collaboration within companies, between companies and among individuals.

Do you recall "the IT revolution" that the business press has been pushing for the last 20 years? Sorry to tell you this, but that was just the prologue. The last 20 years were about forging, sharpening and distributing all the new tools to collaborate and connect. Now the real information revolution is about to begin as all the complementarities among these collaborative tools start to converge. One of those who first called this moment by its real name was Carly Fiorina, the former Hewlett-Packard C.E.O., who in 2004 began to declare in her public speeches that the dot-com boom and bust were just "the end of the beginning." The last 25 years in technology, Fiorina said, have just been "the warm-up act." Now we are going into the main event, she said, "and by the main event, I mean an era in which technology will truly transform every aspect of business, of government, of society, of life."

As if this flattening wasn't enough, another convergence coincidentally occurred during the 1990's that was equally important. Some three billion people who were out of the game walked, and often ran, onto the playing field. I am talking about the people of China, India, Russia, Eastern Europe, Latin America and Central Asia. Their economies and political systems all opened up during the course of the 1990's so that their people were increasingly free to join the free market. And when did these three billion people converge with the new playing field and the new business processes? Right when it was being flattened, right when millions of them could compete and collaborate more equally, more horizontally and with cheaper and more readily available tools. Indeed, thanks to the flattening of the world, many of these new entrants didn't even have to leave home to participate. Thanks to the 10 flatteners, the playing field came to them!

It is this convergence—of new players, on a new playing field, developing new processes for horizontal collaboration—that I believe is the most important force shaping global economics and politics in the early 21st century. Sure, not all three billion can collaborate and compete. In fact, for most people the world is not yet flat at all. But even if we're talking about only 10 percent, that's 300 million people—about twice the size of the American work force. And be advised: the Indians and Chinese are not racing us to the bottom. They are racing us to the top. What China's leaders really want is that the next generation of underwear and airplane wings not just be "made in China" but also be "designed in China." And that is where things are heading. So in 30 years we will have gone from "sold in China" to "made in China" to "designed in China" to "dreamed up in China"—or from China as collaborator with the worldwide manufacturers on nothing to China as a low-cost, high-quality, hyperefficient collaborator with worldwide manufacturers on everything. Ditto India. Said Craig Barrett, the C.E.O. of Intel, "You don't bring three billion people into the world economy overnight without huge consequences, especially from three societies"—like India, China and Russia—"with rich educational heritages."

That is why there is nothing that guarantees that Americans or Western Europeans will continue leading the way. These new players are stepping onto the playing field legacy free, meaning that many of them were so far behind that they can leap right into the new technologies without having to worry about all the sunken costs of old systems. It means that they can move very fast to adopt new, state-of-the-art technologies, which is why there are already more cellphones in use in China today than there are people in America.

If you want to appreciate the sort of challenge we are facing, let me share with you two conversations. One was with some of the Microsoft officials who were involved in setting up Microsoft's research center in Beijing, Microsoft Research Asia, which opened in 1998—after Microsoft sent teams to Chinese universities to administer I.Q. tests in order to recruit the best brains from China's 1.3 billion people. Out of the 2,000 top Chinese engineering and science students tested, Microsoft hired 20. They have a saying at Microsoft about their Asia center, which captures the intensity of competition it takes to win a job there and explains why it is already the most productive research team at Microsoft: "Remember, in China, when you are one in a million, there are 1,300 other people just like you."

The other is a conversation I had with Rajesh Rao, a young Indian entrepreneur who started an electronic-game company from Bangalore, which today owns the rights to Charlie Chaplin's image for mobile computer games. "We can't relax," Rao said. "I think in the case of the United States that is what happened a bit. Please look at me: I am from India. We have been at a very different level before in terms of technology and business. But once we saw we had an infrastructure that made the world a small place, we promptly tried to make the best use of it. We saw there were so many things we could do. We went ahead, and today what we are seeing is a result of that. There is no time to rest. That is gone. There are dozens of people who are doing the same thing you are doing, and they are trying to do it better. It is like water in a tray: you shake it, and it will find the path of least resistance. That is what is going to happen to so many jobs—they will go to that corner of the world where there is the least resistance and the most opportunity. If there is a skilled person in Timbuktu, he will get work if he knows how to access the rest of the world, which is quite easy today. You can make a Web site and have an e-mail address and you are up and running. And if you are able to demonstrate your work, using the same infrastructure, and if people are comfortable giving work to you and if you are diligent and clean in your transactions, then you are in business."

Instead of complaining about outsourcing, Rao said, Americans and Western Europeans would "be better off thinking about how you can raise your bar and raise yourselves into doing something better. Americans have consistently led in innovation over the last century. Americans whining—we have never seen that before."

Rao is right. And it is time we got focused. As a person who grew up during the cold war, I'll always remember driving down the highway and listening to the radio, when suddenly the music would stop and a grim-voiced announcer would come on the air and say: "This is a test. This station is conducting a test of the Emergency Broadcast System." And then there would be a 20-second high-pitched siren sound. Fortunately, we never had to live through a moment in the cold war when the announcer came on and said, "This is a not a test."

That, however, is exactly what I want to say here: "This is not a test."

The long-term opportunities and challenges that the flattening of the world puts before the United States are profound. Therefore, our ability to get by doing things the way we've been doing them—which is to say not always enriching our secret sauce—will not suffice any more. "For a country as wealthy we are, it is amazing how little we are doing to enhance our natural competitiveness," says Dinakar Singh, the Indian-American hedge-fund manager. "We are in a world that has a system that now allows convergence among many billions of people, and we had better step back and figure out what it means. It would be a nice coincidence if all the things that were true before were still true now, but there are quite a few things you actually need to do differently. You need to have a much more thoughtful national discussion."

If this moment has any parallel in recent American history, it is the height of the cold war, around 1957, when the Soviet Union leapt ahead of America in the space race by putting up the Sputnik satellite. The main challenge then came from those who wanted to put up walls; the main challenge to America today comes from the fact that all the walls are being taken down and many other people can now compete and collaborate with us much more directly. The main challenge in that world was from those practicing extreme Communism, namely Russia, China and North Korea. The main challenge to America today is from those practicing extreme capitalism, namely China, India and South Korea. The main objective in that era was building a strong state, and the main objective in this era is building strong individuals.

Meeting the challenges of flatism requires as comprehensive, energetic and focused a response as did meeting the challenge of Communism. It requires a president who can summon the nation to work harder, get smarter, attract more young women and men to science and engineering and build the broadband infrastructure, portable pensions and health care that will help every American become more employable in an age in which no one can guarantee you lifetime employment.

We have been slow to rise to the challenge of flatism, in contrast to Communism, maybe because flatism doesn't involve ICBM missiles aimed at our cities. Indeed, the hot line, which used to connect the Kremlin with the White House, has been replaced by the help line, which connects everyone in America to call centers in Bangalore. While the other end of the hot line might have had Leonid Brezhnev threatening nuclear war, the other end of the help line just has a soft voice eager to help you sort out your AOL bill or collaborate with you on a new piece of software. No, that voice has none of the menace of Nikita Khrushchev pounding a shoe on the table at the United Nations, and it has none of the sinister snarl of the bad guys in "From Russia With Love." No, that voice on the help line just has a friendly Indian lilt that masks any sense of threat or challenge. It simply says: "Hello, my name is Rajiv. Can I help you?"

No, Rajiv, actually you can't. When it comes to responding to the challenges of the flat world, there is no help line we can call. We have to dig into ourselves. We in America have all the basic economic and educational tools to do that. But we have not been improving those tools as much as we should. That is why we are in what Shirley Ann Jackson, the 2004 president of the American Association for the Advancement of Science and president of Rensselaer Polytechnic Institute, calls a "quiet crisis"—one that is slowly eating away at America's scientific and engineering base.

"If left unchecked," said Jackson, the first African-American woman to earn a Ph.D. in physics from M.I.T., "this could challenge our pre-eminence and capacity to innovate." And it is our ability to constantly innovate new products, services and companies that has been the source of America's horn of plenty and steadily widening middle class for the last two centuries. This quiet crisis is a product of three gaps now plaguing American society. The first is an "ambition gap." Compared with the young, energetic Indians and Chinese, too many Americans have gotten too lazy. As David Rothkopf, a former official in the Clinton Commerce Department, puts it, "The real entitlement we need to get rid of is our sense of entitlement." Second, we have a serious numbers gap building. We are not producing enough engineers and scientists. We used to make up for that by importing them from India and China, but in a flat world, where people can now stay home and compete with us, and in a post-9/11 world, where we are insanely keeping out many of the first-round intellectual draft choices in the world for exaggerated security reasons, we can no longer cover the gap. That's a key reason companies are looking abroad. The numbers are not here. And finally we are developing an education gap. Here is the dirty little secret that no C.E.O. wants to tell you: they are not just outsourcing to save on salary. They are doing it because they can often get better-skilled and more productive people than their American workers.

These are some of the reasons that Bill Gates, the Microsoft chairman, warned the governors' conference in a Feb. 26 speech that American high-school education is "obsolete." As Gates put it: "When I compare our high schools to what I see when I'm traveling abroad, I am terrified for our work force of tomorrow. In math and science, our fourth graders are among the top students in the world. By eighth grade, they're in the middle of the pack. By 12th grade, U.S. students are scoring near the bottom of all industrialized nations. . . . The percentage of a population with a college degree is important, but so are sheer numbers. In 2001, India graduated almost a million more students from college than the United States did. China graduates twice as many students with bachelor's degrees as the U.S., and they have six times as many graduates majoring in engineering. In the international competition to have the biggest and best supply of knowledge workers, America is falling behind."

We need to get going immediately. It takes 15 years to train a good engineer, because, ladies and gentlemen, this really is rocket science. So parents, throw away the Game Boy, turn off the television and get your kids to work.

There is no sugar-coating this: in a flat world, every individual is going to have to run a little faster if he or she wants to advance his or her standard of living. When I was growing up, my parents used to say to me, "Tom, finish your dinner—people in China are starving." But after sailing to the edges of the flat world for a year, I am now telling my own daughters, "Girls, finish your homework—people in China and India are starving for your jobs."

I repeat, this is not a test. This is the beginning of a crisis that won't remain quiet for long. And as the Stanford economist Paul Romer so rightly says, "A crisis is a terrible thing to waste."

***Thomas L. Friedman** is the author of "The World Is Flat: A Brief History of the Twenty-First Century," to be published this week by Farrar, Straus & Giroux and from which this article is adapted. His column appears on the Op-Ed page of The Times, and his television documentary "Does Europe Hate Us?" was shown on the Discovery Channel on April 7, 2005.*

Globalization and the American Labor Force

Fred Maidment
Ancell School of Business
Western Connecticut State University

ABSTRACT

The global economy has changed the way national economies recover from recessions and create jobs. This article focuses on the impact of technology and the presence of educated workers in developing countries. Our basic idea is that these two factors have created a market for highly skilled and educated workers that is international in nature and extremely competitive. This article describes this development, analyzes its impact on the United States, discusses public policy alternatives developed in the United States, continental Europe, and Great Britain, and offers some initial ideas that could lead to a solution.

Over the past three years or so, the U.S. economy has struggled to come out of a recession that started as the Bush administration took office in 2001 [1], following a period of historic economic growth and expansion. The U.S. economy peaked in the summer of 1999 and declined slowly until the country experienced three consecutive quarters of negative economic growth as President George W. Bush took office. The economy then began a slow recovery that was set back by a series of events including Sept. 11 and revelations of corporate wrongdoing (e.g., Enron, Global Crossing, and Arthur Anderson) that came to light as the economy was beginning to rebound from the relatively mild recession of 2001. In addition, the dot-com bubble—one of the greatest stock market speculation bubbles of all time—burst, taking with it many of the assets of individual and institutional investors, causing them to be far more cautious and less likely to invest on future promises of high returns [2].

The post-2001 recovery has been slow and painful. Although the nation may be seeing the beginnings of a truly significant recovery, job-growth figures have been disappointing [3]. Although there are many reasons for this lack of job growth, this article argues that a systemic change has occurred: that there is now a global economy, not only for markets and raw materials, but for labor. The jobs that workers held in the United States prior to the last recession are returning, but they are not necessarily returning to American workers.

THE DISAPPOINTING JOB PICTURE

While economic growth figures for the United States in 2004 are impressive, the question remains, "Where are the jobs?" These are some recent figures:

Month	Net New Jobs Added to Payroll
November 2003	57,000
December 2003	1,000
January 2004	112,000
February 2004	21,000
March 2004	308,000
April 2004	288,000
May 2004	249,000
June 2004	112,000
July 2004	32,000
August 2004	144,000

Jobs have always been a lagging indicator, i.e., they follow rather than lead economic growth. Employers would rather have their employees work overtime than hire additional workers when an economic upturn begins because hiring new workers is expensive and, if the upturn is not real, or is cut short, terminating new hires is expensive and painful. Although the numbers reported above are all positive and can be subject to different interpretations (as we saw in the recent presidential campaign), they fall below the numbers of new jobs necessary to keep up with changes in the population.

THE LINK TO TECHNOLOGY

For years, the manufacturing sector of the U.S. economy has been sending jobs to less-costly locations. For example, jobs in the textile and auto industries first left the Northeast and the upper Midwest for the South. Now, the textile industry is in the process of departing from the United States almost completely, and the auto industry is becoming so globalized that it is hard to tell whether a car was made in America, Japan, Korea, or Europe. But the jobs affected in these more-traditional downsizings have almost always been jobs that require limited skills. A job that can be learned in 30 minutes on an assembly line will always be in danger of going to the lowest bidder. It does not take long for a relatively unskilled worker in the Third World to reach the level of proficiency of a much more-expensive employee working in a developed country.

Technology has not only enabled manufacturing workers to become far more productive, but it has also enabled much of that work to be done outside the developed world in plants in the Third World. More recently, in the high technology service industries, the back-office work was moved to workers outside of the developed world. This is especially true in information technology, finance, and other service sectors [4]. Those jobs are never going to return to the United States or to any other developed country.

From Technology to Education

But this is material that is well-known. The focus of this article is the new forces that have come into play. For the first time in developing countries there are critical masses of highly skilled, well-educated workers who are capable, willing, and perfectly able to perform complicated and advanced tasks at a very high level [5]. Throughout most of history, this type of person has been found in substantial numbers only in advanced economies. But that has changed, partly as a result of. more than 50 years of student exchanges between the United States, Europe, and the developing world, especially China and India.

The original exchange students went to the United States and Europe to study at the end of World War II and a stream followed. Some of them stayed, but many of them returned to their homes, where they became teachers and often leaders in their societies. As the generations have passed, universities have been established in countries such as China and India that produce engineers, teachers, accountants, doctors, scientists, and other professionals who are often as skilled as those produced in the West. Perhaps their equipment is not as current as that of MIT or Caltech, but the faculty went to school there or was taught by faculty that went to school there. They read the same journals, go to the same meetings, have many of the same ambitions (for comparison purposes, think of the United States, circa 1920, with middle-class families getting their first cars, houses, and even indoor plumbing), and work on many of the same projects, including putting people into space, as the Chinese recently did [6].

Thus, the institutions of higher education in the developing world have created a significant number of highly qualified workers, and, as is well-known, the costs and standards of living in India and China and other developing countries are very much lower than that of the United States or other developed countries. An engineer or a computer programmer in one of these countries would, obviously, be paid far less than a U.S., Japanese, or European counterpart.

Multinational corporations are fully conversant about the differences in labor costs and the capabilities of their employees and have started to take advantage of them on a wide variety of fronts. Today, smaller organizations are also taking advantage of this, often through the euphemism of "third-party provider," especially in information technology [7]. India's and China's workforces are at least three-and-one-halftimes larger than the American workforce. Even if the technologically advanced workforces in China and India are only one-third of the relative size of that in the United States, then both China and India have as many technology workers as the United States has.

The Historical Lesson

There is historic precedent for the situation facing the developed countries. At the end of World War II, both Germany and Japan were completely devastated. Yet, they still had a large number of highly skilled, well-educated, and trained workers. While their traditional forms of capital had been obliterated by the war, their human capital, while damaged, had more-or-less survived. With the assistance of the United States, through the Marshall Plan and other programs, these two countries were back on their economic and political feet in less than a decade, producing goods and services that were often competitive on the world market, and in 25 years, giving American industry a real challenge.

EXISTING PUBLIC POLICY RESPONSES

The Continental European Approach

The European approach to the more competitive global environment is far more protective of labor than the U.S. approach. This orientation stems from the historic relationship among European unions, their employing corporations, and the governments [8]. The union movement in Europe is far more politically involved than its American counterpart. There are political parties in many of the countries in Europe that are called "Labor" parties, and they tend to be somewhat more closely aligned with more liberal social causes and issues, including extensive holidays, family leave, and significantly fewer working hours. In Germany, for example, it is not uncommon, for a member of the labor union to have a seat on the board of directors of the corporation, something that might bring on a heart attack for an American CEO.

For European corporations, this means that it is very difficult to terminate employees, because they have many protections against being fired. The result is that corporations in Europe hire new employees only when they absolutely must, and once an employee has a job s/he does not leave. This has resulted in at least two unintended consequences.

First, unemployment in Europe has remained relatively high for the past 15 years, especially among the young, as compared to the United States [9]. The major economies of Germany, France, and Italy have had unemployment rates of around 10% or more [10]. Second, this very restrictive labor market, along with very high rates of taxation, has resulted in very low economic growth in Europe over the past 15 years. During the 1990s, the European Union grew by only a little over 8%, while the U.S. economy grew by over 60% [11]. As Michael Burda of Humboldt University in Berlin said, "You have to work to grow," [12, p. A1].

The American Approach

American public policy toward corporate and workplace issues has had three major components. First, stated in its most simple form, the policy has been to keep government out of most of the affairs of business, as long as competitive conditions in the marketplace were maintained. Since the latter part of the 19th century, the country has at least paid lip service to an antitrust policy, focusing on the prohibition of marketing and industrial practices that would restrict trade. These antitrust laws addressed conditions that had developed in the 1800s. These laws were later augmented by New Deal legislation in the 1930s and still later by the social legislation of the Johnson years. These policies were based on the assumption that the relationship between corporations and the people is essentially adversarial in nature; that companies do not necessarily have the best interests of their employees and customers at heart. Many European countries and, in particular, Japan, have not followed this path, and have instead encouraged the development of large, often multi-industry cartels, such as Mitsubishi and Hitachi.

Second, with the exception of unionized organizations, American firms operate under the doctrine of employment at-will. Essentially, this means that employees can be hired or terminated for any reason. While this doctrine has been modified over the years to account for racial, gender, and other forms of specific discrimination such as those covered by the ADA, Title VII, and the ADEA, it is still alive, if not fully well. This allows American organizations to be far more flexible in their hiring practices than their continental European counterparts. There have been efforts to reform the employment at-will doctrine, notably the Model Employment Termination Act [13], but these efforts have so far been largely unsuccessful. When reform arguments of substantial cost savings were presented, they were ignored by U.S. industry, which holds the doctrine of employment at-will near and dear to its heart [14]. Even in unionized environments, American companies are not as restricted as many continental European organizations. What this means is that American organizations can expand or contract their workforces far more easily than their continental European or Japanese counterparts. Unlike in continental Europe or Japan, it places the burden of responding to changes in the economy on the workers, not on the corporations, because in the United States, workers must respond by taking the initiative and making themselves more marketable in the workforce. In continental Europe and Japan, more of the burden is placed on the corporations because it is more difficult to shed workers when the economy slows.

Third, although the doctrine of employment at-will remains viable, public policy has permitted the development of two major classes of exceptions. First, since the 1930s, the government has provided at least some support to the organized labor movement, and it has permitted unions to bargain collectively over topics that would restrict the application of employment at-will. Thus, collective bargaining agreements consistently contain provisions calling for the arbitration of disputes over employee discharge or for seniority rules that influence who will be let go if there is a downturn. However, the U.S. labor movement has never been as politically involved as are the labor movements in many of the other developed countries, and it has never penetrated industry to the extent that unions have in countries such as Great Britain, France, Germany, Italy, and the Scandinavian nations. Today, only a relatively small percentage of American workers are members of a labor union, and those workers do not have the public policy protections their European counterparts possess.

In the United States today, it is well-known that union organizing attempts are often blunted by employer use of tactics of questionable legality [15], and efforts on the part of organized labor to influence elections have rarely succeeded. Some of the more recent failures include organized labor's efforts to elect Vice President Al Gore as president in 2000; campaigning for losing Democratic congressional candidates in 2002, and supporting losing Congressman Dick Gephardt in the 2004 Iowa caucuses [16]. These failures have exposed organized labor's lack of political muscle in the United States.

The results of the American approach are: 1) the U.S. economy has grown faster than virtually any other large developed economy in the world over the past 15 years, especially during the decade of the 1990s; 2) U.S. unemployment has been about half that of Germany, Italy, or France during the 1990s [11]. Even during the past recession, the U.S. unemployment rate would have been the envy of these three nations [17, 18]; and 3) American workers have become far more productive. Over the past 25 years American workers have actually increased the amount of time spent on the job, while their European and Japanese counterparts [19] have gone in the other direction. According to a United Nations study, American workers now spend more than 500 hours per year more on the job than the average German worker and about 125 hours more per year than the average Japanese worker. Only South Korean and Czech workers exceed the amount of time spent on the job by American workers. With the Czechs, the difference is about the same as it is between the Americans and the Japanese workers. South Korea is the only industrialized country where workers still work a six-day week, and the government is attempting to move the country to a five-day week, partially because the government feels that this will actually improve the economy because the people will have more time to spend their money [20].

The British Approach

The approach in Great Britain has been somewhat different from the United States and the other major European economies. In the United Kingdom, it has been more difficult to terminate employees than in the United States, but easier than in the rest of the European Union. At the same time, the British have experienced generally lower tax rates than the rest of Europe, but higher than that of the United States. The combination has lead to an unemployment rate that compares very favorably with that of the United States [11] and an economic growth rate of almost 40% for the 1990s [10,11]. In fact, the European Union, as a whole, would actually have experienced slight negative growth for the decade of the 1990s had it not been for the British economy [21]. However, the United Kingdom may be more like its E.U. partners in the future as the officials in Brussels have started to bring the policies of all of the members of the European Union more in line with each other [22]. Also, the proposed B.U. constitution would appear to move that policy forward [23].

EVALUATION

Neither the American approach to coping with the rate of technological changes and challenges nor the European approach is completely satisfactory. As we have seen, the European approach, coupled with a high rate of taxation, trades high unemployment and low economic growth for job security for those who have jobs. The U.S. approach has produced higher levels of economic growth, a relatively low tax rate, and a lower unemployment rate. However, the cost has been paid in terms of job security, high employee stress, and low employee morale, loyalty, and commitment. The British approach of lower taxation than its E.U. partners, but higher taxation than the United States, coupled with a less-restrictive labor policy than continental Europe, but a more-restrictive policy than the Americans, has resulted in low unemployment and very respectable economic growth. The real question concerns how to achieve economic growth and low unemployment rates without some of the dysfunctional consequences. While there are some who may say that these goals are mutually exclusive, the recent British example demonstrates that they do not have to be.

Under the Thatcher government, the British instituted a series of reforms that were, at the time, very painful to many in the United Kingdom. These actions resulted in the privatization of many industries that had formerly been state monopolies, and the resulting discipline of the marketplace stemming from that privatization made those industries far more competitive than they had been in the past. As such, workers no longer had the same kind of job security frequently associated with state-run monopolies/government jobs. Companies had to compete. While British unions, unlike their American counterparts, possessed sufficient political power to temper this privatization by restricting the ability of the newly privatized and existing companies to hire and fire at will, the firms were able to gain more control over their labor force than their continental European counterparts have been able to achieve. This was then combined with the British approach of comparatively moderate taxation, especially by European standards, that has led to relatively high economic growth and low unemployment.

During the 1990s the British experienced 39% economic growth for the decade [11]. While this did not match the growth rate of the United States, it was farberter than that of the other major economies of Europe. British taxes are high when compared to those in the United States, but not as high as in much of the rest of Europe, and the unemployment rate during the 1990s compared very favorably with that of the United States. Flexibility in hiring and firing in Great Britain was somewhere between the United States and continental Europe. The British may soon have to conform to the rest of the European Union in their employment practices, even though they have opted-out of the European Union's 48-hour maximum workweek [24]. Should they choose to vote yes on the new E.U. constitution, it will be interesting to see how these new rules will affect economic growth and unemployment over the next 10 years in the United Kingdom and continental Europe [22, 23].

Where Will the High-Tech Jobs Be?

In the United States, with the economy on the rise, most organizations should be considering hiring new employees, but the question is, in a global marketplace for products, services, materials, and labor, Where are they going to be doing the hiring? It is not uncommon for "American" corporations to have well over 50% of their employees, markets, and sales outside of the United States. Such common U.S. names as Ford, IBM, and Coca Cola would fall into this category, and more firms are joining them [7]. Companies in India are also outsourcing jobs when it is their interest to do so [25]. The global marketplace is a bazaar where all things are for sale, including the classic economic factors of production: land, labor, capital, and entrepreneurship. Buyers of these factors, like shoppers on the Internet or at the mall, will look for the best possible value for their money—which could very well mean replacing highly skilled and highly expensive American workers with less-expensive but also quite skilled employees in countries such as India or China.

Just as the textile industry moved production and the jobs out of New England and just as the auto industry created the "rust-belt" in the Midwest by moving production to less-costly locations, corporations are now doing the same with high-value/high-tech service sector jobs. This is history repeating itself, with the difference being that these are service jobs that require a relatively high degree of education and training. And these jobs are going to people who are prepared to do them for far less money than the people in the United States. The question for policy makers is how to respond to this shift in the economic environment.

Economists call this an economic dislocation, but to the individual who has been "economically dislocated" it means the loss of one's source of income, damage to one's self-respect, and often an array of social and psychological problems for the person and the community. To the elected policy maker, the individual is a citizen, a constituent and, most importantly, a vote.

The primary responsibility of a corporation in a capitalistic market economy is profitability [26]. These organizations also have secondary responsibilities to various stakeholders of the organization, including their employees, customers, suppliers, the communities in which they do business, as well as others [27], but their primary function today is to achieve survival and profitability in a highly competitive global marketplace. These organizations must ruthlessly control costs, while at the same time continuously maintain, enhance, and improve the quality of their products. These considerations encourage the export of, not only routine manufacturing jobs as in the past, but the high-technology jobs of today, and traditional U.S. public policy encourages this development. This country's historical hands-off policy toward jobs and even toward the migration of entire industries has been in the name of free trade, and the American economy, on the whole, has benefited. Now, however, the industries at risk include the financial sector, information technology, and other areas of high technology, considered to be important to the future of the American economy.

Existing policy proposals are inadequate. President Bush has proposed adding some funds to community colleges to help retrain individuals whose jobs have moved overseas [28], but this is only a response to help people who have lost their jobs in the manufacturing sector, not in the high-tech/service sector. It seems unlikely that these high tech/service sector people would be candidates for welding jobs. Indeed, many of them could teach in the programs. Presidential candidate Kerry repeatedly raised the issue of outsourcing during his campaign, but he did not deal with the issue addressed in this article.

The governments of both the United States and Europe need an industrial policy that addresses the need for employment and economic growth. The European approach has not been successful in either area. The U.S. policy of *laissez faire* may not be adequate to deal with the changing marketplace, as the demand for highly skilled and educated labor becomes both global in nature and far more competitive. Advances in technology cannot be stopped, nor should they, and corporations will not stop seeking to increase their competitiveness by cutting their costs and increasing their profits. But a balance must be struck between what is fair to citizens/workers/consumers of a society and the benefits/costs/changes that advances in technology are certain to bring. The genie of technological advancement and communication is out of the bottle, and nobody wants to or is able to put it back in, but dealing with that genie will not be easy. There are bound to be economic dislocations as willing, capable, and educated workers in developing countries compete with workers in developed societies.

We think that the British have presented at least a middle way. Something closer to a solution to the problem of dealing with outsourcing/technological unemployment, while at the same time providing an environment that encourages economic growth and development—not as Darwinian as the American, but not as protectionist as their continental neighbors. It is still more difficult to terminate employees in the United Kingdom than in the United States, but it is still much easier than in the rest of Europe. The British approach gives firms the flexibility they need to respond to changes in the marketplace, while giving the employees a certain amount of protection from the whims and potential incompetence of management. This spreads the systemic risk of the marketplace to both the employer and the employee, forcing the employer to take a more active role in determining the future human resources needs of the organization, as well as the technological needs the organization will have to address to make those human resources competitive. The employees still have the responsibility to maintain and improve their skills. The difference is that in the British model, there is more sharing of the burden of rapidly changing technology and the resulting outsourcing of the human resources needs of the company.

An Overall View

As a result of the forces discussed in this article, policy makers should consider the following when addressing the needs of the 21st century in employee management relations:

- Corporations have a duty not only to their stockholders to make a profit, but to their other stakeholders and the communities in which they do business;
- Technological change is going to be rapid and both predictable and unpredictable;
- The global marketplace will be hyper-competitive for the foreseeable future and companies must continue to pursue technological change and advancement while at the same time ruthlessly attempting to control costs.
- The cost of addressing the global economy of the 21st century must be paid. The only real question is who will pay for it.
- In the American approach, it is paid directly by the workers, who are subsidized, at least in part, by the government;
- In the continental European model it is paid by the corporations, who are also subsidized, directly or indirectly, by the government;
- In the British model, the labor force and the employers share responsibility, and there is some direct or indirect government support.

Policy makers must select the approach that will be most beneficial and costeffective for their societies. Each approach to the problem of outsourcing technological unemployment has costs associated with it, and each has certain benefits. This author favors an approach more in line with the British model, since it spreads the systemic cost of outsourcing and technological unemployment more evenly among the concerned parties. However, it should also be recognized that American industry has demonstrated that it will be very reluctant to give up the doctrine of employment at-will even if it can be definitively demonstrated that it is in its best interests to do so, and that firms will be generally unwilling to assume any additional costs in the hypercompetitive global marketplace unless either required and/or given incentives to do so.

The history of American industry has demonstrated a reluctance to reform itself, and major reforms have been imposed only from the outside in the form of industrial policy. Unfortunately, these reforms have come only when the abuses of industry have finally demanded they be instituted. Policy makers need to take action to prevent these kinds of abuses from occurring. The need is obvious, but is the political will to act sufficient to avoid the inevitable crisis that has been necessary for action in the past?

SUMMARY AND CONCLUSIONS

The world has become a global marketplace that is more competitive and far less forgiving than the national economies of just a few decades ago. To survive in this hypercompetitive world, corporations must produce the highest quality goods possible while at the same time ruthlessly cutting costs, a major component of which is almost certain to be labor.

Outsourcing jobs to less-expensive venues is nothing new; manufacturing jobs have been outsourced for years. What is new is that service sector jobs, often requiring a high degree of education and training, are now being outsourced to countries where the cost of similarly educated and competent employees is much less than that in developed countries.

Since World War II, many people from the developing world went to the United States and Europe, were educated in the major universities, returned to their home countries and taught others. These educated and skilled workers in places like India and China have reached a critical mass and are now capable of doing many of the jobs that were once the sole domain of workers in developed countries. Corporations have realized this and have transferred much of the work to these less-costly locations because the technology of to day's environment allows them to do so at minimal cost. The workers are highly competent, motivated, and much less costly.

This has presented governments in developed countries with the problem of increased unemployment, not because the company has done away with the job, but because the job has left the country. There have been a variety of responses to these events. In the United States, the burden has fallen primarily on the employees to seek retraining and new jobs. In continental Europe, the burden falls primarily on the firms to retrain the human resources and to provide them with the technology to make them competitive in the global economy. Great Britain has found a middle way, however, that provides the basis for our recommendations concerning the future of labor relations in the 21st century.

Government policy makers have a vested interest in how corporations treat their workers. If the government is going to accomplish its primary task of protecting the citizenry/workers/voters, it will have to take an active role in establishing an industrial policy that will do that, while at the same time allowing private industry to have the necessary flexibility to grow, prosper, and provide a standard of living that will benefit all of the citizens.

ENDNOTES

1. "Hayswire: NBER Mulls Revision of Recession Start Date Backwards," NCC, *American Intelligence Wire*, January 18, 2004.
2. V. J. Rancanelli, "Singing the Earnings Blues," *Barons*, November 5, 2001, V 81, I 45, MW p. 12.
3. R. Foroohar and T. Emerson, "A Heavier Burden: Even as Recovery Spreads Worldwide, Workers Are Finding Themselves Working Harder for Less Money," *Newsweek*, August 23,2004, p. 36.
4. Russell Flannery, "Hiring Hall," *Forbes*, July 26, 2004, p. 80.
5. A. P. D'Costa, "Uneven and Combined Development: Understanding India's Software Experts," *World Development*, January 2003, pp. 211-227.
6. J. Plomfret, "China's First Space Traveler Returns Home a Hero," *The Washington Post*, October 16,2003, p. A. 01.
7. L. Sullivan, "The 0 Word: Outsourcing Overseas: IBM Is Doing It. So Is Dell. Amazon, Cisco Systems, Motorola and Merrill Lynch Are Also in on It. Congress Is Filibustering on the Topic and Presidential Candidates Are Debating It. So What Exactly Is All the Excitement over Outsourcing Jobs Overseas?" *Risk Management*, July 2004, v 51, 7, p. 24-30.
8. C. P. Wallace, "Difficult Labor: German Unions Are Losing Support and Influence. Is Militancy or Moderation the Way to Regain their Clout?" *Time International*, August 4, 2003, v 162, 5, p. 51.
9. F. Maidment, "Germany and the United States: Two Countries, Two Directions," *European Business Review*, v 16, I. 3, 2004. pp. 267-271.
10. *European Marketing and Data Statistics, 2003*, Euromonitor, PLC, London, UK.
11. F. Maidment, "Labor's Role in Driving Economic Growth: A Comparison of the EU and NAFT A, *Proceedings of the Annual Meeting of the Northeast Business and Economics Association*, October 2-4,2003, Parsippany, N.J., pp. 75-77.
12. C. Rhodes, "Short Hours Undercut Europe In Economic Drive, *The Wall Street Journal*, August 8, 2003, p. AI, col. 1.
13. Theodore J. St. Antoine, "The Model Employment Termination Act: A Fair Compromise," *The Annals of the American Academy of Political and Social Science*, November 1994, v. 536, pp. 93-102.
14. Lewis Maltby, "The Projected Economic Impact of the Model Employment Termination Act," *The Annals of the American Academy of Political and Social Science*, November 1994, v. 536, pp. 103-118.
15. B. Israel, "Post-Dispatch Tries to Bust Union," *St. Louis Journalism Review*, April 2003,v.33,255,p.31.
16. S. Greenhouse, "For Labor, a Day to Ask What Went Wrong?" *The New York Times*, January 21,2004, p. A23.

17. Each country determines its unemployment rate somewhat differently, and if the United States calculated its rate the way any of these three European countries calculate their rates, the U.S. rate would be slightly higher. Also, for historic purposes, it is difficulty to directly compare unemployment rates over time because all governments, from time to time, make changes in the way they calculate their unemployment rates [18].
18. F. Maidment, "Unemployment to Rival the Depression," *The New York Times*, January 30, 1983, Sec. III, p. 21.
19. "Koreans, Czechs, American Are Hardest Workers," *EAP Associates Exchange*, September-October 2001, v. 31, is, p. 32.
20. S. Prasso and M. Ihlwan, "Less Work, More Shopping," *Business Week*, September 9,2002, p. 10.
21. F. Maidment, "Should Great Britain Join NAFTA?" *Proceedings of the New England Business Administration Association Annual Meeting*, May 2003, New Haven, Conn., pp. 42-44.
22. "News Analysis: EU Internal Comms Directive Looms," PRWeek, July 16,2004, p. 17.
23. "The Ultra-Liberal Socialist Constitution," *The Economist*, September 18, 2004, v.372,n. 8393,p. 59.
24. Steve Crabb, "The Art of Overdoing It," *The Grocer*, July 17, 2004, p. 68.
25. "Great News! India Is Outsourcing Jobs," *Asia Africa Intelligence Wire*, April 23, 2004.
26. M. Freedman, *Capitalism and Freedom*, University of Chicago Press, Chicago, 1962.
27. G. A. Steiner and J. F. Steiner, *Business, Government and Society*, McGraw-Hill Higher Education, Burr Ridge, Ill., 2001.
28. "Bush Brings Job Growth Message to Fairfax," *The Washington Post*, June 26, 2003, p.T.05.

UNIT 2

Planning

Unit Selections

Key Points to Consider

- What do you think is the best way to make decisions when other people have to implement them? Do you think some ways are better than others? Explain.
- What are some of the different ways that strategies can be implemented, especially by small businesses? How do you feel about talking to your competition?
- Under Sarbanes-Oxley, it is necessary to report to the federal government a whole new list of information that was not required to be reported before. Given some of the scandals in American industry, do you think this is a good idea? How would you go about doing this?
- If you are the leader of an organization, and you have no idea as to how to address a problem, how would you go about doing it? Would you involve others?
- Managers need to keep one eye on the external environment. Why doesn't this always work? Is it that we tend to see only what we are looking for?

Student Website

www.mhcls.com/online

Internet References

Further information regarding these websites may be found in this book's preface or online.

Benchmarking Network

http://www.well.com/user/benchmar/tbnhome.html

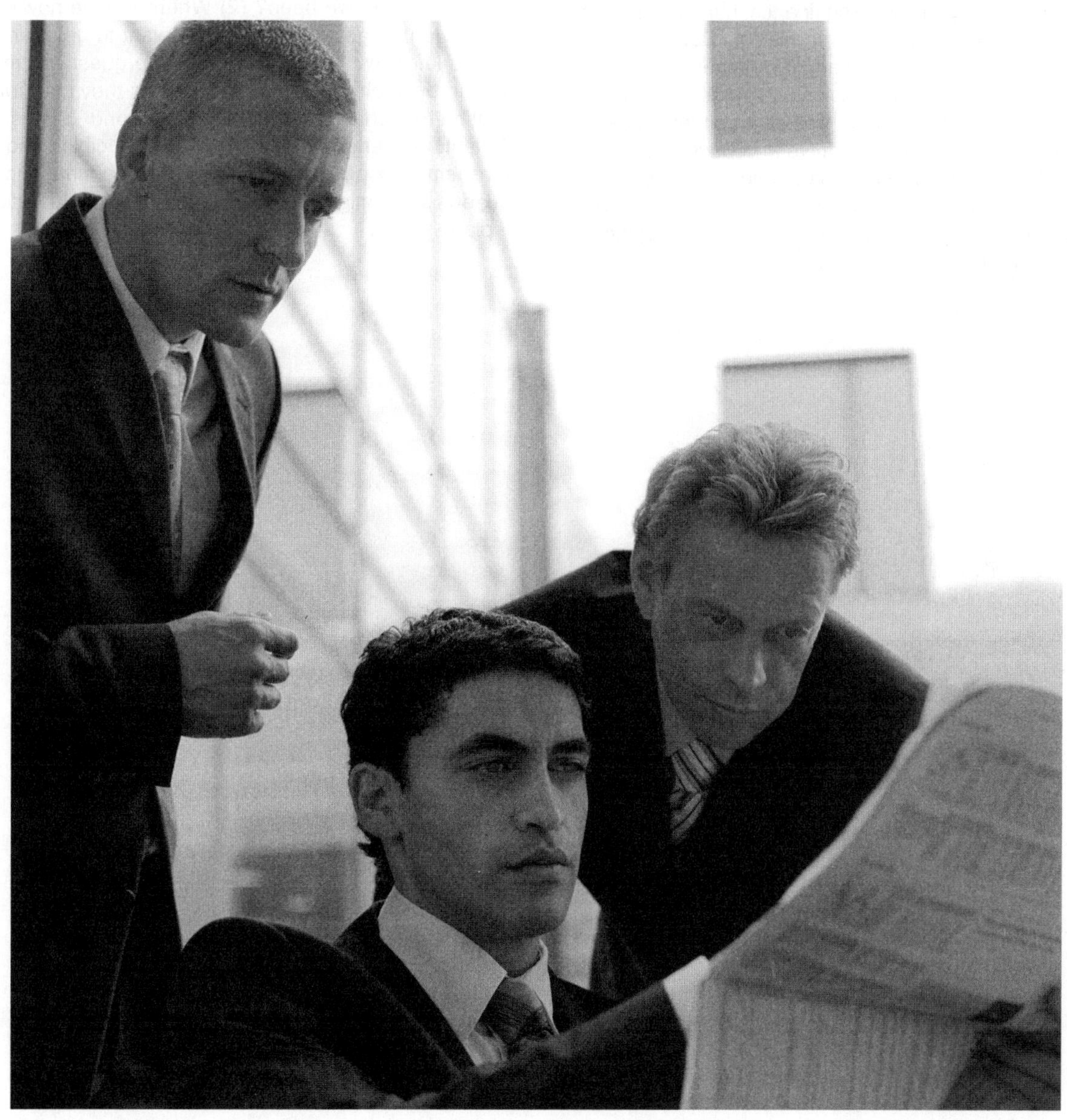

Managers must plan. Planning must be accomplished before action takes place. The question is, how should managers plan and decide on a course of action?

There are various styles, methods, and techniques that a manager can call upon. The way that the decision is made will be a key factor in the implementation of the plan. People who feel that they have some participation in making important decisions that will affect them are far more likely to support the plan enthusiastically than are people who feel that the decision is a fiat from the upper reaches of the organizational chart. Of course, a manager can make some decisions alone or in consultation with a few people. The important part is to select the appropriate planning/decision-making style, so that the action will have the greatest chance for success. The way to accomplish this is to involve the people who will be most directly concerned with the implementation of that decision.

It is basic to the function of a manager that he or she must make decisions. It is not possible for the policy manual to cover every situation that can arise. Managers must be able to interpret the goals and objectives of the plans for the good of the organization—not an easy task. Since there is always a degree of uncertainty in an important decision, the organization is also obligated to provide the manager with support and resources so that the decisions will succeed. Support includes not only a recognition and knowledge of the firm and its plans, but an understanding of the organization's internal and external environment.

This is explored in "Embracing Confusion: What Leaders Do When They Don't Know What to Do," and "Why Environmental Scanning Works Except When You Need It."

Planning must consider the internal strengths and weaknesses of the organization, including finance, human resources, manufacturing, distribution, and marketing. Capitalizing on strengths while minimizing the impact of weaknesses is vital to successful planning. Strategic decision making also involves an assessment of the environment as well as an understanding of the corporate culture, and the imperative to behave in an honest and ethical manner. Those who manage and plan for organizations must recognize that the only constant is change. Everything is fluid—people, places, and things—and managing the strategic agenda will be a key to success.

Finally, there are many ways to plan and make strategy. The effectiveness of the plan depends on the nature and needs of the business, the styles of the people, and the goals and plans of the firm. The five basic questions in strategic planning are: (1) Where have we been? (2) Where are we now? (3) Where do we want to go? (4) How do we want to get there? (5) How will we know we have arrived? These questions must be answered by each firm's management as they plan for the organization in a changing and uncertain world. It is essential that students of management learn these principles and be able to put them into practice. Opportunities abound and are often found in what might be considered less than traditional areas of planning.

Choose the Right Tools for Internal Control Reporting

Time is running out for many businesses to begin the complex process of complying with section 404 of the Sarbanes-Oxley Act of 2002, which tightened internal control and financial reporting requirements.

BY BRUCE I. WINTERS

This article is intended for readers in both industry and public accounting who seek, or need to offer, advice on selecting software—based on the extent to which a company already has compliance systems in place—for meeting section 404's requirements. Although it is not a detailed buyer's guide, it describes the features of specific software categories and thus can serve as a practical guide to what's available in the market and what to look for when examining software for employers and clients and discussing products with vendors.

CPAs can play a valuable role in helping companies choose software tools whose functions include supporting compliance and also enhancing communication with investors, employees and regulators, making financial statements clear and easier to analyze and increasing efficiency by, for example, eliminating redundant or obsolete controls and improving workflow. Acting as a technical adviser on financial internal controls design, financial processes and transaction flows, the CPA can help a client or employer answer three difficult but important questions:

- Is it better to design a compliance program for the short term (one year or less) or a more sustainable one for the long term?
- Which software tools are most capable of fostering complete, effective and sustainable compliance in a given business situation?
- What other investments (new policies and procedures, training and ethics programs, for example) are necessary to achieve section 404 compliance and also to take full advantage of the software chosen?

Companies are eager to contain the already spiraling costs of complying with Sarbanes-Oxley. Some are overhauling their business processes and integrating them into enterprise-wide systems. They also are installing software that produces always-up-to-date business process documentation in terms managers, investors and lenders can understand. This software enables companies to refine their financial controls, improve both their timing and public communication of key company events and provide more detailed evaluations of business results.

They Aim to Do It for Less

Emphasis on cutting Sarbanes-Oxley compliance costs in 2004	Percentage of responding CFO's
Major	23%
Moderate	50
Limited	13
None	7
Not sure	7

Source: Survey of CFOs of 70 U.S. companies with an average annual revenue greater than $6 billion, PricewaterhouseCoopers, 2003.

ASK (AND UNDERSTAND) BEFORE BUYING

CPAs can save clients or employers time and money by strongly recommending the selection of software be based on the criteria listed below in order of importance.

- The software tool's most important functions, not its minor features.
- The vendor's viability as a going concern.

- The vendor's support plans and the software's position in its product line.
- The product's ongoing compatibility with the company's operating systems and its scalability.
- Whether the tool has a Web-based interface and employees can access it online without installing software on their individual PCs.
- Whether customization of the product is available or required.
- The availability of suitable vendor-supplied implementation services.
- The level of training the vendor provides.
- The extent of integration with other tools—for example, how proprietary is the database, and can users easily link it to other programs?
- Price.
- Maintenance, support and upgrade costs (direct and indirect—for example, hardware and staff).
- Availability of information on any infrastructure and operating system changes or updates that could become necessary.

CPAs can play a valuable role in helping companies choose software tools whose functions include supporting compliance and also enhancing communication with investors, employees and regulators, making financial statements clear and easier to analyze, and increasing efficiency.

BUYER, KNOW THYSELF

The extent to which a company has progressed in building a strong control environment will dictate what tools it needs to buy and when. CPAs can use an internal controls maturity framework to help companies determine whether their existing or proposed controls for a given activity or process are rigorous enough to manage related risks and that they are sufficiently documented for review by auditors who must assess section 404 compliance. A version of such a framework, developed by PricewaterhouseCoopers, appears below.

As companies implement tools capable of providing real-time updates of business-process changes, their systems will begin to resemble the higher-numbered descriptions in the maturity model, reflecting greater efficiency and reduced risk.

Here's how to use the model. First, the CPA and the company should review the company's existing controls and identify the level of maturity that best describes them. This comparison will highlight any less than optimal controls, reveal what additional levels of sophistication are possible and enable the company to decide what goals it wants to establish for reinforcing its controls.

The Maturity Framework

Level 1: ***Unreliable.*** Unpredictable environment for which controls have not been designed or implemented.

Level 2: ***Informal.*** Controls are present but inadequately documented and largely dependent on manual intervention. There are no formal communications or training programs related to the controls.

Level 3: ***Standardized.*** Controls are in place and documented, and employees have received formal communications about them. Undetected deviations from controls may occur.

Level 4: ***Monitored.*** Standardized controls are in place and undergo periodic testing to evaluate their design and operation; test results are communicated to management. Limited use of automated tools may support controls.

Level 5: ***Optimized.*** An integrated internal controls framework with real-time monitoring by management is in place to implement continuous improvement. Automated processes and tools support the controls and enable the organization to quickly change the controls as necessary.

Impact of Section 404

This section of the Sarbanes-Oxley Act of 2002 generally requires public companies with a market value of $75 million or more, following the conclusion of their first fiscal year ending on or after June 15, 2004, to begin certain actions—such as including in their annual reports an assessment of whether their systems and financial reporting procedures are capable of providing accurate and complete financial statements. Other businesses must start their compliance efforts after the close of their first fiscal year ending on or after April 15, 2005.

Section 404 directs the SEC to issue rules mandating that companies' annual reports contain an internal control report that

- States the responsibility of management for establishing and maintaining an adequate internal control structure and procedures for financial reporting.
- Contains an assessment, as of the end of the company's most recent fiscal year, of the effectiveness of its internal control structure and procedures for financial reporting.

BE THOROUGH

Given the constant evolution of business processes, it makes sense for companies to adopt—if they're not already using—compliance software that can be fully integrated with company operations and reporting. Yet many companies still use paper-based systems or relatively uncomplicated software—such as spreadsheet, word processing and flowchart programs—to document their business process controls for compliance purposes. But while these products and paper systems can produce initial documentation easily, they aren't well-suited to continually making or tracking changes in it.

The best products provide an internal control architecture that changes to meet the organization's evolving compliance needs.

Companies reluctant to implement more complex systems equipped to track business process changes over time argue that Sarbanes-Oxley guidance and requirements still are not final, making significant software expenditures premature. Postponing the purchase of appropriate tools, however, may require the company to create compliance documentation using spreadsheets and word-processing programs, which can be error-prone. But eventually—perhaps very soon—they will have to recreate that documentation with more robust tools.

Many executives are reaching the same conclusion. In a CFO magazine survey published in March 2003, only 11% of 245 CFOs said spreadsheet-based control reporting—which is very common—was accurate enough to make senior executives confident about certifying their companies' financial statement data, as the Sarbanes-Oxley Act requires

To help guide their employers and clients in choosing the right application to facilitate section 404 compliance, CPAs first need to explore the characteristics and relative merits of several types of software tools.

WHAT TOOLS ARE AVAILABLE

Many of today's commercial software products can help companies comply with the provisions of the Sarbanes-Oxley Act. These tools range from simple, stand-alone programs that focus on a specific issue (for example, a regulatory checklist) to more complex enterprise-wide, real-time systems.

Except for generic tools—discussed below—many of these products provide a framework for adding modules to be offered in the near future—even by other vendors. The best of them establish and maintain a relationship between the overall business and its core systems and provide an internal control architecture that changes to meet the organization's evolving compliance needs.

CPAs should encourage their clients and employers to speak with multiple vendors when evaluating tools and request demonstrations of them to ensure understanding of their potential value to the company.

The tools can be classified into four categories.

■ ***Generic tools*** enable users to document internal controls, reduce potential risks and provide some level of comfort that compliance initiatives are in place. Many companies already have such compliance software built into their general accounting systems (see exhibit 1). But since such software is not dynamic—that is, it can't easily adjust to a company's changing business requirements—it provides only the most basic level of assurance and applies only to a given point in time. Further, since companies often adopt such tools without going through a formal software evaluation process and postpurchase measurement of their use and performance, it's difficult to ascertain their reliability.

These generic tools help companies comply with section 404. Their capabilities are limited, however, and do not match those of other products that are the best in their respective categories. However, vendors of accounting products are augmenting them with self-documenting audit trails that automatically record and provide access to incremental changes, with analysis tools to help auditors examine transactions within the system, with business intelligence tools that

EXECUTIVE SUMMARY

- **CPAs CAN PROVIDE A VALUABLE SERVICE** to their employers or clients by helping them plan their strategic approach to compliance with section 404 of the Sarbanes-Oxley Act of 2002.
- **NEW SOFTWARE PRODUCTS CAN IMPROVE** corporate governance and external communications about financial performance. They also can enhance the efficiency and effectiveness of compliance programs, thus reducing their cost and helping companies track progress toward establishing adequate internal controls and maintaining their effectiveness as business conditions change.
- **IT'S IMPORTANT THAT CPAs BECOME FAMILIAR** with the four categories of software tools: "generic" applications that enhance controls; document management and workflow; data mining, file retrieval, pattern recognition and business intelligence; and business performance management and real-time compliance.
- **COMPANIES SHOULD DETERMINE** which of the four categories of tools their current internal controls fit into, then identify company resources—such as staff and funding—that are available for an upgrade. Next they should select advanced tools that will enhance controls and improve company monitoring of them and compliance reporting to regulators.
- **CPAs SHOULD MAKE CERTAIN THAT BEFORE** their employers or clients buy compliance software they not only understand its characteristics, limitations and the related vendor support plans but also know what additional tools are necessary to ensure the company has in place a system of mature internal controls.

BRUCE I. WINTERS, CPA, is a certified information systems auditor focusing on Sarbanes-Oxley engagements in PricewaterhouseCoopers' systems and process assurance practice. He welcomes comments on this article and can be reached by e-mail at bruce.i.winters@us.pwc.com.

make it possible to delve into or summarize data, with consolidation interfaces linking disparate accounting systems, and with flags and alerts that signal when predetermined cost or other limits have been reached and require review by an analyst

The CPA should emphasize the importance of his or her client's or employer's contacting their accounting software vendors to evaluate their plans for assistance and support in section 404 compliance. This will provide a starting point for their deciding what, if any, additional tools are needed and how best to connect them to the company's existing systems.

Besides accounting products, other subcategories of generic tools include those for communication and collaboration and regulatory and technical reference purposes (see exhibit 1). Security products, of which there are too many to mention, constitute another group of these generic tools.

Exhibit 1: Generic Software Tools

Accounting (products with enhanced internal control capabilities)

- ACCPAC International Inc. (www.accpac.com).
- Best Software (www.bestsoftware.com).
- Creative Solutions Inc. (www.creativesolutions.com).
- Hyperion Solutions Corp. (www.hyperion.com).
- J.D. Edwards & Co. (www.jdedwards.com).
- Lawson Software (www.lawson.com).
- Microsoft Corp. (www.microsoft.com).
- Peoplesoft Inc. (www.peoplesoft.com).
- Oracle Corp. (www.oracle.com).
- SAP AG (www.sap.com).

Communication and collaboration

- Akonix (http://akonix.com).
- FaceTime Auditor (http://facetime.com).
- IM-Age (http://im-age.com).
- IM Logic (http://imlogic.com).
- Iron Mountain (www.ironmountain.com/digital).
- KVS (http://kvsinc.com).
- Legato (http://legato.com).
- Sector (http:/sectorinc.com).
- WiredRed (http:/wiredred.com).
- Zantaz (http://zantaz.com).

Regulatory and technical reference

- BNA Inc: (www.bna.com).
- CCH Inc. (www.cch.com).
- Factiva (www.factiva.com).
- LexisNexis (www.lexisnexis.com).
- PPC (www.ppcnet.com).
- The Thomson Corp. (www.thomson.com).
- WG&L (www.riahome.com/brands/default.asp).

Communication and collaboration tools also are used to set up audit trails and documentation. E-mail, instant messaging, webcast conferences and virtual team workspaces—locations employees share for common projects—all are repositories of critical business and process information that organizations rely on and must document and analyze.

Security-focused generic tools often provide finely detailed analyses for segregation of duties, intrusion detection, encryption, firewall implementation, antivirus protection, enterprise security and disaster recovery plan updates as important components of a strong internal control system.

Regulatory and technical reference tools provide a strong environment for obtaining accurate and up-to-date regulatory information for an organization.

CPAs should focus their clients and employers—when they shop for such tools—on the importance of obtaining from vendors a detailed explanation of how their products might integrate with the company's internal control environment and with other vendors' tools. While such integration is possible, it tends to be less than optimal because generic tools are not designed to link to other products.

■ ***Document management and workflow tools*** are more capable of interacting with other software than are generic products and can address relatively straightforward functions such as report tracking (see exhibit 2). These products monitor workflows and processes—applying a business unit's self-defined rules—to make them more event-driven and thus easier to manage. They allow users to perform detailed indexing and searching of multiple document types, including e-mail, flowcharts and narratives, to organize and retrieve text, images and numeric data.They also enable companies to collect and integrate data from their various accounting systems and to create links between separate business units' discrete business processes. Companies using them can better understand and analyze the frequency of control activities, categorize internal control types, test their effectiveness and re-

Exhibit 2: Document Management and Workflow Software Tools

- Documentum (www.documentum.com).
- eFileCabinet (www.efilecabinet.com).
- EMC Centera (www.emc.com).
- FileNet (www.filenet.com).
- GoFileRoom (http://immediatech.com).
- IBM/Lotus (www.lotus.com).

As an alternative, the following products do not possess Sarbanes-Oxley-specific compliance features but do have content-management capabilities.

- Hummingbird (http://hummingbird.com).
- iManage Worksite MP (www.interwoven.com/products/worksite_mp).
- Onbase by Hyland (http://onbase.com).

veal relationships between key job responsibilities and their place in the workflow.

These tools also are used to analyze risk and controls, rank them in terms of importance, materiality and impact and organize them by work group in a way that can be continuously updated to correspond with changing business conditions and be summarized for quarterly review and management approval.

■ ***Data mining, file retrieval, pattern recognition and business intelligence tools*** can gather data from separate systems and organize and analyze them. This enables companies to detect patterns in financial statement data and thus improve the effectiveness of internal controls and the accuracy of financial information (see exhibit 3).

Exhibit 3: Data Mining, File Retrieval, Pattern Recognition and Business Intelligence Software Tools

Data mining, file retrieval and pattern recognition

- ACL (http://acl.com).
- Caseware's IDEA (www.caseware.com).

Business intelligence

- Brio/Hyperion (www.hyperion.com).
  Business Objects/Crystal (http://businessobjects.com).
- Cognos Inc. (www.cognos.com).
- SAS Financial Management (www.sas.com/solutions/financial).

CPAs should impress upon companies the central role that three types of software in this group—data mining, file retrieval and pattern recognition—play in helping organizations fully understand the information they produce about their activities. Tools that perform these functions typically analyze, manipulate, sample and extract data. They also compare actual trends and patterns in financial statement accounts with expected norms to help identify irregularities that could indicate fraud or errors.

A fourth type of software in this group—-business intelligence tools—makes it possible to examine the results of business operations, delving deep into data and modifying variables to see how they affect a situation. It also enables users to review data for patterns, and it has strong reporting and graphical capabilities. And, with the advent of tools that are easier to connect to financial systems, this kind of software also has become cost-effective.

■ ***Business performance management and real-time compliance tools*** provide management with real-time, enterprise-wide data (see exhibit 4). These tools can smoothly interact with other software and systems and provide one repository for all company information, facilitate the development of consistent and more efficient processes, help optimize information timeliness and accuracy and promptly notify management of compliance problems and supply the means to resolve them, all of which enable the company to respond quickly to changing business conditions.

PRACTICAL TIPS TO REMEMBER

- The CPA should help the company evaluate its environment to determine the maturity level of its internal controls.
- He or she also should assist the entity in assessing its internal control philosophy and control environment.
- The CPA should encourage management to develop an understanding—through discussion with vendors—of the compliance software tools and their characteristics.
- When evaluating such software, companies should speak with multiple vendors in each category and observe a demonstration of every product to understand the value it can add to the organization.

The Gartner Group (www.gartner.com), a technology research and consulting company, estimates that 40% of companies will adopt business performance management (BPM) tools by 2005.

BPM tools add continuous auditing capability to real-time enterprise systems in the form of customized computer screens—called dashboards—that present key performance indicators managers use to decide when and how to react to changing business conditions. Managers' actions might include defining, improving and monitoring business processes on a timely basis, measuring and tracking the workflow of business functions and the changes in resources at each step of a process and—based on these—dynamically adjusting business processes. (An example would be production and inventory adjustments based on sales trends and related changes to approvals and workflow.)

There is a wide range of products in this category. Some link to specific enterprise-resource-planning systems, while others perform specific functions such as setting automatic triggers or real-time alerts to obtain quick responses. Some BPM tools enable you to instruct the system to alert management whenever, for example, company sales goals are missed or surpassed or multiple approvals are needed of large transactions.

Sarbanes-Oxley has begun a new reporting era for public companies, which will need real-time systems to monitor changing business conditions.

Real-time compliance tools store all information in one "data warehouse," provide consistent and efficient processing, optimize timeliness and accuracy, include rapid warning and response systems and make it easier to monitor and manage risks. These tools also provide performance management and workflow functions.

CPAs should ensure that all products being considered serve the needs of organizations in which employees report to a variety of departments in different locations. The software must link controls to processes, analyze and describe

Exhibit 4: Business Performance Management and Real-Time Compliance Tools

Business performance management (BPM)

Vendors are building software products with the ability to exchange data with other software to meet the functional and performance needs of both large and small companies. These products generally are easy to customize for specific situations and can be implemented without redesigning underlying systems. Examples of such software include

- Fuego (http://fuego.com).
- GEAC Enterprise Solutions (http://americas.geac.com).
- SAS (http://sas.com).
- Savvion Business Manager 5 (http://savion.com).

Real-time compliance

These products, many of which have BPM capabilities, are the optimal solution for companies aiming to implement an enterprise-wide internal control system. Among the vendors in this category are

- Approva Bizrights (http://approva.net).
- Axentis Enterprise (http://axentis.com).
- CARDmap (http://carddecisions.com).
- Centerprise Corporate Control Center (http://centerprise.com).
- Certus (www.nthorbit.com).
- CommerceQuest Traxion (http://commercequest.com).
- Compli Enterprise (http://compli.com).
- Concur Control (www.concur.com).
- Handysoft SOXA Accelerator (www.handysoft.com).
- KnowRisk (http://corprofit.com).
- Magique (www.darcangelosoftwareservices.com).
- Microsoft's SharePoint Portal Server (www.microsoft.com).
- Movaris Certainty (http://movaris.com).
- OpenText Livelink and IXOS (www.opentext.com).
- Paisley Focus (http://paisleyconsulting.com).
- Paisley Risk Navigator (http://risknav.com).
- Protiviti (www.protiviti.com).
- Providus RiskResolve (http://providus.com).
- Sarbanes-Oxley Express (www.openpages.com).
- Sempire Enterprise Governance (http://sempire.com).
- S-O Comply (http://onproject.com/soa).
- SOA Director (http://soadirector.com).
- Virtual Commitment (www.virtualcommitment.com).

the processes and link them to objectives and risks. The tools also should enable users to categorize, and set priorities for, risk and business objectives comprehensively in all areas of an organization.

DEAL WITH THE INEVITABLE

Sarbanes-Oxley has begun a new era of reporting for public companies. In order to meet the expectations of employees, shareholders and government, companies will need real-time systems that inform management of changing business conditions, such as changes in revenue, expenses, cash flow, production and employee-related issues as they occur.

Many companies will respond with static, manual "quick fixes" or patchwork solutions—such as spreadsheet-based systems—without lasting value, but others will build the appropriate architecture and tools to monitor processes and ensure their integration into standard operations, thereby providing the mechanisms that ensure the reporting of complete, accurate, valid and reliable information.

Note that this article does not pretend to cover all available products in any of the software categories it discusses. Instead, it presents a starting point from which readers can begin their own exploration of the subject.

Let's Be Friends

It seems nuts. But new research says that CEOs who become pals with their rivals do better than those who don't.

Alison Stein Wellner

MARIANNE D'EUGENIO DIDN'T KNOW what to think. It had been just two weeks since she'd opened Quadrille Quilting, a store in North Haven, Conn. Now she was on the phone with the last person she ever expected to talk to—Marty Childs, proprietor of Calico Etc. in nearby Cheshire and her closest competitor.

Childs was calling to ask if she could come by D'Eugenio's new store the next week to have a look and get acquainted—"a friendly welcome to the quilting community," was how she put it. D'Eugenio said yes because she didn't know what else to say. "What does that woman want from me?" she wondered.

At the very least, she assumed, Childs most likely intended to spy on her. As for the possibility that Childs might simply be a nice person looking to make a new friend, it never crossed D'Eugenio's mind. And who could blame her? After all, everyone knows that rivals can't really be pals.

Or can they? New research suggests that not only is it possible to make friends with your competitors—it's advisable. No matter how competitive their industry, rival CEOs who form friendships are at a distinct advantage over those who go it alone, says James D. Westphal, professor of management at the University of Texas at Austin, who recently completed a study of CEO friendship in 293 companies in a broad range of sectors.

What accounts for the advantage? When CEOs become friends, they talk shop. In the course of casual conversation, they compare notes, share information, and swap impressions about business conditions. That takes some of the uncertainty out of doing business. What's more, because competing CEOs are operating with similar information, they tend to make similar decisions, Westphal says. Say one CEO decides the time is ripe to raise prices. Chances are the rival-friend will do the same. Such informal coordination reduces risk. It's far less dicey, for example, to boost prices if you have a pretty good idea that your rival is too. And if you've both misread the market, at least one of you isn't going to put the other out of business. "A personal relationship between CEOs is going to tend to reduce rivalry," says Westphal. "That can only be good for both companies."

Researchers found that entrepreneurs who believe they're in business to vanquish the competition are less successful.

But before you invite your toughest rival over for tea, there are a few things to consider. Becoming buddies will require you to adjust your attitude about what it means to compete in the first place, says Kaihan Krippendorff, a professor of entrepreneurship at Florida International University. "Our knee-jerk reaction to a competitor's gain is to take it as our loss"—an attitude that is bad for business, he says. Over the past seven years, Krippendorff has analyzed 400 business case studies, the results of which are collected in his 2003 book *The Art of the Advantage*. His key finding: Entrepreneurs who believe they're in business to vanquish the competition are less successful than those who believe their goal is to maximize profits or increase their company's value.

Admittedly, this is not an easy notion to embrace. Bob Weinschenk, for example, is having none of it—despite what the academics have found. For Weinschenk, the CEO of Britestream Networks, a network security company in Austin, friendship with a competitor is simply out of the question. When Weinschenk bumps into a rival, "I'll nod and say hi, but it's really difficult to go beyond that," he says. "I'm not going to say, 'Let's go get a beer,' when what I really want to do is hurt your company." As he sees it, friendship is simply not part of an entrepreneur's job description. "My job is to take the team across the finish line and deliver return to the investors," Weinschenk says. "Anyone that interferes gets put on the bad-guy list."

Given the high stakes involved in running a company, it's an understandable attitude. But Charles O'Hearn, CEO of Summit Educational Group, a tutoring firm in Boston, says moving at least some competitors off the bad-guy list has been a boon for his business. Over the past 10 years, for example, he has developed a strong friendship with Lisa Jacobson, CEO of Inspirica, a tutoring firm in New York City. Jacobson, he says, has been an invaluable sounding board for brainstorming thorny business problems and confirming his sense of business trends.

But two years ago, that friendship was put to the test when Jacobson nervously informed O'Hearn she had decided to open a second office—in Boston, O'Hearn's home turf. O'Hearn considered his options. He could have gotten upset and ended the friendship. He could have made a countermove and opened an office in New York. Instead, he wished his friend luck. Sure, he was worried about losing business. But O'Hearn also knew that a new, smart competitor like Jacobson would only force his company to work harder. An avid basketball player and golfer, he makes the easy comparison to sports. "I like playing with people who are better than me," he says. "That makes me a tougher competitor."

It turned out that Boston has been big enough for both companies. And if O'Hearn does start to lose market share down the line? "I'd be bummed, but I'd just say, 'What do we need to do to compete?'" he says. "I could even see myself calling Lisa and asking, 'What are we doing wrong, and what are you doing right?'" The way O'Hearn sees it, it's better to have your butt whipped by a friend than an enemy. At least that way you're more likely to find out why.

Still, it's important never to forget where friendship ends and business begins. After all, not every apparently friendly rival is going to have pure intentions. There are plenty of things that O'Hearn won't share with even his closest pals in the industry; most new business initiatives, such as a new direct-mail strategy he's investing in, remain close to the vest. Everyone draws the line in a different place, but it's important to set limits and stick to them, particularly as your ties grow stronger.

Assuming your psyche is in order and your business boundaries firmly in place, there's no good reason not to pick up the phone, dial the competition, and see if you can't make yourself a new friend. That's what Marty Childs was doing when she first rang Marianne D'Eugenio at her quilt shop. As it happened, the pair developed a friendship that has paid dividends for both of their businesses. D'Eugenio, for example, prefers to work with floral fabrics, while Childs favors bright colors. Rather than stocking up in the other's area of specialty, they refer customers back and forth. "I think customers appreciate the fact that we're friendly with each other," says D'Eugenio. "When you have a friendship rather than a rivalry, it makes your life a lot easier." Indeed, when yet another quilt shop recently opened in the area, D'Eugenio didn't hesitate. She picked up the phone and gave the owner a call. Sure, it was a new competitor—but perhaps it was a new friend, too.

Embracing Confusion: What Leaders Do When They Don't Know What to Do

Rapid change is making confusion a defining feature of management in the 21st century. Paradoxically, the authors argue, leaders who accept their confusion can turn a perceived weakness into a resource for learning and effective action.

BARRY C. JENTZ AND JEROME T. MURPHY

WHILE we didn't know it at the time, the seed for this article was planted some 20 years ago when Jerome Murphy became the new—and often confused—associate dean of the Harvard Graduate School of Education. Blindsided by unexpected problems and baffled by daunting institutional challenges, Murphy often lost his sense of direction and simply didn't know what to do. To make matters worse, he felt like a phony. "For God's sake," he said to himself, "isn't a Harvard dean supposed to have the answers?"

Enter Barry Jentz, an organizational consultant who helped Murphy learn that confusion is not a weakness to be ashamed of but a regular and inevitable condition of leadership. By learning to embrace their confusion, managers are able to set in motion a constructive process for addressing baffling organizational issues. In fact, confusion turns out to be a fruitful environment in which the best managers thrive by using the instability around them to open up better lines of communication, test their old assumptions and values against changing realities, and develop more creative approaches to problem solving.

THE LOST LEADER SYNDROME

The two of us were recently reminded of our early encounters with confusion when we had the opportunity to work on issues of leadership with a distinguished group of urban school superintendents. Given the challenge of getting to their present positions, all of these superintendents had long since mastered the skill of presenting a confident, take-charge demeanor. But after developing enough trust to talk frankly with one another, these seasoned superintendents admitted that they were often confused and sometimes simply didn't know what they were doing—not that they could ever admit that in public.

This candid discussion revealed a pattern of behavior that we have come to call the Lost Leader Syndrome. The standard pathology may look familiar. No matter how capable or well prepared, managers regularly find themselves confronting bewildering events, perplexing information, or baffling situations that steal their time and hijack their carefully planned agendas. Disoriented by developments that just don't make sense and by challenges that don't yield to easy solutions, these managers become confused—sometimes even lost—and don't know what to do.

Many managers inevitably will respond to these symptoms by simply denying that they are confused. Others will hide their confusion—their search for sense—because they see it as a liability, telling themselves, "I'll lose authority if I acknowledge that I can't provide direction—I'm supposed to know the answers!" Acting as if they are in control while really not knowing what to do, these managers reflexively and unilaterally attempt to impose quick fixes to restore their equilibrium.

Sometimes, these managerial responses may even succeed in making the immediate symptoms of problems go away, but they rarely address underlying causes. More often, they lead to bad decision making, undermine crucial communication with colleagues and subordinates, and make managers seem distant and out of touch. In the long run, managers who hide their confusion also damage their organizations' ability to learn from experience and grow. Yet, despite these drawbacks, few managers can resist hiding their confusion.

We have observed this dysfunctional pattern hundreds of times in the public, private, and nonprofit sectors—in government agencies, corporations, universities, and foundations—

and believe that it is becoming more common as the pace of change accelerates.

Our recent discussions with school superintendents suggest that this pattern of confusion and hiding or covering up is particularly prevalent in the pressure-cooker world of public education. Parents, taxpayers, and political and business leaders expect educators to address issues for which there are no ready answers. Tony Wagner maintains that "the overwhelming majority of school and district leaders do not know how to help teachers better prepare all students for the higher learning standards."[1] Similarly, Richard Elmore argues that "knowing the right thing to do is the central problem of school improvement."[2]

In these pages, we will look at a method by which managers can transform their confusion from a liability into a resource and describe how this resource can be used to promote learning, new ideas, and the ability to take effective action. We call this method Reflective Inquiry and Action (RIA), a five-step process through which managers can assert their need to make sense and enlist individuals and teams without sacrificing their goals, values, or judgment. We believe that in the all too frequent situation of not knowing *what* to do, managers can make progress and maintain their authority by knowing *how* to move forward.

The RIA process is designed primarily for "micro" work, such as that in private meetings between individuals and small groups. But, as we shall see, several of the guiding principles behind RIA—embracing your confusion, structuring a process for moving forward, listening reflectively—can be quite useful on a larger scale and even in public venues. Significantly, these ideas can help leaders make headway while struggling with the daunting "macro" challenge of educating all children in every school, often a cause of confusion.[3]

THE TALE OF THE TAPE

Is "confusion" even the best term for that sense of disorientation caused by having the rug pulled out from under one's feet or by being baffled in the face of an unyielding challenge? It is certainly a loaded word in management circles, and to suggest that an educator should acknowledge confusion, even to close and trusted colleagues, is risky. When a New York City teacher recently posted on her weblog: "I have no idea how to teach these kids, and I'm not sure I ever will," her principal called her in to assess her emotional state.[4]

Even if managers can privately bring themselves to accept their confusion, can they truly use it as a resource for effective management? Many managers dismiss this idea as suspiciously touchy-feely. After all, phrases such as "embracing your confusion" sound too much like "getting in touch with your inner child"—hardly the basis for making progress in a rough-and-tumble world. Some managers may be unsettled by what they see as the "soft" nature of RIA, even if deep down they know that there is truth in the old cliché that real men never ask for directions—instead they end up driving around in circles.[5] (In the RIA model, real managers accept that they are lost and metaphorically ask for directions.)

Nowhere is this skepticism more evident than in RIA workshops. To overcome it and to get managers to take these ideas seriously, we have learned to put participants in front of a video camera and ask them to respond to difficult scenarios that thrust them into confusion. When the tape is played back, participants are surprised to see the discrepancy between how they behave and how they *think* they behave. They watch how their retreat into hiding produces interpersonal dynamics characterized by posturing, guessing, arguing, and accusing—when the truth is that everyone is equally confused.[6]

By contrast, when one of the participants is able to acknowledge her confusion without fear or shame—and to invoke the rigor of a structured inquiry—the videotape reveals a palpable change in the participants' sense of energy, competence, and confidence. For a manager who is capable of creating the conditions necessary for interpersonal learning and for those who have witnessed these methods at work, this moment of discovery raises hope that the RIA process can be the foundation for shared progress. For advocates of RIA, these revelations are a powerful argument against dismissing these ideas as too soft for a tough world.

THE "OH, NO!" MOMENT

Imagine being the head of a team charged with preventing deadly radiation leaks at a nuclear power plant. You hear an alarm sound. Based on years of experience and training—and a quick review of the data—you make an educated guess about what the problem might be. Suddenly, one of your team members reports that a key piece of information from the reactor systems doesn't fit your hypothesis. In fact, it's the exact opposite of what it should be. You have encountered what we refer to as an "Oh, No!" moment. You can't make sense of what is going on. As you sit stunned in front of your reactor-systems console, your team stares at you, waiting for a decision.

Now imagine that you are a member of the team, looking nervously to your leader. The last thing the situation requires is someone who:

- instinctively blames circumstances or other people when things go wrong;
- says he is open to input but regards any feedback as criticism and doesn't listen to others;
- hates uncertainty and opts for action even when totally confused; or
- takes a polarized view of leadership in which anything less than take-charge decision making shows abject weakness.

We all understand that a manager who neither listens to nor learns from others can quickly turn a messy problem into a nightmare. "Oh, No!" moments are familiar to all of us. They are caused not only by emergencies but also by a wide variety of everyday situations that regularly arise out of the blue and call into question our fundamental assumptions. We just can't make sense of what's going on. Taken aback by these situations, managers become distracted from their strategic agenda and reflexively respond to "Oh, No!" moments like the following:

- A change in technology renders a valued program obsolete.
- A promotion that everyone knows to be "ours" goes to a rival.

- A key administrator resigns without warning, offering an explanation that we simply do not believe.
- After repeated efforts to address a strategic challenge, we get feedback that our latest attempt is a failure.
- The long hours that produce triumph at work also produce trouble at home.

In moments like these—and in many situations that are more mundane but no less challenging—our minds begin to teem with questions. Our stomachs churn with emotion. Our old bearings no longer keep us on course. We struggle to reorient ourselves because the assumptions that gave meaning to our daily lives are suddenly rendered inadequate. We grope for new information that can help us make sense of this new situation and its impact. Often this initial investigation fails to reconcile our old assumptions with our new reality, and we find ourselves confused or even lost.

One of the ironies of these disorienting situations (and the "Oh, No!" moments that signal them) is that we often forget how much we rely on our world to make sense until our world is turned upside down by new information or changing circumstances.

GOING INTO HIDING

In the face of an "Oh, No!" moment, few of us are willing to reveal our confusion or our sense that maybe we are lost. To admit such a possibility opens the door not only to the fear of losing authority but also to a host of other troubling emotions and thoughts:

- Shame and loss of face: "You'll look like a fool!"
- Panic and loss of control: "You've let this get out of hand!"
- Incompetence and incapacitation: "You don't know what you're doing!"

At the gut level, many managers believe that saying " I'm at a loss here" is tantamount to declaring "I am not fit to lead."

So, when faced with disorienting situations, most managers deny, hide, or opt for the quick fix, rather than openly acknowledge that they feel confused.[7] Denial takes the form of blaming themselves or others, usually the person who delivers the counterintuitive information. Hiding leads to keeping their mouths shut in self-protection, not wanting to risk exposure as anything other than completely composed and confident. (One former school principal calls this the "art of the bluff.") Many managers unilaterally go for the quick fix, often making the wrong choice or dealing with a symptom rather than a root cause. In time, their unwillingness to consult with others and reluctance to seek out new information isolates these managers even further—having earned a reputation for not getting it, they are offered less and less candid information by their colleagues and staff.

Managers who hide their confusion are also sending out a strong signal that open acknowledgment of confusion is not acceptable behavior. Everyone else learns to hide as well. Organizations can spend thousands of dollars every year on development seminars that teach the power of becoming a "learning organization" that grows and improves over time, but managers who hide their own difficulties send the opposite message. They ensure that no growth occurs, that coworkers have no incentive to communicate openly, and that the organization drives around in circles, making the same mistakes again and again.

THE HIGH COST OF HIDING: A CASE IN POINT

Hiding is not only the natural managerial response to the confusion created by dramatic "Oh, No!" moments but also a common reaction to many mundane, everyday interactions, as illustrated in the following case of a meeting of a school district project team that went disastrously awry.

The superintendent was starting a reform effort with a tight and aggressive timetable. The changes had been long discussed, but never in detail, and now it was time to make definite plans. In her personal kickoff meeting with her business manager, chief deputy, and a senior aide, the superintendent said, "We haven't had much time to talk about the approach, but I'm really not so concerned about that because the problem here is really straightforward." The deputy superintendent was confused. " 'Not much time' is an understatement!" he thought to himself.

He wanted to say, "I don't want to appear stupid, but I need more clarification. I'm not at all sure of the approach you expect." Instead, he chose to hide his confusion, saying, "I think I understand your perspective, but can we talk about the approach a little bit more?" To which the superintendent responded, "I'm afraid I'm overdue for a meeting. If you get stuck, give me a call. I've got full confidence in the team. We should reconvene in two weeks."

By putting into place an overt and orderly process, you not only maintain your authority but also contain the confusion, avoid premature closure, and enlist your team in finding the best way to move forward. You turn your confusion into a resource.

As the superintendent left the room, the deputy thought, "This looks about as clear as mud—but I can't let the others think that I'm not on top of things. They'll lose confidence." Deciding once again to withhold his confusion, the deputy said to the business manager, "It's too bad we didn't have more time with the superintendent, but I think we've got enough to go on. Let's flesh out the work plan." Meanwhile, the business manager was thinking, "Boy, I'm glad I'm not the one who has to make sense of this—but it looks like the deputy is clear. It'll probably work out all right."

When the superintendent saw the draft plan prepared by her team, she was completely caught off guard. "They're only about

60% on target here," she thought to herself. "What the hell is the problem? These are my top people! How could they miss the mark on a plan that should have been as easy as falling off a log?" And what did she do with her confusion? She buried it and admonished the group for not finding the right "focus." Crucial weeks and many hundreds of staff hours had been wasted.

In a project post mortem, the superintendent admitted that she had withheld her confusion after reading the team's first draft and asked why her people had not voiced their own confusion during the first project meeting. Team members gradually acknowledged that they had concealed their confusion because they were afraid of looking stupid, making her angry, disappointing her, and being judged as not up to the job.

THE RIA MODEL

To succeed, managers must learn to embrace a new approach—one that is deceptively easy to describe but remarkably hard to practice. Yet this method can be applied to a wide range of unexpected problems, from time-sensitive emergencies to long-term projects.

Here are five steps for you to consider when you are confused and uncertain about how to get from Point A to Point B (or even unsure of what or where Point B might be). By putting into place an overt and orderly process, you not only maintain your authority but also contain the confusion, avoid premature closure (caused by internal or external pressure to act too quickly), and enlist your team in finding the best way to move forward. You turn your confusion into a resource.

These steps are presented as a sequence, but in practice their implementation should be seen as flexible and opportunistic. They should also be seen as a process within a larger framework: you may need to use them in multiple cycles or multiple venues in order to achieve the best effect.

Because going public with your confusion runs counter to conventional thinking, we suggest care in doing so in circles that go beyond trusted team members, advisors, and confidants. RIA should be tried out initially in limited but critical venues (e.g., with those who report to you directly), and even then you should lay the groundwork carefully by discussing the anticipated change in your problem-solving approach. Schedule a special meeting, distribute this article for discussion, and be open about the potential pros and perceived cons of RIA.

Step 1. Embrace your confusion. When confronted with disorienting problems, you need to do the one thing you least want to do—acknowledge to yourself that you are confused *and* that you see this condition as a weakness. Indeed, the biggest hurdle in getting from Point A to Point B is first getting to Point A—that is, acknowledging your true starting point.

Getting to Point A is extremely difficult because disorienting situations typically produce a painful split between feeling confused and listening to the loud voice that says that "real" leaders are not supposed to feel this way. In the grip of this ambivalence, managers will typically respond in primitive fight-or-flight terms, saying to themselves, "What's wrong with me for getting into this mess?" or "How do I get rid of this awful confusion?" Neither of these predictable responses offers a way to get beyond your inner conflict.

Rather than fight or flee, you need both to recognize and accept your tacit, yet firmly held, assumption that confusion means weakness.[8] You might take a deep breath and say to yourself, "I'm confused and that makes me feel weak." Paradoxically, fully embracing where you start will not lead you to wallow in your confusion, but rather frees you to move beyond your inner conflict.

You can then do what you most need to do—question your assumption that confusion is a weakness that needs to be banished and entertain a new assumption that confusion can be embraced as a resource for leadership. Because changing a firmly held belief is so difficult, it helps to develop a personal mantra. Here are some examples:

- "Confusion is not weakness, but the strength to take in new information at the risk of challenging my basic assumptions."
- "Leadership is being out in front where I have no choice but to encounter situations that make no sense to me."
- "Leadership is not about pretending to have all the answers but about having the courage to search with others to discover solutions."

Step 2. Assert your need to make sense. Having prepared yourself mentally, you now need to engage in dialogue. This face-to-face interaction will normally take the form of a meeting in which you describe your confusion so that others will know the point you (and they) are starting from. You might say any one of the following:

- "This new information just doesn't make sense to me."
- "I have a few thoughts about this, but I'll be the first to say we don't have enough information to suggest a definitive course of action."
- "Before I can make a decision, I need help in understanding this situation and our options for dealing with it."

Unless you come to recognize that being confused is a normal—even necessary—consequence of leadership, it will be difficult for you to state firmly that you are at a loss. How you deliver this message is as important as the words you use. Unless you unambiguously assert, with conviction and without apology, your sense of being confused, others will fulfill your worst expectations—concluding that you *are* weak—and they will be less willing to engage in a shared process of interpersonal learning.

At the same time, publicly asserting your confusion helps others to do the same—to claim their own confusion and begin trying to make sense out of a disorienting situation. By taking the lead, you make it easier for others to follow. Together you and your team will often discover that you share a common problem: how best to structure a process that can turn confusion into a productive, shared search for innovative solutions.

Step 3. Structure the interaction. Publicly acknowledging that you are confused is important, but it is only a beginning. Without skipping a beat, you must next provide a structure for the search for new bearings that both asserts your authority and creates the conditions for others to join you. You provide such a structure by stating [illegible] ering a set of specific steps [illegible] e, providing the timetable, [illegible] ods by which decisions will [illegible] y send the message, "To be [illegible] ay not know what course to [illegible] w how to structure a process [illegible] make sense of our new situ[illegible] words, you announce that yo[illegible] ctions but that you are still i[illegible] duce a clear outcome.

As an example, let's return to our story of the nuclear power plant executive and recall that after hearing the alarm he receives a report telling him the exact opposite of what he expected. Stunned, he is thrown into a state of confusion. While it will not be easy for him, he must acknowledge his confusion in a spirit of inquiry so that others might question his theories or offer explanations for the discrepancy between the expected and the actual report. To establish a good structure for this discussion, the manager might say, "Listen up! We've got two minutes, and then you'll get my decision. Between then and now, I'm going to talk about what's got me confused, and you are going to give me new information, feedback, or explanations for what is going on."

As in this example, it normally makes sense to start a meeting by revealing your state of mind, describing how you propose to structure the interaction, and then offering suggestions about the type of data you need to clarify and resolve the problem.[9]

Step 4. Listen reflectively and learn. You now need to listen reflectively as others respond to you. In the context of the RIA model, "reflective" carries both of its common meanings: you reflect thoughtfully on what other people have to say, and you consciously attempt to reflect your understanding of what was said back to the speaker.[10]

Reflective listening is especially difficult when you most need to do it—in situations where new information threatens to undercut your cherished assumptions. You tend to be blind to what may seem obvious to those around you; to you, their perceptions sound stupid, wrong, and intentionally hurtful.

Reflective listening is not normal listening. Ordinarily, most of us listen from a reflexive mindset that automatically judges the other person. This mindset is embodied in the question: "What's right or wrong with what was just said and what am I going to do about it?" In effect, your first mental act is to judge the worth of what was said, and your first verbal act is to agree or disagree. This typically leads to a confrontation, not a joint inquiry.

By contrast, reflective listening requires you to put yourself in the other person's shoes and, with an open mind, reflect upon her words, tone, demeanor, and nonverbal behavior. You then test what you have heard by reflecting back in your own words the essence of what she was trying to express. Finally, you come to a full stop and allow the other person the time to confirm, retract, or modify what she originally said. Here's the sound of reflective listening:

- "You seem to be saying that *x* caused *y*. Do I have that right?"
- "You're torn between two explanations. On one hand, you think *x* accounts for *z*; on the other hand, you think *y* does?"
- "So you're angry because I am saying one thing and yet doing quite another?"

Reflective listening sounds simple but is actually an acquired skill that requires repeated practice, like hitting a backhand in a fast-paced tennis match. And even after you have learned how to do it, you will still encounter major challenges in applying it to real-world situations. One such challenge is dealing with people who typically are not very good listeners themselves. In conversation with them, it will be only natural to respond to their reflexive style by falling back into the same pattern. Indeed, our habit of responding in kind is such a powerful force that it has a name: the Norm of Reciprocity. ("If you don't listen to me, I'll be damned if I'll listen to you.")

To make matters worse, reflective listening is especially difficult when you most need to do it—in situations where new information threatens to undercut your cherished assumptions. Because you are inside your frame of reference, you tend to be blind to what may seem obvious to those around you; to you, their perceptions sound stupid, wrong, and intentionally hurtful.

For all these reasons, surprisingly little reflective listening goes on in most organizations. Yet, as hard as reflective listening may be, it is an essential tool for checking the depth and accuracy of your understanding and thereby avoiding action based on untested inferences. Reflective listening also ensures that the other people in the discussion feel that they have been heard and understood, thus increasing their inclination to trust and collaborate with you. By mastering and using this skill, you produce conditions for joint inquiry rather than confrontation.

Step 5. Openly process your effort to make sense. Once you have taken in what others are saying—some of which will probably be puzzling and may be upsetting—you need to process your responses out loud. You must suppress the automatic instinct to process internally and simply announce the products of your private search for new bearings. When you find the courage to externalize your intellectual process, you invite others to engage in interpersonal learning. Working together, you can discover the limitations of one another's thinking—limitations that you cannot know as long as you process privately. Here are three examples:

- "That's news to me. I haven't heard that before."
- "That really throws me. How do you get to that from what you were saying?"
- "That helps me a lot by pointing out *x*."

If you end up using all of the available time without coming to a clear resolution, bring closure by explicitly summarizing where you are in the learning and decision-making process and describing next steps. You can say something like, "Clearly, we have a disagreement here. Let's state it and put it aside for now. We should move on and get next steps in place, including agreement on when and how this will be finally decided."

ANOTHER CASE IN POINT: RIA ON A LARGER SCALE

This case illustrates one way that the techniques of RIA apply not only to isolated and limited interactions and meetings but also to larger-scale initiatives.

Two months into a new job, a school superintendent received the results of a statewide literacy assessment: 25% of his district's eighth-graders couldn't read! A flash flood of dismay, blame, and calls for immediate action stormed in from the community, the media, and the schools. Behind the scenes, the school board demanded that the superintendent institute an emergency remedial reading program in all elementary schools and issue a strong "shape up" memo to the entire teaching staff. The teacher union made it clear that teachers were not going to be scapegoats.

Confronted on all sides with demands for action, the superintendent used RIA to interrupt the blame game, gain time for analysis, and avoid a rush to a quick fix, which he thought would exacerbate factional divisions without solving the problem. He was also confident that he could deal with his confusion without appearing weak or out of control.

Meeting privately with each board member, with small groups of the district's administrative staff, and with the head of the teacher union, he asserted his confusion about the test scores; he listened reflectively to accusations, demands, and explanations for the poor results; and he argued that action should follow a better understanding of the problems. He used a similar approach, with only slightly less candor, with business and community leaders, parent groups, and the local media. By listening carefully to everyone's concerns, the superintendent was able to garner support for a period of structured inquiry.

After these initial meetings, the superintendent created an inquiry group of teachers and administrators, charging it to analyze existing student data to evaluate the competing explanations for the poor results. As the group examined the data and tested hypotheses, everyone realized that they were all in the same boat—deeply confused. None of their assumptions or preconceptions seemed to account for the low test scores. That shared recognition freed them to work in concert.

Within weeks, the inquiry group came up with three significant findings: most of the nonreaders had entered the district after the third grade and so had missed the district's exemplary phonics program; the nonreaders were clustered in several schools in disadvantaged neighborhoods; and the transfers of students from one grade to the next were uncoordinated, so that those who needed long-term remedial assistance were not getting it.

On the basis of this new, shared understanding of the problems, targeted programs were implemented to address them, which led to an improvement in test scores the following year. Moreover, the superintendent gained widespread credibility because his more measured and informed approach avoided an ill-considered quick fix and produced results.

" So what?" a skeptic might say. "So the superintendent did his job—big deal." The fact remains that, every day, managers in similar situations don't do their jobs because they are afraid of their own confusion. Instead of acting on it with some version of the steps described in this article, they insist on denying it, hiding it from others, or trying to banish it with a quick fix. And, all too often, the problems get worse.

CONFUSION AS A RESOURCE

In the 21st century, as rapid change makes confusion a defining characteristic of management, the competence of managers will be measured not only by *what they know* but increasingly by *how they behave* when they lose their sense of direction and become confused. Organizational cultures that cling to the ideal of an all-knowing, omnicompetent executive will pay a high cost in time, resources, and progress, and will be sending the message to managers that it is better to hide their confusion than to address it openly and constructively.

Being confused, however, does not mean being incapacitated. Indeed, one of the most liberating truths of leadership is that confusion is not quicksand from which to escape but rather the potter's clay of leadership—the very stuff with which managers work. Managers can be confused yet still be able to exercise competent leadership by structuring a process of reflective inquiry and action. The RIA process can help address the maddening "Oh, No!" moments that can hijack managerial agendas. Equally important, the central principles of RIA can be quite useful on a larger stage (as seen in the school superintendent case) and can help managers make progress when taking on longer-term, strategic challenges, such as meeting the public expectation that all children learn.

The RIA process provides an orderly way for managers to move forward when they don't know what to do, to stay "in charge" when confused and even lost, to contain shared confusion and work on it, and to avoid premature closure. It enlists the manager's team in finding the best way to make progress and promotes honesty, trust, and mutual respect. It turns a perceived weakness—confusion—into a resource for learning and effective action.

Armed with confusion and the RIA process, leaders can take timely, constructive action—even when they don't yet know what to do.

Notes

1. Tony Wagner, "Beyond Testing: The 7 Disciplines for Strengthening Instruction," *Education Week*, 12 November 2003, pp. 28, 30.
2. Richard F. Elmore, "Knowing the Right Thing to Do: School Improvement and Performance-Based Accountability," NGA Center for BEST PRACTICES, August 2003, p. 9, available at `www.nga.org/center`. Click on the center's logo, and search on the author's name.
3. When applied to these "macro" agendas, RIA may be seen as one of many methodologies available to managers to pursue the larger-scale challenges of long-term "adaptive" leadership, as described by Ronald A. Heifetz in *Leadership Without Easy Answers* (Cambridge, Mass.: Harvard University Press, 1994).
4. Mark Toner, "'Blogs' Help Educators Share Ideas, Air Frustrations," *Education Week*, 14 January 2004, p. 8. For many leaders, it's easier and safer to employ humor or euphemism. After a long lifetime of blazing trails on the American frontier, the octogenarian Daniel Boone was asked by a friend if he'd ever been lost. "No, I can't say as ever I was lost," Boone replied, "but I was bewildered once for three days."
5. One of the lessons of our work in leadership and management training is that this pattern of reluctance to seek assistance from others when lost and confused is not limited to male executives. It may be that many female leaders respond to the pressure of gender bias by cultivating a style even more self-contained than that of their male colleagues.
6. The discrepancies between the way managers behave and the way they *think* they behave has been extensively reviewed in the literature on leadership theory. See Chris Argyris and Donald Schön, *Theory in Practice: Increasing Professional Effectiveness* (San Francisco: Jossey-Bass, 1974).
7. Some managers may take their confusion "off-line," revealing it to only one or two trusted confidants. As one veteran executive told us, "I could never say something like that in public. It would be suicide. But there are people I can call on to talk things through with and then say, 'This conversation never happened.'" Unfortunately, while this safety valve provides a valuable sense of relief for managers wrestling with confusion, it doesn't help others in the organization to open up and engage in productive conversation.
8. For a similar argument about the power of basic assumptions, see Robert Kegan and Lisa Laskow Lahey, "The Real Reason People Won't Change," *Harvard Business Review*, November 2001, pp. 85–92.
9. The joint inquiry model can be used on as small a scale as a one-on-one meeting but has obvious applications in larger situations as well. At the macro level, one of the best situations in which to use this model is when a manager starts a new job. Obviously, entering a new workplace is bound to throw a manager into a state of confusion, since historical explanations of key events will vary from source to source and there will be little initial guidance about which sources are reliable (i.e., whom to trust). For a detailed account of "structuring the interaction" at the beginning of a new job, see Barry Jentz et al., *Entry* (McGraw-Hill, 1982; reprint, Leadership & Learning, Inc., available from `www.entry-book.com`).
10. The definitive article on listening remains Carl R. Rogers and F. J. Roethlisberger, "Barriers and Gateways to Communication," *Harvard Business Review*, November/December 1991, pp. 105–11. (Originally published in 1952.)

BARRY C. JENTZ *is an organizational consultant to public and private schools, corporations, and private firms and a lecturer in the Graduate School of Education, Harvard University, Cambridge, Mass.* ***JEROME T. MURPHY*** *is Harold Howe II Professor of Education and dean emeritus, Graduate School of Education, Harvard University, Cambridge, Mass. He is currently a visiting professor at the Graduate School of Education, University of Pennsylvania, Philadelphia.* *The authors would like to thank their colleagues and the participants in the Superintendents Leadership Program, a collaborative effort of the Graduate School of Education and the Kennedy School of Government at Harvard University; Ron Heifetz for his enduring insights; and Samantha Tan for her research assistance and counsel. The authors would particularly like to thank Thomas Champion for his extraordinary contributions to this article, and they are especially grateful to the Wallace Foundation for its support.*

Article 9

Why environmental scanning works except when you need it

Environmental scanning systems are useless in the face of strategic inflection points—the dangerous quantum changes in competitive environments. Top managers and strategic planners lack the will and the intuition, respectively, to deal with those points the system *does* detect. More often than not, however, the system will simply fail to see them at all. To do so requires a synthesis that can only be provided by line managers who have both the right intuitions, by virtue of day-to-day contact with the real world, and access to unfiltered information, by virtue of their lowly station in the corporate hierarchy.

Brian J. Huffman

"Big men don't scare easy."
"Big men get popped off regularly."
—William Conrad (racketeer Castro) and Dick Powell (ex-con Rocky Malloy) in *Cry Danger*

We humans can handle today, but tomorrow often keeps us awake at night. Maybe that's a good thing; some of the top business people in the country seem to be running scared. Andrew Grove, Intel's Chairman, even says he finds fear healthy: "It is fear that makes me scan my e-mail . . . makes me read the trade press...gives me the will to listen to the Cassandras....Fear can be the opposite of complacency" (Grove 1996). Bill "Sleepless-in-Seattle" Gates gloomily predicts that Microsoft will have to weather at least three major crises in the next ten years. As if that weren't bad enough, he adds, "One day an eager upstart will put Microsoft out of business. I just hope it's fifty years from now, not two or five" (Gates 1999).

Why are these guys so worried? Certainly companies as large and powerful as Intel and Microsoft could not be put out of business that fast. Certainly they have environmental scanning "radar systems" to warn their titanic enterprises about the icebergs on the horizon. Maybe they have, but then the original Titanic wasn't really sunk by an iceberg. After all, the berg didn't ram the Titanic; the ship rammed the berg—and went down *very* fast.

The Titanic sank because of facts that its slightly post-Victorian crew were simply not equipped to see. They lived during a time in which technological changes came at a furiously unprecedented rate. Victorian optimism combined with new and unfamiliar technology led to spectacular, technologically driven disasters even before the Titanic's sinking. That optimism was manifest in Titanic's defective hull rivets, in its "watertight" compartments which were open on top, in its radio operator who was annoyed by ice warnings coming from other ships, and in its lack of sufficient lifeboats.

Given Titanic's limited sea trials, the crew would have had to rely on their experience in estimating the proper turning radius, knowledge of which would be needed to determine a safe cruising speed in iceberg-infested waters. Unfortunately, the ship's unparalleled dimensions made nonsense of that "experience."

The Titanic went down because ship design had reached what Grove calls a *strategic inflection point*—a point of massive change. By 1912, when Titanic passed into history, ship designs were changing faster in one year than they had previously changed in decades. The Titanic's fate seems less unlikely when one considers that the most experienced of the vessel's officers had begun their careers when commercial ships were made of wood and powered by wind and sail.

Environmental scanning systems are like the spotters in the Titanic's crow's nest; they are put in place to warn us about icebergs, problems we expect given our perception of the current environment. But what if that perception is wrong? What if the environment has changed? What if, in other words, we have reached a strategic inflection point? In that case, the unexpected and therefore much more dangerous problem slips in undetected. The real danger, the crew's outdated experience, remains unseen.

Expected problems, however dangerous, are still part of the existing game that successful players like Microsoft and Intel know how to win. Strategic inflection points, on the other hand, represent a new game in which the current winners are as amateurish and thus as likely to lose as any other player. Environmental scanning systems, which see only expected problems, warn us about those things that are no real threat in the first place.

Intel was a frog sitting in water that had very slowly been brought to a boil.

The most dangerous strategic inflection points are those that don't just "happen" by themselves but are driven by a competitor (usually a new competitor). In these cases, detection is even more difficult because the competitor can be expected to try to hide the change until it is too late to stop the damage. The military calls these competitor-driven points "asymmetric attacks."

How can firms deal with strategic inflection points and asymmetric attacks? Why do these represent such a serious threat even to large, successful corporations? And why does environmental scanning fail in the face of them?

What is a strategic inflection point?

"Why didn't you come home before?"

"Why didn't I go to China? Some things you do, some things you don't."

—Keith Andes (fisherman Joe Doyle) to Barbara Stanwyck (his sister) in *Clash by Night*

Why did Andrew Grove and his lieutenants at Intel doggedly stick with plans for making memory chips when they knew the Japanese were about to eat their lunch? The answer involves a noxious mixture of corporate identity, cognitive dissonance, and a strategic inflection point. The bottom line is that their environmental scanning system did not help them avoid a near disaster.

Grove defines a strategic inflection point as the point in time "when the balance of forces shifts from the old structure, from the old ways of doing business and the old ways of competing, to the new." The forces to which he refers are Porter's 5 forces (existing competitors, customers, suppliers, new entrants, and substitutes) plus Grove's own force of "complementors"—businesses from which a firm's customers buy products that either work better or work only with its product.

Strategic inflection points differ from run-of-the-mill environmental changes in that they are very large—Grove says ten times larger, or "10X." Because environmental scanning systems are designed to pay attention to the six forces, it seems they would more readily detect strategic inflection points than smaller force shifts. However, just the opposite is true. Despite their size—actually, because of it—these massive shifts turn out to be harder to identify than smaller, more expected ones. As Grove warns, they "build up force so insidiously that you may have a hard time even putting a finger on what has changed, yet you know that something *has*."

Part of the problem is managerial will. Specifically, the will to "see" a force change is inversely proportional to the size of that change. We do not see what we do not want to see, and nobody wants to see his world coming to an end. Sometimes management refuses to see the really bad news even if the scanning system serves it on a silver platter. Intel's experience makes the point.

Intel thrived for many years as a memory chip manufacturer before encountering a strategic inflection point that took it to the brink of bankruptcy. In the late 1970s, the Japanese began to slowly change the rules of Intel's game, eventually devoting far more resources to memory chip development and production processes than any American player. In time, it became inevitable that the Japanese were going to own the entire memory chip market.

Intel's top managers lacked the will to see the warnings from their environmental scanning system and stood frozen as market share eroded. Grove admitted that it was actually impossible for his management team—people who saw themselves as "memory chip makers"—to even consider a future in which they did not make chips. Finally, forced to consider an even more disturbing image of the future, one in which he had been fired for mismanagement, Grove was jolted out of his slumber. He would do what he knew his successor would have to do: take Intel out of memory chips. Grove was shocked that he had to slip so low to be able to see unpleasant facts that had been staring him in the face for years.

Grove's inaction had nothing to do with the speed of the attack. This wasn't Pearl Harbor. In fact, Intel was already aware of the Japanese as competitors in the late 1970s and had even used Japanese producers as subcontractors. It took nine long years for the Japanese share of the worldwide semiconductor market to grow from about 28 percent in 1976 to the point at which it equaled the US share of about 45 percent by 1985. Intel was a frog sitting in water that had very slowly been brought to a boil.

It is interesting to note that the line managers at Intel, whose intuitions were sharpened by close day-to-day contact with the chip game, were not suffering from the same blindness as top management. Says Grove, "These people, like our customers, had known what was inevitable before we in senior management faced up to it." The irony is that those removed from the radar screen of the environmental scanning systems were nevertheless the first ones to see the new reality approaching.

Grove mentions the value of intuition in identifying strategic inflection points, stating that data may be trumped by "anecdotal observations and your instincts." But he fails to mention that the opportunity for anecdotal observation and the right kind of intuition is more and more rare as one climbs higher up the corporate ladder. Top managers are both further from the day-to-day realities of the business and more likely to receive filtered information.

Proponents of environmental scanning will say that these systems can work if the data are properly analyzed and if top management gets the information and forces itself to be receptive to it. But that will not become reality. Remember in *Whatever Happened to Baby Jane?* when the wheelchair-bound Joan Crawford complained that the abusive Bette Davis wouldn't be so mean to her if she weren't stuck in her chair? Davis murderously shoved the chair with Crawford in it over the edge of a large staircase and taunted, "But'cha *aahre*, Blanche. Ya *aahre* in that chair."

What is an asymmetric attack?

"My, my. Such a lot of guns around town and so few brains."

—Humphrey Bogart (private eye Philip Marlowe) in *The Big Sleep*

The United States Army may be the 900-pound gorilla of the world's military forces, but its deep thinkers in War College's Strategic Studies Institute (SSI) are nevertheless very concerned about the strategic inflection points it calls *asymmetric attacks*. The definition of asymmetry in this respect refers to the way the adversary fights. As Metz and Johnson (2001) explain, it is a manner of fighting that has evolved from the somewhat fuzzy "not fighting fair" to "acting, organizing, and thinking *differently* than opponents in order to maximize one's own advantages, exploit an opponent's weaknesses, attain the initiative, or gain greater freedom of action."

The standard (symmetric) attack is like a boxing match in which two people hammer away at each other using roughly the same methods and technology; not surprisingly, the big guy usually wins. In an asymmetric attack, the smaller guy would pull out a gun. On September 11, 2001, al-Qaeda did not box according to the Marquis of Queensbury Rules.

A competitor's use of asymmetry is not always deliberate. According to Metz and Johnson, "More often, antagonists in a conflict or war simply use what they have and do what they know how to do. That the outcome is asymmetric is more accidental than planned." Thus, the concept of asymmetry allows for fortuitous, even inadvertent success—"dumb luck."

Asymmetric attacks, like strategic inflection points in general, are becoming more and more common as the world order changes faster and faster. Mintzberg (1993) notes that the outdated belief of 1960s-era business writers like John Kenneth Galbraith that giant corporations were relatively free from any serious competition seems quaintly ridiculous given recent history. Galbraith also might have said that the American military faced no real challenges. He expressed his notions in the last decade in which they could have been taken seriously—the decade before insignificant Japanese car manufacturers turned powerful GM into one of the biggest money-losing enterprises in history, before Big Blue's share of the computer industry was dramatically cut by whiz kids like Steven Jobs with "toy" computers they built in their garages, before the US military lost a war to a third-world nation.

In the same way the Colt 45 was the "great equalizer" in the Old West, new strategies and technologies such as the Internet have made the business playing field of today more level and far more dangerous. New competitors like Amazon.com have used the Net to come out of nowhere and launch asymmetric attacks on bookstore chains many times their size.

The bad news in the previous section was that top management will not see warnings of strategic inflection points even when the environmental scanning systems detect them. The worse news here is that scanning systems are not likely to detect asymmetric attacks because those who launch them approach with stealth and misinformation, and because the attacks are one-time events and therefore nearly impossible to forecast (more will be said on this later).

Asymmetric attacks are mutations, and like mutations in nature they are usually unsuccessful (fortunately for most existing businesses). Unfortunately, when mutations are successful, they often spell doom for existing species.

Real danger? The Powerball lottery's evil twin

"If you want to play with matches, that's your business. But not in gas-filled rooms."

—Robert Mitchum (ambulance driver Frank Jessup) and Jean Simmons (femme fatale Diane Tremayne) in *Angel Face*

Strategic inflection points are dangerous precisely because it is so difficult to see them coming. An environmental scanning system fails to detect them because in looking for things that are likely to happen, it analyzes, or breaks down information, when it needs to synthesize—put seemingly unrelated pieces of information together. The trick is to somehow synthesize unlikely combinations of these unrelated pieces conceptually before they synthesize themselves physically.

But why worry at all? If strategic inflection points represent such unlikely combinations, they should be unlikely, right? No, weird combinations are common; the issue is not whether a specific unlikely thing will happen, but whether or not *any* unlikely thing will happen. Chiles (2002) explains, "In a multistate lottery the odds of any given person winning are extremely remote, but the likelihood that *someone* is going to win, sooner or later, is certain." Substitute "occurrence of a strategic inflection point" for "someone winning" and we have what Chiles calls the "Powerball lottery's evil twin." Many unlikely things came together to create the Internet, which could have wiped out Microsoft. Thus, Gates's pessimism is not paranoia; the day will come when that "eager upstart" puts him out of business.

However, after an unanticipated disaster strikes, the armchair quarterback is easily able to convince himself that the disjointed (unsynthesized) data provided by the environmental scanning system should have been enough to warn leaders. Disasters are seen as having been inevitable, predictable, and (of course) avoidable. The press and FBI whistleblower Colleen Rawley tell us the FBI should have been able to assemble the bits of information it had prior to 9/11 to prevent that disaster. They are kidding themselves; unlikely connections only look likely in hindsight. James Burke (2003) of "Connections" fame found a connection between the 1804 attack on Tripoli and the invention of fish sticks; he was able to make even that ridiculously unlikely connection look plausible.

An experiment described by Fischhoff (1975) illustrates the point. Subjects in three groups were told about a battle between the British and the Nepalese Gurkhas in 1814. All three groups were truthfully apprised of the conditions prior to the battle, but each group was given a different outcome. The first group was told that the British won, the second that the Gurkhas won, and the third that the battle ended in a tie. Members of each group said that given the conditions before the battle (the data), they would have judged the outcome they heard as most likely even if they had not been told what happened. So much for 20/20 hindsight.

Moreover, according to Kahneman and Tversky (1982), the easier it is for subjects to imagine an alternative ending, the more they will tend to believe that what did happen could have been avoided. Wall-to-wall news coverage after the first space shuttle disaster gave the armchair quarterbacks enough "facts" to make that accident seem almost the result of criminal negligence. However, "the" definitive Challenger disaster study by Vaughan (1996) made it clear that the explosion was not foreseeable.

How are environmental scanning systems supposed to work?

"Maybe she was all right, and maybe Christmas comes in July. But I didn't believe it."

—Humphrey Bogart (war vet Rip Murdock) in *Dead Reckoning*

In order to better appreciate the problems environmental scanning systems have with strategic inflection points, we first need to step back and consider how such systems are supposed to work. According to Thompson and Strickland (1998), environmental scanning "involves studying and interpreting the sweep of social, political, economic, ecological, and technological events in an effort to spot budding trends and conditions that could become driving forces." Those authors dampen expectations by admitting that environmental scanning is "highly qualitative and subjective," but apparently they do not think it so qualitative and subjective as to defy any systematic approach. In fact, they offer two analytical approaches: constructing scenarios (which will be discussed later) and answering key questions:

1. What are the industry's dominant economic features?
2. What is competition like and how strong are the competitive forces?
3. What are the drivers of change in the industry and what impact will they have?
4. Which firms are in the strongest/weakest positions?
5. What strategic moves are rivals likely to make next?
6. What are the key factors for competitive success?
7. Is the industry attractive and what are its prospects for above average profitability?

Proponents of environmental scanning usually recommend that these questions be answered by dedicated strategic planners, staff people removed from day-to-day operations so they are free to concentrate on the big picture. But the use of analytical systems, such as these seven questions, and of dedicated strategic planners is the root cause of environmental scanning system failure.

Problems with strategic planning

"I came to Casablanca for the waters."
"Waters? What waters? We're in the desert."
"I was misinformed."

—Humphrey Bogart (nightclub owner Rick) and Claude Rains (Capt. Louis Renault) in *Casablanca*

Henry Mintzberg is an outspoken critic of textbook recommendations for strategic planning, of which environmental scanning is a part. He captures his objections in three "fallacious assumptions." The first is the *assumption of detachment*, the belief that "thought must be detached from action, strategy from operations, ostensible thinkers from real doers, and therefore 'strategists' from the objects of their strategies" (Mintzberg 1993). Surely, dedicated expert planners freed from day-to-day operations would be better at determining the meaning of data from environmental scanning and therefore better at building strategies than those who must divide their attention between operations and strategy making? Surely not. The real-world experiences and intuitions of line managers are essential in both interpreting environmental data and developing strategy.

But if strategy must be developed exclusively by dedicated planners, couldn't line management experience and intuition still be provided systematically somehow? This illustrates the second fallacy. The *assumption of formalization* is the mistaken belief that analytical systems can be built with the capability of generating intuitions on a par with those of line managers. Mintzberg argues that the belief is due to a misunderstanding of Taylorism, which requires an understanding of any process to be formalized. Since no one understands the process by which humans generate intuition, it cannot be formalized. Mintzberg notes further that even if an intuition-generating system could be built, it would certainly not be analytical, like the seven questions. Rather than breaking up information into pieces, a line manager's intuition is needed for just the opposite purpose—to synthesize fragmented pieces into meaningful wholes.

Rather than breaking up information into pieces, a line manager's intuition is needed for just the opposite purpose—to synthesize fragmented pieces into meaningful wholes.

The third fallacy is the *assumption of predetermination*, the belief that the strategy-making process can be specified in advance of making strategy, and that the consequences can likewise be determined in advance of implementation. This, says Mintzberg, is because "the context for strategy making is (assumed to be) stable, or at least predictable." Mintzberg argues that strategies are often incorrectly relied upon as if they were road maps "with a fixed and well-defined target, as well as the steps to reach that target." Road maps work because roads stay put, but a competitive environment changes from one minute to the next.

This third fallacy is especially significant when one-time events are concerned (as we will see next). For now, it is enough to know that one-time events are difficult to predict and that they are becoming more and more common. Further, whereas the fallacious assumptions discussed here relate to strategic planning in general, we focus next on the specific problems of environmental scanning.

Problems with environmental scanning

"What do you want, Joe, my life history? Here it is in four words: big ideas, small results."

—Barbara Stanwyck (Mae Doyle) to Keith Andes (her brother Joe) in *Clash by Night*

Many big ideas and small results are associated with environmental scanning. The problems with the seven questions should be clearer in light of Mintzberg's objections. First, there is nothing in them, or in the expert strategists who are supposed to answer them, to cause a picture of the future to be synthesized (the fallacy of formalization). Second, questions 1, 2, 4, and 6 are oriented toward considering the status quo, which is apparently assumed likely to be maintained (the fallacy of predetermination). Third, although questions 3, 5, and 7 are more oriented toward the future, it is still hard to say how they would work for a company facing a fundamental shift in its industry. Question 3 seems especially problematic: What good is identifying drivers of change *in* the industry when the changes are coming from *outside* the industry? Question 5 would be irrelevant because, first, the firm's perceived rivals would most likely not be its real rivals and, second, the rivals it does perceive would most likely be in the *current* industry and therefore just as clueless about what to do as the firm itself. Finally, question 7 assumes the firm knows what "the industry" means; again, this is unlikely since the only industry they perceive is the current one, and that one is coming to an end.

Mintzberg pointed out that a major problem with environmental scanning systems is that they cannot predict one-time events (such as 9/11) because there are no patterns or causal relationships from which to construct a model. We can predict the weather (however imperfectly) because the same sort of weather happens over and over again. We have learned that a falling barometer generally precedes precipitation.

The difficulty in scanning for one-time events was demonstrated by hundreds of computer industry analysts who got their predictions way wrong not just once but twice in a single year. Gates tells how newspaper and magazine headlines in 1995 went from mistakenly declaring Microsoft "invincible" in August to mistakenly saying the company "didn't get it" (the Internet) only two months later; Microsoft stock was actually downgraded by Goldman Sachs in mid-November of that year. The analysts had earlier declared the company invincible because they could not see the approach of a one-time event: the sudden commercial viability of the Net. Just off the success of Windows 95, Microsoft suddenly found itself with dangerous new competitors who themselves had almost accidentally stumbled into the perfect position to exploit the Net's unexpected leap in popularity. No consideration of the six forces would have been of any use to Microsoft or the PC industry press in predicting this attack since it came from outside the environment of the software industry, specifically, the US Defense Department and university researchers. Neither of these was a new entrant; neither had any intention of getting into the PC software business; neither would have been on any "new entrant watch list" at Microsoft.

A top executive or dedicated corporate planner would not have been on a recruiting trip in the first place, but even if one had, it is unlikely he would have had the right intuition to appreciate the danger in what was going on at Cornell.

Not only did the Net threat evolve without the intention of an existing force or "player" in the PC software industry, in many ways it evolved without any human intention whatsoever. Corporations put together LANs first to share expensive resources such as laser printers and then later to share local data; there was never a long-range plan or intention to connect to a worldwide web. Java was not designed for the Web, but as a control language to make simple devices like toasters work smarter. And because toasters are not video devices, Java was developed without the intention of supporting graphics, video, or sound. Finally, ARPANET (the original Web) was developed for national defense, not for any commercial purposes. In short, Al Gore was not the only one who didn't invent the Web. Nobody did. Its approach could never have been detected by experts using environmental scanning systems monitoring existing industry forces. Even those who were building its components never really saw "The Net" coming. It was huge, dangerous, but nevertheless undetected.

The extreme danger posed by the Net is hard to appreciate today. It was theoretically possible that future computer users might not buy boxed software at all; instead, they might use Internet browsers to run applications located at remote websites. PC software sales might have plummeted and huge companies like Microsoft, with their proportionately huge overheads, could have gone bankrupt in minutes. Microsoft stayed afloat because software did not migrate to the Web in any substantial way. Moreover, as Gates puts it, his company was never as clueless as the press seemed to think it was. But that strategic inflection point and accompanying asymmetric threats might have caught Microsoft sleeping if it had relied exclusively on top management, professional strategists, or environmental scanning systems to warn it. As Gates modestly admitted, the "impetus for Microsoft's response to the Internet didn't come from me or from our other senior executives. It came from a small number of dedicated [operating level] employees who saw events unfolding."

By 1995, operating employees at Microsoft had already begun to have bad feelings about the Net; their intuition-driven fears were the product of the day-to-day grind of running the business. Steven Sinofsky, for example, had a wake-up call when he was stuck at Cornell University in a snowstorm during a recruiting trip and just happened to see how the Net had become a normal part of the Cornell student's everyday life. He was shocked to observe students already living what Gates later called the "Internet lifestyle." A top executive or dedicated corporate planner would not have been on a recruiting trip in the first place, but even if one had, it is unlikely he would have had the right intuition to appreciate the danger in what was going on at Cornell.

While anyone might agree that dedicated corporate planners may be too far out of touch to make sense of data from environmental scanning systems, it is harder to believe that top management would not be able to put together the right picture. Indeed, Harvard Business professors Watkins and Bazerman (2003) actually recommend that corporate management play the role of synthesizer. But then, they hedge, "the barriers to this happening are great....Those at the top inevitably receive incomplete and distorted data. That's exactly what happened in the months and years leading up to September 11." These authors seem to want it both ways, finding crisis predictable but still "inevitable" (their word) due to a lack of synthesis caused by the existence of organizational silos. In other words, top management should synthesize— except that it can't.

Top executives would probably like to believe Watkins and Bazerman since they would be understandably reluctant to face the fact that the fate of their company is not entirely (or perhaps even primarily) in their hands. Indeed, Mintzberg believes that company leaders continue to pursue the holy grail of formalized strategic systems because they would rather not rely on the idiosyncrasies of human intuition, especially when that intuition is not their own. Still, as the Sinofsky case demonstrates, top managers are stuck with relying on human intuition and even dumb luck—what if it hadn't snowed in Ithaca?

The Sinofsky case also demonstrates the impossibility of designing an environmental scanning system capable of capturing the relevant data where one-time threats are concerned. How could those charged with developing such a system at Microsoft possibly have known that the habits of Cornell students would have any relevance in trying to determine the future of the PC software industry?

Although Watkins and Bazerman's confidence in top management may be misplaced, their comment about organizational silos does add another problem to the synthesis issue. Individual line managers spend most of their time attending to their own departments and so do not often get together to exchange information; thus, they may not come across all the information needed to synthesize a complete picture of coming inflection points. More about this later.

Finally, Gates specifically takes issue with one well-regarded approach to environmental scanning: staying close to the customer—a major recommendation in Peters and Waterman's 1982 must-read *In Search of Excellence*. It is common knowledge that several of the "excellent" companies mentioned in that book subsequently failed despite staying very close to their customers. Their failure is especially significant given that every one of them was enjoying tremendous success at the time the book was written. But how, Gates asks, could the customers of, say, Wang Labs have been of any use in warning the firm that word processing would soon be done by software running on small but powerful PCs while dedicated word processors were going to go the way of the dinosaur?

Defenses against strategic inflection points

"That isn't the way to play it."

"Why not?"

"Cause it isn't the way to win."

"Is there a way to win?"

"Well, there's a way to lose more slowly."

—Robert Mitchum (private eye Jeff Bailey) and Jane Greer (racketeer's girl Kathie Moffet) in *Out of the Past*

Synthesis of something unlikely is much harder than synthesis of something likely; only line managers are down low enough to see unfiltered information and have the intuition born of experience to connect the dots. But individual line managers may not have all the information needed to do the synthesis alone.

Bill Gates and Andrew Grove both recommend a periodic forum for line managers so they can come together to collectively synthesize information about approaching strategic inflection points. Grove states that the "most important tool in identifying a particular development as a strategic inflection point is a broad and intensive debate" involving technical issues, marketing issues, and strategic repercussions. He makes it clear that operations people must be involved in that debate, but he also recommends that managers at all levels and even outsiders (customers and partners) be heard.

Similarly, Gates recommends biannual "Think Weeks" such as those at Microsoft, in which his employees set aside "all other issues to concentrate on the most difficult technical and business problems facing the company." This approach capitalizes on the intuition of line managers and gets them together outside their corporate silos.

The Army's SSI think tank addresses the issue of getting line managers together under the topic of "focused intelligence" (one of its recommendations for dealing with asymmetric attacks). Specifically, it recommends looking "somewhere else" and breaking down barriers between intelligence agencies. Of course, barriers exist not only between but *within* intelligence agencies. The FBI headquarters rejected a large number of requests for wiretaps and other surveillance means from field agents prior to 9/11; either the agents were asking for too much or headquarters was denying too much, but the two parts of that organization were not on the same sheet of music.

Frederick Forsyth (2002), successful novelist and former soldier of fortune, also advocates both aspects of focused intelligence. He notes, "What went wrong before Sept. 11 was not that nobody knew anything; it was that various agencies knew (or suspected) bits of something looming but could not put the jigsaw together alone." Forsyth thought the British Joint Intelligence Committee, which consists of "top people" from the British equivalents of the CIA, FBI, and NSA, might serve as a model for the right type of synthesis. But "top people" alone cannot do the required synthesis, so Forsyth is wrong—unless he assumes they would be supported by more lowly operations-level managers. In his own novel *The Day of the Jackal*, top government leaders did meet around a table (to try to prevent the assassination of Charles de Gaulle), but their meetings were chaired by a lowly police detective who was the only one capable of putting the final picture together.

Synthesis is nothing, of course, if the organization cannot react to the picture it synthesizes. Therefore, the

SSI recommends "maximizing organizational conceptual adaptability" as a second defense. According to Metz and Johnson, firms can maximize adaptability by "making modularity a central criterion in the force development process." This means acquiring people and systems that will "plug-and-play" so task-specific organizations can quickly be snapped together. The SSI uses the term "agility" to describe this capability. The same term (describing the same concept) has been widely used in the business literature since it was popularized by Goldman in 1995.

Finally, it is better if a firm never has to react to a strategic threat in the first place. Perhaps the SSI's best recommended defense against asymmetric attacks is to reduce one's vulnerability. For the US Army, this boils down to two things: keep moving (moving targets are harder to hit) and do not depend on *one* of anything (dependency equals vulnerability). In business, the advice to keep moving might translate to pursuing a policy of adequately funding both R&D and continuous improvement. Not relying on more than one of anything takes more explaining.

When the SSI recommends not depending on one thing, it means one of anything—not just one material thing (such as one weapon), but also one method, one system, and so on. For example, the SSI is concerned that the US military is too dependent on information superiority and digital technology. The problem with this dependence was demonstrated in a 1994 Naval War College war game set in the year 2015. According to Gold (2002), "China savaged the US Seventh Fleet without ever putting a hull of their own in the water. They did it with land-based antiship missiles and anti-satellite capability that knocked vital communications and intelligence assets out of business faster than we could replace them." The business results from relying on one of something can also be disastrous; Intel nearly went bankrupt because it relied on just one type of business, its memory chips.

Defenses Part II: What not to do

"If you'll take my advice, son—I wouldn't start shooting in that get-up."
"Why not?"
"I've never seen a better target."

—Charlie Grapewin (Grandpa Maple) and Porter Hale (would-be vigilante Jason Maple) in *The Petrified Forest*

Grove warns that managers dealing with a strategic inflection point may suffer from the same emotional problems associated with grief: denial, anger, bargaining, depression, and acceptance. Unfortunately, a few managers will be too vested in the status quo to be able to get all the way to acceptance. They will be too afraid or too much in denial to swing at the baseball, and Grove says they cannot be left in charge.

Do not, however, expect the paralyzed manager to appear paralyzed. Grove notes that some managers may be so deluded they actually think they are acting and talk like they are acting when they are not. Don't be fooled. These problems, says Grove, will be more common for upper management who are necessarily removed and protected from the day-to-day realities of the business. They will have their information filtered by those who do not like being the bearers of bad news (everyone) and therefore feel less pressure from the resulting "strategic dissonance." Given that, Grove recommends that more freedom to act be given to lower managers, who will be the first to feel the pressure to try something new.

Does anyone really believe that terrorists flying aircraft into the World Trade Center would have been anywhere on that list of scenarios?

Do not procrastinate. Strategic inflection points should be dealt with as soon as possible. Grove warns that almost no matter what a company's intentions are, it is unlikely to react as soon as it should. He confesses, "I have never made a tough change, whether it involved resource shifts or personnel moves, that I haven't wished I had made a year or so earlier."

Do not expect too much from Broad and Intensive Debates or Think Weeks. Although Gates plans Think Weeks to make actual decisions, Grove says the purpose of a debate is not to find unanimity but merely to get to the place where everyone in the debate understands the others' points of view. Strategic inflection points are generally very murky and debate will make them a little bit clearer, but that's it. Grove's more humble expectations are probably more realistic.

Watkins and Bazerman recommend that a "knowledgeable and creative group of people from inside and outside the organization" should be brought together to try to construct "a plausible set of scenarios for potential surprises that could emerge over, say, the coming two years." The scenarios are to cover those events that, though unlikely, would have a very large impact on the organization if they occurred.

Despite their recommendation, however, one should not expect the exact strategic inflection point ever to be identified. Although a line manager might synthesize something similar to what is coming, there is no such thing as "likely" where these points are concerned. Mintzberg is especially critical of corporate strategists' attempts to construct likely scenarios. He asks how anyone could possibly know how many scenarios to develop to cover all important contingencies. He also asks what a firm is to do after developing the scenarios. Prepare for just one? Prepare for them all?

How would an approach like Watkins and Bazerman's work in practice? Suppose that prior to 9/11 those managing the "business" of this nation's defense had tried to enumerate every scenario that "though unlikely, would have a large impact" on the country. Does anyone really believe that terrorists flying aircraft into the World Trade Center would have been anywhere on that list?

Their approach also leaves us with the problem of determining exactly who is "an outsider." Before 9/11, the FBI headquarters in Washington might not have regarded its own people in Minneapolis as outsiders, but the subsequent whistle blowing shows that they were. Thus, "insiders" can be "outsiders." The opposite is also true, since an outsider's thinking will always eventually become captured by insiders; outsiders don't come with "use by" dates, so how does one know when they have "gone native?" Moreover, some genuine outsiders can be so far outside that soliciting their thoughts would seem ridiculous. What possible use could there have been in talking to a Hollywood actor who was concerned about what he saw on a flight from Boston to Los Angeles? But one week before 9/11, actor James Woods took the same flight that later crashed into one of the WTC towers; it is now clear that he witnessed the dress rehearsal for 9/11, but nobody paid attention to him before the disaster.

"Hey, I like this: Early nothing."

—Gloria Grahame (gangster moll Debby Marsh) about a fleabag hotel room in *The Big Heat*

The world in general and business in particular are a lot more dangerous than we like to pretend they are, and the situation is getting worse fast. Knowledge doubles every few years, and according to Moore's Law, microprocessor power doubles every 18 months. Rapidly increasing knowledge and computing power means a rapidly changing world, and that means strategic inflection points becoming more and more common.

Faced with rapid and severe changes, managers clamber for ways to predict the future, and the academic tries to provide it (despite the fact that the pace of change makes the future less and less predictable). Thus, the academic provides environmental scanning—a false security that is worse than fear.

But some things can be done to help spot and deal with approaching strategic inflection points. Line managers need to be brought together to use their collective intuitions to synthesize a picture of future threats. Firms need to have "broad and intensive debates" or "think weeks." Organizations must be designed to be flexible so they can adapt to change. Top managers unable to adapt need to be replaced. More power needs to be given to lower level managers who are the first ones to see the writing on the wall. Decisions need to be made fast. Finally, firms need to reduce their vulnerability by continuing to move and ensuring that they do not depend on one of anything.

In the end, nothing that has been offered here should make anyone feel very secure. Maybe that's a good thing. If Bill Gates and Andrew Grove are both paranoid, then paranoia must be respectable. The regrettable truth is that the advice given here will not always be enough; managers will also need a little luck, and any academics who offer that should probably be searched before they leave the building.

References and Selected Bibliography

Burke, James. 2003. *Twin tracks: The unexpected origins of the modern world.* New York: Simon & Schuster.

Chiles, James R. 2002. *Inviting disaster: Lessons from the edge of technology.* New York: HarperCollins Publishers, Inc.

Fischhoff, Baruch. 1975. Hindsight foresight: The effect of outcome knowledge on judgment under uncertainty. *Journal of Experimental Psychology: Human Perceptions and Performance* 1: 288–299.

Forsyth, Frederick. 2002. Your spies could be more like our spies. *Wall Street Journal* (12 December): A18.

Gates, William. 1999. *Business @ the speed of thought.* New York: Warner Books.

Gold, Philip. 2002. *Against all terrors: This people's next defense.* Seattle: Discovery Institute Press.

Goldman, Steven L., Roger N. Nagel, and Kenneth Preiss. 1995. *Agile competitors and virtual organizations: Strategies for enriching the customer.* New York: Van Nostrand Reinhold.

Grove, Andrew S. 1996. *Only the paranoid survive.* New York: Doubleday.

Kahneman, Daniel, and Amos Tversky. 1982. The psychology of preferences. *Scientific American* 246: 161–173.

Metz, Steven, and Douglas V. Johnson II. 2001. Asymmetry and US military strategy: Definition, background, and strategic concepts. White paper, US Army War College, Strategic Studies Institute. @ carlisle-www.army.mil (January).

Mintzberg, Henry. 1993. *The rise and fall of strategic planning.* New York: Simon & Schuster.

Peters, Thomas J., and Robert H. Watermman, Jr. 1982. *In search of excellence.* New York: Warner Books.

Thompson, Arthur A., and A.J. Strickland III. 1998. *Strategic management: Concepts and cases.* Boston: Irwin McGraw-Hill, 1998.

Thompson, Peggy, and Saeko Usukawa. 1995. *Hard boiled: Great lines from classic noir films*. San Francisco: Chronicle Books.

Vaughan, Diane. 1996. *The Challenger launch decision: Risky technology, culture, and deviance at NASA*. Chicago: University of Chicago Press.

Watkins, Michael D., and Max H. Bazerman. 2003. Predictable surprises: The disasters you should have seen coming. *Harvard Business Review* 81/3 (March): 72–80.

Brian J. Huffman, *Associate Professor of Management, University of Wisconsin-River Falls (brian.j.huffman@uwrf.edu)*

---

where do you scan?

Article 10

SIX PRIORITIES THAT MAKE A GREAT STRATEGIC DECISION

Good strategies don't arise spontaneously, they come from attention to a spectrum of important priorities.

Mary Burner Lippitt

When telecom companies were the darlings of Wall Street, Iridium seemed to have everything going for it. The company was committed to a far-sighted vision for a satellite phone system; had identified and targeted a potentially profitable niche—consumers not served by cellular communications; and was part of a worldwide consortium that included heavy-hitters Motorola and Sprint. In pursuit of its vision, Iridium spent $5 billion to launch a first-to-market product and another $150 million in advertising. Iridium faced, and conquered, the daunting technical challenge of putting 66 satellites into space and creating a worldwide telecommunication system.

Iridium had the jump on its competitors when it opened for business in 1998 offering a global communication network for international voice, data, and fax communication. It filed for bankruptcy a year later.

How did such a promising venture fall? Hindsight makes it clear that Iridium overlooked external realities. At a time when the cell market saw hardware prices falling, wireless standards coalescing, and new features being added, Iridium pursued its own course. Its hardware was expensive and bulky, and, worse, it couldn't be used indoors. A competitor, Globalstar, was 18 months behind Iridium, but operated with a business plan that targeted the international businessperson and local service in developing areas. It also offered less expensive and lighter equipment along with "get-acquainted" pricing as low as $.50 per minute in the U. S. versus a $2 to $7 per minute charge from Iridium.

Could Iridium's leaders have foreseen these problems? The answer is yes—if their thinking had been broad, deep, and comprehensive, rather than pre-cooked or disconnected from reality. Iridium focused all of its resources on just one priority—becoming the technical leader. It ignored five other important priorities that would have provided a more balanced, and realistic, perspective.

Critical Thinking Framework

A critical and comprehensive analysis must go beyond traditional SWOT analysis. What we see as opportunities, threats, strengths, and weaknesses depends on our perceptions, and perception clouds reality more often than revealing it. Strategic thinking must also go beyond belief in a one-stop strategic fix. Putting all strategic eggs in a basket named quality, Six Sigma®, customer relationship management, niche selection, first to market, or innovation can lead to disaster.

The single strategy solution leads us astray if it assumes stability in our era of turbulence just as surely as if it assumes everything will change. Using one lens to view strategic options magnifies potential benefits, overlooks limiting variables, and confirms preexisting inclinations. Taking into account a wide array of factors during decision making may appear to muddy the analytic process, but it also increases the likelihood of success.

Information doubles on the World Wide Web every 2.8 years. Clearly, therefore, it is not the availability of information that is the issue, it is our ability to grasp it and use it wisely. Leaders must not only drill into the details when red flags start to surface, but also confront conventional practices and ascertain opportunities more quickly than ever before. Escalating speed and complexity cannot be handled with linear thinking. It requires continuous reassessment through an objective and exhaustive inquiry.

Strategic leaders must concentrate on asking questions that tap multiple perspectives in order to avert the single lens trap as well as develop strategic thinking throughout their organization. Six priorities or desired outcomes can be used to generate balanced decisions, manage risk, and build a communication plan. The six priorities are:

1. Keeping products/services up-to-date and/or being state-of-the art.
2. Gaining and maintaining market share and/or serving customers.
3. Minimizing confusion by building an infrastructure and systems to establish and sustain high performance.
4. Improving processes and procedures for efficiency, quality, and return.
5. Developing committed and competent workforce and/or building a supportive environment and identity.
6. Positioning for the long-term by identifying trends, assumptions, and issues that offer opportunities or potential threats.

These priorities represent the pressing business issues leaders must address if they hope to sleep through the night. Leaders who understand and continuously adjust priorities to reflect workforce and business realities develop more solid strategies. Priorities are objective and dynamic, reflecting information, alternatives, and consequences as events shift or erupt. Knowing the priorities enhances flexibility, commitment, focus, and success.

Being able to interpret trends, judge events, predict opportunities, and persuade an organization is not a matter of charisma or conviction. It relies on an accurate assessment of reality derived from an inclusive and extensive examination of six priorities.

Product Leadership

Intel strives for faster chips and new products because it recognizes the transient benefits of technology. The current recession has not sidetracked Intel's research and development spending, which grew from $2.7 billion in 1998 to $4 billion in 2002. The reliance on this proven strategy drew both praise and concern from Wall Street. The research and development investment positions Intel effectively for the recovery, but it also could hurt the company's financial performance in a prolonged recession. The added lens complicates strategy, but strategy cannot be an easy call. Leaders face a tough act to create a sound direction.

Iridium, too, focused on technical leadership, but with considerably less success. It is possible that its leaders failed to ask the right questions about this priority. Those questions include:

1. What are the options, new alternatives, and synergies?
2. If there were no constraints, what could we do?
3. How can we take our existing procedures/methods to a new level?
4. What has never been tried before?
5. What have we given up on in the past that might be viable now?

This analysis can extend product range. The zipper was limited to securing bales of grain, until it was expanded to clothing. Likewise, Novocaine was developed as a nonaddictive anesthesia for treating battlefield wounds, until practical applications in dentistry eclipsed the original purpose. In addition to these extensions, breakthrough products from the Walkman to the personal digital assistant have surfaced using these questions.

Problems associated with alluring, groundbreaking products can derail efforts, consume funds, and waste time.

But a new idea is not necessarily a good idea. Problems associated with alluring, groundbreaking products can derail efforts, consume funds, and waste time. Genetically modified foods have tremendous appeal for producers and distributors. But from another perspective, the substantial hurdle of customer acceptance looms large. A one-pound Iridium phone had customer problems as well as competitive forces working against it. A promising idea cannot equate with a successful strategy.

Customer Focus

The second threshold of analysis centers on the customer, market share, and meeting customer expectations.

Understanding current customers reveals cross-selling opportunities, identifies potential customers, and pinpoints the level of customer loyalty.

Questions to test the feasibility of an original game plan include:

1. What is our competitive advantage?
2. How can we grow our existing key customers?
3. Who is the competition?
4. What new customers can be targeted?
5. What is the expected market share?

Understanding current customers reveals cross-selling opportunities, identifies potential customers, and pinpoints the level of customer loyalty. The experiences of Target and Home Depot demonstrate that strong benefits stem from understanding your customer and meeting their needs. Firms such as Harley-Davidson benefit from following customers after the sale; Harley's customer rallies enhance customer retention as well as sell clothing and ancillary products.

But you can get so close to the customer that you can miss opportunities. SmithKline and Glaxo focused on relieving customers' pain when they developed Tagament and Zantac. Ulcer and heartburn patients flocked to the new products, which blocked the production of stomach acid. But customer desire for relief and strong market share overshadowed an even more critical need—preventing ulcers that stimulated acid secretion in the first place. Johnson & Johnson pursued this avenue, and the success of its purple pill, Prilosec, has been astounding. J & J recently reformulated the medication to address the erosion in the esophagus. The firm has advertised Nexium heavily in the hope that it would attract new patients as patent protection on Prilosec expires.

Infrastructure Development

Knowing what customer wants is not enough. The organization has to deliver the goods. The third priority area explores aspects from an internal systems viewpoint.

The third priority questions include:

1. What are the risks?
2. What is the best distribution channel?
3. Are there potential partners or allies?
4. Are our current systems capable of sustained excellence?
5. How should the structure/governance change to deliver results?

This structural analysis frequently results in a quest for mergers, acquisitions, or alliances. The promise of reduced overhead, increased system efficiencies, and cross-selling within the firm produces larger and larger firms.

With demographic trends warning of a dire shortage of talent in a decade, the ability to be an employer of choice and retain talent is vital.

However, goals of increasing business breadth, rolling-up local firms into national firms, or building market cap are not, by themselves, successful strategies. ITT could not maintain its size and was dismantled. The expected synergies evaporated in the AOL Time Warner merger, while culture clashes and flagging stock price distracted management. Magellan Health Services' acquisition spree to become the nation's largest provider of mental health services burdened the firm with so much debt that it was delisted from the New York Stock Exchange.

Efficiency, Quality, and Return

Being first to market, commanding strong customer loyalty, and having a solid infrastructure, without also being profitable makes little sense. The fourth priority digs into the details to discover whether an option can build a sustainable business.

Questions addressing the issues of quality and efficiency include:

1. Is the option financially viable in the short and long term?
2. What economies of scale exist?
3. What level of quality can be attained?
4. What data and measures can be used to monitor progress?
5. How can technology increase efficiencies?

In our competitive and complex environment, excellence in one area can be a recipe for disaster. For example, although other firms benchmark their systems, cycle time, or resource utilization efforts against Amazon.com's vaunted systems, these alone cannot guarantee success. And while Motorola developed legendary Six Sigma skills, it lost market share in hand-held phones to Nokia.

A Workforce Advantage

Getting it right means mastering multiple priorities, the easily quantifiable facets as well as the quality aspects of the workforce and the work environment. In the information age, the workers' discretionary effort creates the high-performing workplace. Even though individual behavior cannot be effectively monitored constantly, performance can be measured.

To discover the scope of this fifth priority, the questions include:

1. Do we currently have the talent needed? Can we develop it internally?
2. Are we an employer of choice? Can we retain key talent?
3. What is consistent with our culture, operations, values, and practices?
4. What level of commitment is needed? Can we gain support in the requisite time frame?
5. What are the applicable lessons we have learned about our culture and workforce?

This may sound soft or just nice to have, but evidence is clear, a workforce advantage is a must have. In an industry noted for slim margins and decidedly hostile labor-management relations. Southwest Air has maintained both a profit and strong worker support for 26 years. While the former CEO's practice of dressing as

Elvis Presley at employee meetings or hiding in a baggage compartment can be duplicated, the high-performing environment and fast plane turnaround times cannot be. In fact, the competitive advantage that is the hardest to replicate is internal culture.

The power of culture was evident in the highly charged debate prior to Hewlett-Packard's merger with Compaq. Concerned that their culture, the HP Way, would be sacrificed, several stakeholders vigorously fought the merger. This priority may seem bound to the past, but it also positions the firm for the future.

Only a priority framework produces an in-depth understanding and avoids the traps inherent in the narrow view.

Slogans, promises, or parties cannot manufacture a high performance culture. Only a sound strategic choice—supported by action—can. Although most technological advances can be easily adopted, culture and talent are difficult to replicate. With demographic trends warning of a dire shortage of talent in a decade, the ability to be an employer of choice and retain talent is vital.

Tracking the External Environment

Leaders must understand trends and competitive opportunities if they are to ensure that their firms are effectively positioned for the long term. Evaporating trends strand grand plans and drain resources. Even when the crystal ball can be deciphered, reading the impact and implications requires both art and science.

Questions that can uncover the sixth priority include:

1. What assumptions are no longer valid?
2. What are the nontraditional threats from regulators, technology, or competitors?
3. Are our short- and long-term goals aligned?
4. What are the opportunities or trends on the horizon?
5. How can we capture emerging trends?

Unanticipated circumstances and consequences both erode and erupt. Linux, the open source operating system, has taken market share from Microsoft in Spain. The locally coordinated effort has spurred other "open source" efforts. Whether this is an isolated incident or emerging trend requires study, but the benefit of reevaluating assumptions and operating practices is solid, even in established industries.

A Spanish retailer, Zara, challenged standard retail operating practices by designing new merchandise and restocking every two weeks instead of following the traditional 12-week cycle. Its manufacturing costs are about 15% higher than other firms' because it relies on higher cost factories in developed countries to respond quickly to fashion trends. However, Zara's strong brand reputation translates into reduced marketing costs and profit margins 43% higher than at the Gap.

Putting Priorities to Work

Successful strategy neither emerges magically nor is it contingent on bet-the-ranch hunches. Solid corporate blue-prints emerge from probing and balancing six priorities. Judgment plays a part, but it must follow the identification, quantification, and evaluation of information. Starting with a strong premise means that facts conform to expectations and assumptions go untested.

Iridium Satellite LLC purchased Iridium's assets for $25 million and repositioned the business. Rejecting the predecessor firm's reliance on the commercial sector, the new Iridium negotiated a long-term contract with the U. S. Department of Defense and cut costs. This strategy appears viable, since it reflects reality rather than promise.

When there are so many variables to consider, only a priority framework produces an in-depth understanding and avoids the traps inherent in the narrow view. It has the added benefits of promoting the development of feasible plans, milestones, and checkpoints; providing a map to develop critical thinking skills in others; and drawing attention to the benefits that must be communicated to gain support for a strategic decision. Getting it right is not easy, but it gets easier when a systematic examination precedes the strategic decision.

Dr. Mary Burner Lippitt is a trainer, consultant, researcher, and speaker in the areas of leadership/executive development and the optimization of strategic and tactical thinking within the organization. She is the author of The Leadership Spectrum: 6 Priorities That Get Results. *Her inventory,* Leadership Spectrum Profile® *(Davies-Black, 2002), was cited among the top 10 training tools by* Human Resource Executive *magazine. She can be reached at mlippitt@enterprisemgt.com*

From *Journal of Business Strategy*, January/February 2003, pp. 21-24.

UNIT 3
Organizing

Unit Selections

11. **Classifying the Elements of Work**, Frank B. Gilbreth and Lillian M. Gilbreth
12. **The Dark Side of Change**, G. Neil Karn and Donna S. Highfill
13. **The Change-Capable Organization**, Patricia A. McLagan
14. **Build Your Own Change Model**, Robert H. Schaffer and Matthew K. McCreight

Key Points to Consider

- Some of the early work that was done by management theorists was in classifying and analyzing jobs. Do you think that this type of analysis style still applies? Explain.
- There are a variety of ways for an organization to organize. What are some of the ways that you could see a company organizing? Is there any "best" way?
- Do you think that all change is necessary? Are there some instances when change is done for change's sake?
- Change is something that all organizations need to address. Do you think there is any "best" way to change, or do you feel that all organizations are unique and need to develop their own approach to change?

Student Website

www.mhcls.com/online

Internet References

Further information regarding these websites may be found in this book's preface or online.

From Foosball to Flextime: Dotcommers Are Growing Up
http://www.fastcompany.com/articles/2000/12/act_childcare.html

Sympatico: Careers
http://www.ntl.sympatico.ca/Contents/Careers/

U.S. Department of Labor (DOL)
http://www.dol.gov

Work and Organizational Psychology, Stockholm University
http://www.psychology.su.se/units/ao/ao.html

After the managers of an organization have planned a course of action, they must organize the firm to accomplish the goals. Many early writers in management were concerned with organization. Frederick W. Taylor was one of the first to apply scientific principles to organizing work. He was followed by Frank and Lillian Gilbreth, pioneers in the field of time and motion studies. Their work contributed to the development of the assembly line and other modern production techniques and is shown in the classic essay "Classifying the Elements of Work."

The questions that constantly confront managers today are how best to organize the firm, given the internal and external environment, and how to approach the problem, not only from the company's perspective, but also from the perspective of the economy as a whole. Are large organizations better than small ones? Each has advantages and disadvantages. Which is better able to compete in the global environment against organizations from different countries with different expectations and rules? Add to this the fact that society is evolving, so that new types of organizations will be needed in the future as well as new forms of commerce.

There are several ways that a company can grow. One is to merge with and acquire other firms. The second is to expand the current businesses internally by building on their already established business units. A third is to utilize the new technology that is available as we continue into the twenty-first century. A recent trend in U.S. industry has been to grow via the merger and acquisition route, but growing internally or through the use of new technology can often be more rewarding.

People are not machines; they are looking for fulfilling and enjoyable work. Managers, therefore, must design jobs to be interesting and rewarding. The days of assembly-line workers doing the same task over and over are numbered. Such positions are being replaced by jobs that vary in the types of tasks the worker performs each day. The content is also changing for jobs that have traditionally required lower-level skills and less effort. Technology is forcing organizations to change the way that they do business and how people do their jobs.

Today, firms must be designed to meet the increasingly competitive environment of a global economy. Organizations must learn to do more with fewer resources and fewer people, management overlap and deadwood can no longer be tolerated. Organizations, therefore, try to be lean and mean, but, as questioned in "The Dark Side of Change," is that necessarily the best way to go? As firms cut back, are they crippling the future of the organization by looking only at the short term? The opposite side of this coin is that the middle manager who is able to survive and prosper in this environment will be a better leader, having been tempered in a much hotter furnace than his or her predecessors.

To remain competitive in a rapidly changing environment, organizations must evolve to meet the rapidly developing global economy with which they will have to interact. Change will be a top priority for all organizations as new challenges appear for them to overcome. But, it cannot be change for the sake of change. Organized, focused change that has been well thought-out and executed will be the only type of change that will be successful, as argued by Schaffer and McCreight in "Build Your Own Change Model." Managers will have to trust their employees more and share information with them.

In the future, organizations will have the world as their market and their competitor. They must be able to foresee changes in their environment and react quickly to turn those changes to their advantage. Organizations will need strength and flexibility to meet change or they will suffer the fate of the dinosaurs, which failed to adapt to new environments.

Article 11

Classifying the Elements of Work

Frank B. Gilbreth and Lillian M. Gilbreth

This paper presents a complete method of visualizing a classification of all the subdivisions and the true motion-study elements of The One Best Way to Do Work.

NEED FOR SUCH A CLASSIFICATION

Such a classification is vitally necessary in order that fundamental super-standards shall be made by the scientific method of selecting and measuring the best units, for synthesis into methods of least waste.

This classification furnishes the basis of a definite mnemonic classification for filing all motion-study and time-study data for the work of the industrial engineer, the machine designer, and the behavior psychologist—that their various pieces of information, usually obtained through entirely different channels and methods of attack, may be automatically brought together, to the same filing folders, under the same filing subdivisions.

So far as we are able to learn, there are no other classifications or bases for filing that accomplish this purpose, and we have found that such a classification is absolutely necessary for our work of finding The One Best Way to Do Work, standardizing the trades, and making and enforcing standing orders for best management.

It is hoped that teachers of industrial engineering in our colleges will learn that *one* demonstration of building up The One Best Way to Do Work from the ultimate elements, in any kind of activity, will do more to teach a student the principles of motion study and most efficient methods of management than dozens of lessons dealing with generalities.

The coming generation should be taught a definite filing system for data of scientific management, laid out under a complete classification of all work; should be taught the method of selecting the right units to measure and the methods of measuring these units; and should be furnished with the devices for making the cost of measuring cheap, and with a method for synthesizing the resulting information. This would result in a general progress in world efficiency and an increase in quality of living that would mark an epoch in the history of industry and civilization.

USE OF FUNDAMENTAL ELEMENTS

The literature of scientific management abounds with examples of units of work improperly called "elements," which are in no sense elements. A classification for finding The One Best Way to Do Work must deal with *true elements*, not merely with subdivisions that are arbitrarily called "elements."

There has recently appeared a well-written biography of a great engineer[1] in which subdivisions of operations, requiring in many instances more than 30 seconds to perform, have been erroneously described as "elements." That error will again mislead many people. These so-called elements should be taken for what they really are, namely subdivisions and not elements, and not confused with true elements, or fundamental units which cannot be further subdivided.

SCOPE OF THE CLASSIFICATION

This classification for finding The One Best Way to Do Work is applicable to all kinds of work. It was used by one of the authors while serving as ranking officer in the field under the training committee of the General Staff, standardizing the methods of The Best Way to Do Work for teaching the five million men and officers in the World War. It has also been used in analyzing the work of the surgeon, nurse, hospital management, large department stores, selling a great many kinds of manufacturing, accounting, office work in general, and many other kinds of work.

TRUE ELEMENTS OF WORK

The classification of all work of any and all organizations for the purpose of finding The One Best Way to Do Work may be visualized as follows:

I. A complete organization, which consists of
II. Processes, such as
(a) Financing
(b) Advertising
(c) Marketing
(d) Distributing
(e) Selling
(f) Accounting
(g) Purchasing
(h) Manufacturing
(i) Planning
(j) Teaching
(k) Charting
(l) Maintaining
(m) Filing
These processes consist of
III. Operations, which consist of
IV. Cycles of motions, which consist of
V. Subdivisions, or events, or therbligs[2] of a cycle of motions which consist of
(a) Search
(b) Find
(c) Select
(d) Grasp
(e) Transport loaded
(f) Position
(g) Assemble
(h) Use
(i) Disassemble
(j) Inspect
(k) Pre-position for next operation
(l) Release load
(m) Transport empty
(n) Rest for overcoming fatigue
(o) Other periods of unavoidable delay
(p) Avoidable delay
(q) Plan
VI. Variables of motions
(a) Variables of the worker
1. Anatomy
2. Brawn
3. Contentment
4. Creed
5. Earning power
6. Experience
7. Fatigue
8. Habits
9. Health
10. Mode of living
11. Nutrition
12. Size
13. Skill
14. Temperament
15. Training
(b) Variables of the surroundings, equipment, and tools
1. Appliances
2. Clothes
3. Colors
4. Entertainment, music, reading, etc.
5. Heating, cooling, ventilating
6. Lighting
7. Quality of material
8. Reward and punishment
9. Size of unit moved
10. Special fatigue-eliminating devices
11. Surroundings
12. Tools
13. Union rules
14. Temperament
(c) Variables of the motion
1. Acceleration
2. Automaticity
3. Combination with other motions and sequences
4. Cost
5. Direction
6. Effectiveness
7. Foot-pounds of work accomplished
8. Inertia and momentum overcome
9. Length
10. Necessity
11. Path
12. "Play for position"
13. Speed

Under I, a complete organization, are included all kinds of organizations, including financial, industrial, commercial, professional, educational, and social.

Under II, processes, it should be noted that processes are divided in the same way from a motion-study analyst's standpoint, regardless in which department or in which function they are found.

Under III, operations, the operations include mechanical as well as physiological, and mental as well as manual. The reasons for these inclusions are:

1. From the motion-study standpoint there are not always clear dividing lines between the *operations of devices* and the *mental and manual operations of the human being*, for they are often mutually interchangeable, sometimes in part and sometimes as a whole.[3]

2. Records of many and probably all mental operations can now be obtained by the chronocyclegraph and micromotion photographic methods, and each year such photographic records can more and more be deciphered and used to practical advantage. Enough can already be read and used to serve our present needs. Careful examination of all our old micromotion and chronocyclegraph films taken under conditions of actual practice show that they are literally full of examples of such records of mental processes.

Under IV, cycles of motions are arbitrary subdivisions of operations. They have distinct and natural boundaries of beginning and ending. Usually and preferably there are certain sequences of therbligs that are especially suitable for standardization and transference to other kinds of work, and serve every purpose of finding The One Best Way to Do Work.

Under V, therbligs, we would emphasize that we do not place "motions" as the next subdivision under "cycle of motions" because "motions" have neither distinct and definite boundaries nor beginnings and endings. For example: It is difficult to determine correctly how many "motions" are required to take a fountain pen from the pocket and prepare to write with it. It will be found difficult to agree on just how many "motions" are made and as to where are located the boundaries of the "motions" of so simple a cycle as this, or of any other similarly common cycle of motions.

However, the 17 subdivisions, or events, or therbligs, as they are variously called, seem to be all that are necessary from which to synthesize all of the *cycles of motions* of all the *operations* of all the *processes* of all the *organizations* of every kind whatever. The science of motion study consists, therefore, of finding The One Best Sequence of therbligs for each kind of work and the science of management consists of deriving, installing, and enforcing the conditions that will permit the work to be done repeatedly in The One Best Way. It is conceivable that sometime in the future an eighteenth and possibly more therbligs will be found, and we seem near to their discovery at the present time. The discovery of additional therbligs pertaining to the phenomena of skill and automaticity seems inevitable.[4]

Under VI, variables of motions, provision is made for filing all information regarding any kind of motion made by either hand, device, or machine. It provides for all information regarding the structures in which work is performed. It provides for filing all data regarding human behavior—supernormal, normal, and subnormal. It supplies the basis of filing all data of the educator, psychologist, psychiatrist, and the expert in personnel, placement, and promotion problems.

This classification can be carried on and subdivided indefinitely. It furnishes an efficient and quickly usable plan for synthesizing the components of The One Best Way to Do Work in such shape that they can be cumulatively improved.

However, our present information regarding the 17 therbligs is sufficient to revolutionize all kinds of work, and if the industries of the various nations would eliminate the obviously unnecessary therbligs and standardize the kinds, sequences, and combinations of the remaining efficient therbligs, the resulting savings each year would be sufficient to pay the outstanding debts of most nations.

HISTORY OF THIS CLASSIFICATION

For many years we have used these therbligs as divisions for dissecting cycles of motions of a great many different kinds of work, but it was not until we began to use photography in motion study in 1892 that we made our greatest progress. It was not until 1912, when we used our first micromotion processes intensively, that we were able to make such great advances as projecting the motions of experts faster and slower, as well as at the speed of experts' demonstration. We were then also able to project and examine therbligs backwards, or in the reversed directions. This enabled us to get a new fund of information that resulted in many suggestions from seeing, measuring, and comparing the therbligs performed in the reversed sequence and opposite directions. This was used to great advantage in finding the methods of least waste and especially in the process of taking machines apart and putting them together again in front of a motion picture camera, and then running the film backwards, showing the films of assembling as dissembling and vice versa.

EXAMPLES OF PROFITABLE USE

Running films of superexperts backwards, to see what we could get for automatically suggesting inventions, or as "thought detonators" when seeing the operation done thus, presented peculiarities and combinations of therbligs never seen before. This was, of course, supplemented by examining one picture, or frame, at a time which, with motion study experts, will always be the most efficient method for getting facts from the films. Great progress was made, for example, in *pre-positioning for next operation* (therblig *k*) parts and tools so that *grasp* (therblig *d*) was performed with quite the same motions and actions and performed within a time equal to that of *release load* (therblig *l*).

As an example of the importance of recognizing the therblig as the fundamental element, the result of that particular study in 1912 was that our organization enabled a client to have his machine assemblers put together 66 machines per day with less fatigue than they had previously accumulated while assembling 18 machines per day. Because this method was synthesized from fundamentally correct units, the same methods are still in use today in this same factory.[5]

This increase in output should not be considered as an exceptional case. On the contrary, it is quite typical. In fact we have a great many illustrations that we could give where the savings were much greater. For example: One large motion-study laboratory, as a result of this method of attack, synthesized and demonstrated new methods which averaged an output of five times as much product per man. This method used in assembling carburetors enabled messenger boys to do the work in one-tenth the time required by skilled mechanics.[6] It has been used on work of assembling pumps with still greater results.[7]

THERBLIG SEQUENCES

It was early recognized that certain similar operations have similar sequences of therbligs. For example: The operations of feeding pieces into a drill press or into a punch press, time tickets into a time stamp, and paper into a printing press, have practically the same sequence of therbligs. A typical sequence of therbligs for one complete cycle of handling one piece on a drill press is *search, find, select, grasp, transport loaded, position, assemble, use, disassemble, inspect, transport loaded, pre-position for next operation, release load* and *transport empty.* This cycle of motions can and should be done with the following therbligs: *grasp, transport loaded, position, assemble, use, release load* and *transport empty,* which are half the number of therbligs of the usual method.

While the former is the usual sequence of therbligs on a drill press, it is by no means the best one. There is The One Best Sequence of therbligs on each machine and each kind of work, and it should always be found, standardized, taught, and maintained.

Table 1		
PAIRED THERBLIG USUALLY PERFORMED BEFORE USE		PAIRED THERBLIG USUALLY PERFORMED AFTER USE
d. Grasp	Use	*l.* Release load
e. Transport loaded	Use	*m.* Transport empty
f. Position	Use	*k.* Pre-position for next operation
g. Assemble	Use	*i.* Disassemble
q. Plan	Use	*j.* Inspect

Table 2 Unpaired Therbligs		
ORDER NO. 4		ORDER NO. 5
a. Search	Use	*n.* Rest for overcoming fatigue
b. Find	Use	*o.* Other forms of unavoidable delay
c. Select	Use	*p.* Avoidable delay

ANOTHER WORK CLASSIFICATION

Now let us look at another method of subdividing and classifying all work. There is another and better known type of division and classification for visualizing all activity which was early recognized. The importance of considering this simple classification can be seen in the unfairness and trouble that have been caused by giving the same piece rate for large lots as for small. This classification divides all work, both large and small, into three parts, as follows:

1. Get ready
2. Do it, or make it.
3. Clean up.

Now, applying this division to one piece on the drill press, we have:

1. *Get ready,* or pick up the piece and put it under the drill. This consists of all therbligs that come before *use* (therblig *h*).
2. *Drill it* (do it or make it). This consists of only one therblig, namely *use* (therblig *h*).
3. *Clean up,* or take the piece out from under the drill and inspect it and lay it down. This consists of all therbligs that come after *use* (therblig *h*).

THE IMPORTANCE OF USE

It should be recognized that the therblig *use* is the difficult one to learn in mastering a trade. It is the most productive and, therefore, the most important therblig of all.

All other therbligs of all kinds of work are desirable and necessary only so far as they facilitate, prepare for, or assist in increasing *use.* Any therbligs that do not foster *use* should be under suspicion as being unnecessary. Use is the highest paid therblig, because it usually requires the most skill. The more of the therbligs of "get ready" and "clean up" that are performed by less skilled and consequently lower priced workers the better for all workers, for they all will be employed a larger portion of the day at the highest priced work at which they are each individually capable. This is true not only in the consideration of the therbligs

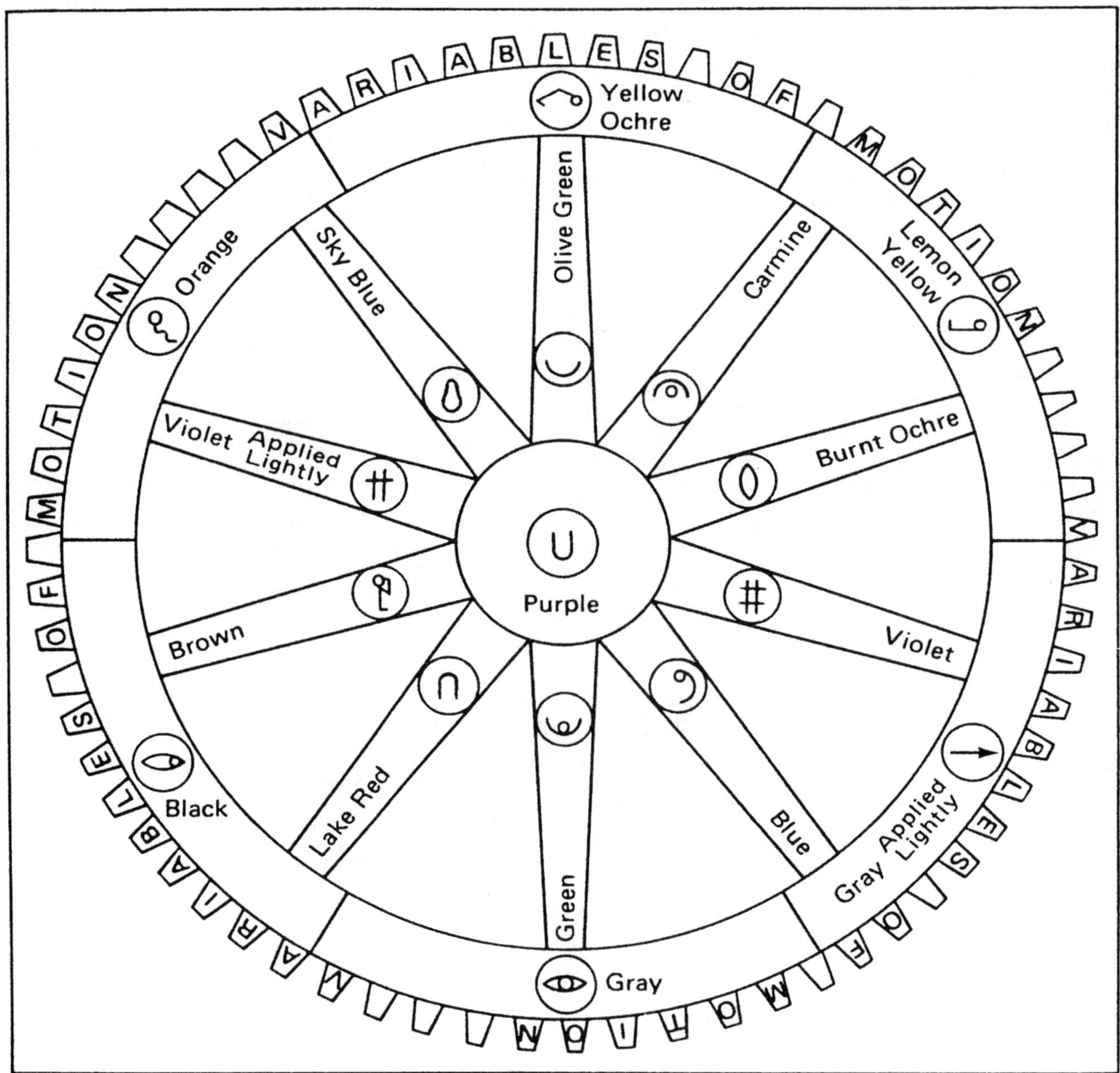

Figure 1. The Wheel of Motion

but also in the trades in general. For example: The bricklayer, the plumber, the steamfitter, the office executive, and many others, each have their specially assigned helpers, but they still habitually do much pay-reducing work for which in the long run they suffer a loss due to less personal activity. It will help to analyze and classify all work if it is recognized that the hod carrier bears the same relation to the bricklayer, and the secretary to the executive, as do the therbligs that compose "get ready" bear to the therblig *use;* and the laborer's work of "clean up" after the work of the bricklayer, is quite the same as the therbligs that compose "clean up" after therblig *use.*

Further investigations of a typical sequence of therbligs, such as on the drill press or other examples cited, from the standpoint of the classification of the therbligs show that *grasp* (therblig *d*) of "get ready" is used before *use* (therblig *h*) and that *release load* (therblig *l*) done after *use* may be quite the same except that it is performed in motions that are the reverse of those of *grasp.*

PAIRED THERBLIGS

There are a number of such paired therbligs which are almost always separated by the therblig *use.*

For example:

It was the absence of a therblig on the other side of *use* to pair with *inspect,* together with the fact that *plan* is actually found in the photographic records regardless of how much planning may be done prior to the beginning of an operation, that caused us to add to the list of therbligs, *plan* (therblig *q*). The therblig *plan* may occur in any place in the sequence of therbligs, but we have put it last in the list before cited because it was added last, and also to distinguish it from the "planning" that should be done before any "performing" of the operation is begun.

There are two more kinds of divisions, or orders, making a total of five orders of therbligs, namely one consisting of *search, find* and *select* (therbligs *a, b,* and *c*) which usually come before *use,* and *rest for overcoming fatigue, other forms of unavoidable delay* and *avoidable delay* (therbligs *n, o,* and *p*) which usually come after *use.* Thus we have two orders of unpaired therbligs separated by *use,* as follows:

In analyzing an operation of any kind a simultaneous motion cycle chart is prepared. The therbligs of motion are applied to this chart in studying it for present methods and determining the altered sequence which should be adopted to establish The One Best Way to Do Work. This brought up the problem of graphic presentation of the therbligs for ready identification.

To make these 17 therbligs more real, tangible, and easier to visualize and remember, different colors are used to distinguish them on the simultaneous motion cycle chart.[8] One member of our organization, Paul M. Vanderhorst, who conceived the idea of adding *plan* to our list of therbligs, also suggested the idea of showing the 17 therbligs in the design of a wheel, and we have adopted a "Wheel of Motion" not altogether unlike the "Wheel of Life" of Hindus, for explaining therblig study to the employees of our

STANDARD SYMBOLS, COLORS AND PENCILS FOR SIMO-CHARTS (Simultaneous Motion Cycle Charts)				
Symbol	Name of Symbol	Symbol Color	Name of Color	Name and Number of Pencil or Crayon
	Search		Black	Dixon's Best Black #331
	Find		Gray	Dixon's Best Gray #352½
	Select		Light Gray	Dixon's Best Gray #352½ Applied Lightly
	Grasp		Lake Red	Dixon's Best Lake Red #321½
	Transport Loaded		Green	Dixon's Best Green #354
	Position		Blue	Dixon's Best Blue #350
	Assemble		Violet	Dixon's Best Violet #323
	Use		Purple	Dixon's Best Purple #323½
	Dis-assemble		Light Violet	Dixon's Best Violet #323 Applied Lightly
	Inspect		Burnt Ochre	Dixon's Best Burnt Ochre #335½
	Pre-position for Next Operation		Sky Blue	Dixon's Best Sky Blue #320
	Release Load		Carmine Red	Dixon's Best Carmine Red #321
	Transport Empty		Olive Green	Dixon's Best Olive Green #325
	Rest for Overcoming Fatigue		Orange	Ruben's "Crayola" Orange
	Unavoidable Delay		Yellow Ochre	Dixon's Best Yellow Ochre #324½
	Avoidable Delay		Lemon Yellow	Dixon's Best Lemon Yellow #353½
	Plan		Brown	Dixon's Best Brown #343

Figure 2. Symbols, Colors, and Pencils for Simo-Charts. In practice, column 3 is solid colors, not crosshatching.

clients. Each part of the wheel representing a therblig has its own individual color, and each of the colors has a special meaning and is also mnemonic. See Figs. 1 and 2.

It should be noted that *use* is the hub of the wheel. *Use* is the most important therblig. The more *use,* the more production.

The therbligs that have like characteristics, although they may represent reversed action, are shown as paired spokes on opposite sides of the wheel.

The rim of the wheel consists of two different kinds, or orders, of three parts each, and the cogs on the rim are shaped like the letter V and are to remind the motion-study student that the variables affect all of the therbligs and must be all carefully considered in order to obtain The One Best Way to Do Work. There are at least a hundred variables that are important on nearly all kinds of work and our complete list contains several thousand variables. It is extremely important to recognize that information relating to the variables is applicable to all kinds of work. The application of this information is simply a matter of degree required in the particular study in hand.

The same colors are always used on the same therbligs wherever they are represented or shown. This permits instant visualization of all the therbligs of any one kind. These colors are specially important in connection with quickly visualizing, grouping, comparing, and interpreting the behavior and happenings on simultaneous motion cycle charts. The use of the standard colors enables the micromotion study engineer to acquire a proper sense of the proper time for each therblig, even before a new study is made. This is particularly important when studying an operator for his first time, as it will show whether or not he is fully cooperating.

In fact, too much stress can hardly be laid on the importance of showing each and every therblig and all possible happenings on the simultaneous motion cycle chart in finding The One Best Way to Do Work. We know of no other method in finding The One Best Way to Do Work. It answers all purposes satisfactorily.

After sufficient experience and study, preferably in a motion-study laboratory, the interrelations, peculiarities, and suitabilities of the therbligs on several simultaneous motion cycle charts of different kinds of work will be recognized by an engineer trained in motion study. When he has the proper training he is invariably able to improve and completely revolutionize any work on which the micromotion study method of attack has not already been used.

RELATION OF THERBLIG STUDY TO STOPWATCH TIME STUDY

The symbols here shown furnish a sort of shorthand which makes for greater speed in making notes regarding best sequences of therbligs and motion study in general, and for remembering the therbligs easily. The results of careful study of the peculiarities of the therbligs individually and in combination with those that immediately precede and immediately follow, as well as those that are executed simultaneously by other anatomical members, will remove for all time any idea that scientific motion study of the behavior of the workers can be accomplished with any such obsolete device as a stopwatch, or that time study and motion study are the same thing or even similar.

The literature of scientific management is full of examples where time study and motion study are confused. This confusion abounds even in books that are considered classics. It should be recognized that "Time study is the art of finding how long it takes to do work." This was Taylor's original definition, and it is still good. Time study is the great invention of Dr. Taylor. Taylor never did any motion study[9] of any kind whatever.[10]

The definition of motion study is: "Motion study is the science of finding The One Best Way to Do Work." Of course micromotion study gives records in indisputable permanent form of the motions and behavior of the demonstrator of the methods and of the individual errorless times of each therblig of each cycle of motions and of the overall times of the operator.

TRANSFERABLE DATA

Intensive study of the resulting therbligs furnishes information that is interchangeable in all kinds of work for finding The One Best Way to Do Work. It is this feature of the great value of the interchangeability of the indisputable detailed data that makes it most desirable to select as demonstrator of a method that person only who is *the best demonstrator obtainable* of the best methods extant or the best known, and in a motion-study laboratory[11] equipped for the purpose, and under controlled conditions.

It is obvious that records of the methods of recognized champions are most desirable. It must be recognized, however, that champions are usually champions because others are so inefficient. The synthesis of the best components of the methods of two or more champions will make a method better than that of the method of the champion of champions and better than the method of *the one best demonstrator obtainable.*

Data regarding the therbligs of a champion or a superexpert in any one kind of work are usable on a great many different kinds of work, for the times and skill on each therblig are transferable. It is also desirable, but not absolutely necessary, that *the best demonstrator obtainable,* of the best method extant, shall have sufficient experience to perform the cycles of motions and the complete operation in the shortest time for that operation. However, it is often difficult to obtain anyone who can demonstrate the combination of the *best method known* and also the *best speed of performance.* Oftentimes the expert of motion study can demonstrate the sequence of therbligs which constitute The One Best Way to Do Work, yet, because of his lack of practice and speed, is not able at first to equal the times nor the relativity of simultaneity of therbligs performed by different anatomical members of those with a much poorer method, but with much greater natural dexterity who have had so much practice that they have arrived at a state of motion automaticity.

> The usual standards obtained by rule-of-thumb methods will always be temporary and transitory.

It is here that the method of recording lateness of therbligs previously cited is of importance. Here again the detailed records of the therbligs are of great value for the correct times of individual therbligs and the proper relativity of simultaneity can be obtained even from inferior sequences where great dexterity and automaticity have been recorded under the wrong method. When the best sequence is known, the correct time for task management for performing The One Best Way to Do Work *can be prophesied before anyone can demonstrate it.* The importance of prophesying the time for accomplishing The One Best Way to Do Work before it can be demonstrated will be appreciated when it is realized that there is not a single case on record where The One Best Way to Do Work has been derived by the wasteful fumbling methods of evolution.

RELATION OF THIS CLASSIFICATION TO FATIGUE STUDY

Much has been written in generalities regarding unnecessary fatigue. Because of the dreadful working conditions in nearly all factories, some improvements can almost always be made by anyone with good intentions and authority together with sufficient continuity of purpose. However, such improvements are only part of what could be done and often lapse after the passing of the regime of the untrained enthusiast who is merely interested in the elimination of unnecessary fatigue. The One Best Way to Do Work is that sequence of therbligs which permits the work to be done in least time, with least fatigue, and entails having the periods of *unavoidable delay* (therblig *o*) and *avoidable delay* (therblig *p*) utilized for *rest for overcoming fatigue* (therblig *n*).

The data relating to therbligs that cause or eliminate unnecessary fatigue can be filed in orderly fashion for future use under the classification shown herein.

Unnecessary fatigue should be recognized as the badge of ignorance of the therbligs and consequently of motion study. To eliminate unnecessary fatigue, there must be complete recognition that the therbligs are the fundamental elements of The One Best Way to Do Work, and are units for the application of the laws of motion study and fatigue study.

RELATION TO STANDARDIZATION

Much has been written also of standardization, and The One Best Way to make standards is to proceed from the standpoint that the best standard is the one that best complies with the laws of motion study. It is quite impossible to standardize a method for quickest achievement of the state of automaticity without recognition and standardization of the individual therbligs involved and their combinations and sequences.

Automaticity of the wrong method, so prevalent in highly repetitive vocations like those of the textile trades, is the shame and disgrace of industry today. However, it will be quite useless for executives and managers to talk standardizations of the correct sequences of the therbligs for The One Best Way to Do Work until they know from personal experience the possibilities of micromotion study and set the example in their own duties. For this purpose the simplest device is the executive's cross-sectioned desk which serves as a permanent reminder, and if used properly will furnish a permanent proof. It permits doing all manual work with almost exactly the same motions every time. It soon becomes strikingly evident how much faster work can be accomplished when the motions are made over the same locations each and every time. The next step is the search for The One Best Way to Do Work.

> ... the evils of deadening monotony do not exist where there is sufficient knowledge of the therblings ...

Because of the rule-of-thumb methods used in the past for obtaining standards, almost anyone can make improvements in the present state of standardization encountered in all organizations. The usual standards obtained by rule-of-thumb methods will always be temporary and transitory. If standards are based upon the permanent records of indisputable knowledge of the ultimate components of the cycles obtained by the micromotion methods, they will be in shape for cumulative improvement without any additional study. Comparatively few organizations have given proper attention to the possibilities of standardization built upon indisputable measured elements, and but few standards have been made with due regard to the extra outputs in the savings of time and fatigue that result if the standards are made to conform with the laws of automaticity, which is the greatest free asset of the working man, whatever his occupation.

RELATION TO THE LEARNING PROCESS

For greatest speed with least effort and fatigue in learning, The One Best Sequence of therbligs should be used whenever possible from the very beginning of the learning period so that automaticity may be achieved in the shortest possible learning period and with least habit interference. The study of the 17 therbligs of this classification furnishes a means to shorten the period required to learn any kind of art, trade, profession, or other activity. Hence, there will be more time available to learn more jobs and thus gain promotion, and, by reason of more knowledge of the theory combined with the practice, prolong one's earning periods by teaching others, when one is too old to do a young man's total quantity of output.

Finally, the evils of deadening monotony do not exist where there is sufficient knowledge of the therbligs and the variables affecting them. As two cycles of motions can never be made exactly alike, the quest of perfection of methods is much more interesting and absorbing than the desire to know which part of the whole structure is the piece which is being worked upon, although the latter is supposed to be the millennium by the academic enemies of standardization.

Knowledge of measuring, selecting, and studying of therbligs makes all work fascinating, for while the best method known and performed under given conditions may be called for practical purposes "The One Best Way to Do Work," a still better method with new tools and conditions is ever possible. There is no instance or example that cannot be improved with greater knowledge of the therbligs pertaining to that work. There are so many possible combinations of therbligs that the skilled worker with the knowledge of therbligs performing any work ordinarily considered monotonous has the opportunity to improve the temporary One Best Way to Do Work almost without limit.

It is not the fault of the skilled worker, if he has not been taught to visualize the therbligs, that he has not been given sufficient incentives to enlist and hold all of his zeal continuously, has not been taught the science that underlies his work, has not been induced to search for the scheme of perfection, has not been taught a filing method for his knowledge that he may have systematized improvement from his additional experience, and has not desired to teach the apprentices and other learners the best way that he knew.

The results derived under the method of attack that this classification embodies have been successful in every kind of work in which it has been used.

It is hoped that this description of this filing classification will be of service to those who are interested in efficiency, in making waste elimination attractive, and in finding and enforcing the managerial conditions which will permit The One Best Way to Do Work.

NOTES AND REFERENCES

1. See *Frederick W. Taylor* by E B. Copley.
2. This word was coined for the purpose of having a short word which will save the motions necessary to write such long descriptions as "The 17 categories into which the motion-study elementary subdivisions of a cycle of motions fall."
3. In 1910 and the years following, we collected and specially devised in our own laboratory, many devices for supplying, mechanically, the therbligs of cycles of motions that the crippled soldiers could not perform, due to their injuries. Such collections should be made by all museums and colleges that intend to teach motion study.
4. See Society of Industrial Engineers Bulletin, November 1923, pp. 6-7. "A Fourth Dimension for Recording Skill," by Frank B. Gilbreth and L. M. Gilbreth. The lateness in starting or finishing of a therblig performed by any one anatomical member as compared with the time of beginning or finishing of a therblig performed by another anatomical member is a most important unit for measuring skill and automaticity.
5. See *Management Engineering*, February 1923, p. 87. "Ten Years of Scientific Management," by John G. Aldrich, M. E., and also his discussion of paper 1378 on page 1131, vol. 34, 1912, American Society of Mechanical Engineers Transactions.
6. See Proceedings of the Institution of Automobile Engineers (English), "The Fundamentals of Cost Reduction," by H. Kerr Thomas, Member of the Council.
7. See Society of Industrial Engineers Transactions, vol. 2, 1920, "The One Best Way to Do Work," by Frank B. Gilbreth and L. M. Gilbreth.
8. See "Applied Motion Study" by Frank B. Gilbreth and L. M. Gilbreth, p. 138.
9. See Bulletin of The Taylor Society, June 1921.
10. This can easily be proved by reading Taylor's own writings, and it is also a matter of record in our own office. This fact is entirely missed, perhaps unintentionally, by Taylor's biographer, Copley.
11. Laboratory motion study has been criticized as being done under conditions of the shop. The conditions of the shop should be changed until they duplicate the most desirable conditions of the laboratory.

Frank Bunker Gilbreth graduated from the English high school in Boston in 1885, passed the entrance examinations at M.I.T., but decided to work for a firm of consulting engineers and to complete his technical training at night. In 1911, he established Gilbreth, Inc., an engineering consulting firm, which advanced the specialty of Motion Study. His achievements in scientific engineering were recognized by the University of Maine, which conferred on him an LL.D. degree in 1920. Gilbreth died in 1925.

Lillian Moller Gilbreth married Frank Gilbreth in 1904. Her education included a Bachelor of Letters and a Master of Letters from the University of California and a Ph.D. from Brown University (1915). She traveled widely as a lecturer on technology and human relations problems, served as president of Gilbreth, Inc., and received numerous awards and medals. Lillian Gilbreth died in 1972.

From *Management Classics*, 1977, pp. 150–165. Published by Goodyear Publishing Company. Originally from *Management and Administration*, August 1924, pp. 151–154, and September 1924, pp. 295–298.

The Dark Side of Change

Could that ambitious initiative be a form of character assassination?

By G. Neil Karn and Donna S. Highfill

In the spring of 2002, Linda Howell joined a leading player in the financial-services industry as director of corporate training, replacing Gayle Smithers. Gayle wasn't forced out—in fact, she left the company in fine standing, for a new opportunity. But the good feelings didn't long survive her departure. "When Linda got in there, she found a lot of problems," commented the executive in charge. "Apparently, it was a real mess. Fortunately, Linda is getting her arms around it. But it will take us six months to dig out of this hole."

How did the situation go south so quickly? Was a fresh broom really needed to sweep the department clean? Or did Linda *concoct* a mess—consciously or unconsciously—so it could then be tidied up?

A business world obsessed with constant improvement breeds *faux change*. Leadership texts implore, "If it ain't broke, break it!" Often, however, faux change is more than changing for the sake of change: It's changing for the sake of the changer. It's possible that Gayle, our incumbent (we've used pseudonyms, but all of the characters and situations are genuine), had successfully covered up incompetence or ineffectiveness during her tenure. But if she indeed deserved her solid reputation, Linda may have positioned her—like a straw man—for a quick and easy knockout punch.

Linda's impulses are hardly unusual. Too many executives have become change junkies, and their habit is being fed with constant innovation, whether or not it results in improvement. In this environment, new leaders feel pressured to produce a transformation where only a minor correction may be warranted. And those who want to create a bang often supply their own gunpowder.

No Problems? Create One

At the root of faux change: a superficial needs assessment made by the incoming manager. A variety of sources can produce the misguided—and predetermined—conclusion that something is wrong and needs fixing.

The least malicious source is the tendency to overlook systems or practices that already exist. As unlikely as it may seem, many new managers are and remain oblivious to what has gone on before. One departed service-industry manager learned that his successor was "having to start from scratch" on a certain initiative. Fortunately, he was able to correct that impression: By spinning his chair a half rotation, he suggested, the new manager could locate three notebooks—documenting the entire process—on the shelf behind him. Absent familiarity with the preceding operation, the successor had leaped to the assumption that nothing existed at all. Then, having established a void, he was prepared to sweep in with a quick fix.

The more frequent occurrence is the successor's inability to fully appreciate the effectiveness of the systems—formal or informal—that do exist. This is especially likely if the new manager arrives with an arsenal of best practices learned in a previous managerial life: He is simply predisposed to a favorite solution.

William Hagle, an HR executive retained by a top financial-services company, arrived with a variety of cost-cutting tools. He was particularly adept at reducing benefits costs. While his savings were substantial, executive management had not mandated these inroads into employees' benefits package. In a company that prided itself on being an employer of choice, this best practice ran counter to the prevailing culture. Faux-change artists, however, have a single-mindedness when it comes to deploying their pet practices.

The dilemma with best practices is that they consistently evolve out of the most conducive circumstances—an executive's special interest or guiding sponsorship, an internal competence, a special market condition, a unique business circumstance, or a crisis that demands a dramatic response. But sadly, as Heraclitus observed, you can't step into the same river twice.

And just when the new practice, transplanted to a different environment, is destined to achieve sub-optimal results, the efficacy of the established practice is suddenly undervalued as the change artist encourages doubt. Although a company's practices usually have evolved as a commonsense response to the organization's people, culture, and operating model, they are suddenly suspect. William, our HR executive, revealed a weak spot that really didn't trouble anyone, but he got the desired attention by defining the situation as near disaster.

Faux change starts when the new manager conjures up a faux crisis. It is a form of character assassination, committed against the predecessor's body of work.

Weeding Out the Fakes

Faux change frequently comes at considerable cost because it entails an investment in fixing something that does not require repair. The superfluous change starts with the disruption of the status quo, which in turn interrupts progress and sometimes suspends service altogether: It is not unusual for a system in transition to be dead in the water, stuck between what it was and what it is trying to become. Energy is misused as people's time and efforts are diverted to defending what went before. And even when those affected are persuaded and ready to move, there is a significant learning curve with the new process.

In the opening scenario of the new corporate-training director, Linda's discrediting of Gayle's work was at the cost of any forward movement in her department. She would have done well to heed the wisdom of the CFO of one regional bank, who told us, "I've learned to be something of a cynic. Rare is the improvement that will ever repay the time lost in installing it."

Worse, faux change is on the rise. Research indicates that reengineering initiatives achieve their business cases only 40 to 60 percent of the time. With change having such a disappointing track record, loss prevention becomes a worthwhile objective.

If organizations are increasingly at risk of being victimized by faux change, how do we effectively diagnose and treat the problem? We propose seven concrete strategies to avoid being victimized by faux change—and to recognize the real McCoy. Management can't discount a new manager's recommendation for change as "faux" in order to avoid making needed investments or to protect some vestige from the past that has outlived its usefulness. Legitimate change is the lifeblood of organizational renewal. What we need is a quick and effective way to identify faux change.

Don't be taken in by enthusiasm alone. If a new manager recommends major change immediately and, particularly, if dissatisfaction with the current state seems to have escalated with her arrival, be skeptical. Ask questions like, "If I didn't think it was broken before, why should it suddenly be now?" If you didn't think you had a problem, there is a fair chance you didn't.

Our HR executive, William, was infatuated by technology. His first venture was a reasonable success: a new HR management system. He followed this with the introduction of an electronic management portal—a keystroke would make available anything from org charts to headcount to last month's turnover rate. "These folks haven't seen anything like this," he was fond of crowing. Unfortunately, what his fellow managers would have preferred seeing was a serious dent in the time-to-fill rate on recruitments. William was delivering solutions nobody wanted.

Insist on a thorough diagnosis of the problem. When a new manager recommends change, poll leaders and customers of the affected area. Ask the manager to get their input when answering the following questions:

- Is the current situation really broken? Show me proof.
- What solutions have been attempted in the past? Did they work? Why or why not?
- Why is the proposed solution better than what's been tried before?
- Exactly how is the proposed fix going to be *demonstrably* better than what has been done in the past?

The head of commercial banking at a mid-sized bank told us, "I insist on fact-based business cases. I like to do breakthrough thinking as well as the next guy, but before I give the go-ahead, I want empirical data."

Check the fit of the solution with your organization. If the new manager wants to adopt a best practice that he has used before, determine if this is a favorable environment for replication. Go to the source of the best practice and interview objective observers. Upon assessment with reliable sources, determine if the fix is proportionate to the need. Identify the ingredients that made this "best practice" best in its original application. Finally, frankly assess whether the incumbent staff can run this new offense.

A new training director who did it right at a mid-sized organization told us, "I have a lot of training interventions in my back pocket. Some of them are quite elegant. The question is: What does this company need right now?"

Require a detailed implementation plan. Insist that the change advocate get granular. Lofty aspirations have their place, but executives must be adamant about the details of what will be done to make it work. Start by asking if the change can be executed with the resources at hand.

Our HR executive, William, was confounded by the details of implementation. Not one of his initiatives was delivered on time and as promised, Before long, his group was tagged as "the gang that couldn't shoot straight." His last venture—an associate portal that promised to be the employee counterpart to the management portal—was aborted at the last minute when implementers realized that the plan would require an expensive new server to avoid a degradation of service on the HR management system. William's sin of advocating changes that nobody ordered was exacerbated by his inability to deliver them.

Determine if the costs outweigh the benefits. Know from the outset that there is *always* a cost of change. Insist that the change agent fully anticipate, articulate, and quantify the downside of any initiative. Prepare for the rule of unintended consequences: Any new activity will introduce problems that are unlikely to be foreseen. Wouldn't any Southerner appreciate a chance to reconsider the introduction of kudzu as cattle fodder?

Confront the cold reality that the business case may not be achieved. Ask, "Could I live with 50 percent of what is promised?" "Can I endure a lengthy recovery cycle until the fruits of this change are realized?" The burden of proof should be on whether the new end game would still be demonstrably better if only partially achieved.

We shouldn't be fooled, and we shouldn't be foolish.

A CEO of a major financial-services firm told us, "If we achieved 50 percent of the business cases our executive committee was promised for new initiatives funded in the last five years, this company wouldn't have an earnings problem."

Keep a close watch, because your savior may soon depart for greener pastures to resell the same ideas in the same way. You'll be left with months or even years of cleanup—from both a systems and people perspective. Of course, his premature flight may be a blessing. Both William and Linda were ultimately let go, but they stayed long enough to do considerable damage.

We have to beat our addiction to the snake oil of change. We cannot take our eyes off of what change is supposed to do: produce genuine and sustainable improvement. We shouldn't be fooled, and we shouldn't be foolish. Don't let your own need for the rush of change result in a situation that could take years from which to recover.

G. NEIL KARN is at Arrabon Consulting, Inc., a management consulting practice.

DONNA S. HIGHFILL is founder and president of Highfill Performance Group Inc., a Richmond, Va.-based consultancy.

– Organizations are at risk of being victimized by faux change (new managers)
- disruption of the status quo
- fixing something that does not require repaire
- considerable cost of changes
- faux change is on the rise

What change is supposed to do: produce genuine and sustainable improvement

The Change-Capable Organization

Part 3 of this series focuses on transforming your organization so that it embraces change as an ongoing way of life. Parts 1 and 2 appear in the November and December 2002 issues of T+D.

By Patricia A. McLagan

Change is a relatively recent management topic everywhere in the world. While it has always been an issue, it's now one of *the* issues. The number of books and articles on change management has increased more than 100 times since the 1960s. In addition, the costs of change failures are rising as organizations try (and fail) or make costly and repeated mistakes to implement complex and organization-wide initiatives such as reengineering, diversity awareness, globalization, quality and productivity programs, as well as complex alliances, mergers, and acquisitions. Many surveys put change management at the top of the list of executive concerns.

One way to deal with change is to notice when major changes are happening and to implement each change using methods such as those described in part 2 of this series. (**"Success With Change," November *T+D***) A managing change approach is especially important when an organization isn't fundamentally designed for success with change—and most organizations aren't. A managing change approach is needed when, in order to implement change, you must override and supplement the normal processes of the business. But managing changes as they occur isn't enough these days. With the number and complexity of changes increasing, it's time to rethink how we design organizations. It's time to admit that change is a way of life and not an appendage to "business as usual." It's time to take a new view of how your organization works and must work every day so that it isn't constantly trying to override the usual organizational processes. That requires a structural and mental redesign of the organization—a transformational approach.

Transformation

The world's research is beginning to provide insights about the qualities of organizations that have an inbuilt capacity for change. Specifically, these organizations

- link present and future
- make learning a way of life
- actively support and encourage day-to-day improvements and changes
- ensure diverse teams
- encourage mavericks
- shelter breakthroughs
- integrate technology
- build and deepen trust.

How to implement those practices is just becoming clear. Creating a change-friendly organization is a new and still emerging pursuit. There are many experiments and some promising results, but there are as yet no robust models. We live in a time of transition, in which our concept of *organization* is being challenged and changed. One thing we can say with certainty is that what we mean by *organization* will be vastly different in the future. We can also say that the following practices are proving to create what Daryl Conner calls a "nimble" organization.

Link the present and the future. Research suggests that change occurs more fluidly when people bring the future into current work. That means that instead of—or in addition to—seeing work as an extension of the past, we need to think about the world, markets, competitors, and opportunities that may exist months and years hence, and factor them into today's decisions.

There are several ways to do that. Several studies suggest that when teams consist of some people who are present-oriented and others who are future-oriented, the teams perform better over time. One study of 108 executives in technology-based startups assessed whether each executive was more present- or future-oriented. Then they looked at communication among the executives. The findings were that significantly better performance occurred when a team contained both present- and future-oriented executives and when there was a lot of communication among the exec team.

Another way to link the present and future is to conduct low-cost experiments with new ideas in the current markets. One study of changes in eight computer companies in the United States, Europe, and Asia made this discovery: Successful projects often incorporate emerging ideas into present products, rather than just developing entirely new products.

For example, Swatch added communications capability to its watches, creating a pager watch, representing a futuristic yet anchored approach to innovation. The company has one eye on what it does well and one eye on the possibilities beyond current capabilities—with the intent to bring them together in the present. Part of the lesson from those and other studies is to be continually looking for new ideas that build on core competencies.

Make learning a way of life. Knowledge is becoming an increasingly more important source of competitive advantage. That includes knowledge about markets and the outside world, about what works and what to avoid doing, and about where to find expertise and information. Organizations that find, spread, and manage knowledge well can respond and innovate faster. They have less waste from people failing in the same way over and over. Recent research tells us that change-friendly organizations excel in knowledge movement and management. Another way to say that is they excel in learning.

Several important themes related to accelerating learning are emerging. One, it's important to expose frontline people to new ideas. Many—perhaps most—innovations and performance improvements happen in the course of daily work. Such improvements and innovations spread when frontline people talk to each other and to suppliers. But people at the top of the organization focused on the big picture often don't support worker communication with suppliers and across work groups. Worse, they may even discourage such contacts. One interesting study examined 73 technical innovations in a 38,000-person firm with 13 different locations. Only seven of the 73 innovations spread between units. The innovations that did spread did so primarily through direct contact between employees and suppliers. The conclusion: Make it easy for workers to talk with and learn from each other and from suppliers, or else develop more formal ways to keep frontline people aware of what's going on related to their work. Some ways to do that are field trips to suppliers and involving frontline people in purchasing decisions.

On a more formal level, accumulating evidence indicates that designing organizations to manage knowledge more systematically and effectively has high payoffs. One study of 158 global companies in North America, Europe, and Asia discovered such benefits as productivity improvements, faster speed to market, increased market share, improved sales volume, and cost reductions and avoidance.

Another study examined 24 companies to discover the keys to using knowledge in an organization successfully. Success occurred in these conditions:

- a knowledge-friendly culture
- a reward system for sharing knowledge
- multiple channels for knowledge transfer, especially encouragement of personal contact across work groups.

All of those are embedded conditions that go beyond any specific change project or program.

It's all about creating and supporting a learning and information-sharing orientation. A study of 268 Australian organizations found that customer retention, new product success, sales growth, and return-on-investment are significantly better in companies with a learning orientation. That is, such companies are better at creating, acquiring, and spreading knowledge and helping people bring that knowledge into action. That study also indicates that a learning orientation has a more positive impact on overall performance than just a market orientation, which focuses on needs that customers say they have. Market orientation is good for adaptive change but seems to prevent radical change: Customers usually want refinements but don't request products when they don't yet feel a need. Learning orientation appears to go beyond that, supporting the kind of creativity that anticipates and even creates new customer demands.

The behaviors of top management have a significant effect on an organization's learning. If the top team actively supports learning, learning orientation goes up significantly. If the team is risk-averse, learning orientation goes down.

Support and encourage day-to-day improvements and changes. Most management interest focuses on the big and planned changes driven by formal strategies or specific challenges. Though some change occurs within a framework of strategic priorities, most change happens almost imperceptibly on local and team levels. One typical study of changes in four industries (biochemical, animal feed, steel, electronics) found that 77 percent of changes at the work-group level were reactions to a specific, current problem or to a suggestion from someone outside of the team; 68 percent of those changes occurred in the course of day-to-day work. Those changes focused on work processes not directly related to work tasks, product and service changes, or changes in how group members work together.

The point is that change is occurring all of the time in organizations. Great organizations encourage—or at least don't inhibit—ongoing change at the individual, team, and inter-team levels. This topic deserves more study, but research-based insights do support that conclusion.

A massive review of the world's organization change literature concludes that in organizations constantly improving, change is "a way of life for the entire organization, not a one-time program." Collins reached the same conclusion after identifying the 11 companies (out of 1435) that achieved breakthrough performance that continued to exceed industry standards. In those few organizations, "relentless commitment" to excellence, rather than a grand program, was part of the success secret. A study of eight computer companies on three continents used the same word, *relentless*, saying that optimal innovation occurred when there was a "relentless pace of change," in which continuous innovation was punctuated by periodic formal innovation planning sessions.

It's clear that the most change-friendly organizations are developing and encouraging skills for ad hoc and emergent change actions—not only for formal and planned change.

Ensure diverse teams. Diversity is an antidote to business as usual. It seems to help stir the pot. And diversity at senior-management levels is especially important to having a nimble organization. When top management teams are diverse in time orientation (combing present and past); tenure; and experience, strategic change is more likely. A global, 14-year study of 67 semiconductor firms found that the most strategic change occurred when the top executive and his or her team had relatively short but different lengths of time on the job. Another comprehensive study based on a six-year review of the two largest companies in each of 16 industries found that more diverse top management teams implemented more complex changes, though the tendency was not to sustain them. The challenge is keeping all diversity headed in the same direction.

Diversity isn't only important at the top. Research has long shown that diversity within any team, though it increases the potential for conflict and sometimes makes it difficult to sustain new directions, leads to more innovative solutions.

Encourage mavericks. Mavericks frequently are essential champions of the new directions that create an organization's future. Mavericks take the risks and do the early experimentation that an organization won't easily fund. By definition, mavericks are not part of the mainstream. They stand for radical change, not evolutionary change. Their ideas and approaches aren't standard and, therefore, cause a lot of resistance and reaction. Evidence is growing that to have transformational capacity, an organization must encourage and be a home for mavericks.

Research is helping to clarify the qualities of disturbers of the status quo. In one study, executives in each of 24 companies of various sizes in the United States, the United Kingdom, and Canada describe the qualities of people who had led small but effective changes in their organizations. The executives said those change leaders were energetic, independent but committed to the organization, questioning of the system, impatient and not put off by resistance, and willing to go beyond the requirements of their jobs to make a difference. These mavericks usually didn't get formal support until they'd proven their ideas. They were driven by the needs of the organization, not by rewards or promotion.

Another report describes 300 people who had led successful customer-focus transformations. They had these qualities: enthusiasm and energy, knowledge of customer needs, communicativeness, and the ability to not only understand customer needs, but also to interpret them creatively.

A large international study of 4405 respondents from 43 companies in 68 countries sums up the maverick profile: "These change champions have the same profile as entrepreneurs."

Sadly, many mavericks who are inside organizations don't find ongoing support there, especially when their ideas challenge the status quo radically. They usually leave and start new businesses. An extensive global review of innovations in several industries found that although every breakthrough innovation in the computer industry from 1973 to 1995 was born in an established organization, none were developed and commercialized in those organizations. A quote from the findings: "Some changes that will make an organization viable are radical changes. When these present themselves, most leaders go where the customers, budget processes, and promotions systems drive them—to incremental and safe decisions." Under those conditions, mavericks leave.

Research is beginning to tell us that it is possible for mavericks to live and prosper in organizations. Creating an environment that doesn't evict them appears to be important to ongoing organizational transformation.

Shelter breakthroughs. When breakthroughs occur in an existing organization, they meet enormous resistance. The resistance forces are so powerful and integrated (the whole organization is often set up for the old ways) that the best course of action may be to create a new organization to

The World's Research

Here's a sampling of the studies and literature on which this article is based.

- *Good to Great: Why Some Companies Make the Leap... and Others Don't,* by Jim Collins (Harper, 2001)
- "Navigating the Competitive Landscape: The Drivers and Consequences of Competitive Aggressiveness," *Academy of Management Journal* (August 2001)
- *The Innovator's Dilemma,* by C. Christensen (Harper Business, 2000)
- "The Development of Product and Process Improvement in Work Groups," *Group and Organization Management* (September 2000)
- "Developing a Market-Oriented Learning Organization," *Australian Journal of Management* (September 2000)
- "Beyond Knowledge Management: New Ways to Work and Learn," *The Conference Board* (March 2000)
- *Research in Organizational Change and Development, vol. 12: An Annual Series Featuring Advances in Theory, Methodology, and Research,* Editors Passmore and Woodman (JAI Press, 1999)
- "Change and Complementarities in the New Competitive Landscape: A European Panel Study, 1992–1996." *Organization Science* (September/October 1999)
- "What's a Good Reason to Change? Motivated Reasoning and Social Accounts in Promoting Organizational Change," *Journal of Applied Psychology* (August 1999)
- *Leading at the Edge of Chaos: How to Create the Nimble Organization,* by D. Conner (John Wiley & Sons, 1998)
- *Enhancing Organizational Performance,* Editors Druckman, Singer, and Van Cott (National Academy Press, 1997)
- "The Corporate Entrepreneur: Leading Organizational Transformation," *Long-Range Planning* (June 1997)
- "Igniting Organizational Change From Below: The Power of Personal initiative," *Organizational Dynamics* (May 1997)
- "The Art of Continuous Change: Linking Complexity Theory and Time-Paced Evolution in Relentlessly Shifting Organizations," *Administrative Science Quarterly* (March 1997)
- "Strategic Change: The Influence of Managerial Characteristics and Organizational Growth," *Academy of Management Journal* (February 1997)
- "Temporal Dimensions of Opportunistic Change in Technology-Based Ventures," *Entrepreneurship Theory and Practice* (Winter 1997)
- "Success Stories in the Strategic Use of Telecommunications: Companies That Made It Work," *Telecommunication* (September 1996)
- "Are Champions Different From Non-Champions?" *Journal of Business Venturing* (September 1994)
- "The Diffusion of Innovation Within Multi-Unit Firms," *International Journal of Operations and Production Management* (October 5, 1990)

shelter and grow the change. Change-friendly organizations have institutionalized ways to provide such shelters.

Christensen's intense and thorough study of breakthrough innovations in the computer, retail, printer, and mechanical excavator industries makes this lesson clear: Successful changes are more frequent in organizations that routinely create small, independent units, in which breakthroughs have their own budgets, suppliers, markets, and cultures. These independent units also receive more resources for learning and trial-and-error. They tend to have different attitudes to the market, often leading the market rather than following its stated needs.

Companies known for their high rates of innovation and large proportion of new-to-old products have long had a policy of sheltering breakthrough ideas. 3M is a good example. It has a formal process for moving new ideas into a protected organization with a separate budget and where those ideas can grow.

Integrate technology. Technology isn't just nice to have; it's critical for creating transformational capacity. However, technology must be a means to an end, not an end in itself. The largest global and ongoing study of changes occurring in organizations throughout the world drew a surprising conclusion: Of all factors reviewed, only IT had a significant and positive relationship to performance. But that was true only when it was integrated with other changes related to creating a more network-like and less top-down organization. Another comprehensive study of companies that achieved and sustained breakthrough performance in their industries concludes that those companies don't use technology as a change driver. But they aren't technology-shy. They use technology to help implement their strategies and enhance their core competencies.

Build and deepen trust. Trust as a theme emerges throughout the change research. People are more likely to support changes when the general atmosphere in and around their organization is trusting and when formal leaders have personal credibility. One study found that nurses were more likely to believe a change was legitimate when they trusted management. If trust was low, they were more likely to resist and look for reasons what managers wanted wasn't right.

Trust is also key theme from a 1999 review of change research to discover barriers to change success. When the researchers asked what affected people's commitment to change, they found that the credibility and honesty of the change agent were critical. They also found that those trust-related qualities were built over time, making them bigger than any single change program or initiative. That partly explains why opinion leaders make such good change agents: They're people others trust.

Trust is a fragile condition in organizations, as in all relationships. A comprehensive report notes: "Many current change practices (such as downsizing) erode trust, making future change initiatives harder to implement." Because trust takes time to build, it must be developed on a day-to-day basis so that it becomes a ready foundation supporting ad hoc and planned changes as they arise.

What all this means

Change isn't just something to manage when strategies shift or crises occur. It's an ongoing challenge and condition in organizational life. Yet, most organizations are designed to support stability. We plan, organize, and control. We operate according to rigid organizational charts and old-style decision and innovation processes. Though we need some of that, most organizations overemphasize control, rules, decision and communication lines, and precedence. Increasingly, success depends on fluidity, openness, learning, and a pervasive capacity to make evolutionary and even radical changes.

In order to open up to change as a natural and ongoing aspect of our organizations, we have to adopt some new ways of thinking about life as well as organizations. Many actions managers and others take indicate that we think organizations are rational systems that we can plan and control from the top and break into functional units for ease of control. The model for that thinking comes from 17th-century science and mechanics, in which the machine is a key metaphor for an organization and a key challenge is how to make things work routinely and consistently. In that world order, change is something to be managed and minimized. The emphasis is on stopping undesirable changes, overcoming resistance, and ensuring that rationally developed strategies will be implemented with limited failure and error.

Now things are different. The mechanical, top-down view of organizations doesn't work well in our global and networked economy and world, except for simple and predictable problems. Research confirms that principles from life sciences are a better framework for thinking about organizations. Life sciences examine how living systems perform and change. Here are a few characteristics from biology and the life sciences that reflect and shed light on many of the research-based findings mentioned in this article.

- As an organism's environment becomes more complex and unpredictable, the organism must develop adaptive and transformative capabilities. The evolution of the brain is a prime example.
- The organism's own capabilities interact with the environment to produce a unique path of evolution. No change can happen that doesn't build on existing capacity.
- When stress and tension build to a breaking point, surprising and unpredictable new actions and directions often occur in nature (for example, feet on fish) that may lead to dramatically improved capabilities. Organisms must have an ability to create their own breakthroughs—and so must organizations. In organizations, people who don't feel they have to preserve the status quo often initiate breakthroughs. Sadly, many organizations aren't designed to embrace breakthroughs and mavericks, so those creativities leave and grow somewhere else.
- In complex, unpredictable environments, all parts of the organism are mobilized for action. That is, parts of any organism operate with a great deal of local authority and responsibility. In the human body, it's not just up to the brain (top management) to decide what to do. Without consulting the thinking part of the brain, the body reacts instantly to stress, temperature changes, air-quality changes, viruses, and so forth. That capacity to respond at all levels becomes more important as more forces challenge and stress the organism. In other words, thinking and acting have to be delegated to the body (people) for adaptive action. That means change is everybody's business and everyone needs the skills and mindset to play an active role.

Next month in the final article in this series, we'll look more closely at the idea that change is everybody's business. We'll stress that in change, there are and can be no bystanders. Leaders can't make changes alone. People throughout the organization are powerful even when they don't act or when they resist.

Editor's note: You can order Parts 1 and 2 of this article at *store.astd.org*

Patricia A. McLagan *is chairman of McLagan International and the author or co-author of many books and articles on management, change, and organization effectiveness, including the newly released* Change Is Everybody's Business. *She's also publisher of a series of research-to-practice reports,* theRITEstuff Reports, *and is co-host of an Internet radio show,* The Changing World of Work; *www.thechangingworldofwork.com.*

This article was based, in part, on her research reported in "Success With Change: Lessons From the World's Research." The full report is available for purchase at www.mclaganinternational.com.

Build your own change model

For decades, CEOs have been looking for the holy grail of corporate transformation, asking, "What is the best way to transform my company? Which model should I use?" Management consultants and academics have been working overtime to supply the answer. They haven't succeeded, however, because the search is a futile one. Every organization is unique. Leaders can adopt ideas that have worked elsewhere, but they need to create their own one-of-a-kind change model through experimentation, learning, blueprint creation, and, most of all, a strong focus on results.

Robert H. Schaffer and Matthew K. McCreight

Of all the CEOs who will toss and turn tonight, you can bet that a large number of them are wondering how to carry out major transformations in their companies: reversing profit deterioration, adapting to radical technological shifts, accelerating slow growth, breaking into new markets, absorbing major acquisitions, and so on. They want to know how to execute these changes in ways that make them winners. An army of consultants and academics have invested major efforts in trying to create the right formula but without success. Each group of gurus has generated its own models, some of which have cut a vast swath through the corporate world. However, none have really proven effective.

One reason for this failure is the fact that even though transformational change is quite complex, change models generally attempt to provide a simplified, one-size-fits-all solution. Some formulas consist mainly of lofty principles but with no implementation guidelines. Some specify detailed action steps without regard to the appropriateness for different firms. Because each firm has its own work processes, culture, and competencies, a given change formula may work well in one but fail miserably in the next.

Moreover, almost all of the change formula creators adhere to the classic begin-with-preparations change paradigm: Only after endless preparatory tasks such as strategic planning, new information systems, training, reorganization, and so on can progress be expected. This rigidly logical paradigm is neat on paper but bears no resemblance to how firms really carry out changes.

These are only a few of the vulnerabilities of most change theories. There are many others. So it should not be surprising that, despite the public hoopla that has accompanied the unveiling of a number of such theories, not a one has been validated by repeated success over time.

The weakness of master models was demonstrated in a landmark Harvard Business School study in the 1980s by Beer, Eisenstat, and Spector (1990). After examining several attempted major transformations in a variety of corporations, the researchers primarily concluded that company-wide change efforts based on formally structured programs failed to achieve their aims. As Beer et al. colorfully put it, "Wave after wave of programs rolled across the landscape with little positive impact." By contrast, the successful efforts tended to be empirically developed by the firms themselves. And in those firms, the change process emanated not from top down, but from bottom up.

Our own experiences with and observations of dozens of attempted major transformations match these findings exactly. Firms can certainly benefit from the cumulative experience of others, but there is no universal change template waiting to be discovered. Each firm must create the change pattern that works best for itself.

Here we sketch a framework by which management teams can carry out the necessary experimentation and learning. It is not a change architecture per se, but a framework for enabling each firm to construct its own change architecture—to design its transition as a unique creative work.

A radical departure

Major transformations should be carried out as a series of discrete staged advances, each about four to six months long, with a beginning and an end. Within each of these bounded periods a number of *rapid cycle projects* are carried out, each designed to produce (a) urgently needed business results, (b) new capability in implementing change, and (c) new insights about the firm's strategy. The wisdom gained during each period is exploited in designing the subsequent one. The successes provide the zest and confidence for moving ahead. Thus, both the number and the scope of the projects expand in every successive stage.

Chicken-and-egg: Strategic plans guide rapid cycle projects that guide strategic planning

The rapid cycle projects are designed both to achieve important business goals and to advance key strategic objectives. Because actually achieving measurable results helps develop implementation capability, it is important to get action under way fairly quickly. Then, while successful work on the projects goes forward, helping to generate an upbeat feeling throughout the firm, senior management can continue to sharpen the strategic plans.

Many purists will be affronted by the idea of initiating change projects before a comprehensive strategic change plan is set in concrete. They will assert that these rapid cycle projects could lead the firm in the "wrong direction." That is a fantasy. The initial projects are designed to yield urgently needed results quickly without major investment, so there is no such risk. Of course, the projects need to cohere with the existing corporate strategy, just as the strategic plans need to be influenced by what is being learned about the firm's implementation capability. Planning and implementation are the chicken-and-egg of corporate transformation. And they should proceed in parallel, each nourishing the other.

> *Firms can certainly benefit from the cumulative experience of others, but there is no universal change template waiting to be discovered.*

In getting started, the CEO and a group of senior managers form a change leadership steering committee to create and orchestrate the overall process. Their first step is to agree, as rapidly as possible, on

- their best current picture of the main transformation goals and strategy
- within that framework, the most urgent performance improvement and strategic change goals they need to attack immediately

They make these priorities as clear as they can to the entire organization. Specific managers are then named to launch rapid-cycle, results-focused projects on the critical goals. Each project should be implemented and completed within the four- to six-month cycle, which means that large-scale, long-term goals need to be carved into incremental steps.

How it began at Eagle Star–Zurich in the UK

In the late 1990s, 100-year-old Eagle Star Insurance was in serious difficulty. The company was the third-largest general insurance firm in the United Kingdom. However, its losses were high, mainly as a result of striving for market share at almost any cost. When Patrick O'Sullivan entered the scene, he was the company's sixth chief executive in as many years. Within a few weeks it became apparent to him that many of the managers were in denial about the company's difficult situation. And to complicate his task, two months into his new job came the announcement that the company was being merged into Zurich Financial Services in what would be a long and involved process.

To launch his transformation, O'Sullivan gathered a few senior executives and made clear that they had to stem their losses very quickly. All of the rapid cycle projects in the immediate future would have to focus on quick cost reduction. At the same time, the team would have to conduct a major strategy review to determine where the company should be headed.

It was easy to decide where to begin: Claims "leakage"—payments in excess of the amount that well-managed claims would require—were running about 10 to 20 percent. With over a billion US dollars in claims each year, these overpayments were an obvious early target. Moreover, the lengthy delays and poor claim service were driving customers into the arms of competitors.

The first rapid cycle projects were planned in just a few weeks. Early in January 1998, 50 front-line staff members, supervisors, and technical experts from 12 different claims locations assembled for a two-day off-site meeting, using a version of the GE WorkOut process. The participants, who had not been asked to work on claims improvements before, were charged with planning steps that in the next few months would reduce the cost of automobile claims by at least $10 million that year.

Though it seemed a very ambitious target, the participants were able to develop more than a dozen major improvement recommendations. Action plans to implement those ideas were quickly approved by senior management at the end of the session. Some were simple ideas, such as collecting more of the millions of dollars in reimbursements legitimately due the company. Others were more complex, such as revamping the company's network of auto repair shops and helping the dozens of claims representatives across the company to actively manage costs.

Other rapid cycle cost reduction projects were launched in that first six months, most in WorkOut sessions similar to the claims session. The leadership team initiated its own efforts to stop activities that were not really essential, thus modeling such initiatives for the rest of the firm. They found many ways to put the brakes on the spending momentum. Certain marketing expenses were cut, for example, and IT projects that were running millions over budget were reined in and brought under greater control.

Rapid cycle projects: Implementation capacity, confidence, enthusiasm

By generating tangible success, rapid cycle projects reinforce senior management's message that the firm can do better. They help people overcome their self-doubts, providing evidence that more can indeed be achieved. At Eagle Star, where denial served as a defense against taking action, rapid results were crucial.

In addition to achieving needed results, these projects are carried out as learning experiences, aimed at building the company's change management skills. Here are some examples of the developmental ingredients that are designed into the projects.

1. Go for results at once.

By demonstrating that the firm has the capacity to produce tangible results at once, rapid cycle projects overcome the frequent tendency to begin change efforts with endless preparations and studies. That is why it is important to carve out goals that participants feel they can attain.

When asked why the change had not been carried out previously, a front-line member of the finance group replied, "No one would listen."

The first claims project at Eagle Star succeeded in eliminating several million dollars in claims costs, even though it fell somewhat short of its ambitious goal. It also gave participants the confidence to do much more. A series of rapid cycle projects were then launched in key branches to expand on the first improvements. One major branch—with more than 150 claim handlers—focused on helping each representative work to reduce overpayments, then saw savings quickly total more than $100,000 a month. It also instilled a new sense of pride among these claims reps.

The finance group tackled ways to improve cash flow, starting with the goal of a $30 million improvement in two months. By launching a series of rapid cycle projects and making some immediate changes in financing strategy, the group exceeded its goal and added over $2 million to the company's bottom line—within a few weeks! When asked why the change had not been carried out previously, a front-line member of the finance group replied, "No one would listen."

No amount of planning or training or number of new systems can provide the zest and reinforcement yielded by the achievement of rapid results like these. At Eagle Star, employees reinforced O'Sullivan's determination to push for ever faster progress and began to dissolve the web of denial the staff had woven around themselves.

2. Develop managerial skills.

The rapid development of new skills and capabilities among management is crucial to the success of any transformation. Rapid cycle projects are designed as learning laboratories to help managers expand their capabilities in handling change. Modifying their management styles, instituting new ways to sponsor and support change efforts, reorienting processes and metrics to focus on crucial goals—and more—can all be built into such projects (see **Figure 1** for examples).

At Zurich UK (as Eagle Star was called after September 1999), the rapid cycle projects were designed with a deliberate developmental agenda for managers. As projects were defined, accountable managers were named. They participated in just-in-time training and coaching sessions to develop the skills they would need to sponsor the projects. As part of the push to accelerate the pace, a small group of manager-level staff were trained as internal consultants. In turn, under the leadership of Organization Development Director Mo Kang, they helped managers learn to drive for rapid results and build their own skills in the process.

3. Introduce new tools and business processes.

Rapid cycle projects can be used to test new ways of getting things done. Streamlining business processes, partnering with customers, managing inventory, developing new

Figure 1

Kinds of management skill development that can be built into rapid cycle projects

- Project management disciplines
- Sharper measurement of results
- One-person accountability for results no matter who is involved
- Engaging lower-level associates in innovative projects
- Tougher and more explicit demand making
- Formation of temporary teams to attack a task creatively
- Business process mapping and process redesign
- Quality management techniques
- Cost analysis
- Experiments in customer and vendor partnerships
- Economic value added experiments
- Collaboration across organization boundaries

products, and so on can all be advanced—as can new elements of IT, new budgeting processes, new measurement and management information schemes, and other disciplines that are needed to drive ever higher organizational performance.

When the first claims projects at Eagle Star were under way, the internal consulting team began issuing monthly updates of the results being achieved. The initial reaction was one of anger. As Mo Kang put it,

> When we issued the first update on the results being achieved by the various work teams, it was revealed that a number of teams were not yet making any progress. I received a number of angry calls over the next few days. "How dare you publish that kind of stuff!" But Patrick [O'Sullivan] pushed right back and told the whole company that this sort of update would be done every month. People got the message pretty quickly that results mattered.

O'Sullivan and CFO Bryan Howett then initiated a series of monthly operating reviews in which each business unit leader and his team had to report on current achievements. They also had to state the actions they would take to close any gaps in performance against plan.

4. Advance strategic thrusts.

Rapid cycle projects can be used to test and advance important strategic thrusts, such as new product launches, new market ventures, and acquisition integrations. These pilot efforts mitigate the "bet your company" feeling associated with major strategic moves. For example, the initial rapid cycle projects in claims provided the basic data needed for a far-reaching strategic transformation of the entire function to further reduce claims overpayments.

Rather than attacking the project on a company-wide basis, Roger Day, head of claims, formed a small team of representatives from various offices who made a quick survey in just one part of the business. The large claims losses they found—and the improvements they quickly effected—validated the fundamental changes they were proposing, even to the most skeptical claims managers. Similar reviews were then held throughout the business, with similar benefits.

Strategic planning and implementation both advance simultaneously, each providing fresh insights and lessons for the other.

These strategic reviews highlighted the need to reorganize the five major claims branches in the Commercial Division. Effective cost control would require much more uniformity and discipline among offices. Claims leader Geoff McMahon challenged a crossfunctional team to get the new processes designed and put into place in all offices in just twelve weeks, instead of taking many months just to conduct the studies and develop the plan. And the team succeeded. This was one of many examples of how the company's strategy began to be shaped from the bottom up as well as the top down.

Another strategic drive that was advanced with rapid cycle projects was the very process of integrating Eagle Star into the global Zurich organization. One WorkOut session, involving both Zurich and Eagle Star people, was held to plan the integration. By the end of the few days they had a plan on how to do it and launched a number of actions that would soon save hundreds of thousands of dollars. Just as important, they had quickly begun to build a common organization. In the words of one participant, "We started as two separate groups. Now, just a few days later, I feel like we are one company."

End of each cycle: What are we learning? What should we accomplish next?

Michael Beer and his team at HBS advise that "Change is about learning." That is the essence of this "build your own" strategy we are advocating. When a cycle is completed, senior management can assess what it achieved and what can be learned from the experiences. As part of these reviews, the steering committee might meet with the managers of all the projects to get some details of the experiences: What did we accomplish? What did we learn? What are the possible implications for the next steps? They can then decide what work should be launched in the next cycle.

The managers who lead projects need to make deliberate choices about what to include in the way of managerial and methodological innovations. When the project plans are written, they must include not only a description of the project and its goal, but also a description of what innovations are to be tested and how their effectiveness will be assessed.

Every company has to test the cycle time that is best for it. In our experience, four to six months is about right, but some firms prefer shorter cycles in the early stages. A one year cycle, even though it matches many other scheduled events in a firm's life, is usually too long until the achievement/learning process is sufficiently embedded.

At the very beginning, the assessment/learning/planning cycle must be initiated and led by the senior-level steering committee. Once under way, the process can spread out. Different units might create their own steering committees to support and manage the change efforts within their own spheres. When useful, other steering groups might be established on a pro tem basis to manage certain key change initiatives. Gradually, as appropriate, the change process becomes an organization-wide shared experimentation and learning experience, with a growing number of rapid cycle projects of broadening scope being carried out in each phase.

Strategic planning continues

In the traditional view of corporate transformations, it is an article of faith that strategic planning must be the first step. Only then may implementation follow. As stated earlier, we advocate that strategic planning and implementation both advance simultaneously, each providing fresh insights and lessons for the other.

At Zurich UK, as bottom line results improved, the strategic focus shifted from stemming losses to expanding profits. The leadership team met early in 2000 and charted a course to move ahead of the competition in terms of cost levels (requiring them to beat the profit targets they had just set for themselves). A few years before, when a large consulting firm had presented the company with a set of ambitious strategic plans, it had lacked the capacity to implement them. Now, with the confidence bred of the success of dozens of rapid cycle projects, the managers knew they could accomplish their goals.

While the change projects are under way, those responsible for overall strategic planning keep the process going. The short-term projects are always chosen and designed so as to best advance the strategic plans (as they exist at the time). But the influence travels the other way as well—as the incubation projects yield results and provide new experiences, those lessons are deliberately factored into ongoing planning.

Institutional changes to support the transformation process

As the result-focused action experiments create momentum and introduce a variety of managerial innovations, the steering committee can begin to design and implement the major institutional changes, cement the progress to date, and advance the process. These major changes include

- organization structure changes
- staffing of key positions
- capital investment and modes of financing
- information and decision systems
- new compensation practices
- major process redesign

At Zurich, one early innovation was the formation of the central internal consulting group of about six people to champion the company's change process and help instill a result focus into its change efforts. This group trained and developed all 200-plus members of the management team and more than 300 others (almost 10 percent of the workforce) in various change leadership and change facilitation skills and roles. The training was result-oriented and conducted within the context of the ongoing rapid cycle projects.

The company's management conferences, which before had largely been set piece events focused mostly on speeches and socializing, became "change acceleration events." The first conference of the top 150 managers after the Eagle Star–Zurich merger was announced was a two day event in which teams developed plans for achieving an additional $15 million in savings—above the amount already budgeted. At the conference, a series of additional rapid cycle projects were launched in underwriting, pricing, claims, and cost management.

Subsequent management conferences launched other rapid cycle efforts under this new strategic banner. One was focused on "innovation" and launched a series of new business ventures, all of which had to be developed and tested within a few months. Success in these new business thrusts led to a more ongoing "boundaryless" attack on innovation, with a cross-business innovation council meeting regularly to review ideas, sponsor projects, and agree on funding for proven ideas.

At the end of four-plus years, Zurich UK is a very different company from the old Eagle Star. It has shifted earnings from a significant loss to strong, sustained profits. It has improved the bottom line by over $100 million a year (as verified by the company's actuaries) and, according to O'Sullivan, multiples of that amount in additional benefits that are not easily measurable. It has moved into new markets and is experimenting with new products and ways of doing business. Instead of the old inertia, change has become a routine. The company is the master of its fate, not a victim of circumstance.

The rapid cycle projects, accelerating and expanding, achieved the bottom line results. At the same time, they helped introduce the many new skills and tools that would be the key to continued performance gains. And all the while, driving dozens of rapid cycle improvement projects, senior managers were constantly analyzing what they were learning and how to move it forward.

Most important, although they exploited the GE Work-Out process and some other specific change techniques as their way to identify and launch the projects, the overall change architecture was their own creation. It was a model over which they labored long and which evolved and changed over time, nourished by a steady stream of positive results. Other companies might want to use different tools, but they can accomplish the same success.

References and selected bibliography

Beer, Michael, Russell A. Eisenstat, and Bert Spector. 1990. Why change programs don't produce change. *Harvard Business Review* 68/6 (November-December): 158 –166.

Robert H. Schaffer *Principal, Robert H. Schaffer & Associates, Stamford, Connecticut (rhs@rhsa.com)*

Matthew K. McCreight *Principal, Robert H. Schaffer & Associates, Stamford, Connecticut (mkm@rhsa.com)*

UNIT 4
Directing

Unit Selections

15. **A Theory of Human Motivation**, Abraham H. Maslow
16. **The True Measure of a CEO**, James O'Toole
17. **The Myth of Charismatic Leaders**, Joseph A. Raelin
18. **Can One Man Save GM?**, Alex Taylor III
19. **Disaster's Future**, Simon Moore

Key Points to Consider

- Why do you think there are so many ideas about human motivation? Why is it so important for people to be motivated?
- To be effective, a leader has to be able to achieve results and be accountable for those results. Do you see that happening in today's world?
- Do you think it is the task of a leader to create conditions under which all followers can reach their full human potential? Defend your answer.
- What are some of the keys that make organizations really work? How can an organization institute these characteristics so that it can achieve high performance?

Student Website

www.mhcls.com/online

Internet References

Further information regarding these websites may be found in this book's preface or online.

ADR (Alternative Dispute Resolution): General
http://www.opm.gov/er/adrguide/

Equity Compensation, Employee Ownership & Stock Options
http://www.fed.org

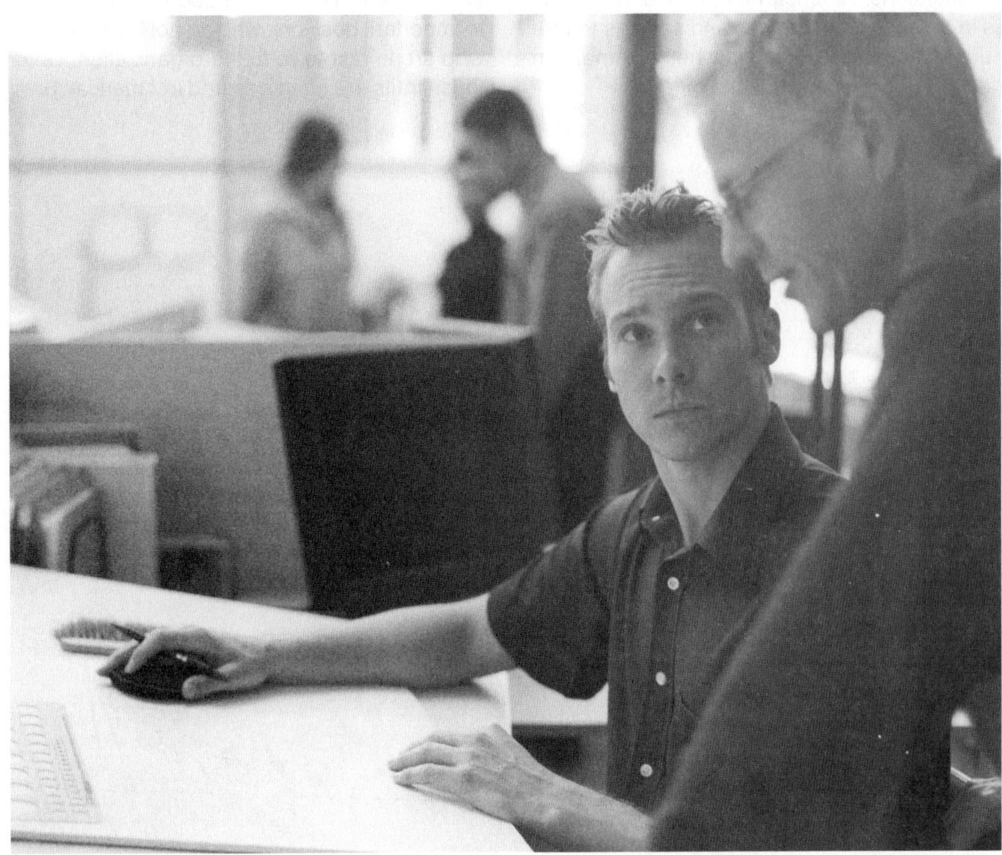

Managers spend most of their time directing the organization. They have learned, however, that just telling people what to do is not good enough. To achieve the maximum possible results, people must first clearly understand the firm's goals, and then management must find a way to motivate them. Miscommunication and assumptions can often lead to poor choices and highly ineffective courses of action. Understanding why people work, how they work, and the circumstances under which they work is important to understanding their motivation as Abraham Maslow discusses in his classic article "A Theory of Human Motivation."

People enter business situations with a history of experiences, attitudes, and beliefs, and effectively communicating with them can be difficult. Open communication must be based upon trust. If there is fear, confusion, or lack of understanding, then communication will not be as effective as it could be. Managers must be able to communicate both in writing and orally. Effective communication involves the ability to design a letter, memo, or conversation so that both the sender and the receiver have a clear understanding of what was said and what is now expected of both parties. This frequently involves telling the receiver not only the message, but how the message was generated, because an employee's understanding of the reasons for an instruction can be the key to effective motivation. In today's environment, the problem is not a lack of ways to communicate, but rather selecting the important information from that which is not. This is particularly important when the organization is faced with a crisis. In these types of situations, communication is even more important than in the regular course of business, when there is no emergency. Organizations must learn to practice excellent communication skills so that when a crisis does hit, they are able to adjust, as seen in "Disaster's Future."

Of all the various components of management, leadership is probably the most discussed, analyzed, and misunderstood. Indeed, some would argue that leadership and management are two separate and distinct activities. Leadership may be over discussed, but it is not well understood. Leadership has been studied since ancient times and was investigated by Aristotle as shown in "The True Measure of a CEO." Leaders come in all shapes and sizes, and all styles, but they need to be developed and they need to demonstrate leadership. There have been good leaders and evil leaders, saints and brutes. But, they all share certain characteristics. One is the ability to communicate an idea to their followers and have them accept it as their own. This results in motivation of the followers. The second characteristic is genuine caring, enthusiasm, and dedication to the dream. A manager who is successful in communicating with, motivating, and leading people will experience enhanced performance and productivity. The Japanese have led other nations in this area with the application of many techniques, such as quality circles. However, not all forms of worker participation have resulted in enhanced productivity.

There are those who would say that there is a leadership crisis facing industry as not enough qualified people are available for these kinds of positions. But there are also those that would disagree with that assumption, and not all types of leaders are right for all types of situations. American firms have also been applying new ideas in a variety of industries and settings to motivate employees, but a cause for concern is whether American workers will continue to be motivated.

Effective managers are people who are able to direct an organization successfully. They know how to communicate, motivate, and lead, achieving enhanced productivity and performance that will accomplish the goals and mission of the organization in a fluid environment. There have been those managers that have risen to important positions who do not have these characteristics, and who are in fact toxic to the organization. Unfortunately, many of these traits are often admired in American business and industry.

A Theory of Human Motivation

Abraham H. Maslow

In a previous paper (13) various propositions were presented which would have to be included in any theory of human motivation that could lay claim to being definitive. These conclusions may be briefly summarized as follows:

1. The integrated wholeness of the organism must be one of the foundation stones of motivation theory.
2. The hunger drive (or any other physiological drive) was rejected as a centering point or model for a definitive theory of motivation. Any drive that is somatically based and localizable was shown to be atypical rather than typical in human motivation.
3. Such a theory should stress and center itself upon ultimate or basic goals rather than partial or superficial ones, upon ends rather than means to these ends. Such a stress would imply a more central place for unconscious than for conscious motivations.
4. There are usually available various cultural paths to the same goal. Therefore conscious, specific, local-cultural desires are not as fundamental in motivation theory as the more basic, unconscious goals.
5. Any motivated behavior, either preparatory or consummatory, must be understood to be a channel through which many basic needs may be simultaneously expressed or satisfied. Typically an act has *more* than one motivation.
6. Practically all organismic states are to be understood as motivated and as motivating.
7. Human needs arrange themselves in hierarchies of prepotency. That is to say, the appearance of one need usually rests on the prior satisfaction of another, more prepotent need. Man is a perpetually wanting animal. Also no need or drive can be treated as if it were isolated or discrete; every drive is related to the state of satisfaction or dissatisfaction of other drives.
8. *Lists* of drives will get us nowhere for various theoretical and practical reasons. Furthermore any classification of motivations must deal with the problem of levels of specificity or generalization of the motives to be classified.
9. Classifications of motivations must be based upon goals rather than upon instigating drives or motivated behavior.
10. Motivation theory should be human-centered rather than animal-centered.
11. The situation or the field in which the organism reacts must be taken into account but the field alone can rarely serve as an exclusive explanation for behavior. Furthermore the field itself must be interpreted in terms of the organism. Field theory cannot be a substitute for motivation theory.
12. Not only the integration of the organism must be taken into account, but also the possibility of isolated, specific, partial or segmental reactions.

It has since become necessary to add to these another affirmation.

13. Motivation theory is not synonymous with behavior theory. The motivations are only one class of determinants of behavior. While behavior is almost always motivated, it is also almost always biologically, culturally and situationally determined as well.

The present paper is an attempt to formulate a positive theory of motivation which will satisfy these theoretical demands and at the same time conform to the known facts, clinical and observational as well as experimental. It derives most directly, however, from clinical experience. This theory is, I think, in the functionalist tradition of James and Dewey, and is fused with the holism of Wertheimer (19), Goldstein (6), and Gestalt Psychology, and with the dynamicism of Freud (4) and Adler (1). This fusion or synthesis may arbitrarily be called a 'general-dynamic' theory.

It is far easier to perceive and to criticize the aspects in motivation theory than to remedy them. Mostly this is because of the very serious lack of sound data in this area. I conceive this lack of sound facts to be due primarily to the absence of a valid theory of motivation. The present theory then must be considered to be a suggested program or framework for future research and must stand or fall, not so much on facts available or evidence presented, as upon researches to be done, researches suggested perhaps, by the questions raised in this paper.

THE BASIC NEEDS

The 'Physiological' Needs

The needs that are usually taken as the starting point for motivation theory are the so-called physiological drives. Two recent lines of research make it necessary to revise our customary notions about these needs, first, the development of the concept of homeostasis, and second, the finding that appetites (preferential choices among foods) are a fairly efficient indication of actual needs or lacks in the body.

Homeostasis refers to the body's automatic efforts to maintain a constant, normal state of the blood stream. Cannon (2) has described this process for (1) the water content of the blood, (2) salt content, (3) sugar content, (4) protein content, (5) fat content, (6) calcium content, (7) oxygen content, (8) constant hydrogen-ion level (acid-base balance) and (9) constant temperature of the blood. Obviously this list can be extended to include other minerals, the hormones, vitamins, etc.

Young in a recent article (21) has summarized the work on appetite in its relation to body needs. If the body lacks some chemical, the individual will tend to develop a specific appetite or partial hunger for that food element.

Thus it seems impossible as well as useless to make any list of fundamental physiological needs for they can come to almost any number one might wish, depending on the degree of specificity of description. We can not identify all physiological needs as homeostatic. That sexual desire, sleepiness, sheer activity and maternal behavior in animals, are homeostatic, has not yet been demonstrated. Furthermore, this list would not include the various sensory pleasures (tastes, smells, tickling, stroking) which are probably physiological and which may become the goals of motivated behavior.

In a previous paper (13) it has been pointed out that these physiological drives or needs are to be considered unusual rather than typical because they are isolable, and because they are localizable somatically. That is to say, they are relatively independent of each other, of other motivations and of the organism as a whole, and secondly, in many cases, it is possible to demonstrate a localized, underlying somatic base for the drive. This is true less generally than has been thought (exceptions are fatigue, sleepiness, maternal responses) but it is still true in the classic instances of hunger, sex, and thirst.

It should be pointed out again that any of the physiological needs and the consummatory behavior involved with them serve as channels for all sorts of other needs as well. That is to say, the person who thinks he is hungry may actually be seeking more for comfort, or dependence, than for vitamins or proteins. Conversely, it is possible to satisfy the hunger need in part by other activities such as drinking water or smoking cigarettes. In other words, relatively isolable as these physiological needs are, they are not completely so.

Undoubtedly these physiological needs are the most prepotent of all needs. What this means specifically is, that in the human being who is missing everything in life in an extreme fashion, it is most likely that the major motivation would be the physiological needs rather than any others. A person who is lacking food, safety, love, and esteem would most probably hunger for food more strongly than for anything else.

If all the needs are unsatisfied, and the organism is then dominated by the physiological needs, all other needs may become simply nonexistent or be pushed into the background. It is then fair to characterize the whole organism by saying simply that it is hungry, for consciousness is almost completely preempted by hunger. All capacities are put into the service of hunger-satisfaction, and the organization of these capacities is almost entirely determined by the one purpose of satisfying hunger. The receptors and effectors, the intelligence, memory, habits, all may now be defined simply as hunger-gratifying tools. Capacities that are not useful for this purpose lie dormant, or are pushed into the background. The urge to write poetry, the desire to acquire an automobile, the interest in American history, the desire for a new pair of shoes are, in the extreme case, forgotten or become of secondary importance. For the man who is extremely and dangerously hungry, no other interests exist but food. He dreams food, he remembers food, he thinks about food, he emotes only about food, he perceives only food and he wants only food. The more subtle determinants that ordinarily fuse with the physiological drives in organizing even feeding, drinking or sexual behavior, may now be so completely overwhelmed as to allow us to speak at this time (but *only* at this time) of pure hunger drive and behavior, with the one unqualified aim of relief.

Another peculiar characteristic of the human organism when it is dominated by a certain need is that the whole philosophy of the future tends also to change. For our chronically and extremely hungry man, Utopia can be defined very simply as a place where there is plenty of food. He tends to think that, if only he is guaranteed food for the rest of his life, he will be perfectly happy and will never want anything more. Life itself tends to be defined in terms of eating. Anything else will be defined as unimportant. Freedom, love, community feeling, respect, philosophy, may all be waved aside as fripperies which are useless since they fail to fill the stomach. Such a man may fairly be said to live by bread alone.

It cannot possibly be denied that such things are true but their *generality* can be denied. Emergency conditions are, almost by definition, rare in the normally functioning peaceful society. That this truism can be forgotten is due mainly to two reasons. First, rats have few motivations other than physiological ones, and since so much of the research upon motivation has been made with these animals, it is easy to carry the rat picture over to the human being. Secondly, it is too often not realized that culture itself is an adaptive tool, one of whose main functions is to make the physiological emergencies come less and less often. In most of the known societies, chronic extreme hunger of the emergency type is rare, rather than common. In any case, this is still true in the United States. The average American citizen is experiencing appetite rather than hunger when he says "I am hungry." He is apt to experience sheer life-and-death hunger only by accident and then only a few times through his entire life.

Obviously a good way to obscure the 'higher' motivations, and to get a lopsided view of human capacities and human nature, is to make the organism extremely and chronically hungry or thirsty. Anyone who attempts to make an emergency picture into a typical one, and who will measure all of man's goals and desires by his behavior during extreme physiological deprivation is certainly being blind to many things. It is quite true that man lives by bread alone—when there is no bread. But what happens to man's desires when there is plenty of bread and when his belly is chronically filled?

At once other (and 'higher') needs emerge and these, rather than physiological hungers, dominate the organism. And when these in turn are satisfied, again new (and still 'higher') needs emerge and so on. This is what we mean by saying that the basic human needs are organized into a hierarchy of relative prepotency.

One main implication of this phrasing is that gratification becomes as important a concept as deprivation in motivation theory, for it releases the organism from the domination of a relatively more physiological need, permitting thereby the emergence of other more social goals. The physiological needs, along with their partial goals, when chronically gratified cease to exist as active determinants or organizers of behavior. They now exist only in a potential fashion in the sense that they may emerge again to dominate the organism if they are thwarted. But a want that is satisfied is no longer a want. The organism is dominated and its behavior organized only by unsatisfied needs. If hunger is satisfied, it becomes unimportant in the current dynamics of the individual.

This statement is somewhat qualified by a hypothesis to be discussed more fully later, namely that it is precisely those individuals in whom a certain need has always been satisfied who are best equipped to tolerate deprivation of that need in the future, and that furthermore, those who have been deprived in the past will react differently to current satisfactions than the one who has never been deprived.

The Safety Needs

If the physiological needs are relatively well gratified, there then emerges a new set of needs, which we may categorize roughly as the safety needs. All that has been said of the physiological needs is equally true, although in lesser degree, of these desires. The organism may equally well be wholly dominated by them. They may serve as the almost exclusive organizers of behavior, recruiting all the capacities of the organism in their service, and we may then fairly describe the whole organism as a safety-seeking mechanism. Again we may say of the receptors, the effectors, of the intellect and the other capacities that they are primarily safety-seeking tools. Again, as in the hungry man, we find that the dominating goal is a strong determinant not only of his current world outlook and philosophy but also of his philosophy of the future. Practically everything looks less important than safety, (even sometimes the physiological needs which being satisfied, are now underestimated). A man, in this state, if it is extreme enough and chronic enough, may be characterized as living almost for safety alone.

Although in this paper we are interested primarily in the needs of the adult, we can approach an understanding of his safety needs perhaps more efficiently by observation of infants and children, in whom these needs are much more simple and obvious. One reason for the clearer appearance of the threat or danger reaction in infants, is that they do not inhibit this reaction at all, whereas adults in our society have been taught to inhibit it at all costs. Thus even when adults do feel their safety to be threatened we may not be able to see this on the surface. Infants will react in a total fashion and as if they were endangered, if they are disturbed or dropped suddenly, startled by loud noises, flashing light, or other unusual sensory stimulation, by rough handling, by general loss of support in the mother's arms, or by inadequate support.[1]

In infants we can also see a much more direct reaction to bodily illnesses of various kinds. Sometimes these illnesses seem to be immediately and per se threatening and seem to make the child feel unsafe. For instance, vomiting, colic or other sharp pains seem to make the child look at the whole world in a different way. At such a moment of pain, it may be postulated that, for the child, the appearance of the whole world suddenly changes from sunniness to darkness, so to speak, and becomes a place in which anything at all might happen, in which previously stable things have suddenly become unstable. Thus a child who because of some bad food is taken ill may, for a day or two, develop fear, nightmares, and a need for protection and reassurance never seen in him before his illness.

Another indication of the child's need for safety is his preference for some kind of undisrupted routine or rhythm. He seems to want a predictable, orderly world. For instance, injustice, unfairness, or inconsistency in the parents seems to make a child feel anxious and unsafe. This attitude may be not so much because of the injustice per se or any particular pains involved, but rather because this treatment threatens to make the world look unreliable, or unsafe, or unpredictable. Young children seem to thrive better under a system which has at least a skeletal outline of rigidity, In which there is a schedule of a kind, some sort of routine, something that can be counted upon, not only for the present but also far into the future. Perhaps one could express this more accurately by saying that the child needs an organized world rather than an unorganized or unstructured one.

The central role of the parents and the normal family setup are indisputable. Quarreling, physical assault, separation, divorce or death within the family may be particularly terrifying. Also parental outbursts of rage or threats of punishment directed to the child, calling him names, speaking to him harshly, shaking him, handling him roughly, or actual physical punishment sometimes elicit such total panic and terror in the child that we must assume more is involved than the physical pain alone. While it is true that in some children this terror may represent also a fear of loss of parental love, it can also occur in completely rejected children, who seem to cling to the hating parents more for sheer safety and protection than because of hope of love.

Confronting the average child with new, unfamiliar, strange, unmanageable stimuli or situations will too frequently elicit the danger or terror reaction, as for example, getting lost or even being separated from the parents for a short time, being confronted with new faces, new situations or new tasks, the sight of strange, unfamiliar or uncontrollable objects, illness or death. Particularly at such times, the child's frantic clinging to his parents is eloquent testimony to their role as protectors (quite apart from their roles as food-givers and love-givers).

From these and similar observations, we may generalize and say that the average child in our society generally prefers a safe, orderly, predictable, organized world, which he can count, on, and in which unexpected, unmanageable or other dangerous things do not happen, and in which, in any case, he has all-powerful parents who protect and shield him from harm.

That these reactions may so easily be observed in children is in a way a proof of the fact that children in our society, feel too unsafe (or, in a word, are badly brought up). Children who are reared in an unthreatening, loving family do *not* ordinarily react as we have described. In such children the danger reactions are apt to come mostly to objects or situations that adults too would consider dangerous.[2]

The healthy, normal, fortunate adult in our culture is largely satisfied in his safety needs. The peaceful, smoothly running, 'good' society ordinarily makes its members feel safe enough from wild animals, extremes of temperature, criminals, assault and murder, tyranny, etc. Therefore, in a very real sense, he no longer has any safety needs as active motivators. Just as a sated man no longer feels hungry, a safe man no longer feels endangered. If we wish to see these needs directly and clearly we must turn to neurotic or near-neurotic individuals, and to the economic and social underdogs. In between these extremes, we can perceive the expressions of safety needs only in such phenomena as, for instance, the common preference for a job with tenure and protection, the desire for a savings account, and for insurance of various kinds (medical, dental, unemployment, disability, old age).

Other broader aspects of the attempt to seek safety and stability in the world are seen in the very common preference for familiar rather than unfamiliar things, or for the known rather than the unknown. The tendency to have some religion or world-philosophy that organizes the universe and the men in it into some sort of satisfactorily coherent, meaningful whole is also in part motivated by safety-seeking. Here too we may list science and philosophy in general as partially motivated by the safety needs (we shall see later that there are also other motivations to scientific, philosophical or religious endeavor).

Otherwise the need for safety is seen as an active and dominant mobilizer of the organism's resources only in emergencies, e.g., war, disease, natural catastrophes, crime waves, societal disorganization, neurosis, brain injury, chronically bad situation.

Some neurotic adults in our society are, in many ways, like the unsafe child in their desire for safety, although in the former it takes on a somewhat special appearance. Their reaction is often to unknown, psychological dangers in a world that is perceived to be hostile, overwhelming and threatening. Such a person behaves as if a great catastrophe were almost always impending, i.e., he is usually responding as if to an emergency. His safety needs often find specific in a search for a protector, or a stronger person on whom he may depend, or perhaps, a Fuehrer.

The neurotic individual may be described in a slightly different way with some usefulness as a grown-up person who retains his childish attitudes toward the world. That is to say, a neurotic adult may be said to behave 'as if' he were actually afraid of a spanking, or of his mother's disapproval, or of being abandoned by his parents, or having his food taken away from him. It is as if his childish attitudes of fear and threat reaction to a dangerous world had gone underground, and untouched by the growing up and learning processes, were now ready to be called out by any stimulus that would make a child feel endangered and threatened.[3]

The neurosis in which the search for safety takes its dearest form is in the compulsive-obsessive neurosis. Compulsive-obsessives try frantically to order and stabilize the world so that no unmanageable, unexpected or unfamiliar dangers will ever appear (14); They hedge themselves about with all sorts of ceremonials, rules and formulas so that every possible contingency may be provided for and so that no new contingencies may appear.

They are much like the brain injured cases, described by Goldstein (6), who manage to maintain their equilibrium by avoiding everything unfamiliar and strange and by ordering their restricted world in such a neat, disciplined, orderly fashion that everything in the world can be counted upon. They try to arrange the world so that anything unexpected (dangers) cannot possibly occur. If, through no fault of their own, something unexpected does occur, they go into a panic reaction as if this unexpected occurrence constituted a grave danger. What we can see only as a none too strong preference in the healthy person, e.g., preference for the familiar, becomes a life-and-death. necessity in abnormal cases.

The Love Needs

If both the physiological and the safety needs are fairly well gratified, then there will emerge the love and affection and belongingness needs, and the whole cycle already described will repeat itself with this new center. Now the person will feel keenly, as never before, the absence of friends, or a sweetheart, or a wife, or children. He will hunger for affectionate relations with people in general, namely, for a place in his group, and he will strive with great intensity to achieve this goal. He will want to attain such a place more than anything else in the world and may even forget that once, when he was hungry, he sneered at love.

In our society the thwarting of these needs is the most commonly found core in cases of maladjustment and more severe psychopathology. Love and affection, as well as their possible expression in sexuality, are generally looked upon with ambivalence and are customarily hedged about with many restrictions and inhibitions. Practically all theorists of psychopathology have stressed thwarting of the love needs as basic in the picture of maladjustment. Many clinical studies have therefore been made of this need and we know more about it perhaps than any of the other needs except the physiological ones (14).

One thing that must be stressed at this point is that love is not synonymous with sex. Sex may be studied as a purely physiological need. Ordinarily sexual behavior is multidetermined, that is to say, determined not only by sexual but also by other needs, chief among which are the love and affection needs. Also not to be overlooked is the fact that the love needs involve both giving and receiving love.[4]

The Esteem Needs

All people in our society (with a few pathological exceptions) have a need or desire for a stable, firmly based, (usually) high evaluation of themselves, for self-respect, or self-esteem, and for the esteem of others. By firmly based self-esteem, we mean that which is soundly based upon real capacity, achievement and respect from others. These needs may be classified into two subsidiary sets. These are, first, the desire for strength, for achievement, for adequacy, for confidence in the face of the world, and for independence and freedom.[5] Secondly, we have what we may call the desire for reputation or prestige (defining it as respect or esteem from other people), recognition, attention, importance or appreciation.[6] These needs have been relatively stressed by Alfred Adler and his followers, and have been relatively neglected by Freud and the psychoanalysts. More and more today however there is appearing widespread appreciation of their central importance.

Satisfaction of the self-esteem need leads to feelings of self-confidence, worth, strength, capability and adequacy of being useful and necessary in the world. But thwarting of these needs produces feelings of inferiority, of weakness and of helplessness. These feelings in turn give rise to either basic discouragement or else compensatory or neurotic trends. An appreciation of the necessity of basic self-confidence and an understanding of how helpless people are without it, can be easily gained from a study of severe traumatic neurosis (8).[7]

The Need for Self-Actualization

Even if all these needs are satisfied, we may still often (if not always) expect that a new discontent and restlessness will soon develop, unless the individual is doing what he is fitted for. A musician must make music, an artist must paint, a poet must write, if he is to be ultimately happy. What a man *can* be, he *must* be. This need we may call self-actualization.

This term, first coined by Kurt Goldstein, is being used in this paper in a much more specific and limited fashion. It refers to the desire for self-fulfillment, namely, to the tendency for him to become actualized in what he is potentially. This tendency might be phrased as the desire to become more and more what one is, to become everything that one is capable of becoming.

The specific form that these needs will take will of course vary greatly from person to person. In one individual it may take the form of the desire to be an ideal mother, in another it may be expressed athletically, and in still another it may be expressed in painting pictures or in inventions. It is not necessarily a creative urge although in people who have any capacities for creation it will take this form.

The clear emergence of these needs rests upon prior satisfaction of the physiological, safety, love and esteem needs. We shall call people who are satisfied in these needs, basically satisfied people, and it is from these that we may expect the fullest (and healthiest) creativeness.[8] Since, in our society, basically satisfied people are the exception, we do not know much about self-actualization, either experimentally or clinically. It remains a challenging problem for research.

The Preconditions for the Basic Need Satisfactions

There are certain conditions which are immediate prerequisites for the basic need satisfactions. Danger to these is reacted to almost as if it were a direct danger to the basic needs themselves. Such conditions as freedom to speak, freedom to do what one wishes so long as no harm is done to others, freedom to express one's self, freedom to investigate and seek for information, freedom to defend one's self, justice, fairness, honesty, orderliness in the group are examples of such preconditions for basic need satisfactions. Thwarting in these freedoms will be reacted to with a threat or emergency response. These conditions are not ends in themselves but they are *almost* so since they are so closely related to the basic needs, which are apparently the only ends in themselves. These conditions are defended because without them the basic satisfactions are quite impossible, or at least, very severely endangered.

If we remember that the cognitive capacities (perceptual, intellectual, learning) are a set of adjustive tools, which have, among other functions, that of satisfaction of our basic needs, then it is clear that any danger to them, any deprivation or blocking of their free use, must also be indirectly threatening to the basic needs themselves. Such a statement is a partial solution of the general problems of curiosity, the search for knowledge, truth and wisdom, and the ever-persistent urge to solve the cosmic mysteries.

We must therefore introduce another hypothesis and speak of degrees of closeness to the basic needs, for we have already pointed out that *any* conscious desires (partial goals) are more or less important as they are more or less close to the basic needs. The same statement may be made for various behavior acts. An act is psychologically important if it contributes directly to satisfaction of basic needs. The less directly it so contributes, or the weaker this contribution is, the less important this act must be conceived to be from the point of view of dynamic psychology. A similar statement may be made for the various defense or coping mechanisms. Some are very directly related to the protection or attainment of the basic needs, others are only weakly and distantly related. Indeed if we wished, we could speak of more basic and less basic defense mechanisms, and then affirm that danger to the more basic defenses is more threatening than danger to less basic defenses (always remembering that this is so only because of their relationship to the basic needs).

The Desires to Know and to Understand

So far, we have mentioned the cognitive needs only in passing. Acquiring knowledge and systematizing the universe have been considered as, in part, techniques for the achievement of basic safety in the world, or, for the intelligent man, expressions of self-actualization. Also freedom of inquiry and expression have been discussed as preconditions of satisfactions of the basic needs. True though these formulations may be, they do not constitute definitive answers to the question as to the motivation role of curiosity, learning, philosophizing, experimenting, etc. They are, at best, no more than partial answers.

This question is especially difficult because we know so little about the facts. Curiosity, exploration, desire for the facts, desire to know may certainly be observed easily enough. The fact that they often are pursued even at great cost to the individual's safety is an earnest of the partial character of our previous discussion. In addition, the writer must admit that, though he has sufficient clinical evidence to postulate the desire to know as a very strong drive in intelligent people, no data are available for unintelligent people. It may then be largely a function of relatively high intelligence. Rather tentatively, then, and largely in the hope of stimulating discussion and research, we shall postulate a basic desire to know, to be aware of reality, to get the facts, to satisfy curiosity, or as Wertheimer phrases it, to see rather than to be blind.

This postulation, however, is not enough. Even after we know, we are impelled to know more and more minutely and microscopically on the one hand, and on the other, more and more extensively in the direction of a world philosophy, religion, etc. The facts that we acquire, if they are isolated or atomistic, inevitably get theorized about, and either analyzed or organized or both. This process has been phrased by some as the search for 'meaning.' We shall then postulate a desire to understand, to systematize, to organize, to analyze, to look for relations and meanings.

Once these desires are accepted for discussion, we see that they too form themselves into a small hierarchy in which the desire to know is prepotent over the desire to understand. All the characteristics of a hierarchy of prepotency that we have described above, seem to hold for this one as well.

We must guard ourselves against the too easy tendency to separate these desires from the basic needs we have discussed above, i.e., to make a sharp dichotomy between 'cognitive' and 'conative' needs. The desire to know and to understand are themselves conative, i.e., have a striving character, and are as much personality needs as the 'basic needs' we have already discussed (19).

FURTHER CHARACTERISTICS OF THE BASIC NEEDS

The Degree of Fixity of the Hierarchy of Basic Needs

We have spoken so far as if this hierarchy were a fixed order but actually it is not nearly as rigid as we may have implied. It is true that most of the people with whom we have worked have seemed to have these basic needs in about the order that has been indicated. However, there have been a number of exceptions.

(1) There are some people in whom, for instance, self-esteem seems to be more important than love. This most

common reversal in the hierarchy is usually due to the development of the notion that the person who is most likely to be loved is a strong or powerful person, one who inspires respect or fear, and who is self-confident or aggressive. Therefore such people who lack love and seek it, may try hard to put on a front of aggressive, confident behavior. But essentially they seek high self-esteem and its behavior expressions more as a means to an end than for its own sake; they seek self-assertion for the sake of love rather than for self-esteem itself.

(2) There are other, apparently innately creative people in whom the drive to creativeness seems to be more important than any other counterdeterminant. Their creativeness might appear not as self-actualization released by basic satisfaction, but in spite of lack of basic satisfaction.

(3) In certain people the level of aspiration may be permanently deadened or lowered. That is to say, the less prepotent goals may simply be lost, and may disappear forever, so that the person who has experienced life at a very low level, i.e., chronic unemployment, may continue to be satisfied for the rest of his life if only he can get enough food.

(4) The so-called 'psychopathic personality' is another example of permanent loss of the love needs. These are people who, according to the best data available (9), have been starved for love in the earliest months of their lives and have simply lost forever the desire and the ability to give and to receive affection (as animals lose sucking or pecking reflexes that are not exercised soon enough after birth).

(5) Another cause of reversal of the hierarchy is that when a need has been satisfied for a long time, this need may be underevaluated. People who have never experienced chronic hunger are apt to underestimate its effects and to look upon food as a rather unimportant thing. If they are dominated by a higher need, this higher need will seem to be the most important of all. It then becomes possible, and indeed does actually happen, that they may, for the sake of this higher need, put themselves into the position of being deprived in a more basic need. We may expect that after a long-time deprivation of the more basic need there will be a tendency to reevaluate both needs so that the more pre-potent need will actually become consciously prepotent for the individual who may have given it up very lightly. Thus, a man who has given up his job rather than lose his self-respect, and who then starves for six months or so, may be willing to take his job back even at the price of losing his a self-respect.

(6) Another partial explanation of *apparent* reversals is seen in the fact that we have been talking about the hierarchy of prepotency in terms of consciously felt wants or desires rather than of behavior. Looking at behavior itself may give us the wrong impression. What we have claimed is that the person will *want* the more basic of two needs when deprived in both. There is no necessary implication here that he will act upon his desires. Let us say again that there are many determinants of behavior other than the needs and desires.

(7) Perhaps more important than all these exceptions are the ones that involve ideals, high social standards, high values and the like. With such values people become martyrs; they give up everything for the sake of a particular ideal, or value. These people may be understood, at least in part, by reference to one basic concept (or hypothesis) which may be called 'increased frustration-tolerance through early gratification.' People who have been satisfied in their basic needs throughout their lives, particularly in their earlier years, seem to develop exceptional power to withstand present or future thwarting of these needs simply because they have strong, healthy character structure as a result of basic satisfaction. They are the 'strong' people who can easily weather disagreement or opposition, who can swim against the stream of public opinion and who can stand up for the truth at great personal cost. It is just the ones who have loved and been well loved, and who have had many deep friendships who can hold out against hatred, rejection or persecution.

I say all this in spite of the fact that there is a certain amount of sheer habituation which is also involved in any full discussion of frustration tolerance. For instance, it is likely that those persons who have been accustomed to relative starvation for a long time, are partially enabled thereby to withstand food deprivation. What sort of balance must be made between these two tendencies, of habituation on the one hand, and of past satisfaction breeding present frustration tolerance on the other hand, remains to be worked out by further research. Meanwhile we may assume that they are both operative, side by side, since they do not contradict each other, In respect to this phenomenon of increased frustration tolerance, it seems probable that the most important gratifications come in the first two years of life. That is to say, people who have been made secure and strong in the earliest years, tend to remain secure and strong thereafter in the face of whatever threatens.

Degree of Relative Satisfaction

So far, our theoretical discussion may have given the impression that these five sets of needs are somehow in a stepwise, all-or-none relationships to each other. We have spoken in such terms as the following: "If one need is satisfied, then another emerges." This statement might give the false impression that a need must be satisfied 100 percent before the next need emerges. In actual fact, most members of our society who are normal, are partially satisfied in all their basic needs and partially unsatisfied in all their basic needs at the same time. A more realistic description of the hierarchy would be in terms of decreasing percentages of satisfaction as we go up the hierarchy of prepotency, For instance, if I may assign arbitrary figures for the sake of illustration, it is as if the average citizen is satisfied perhaps 85 percent in his physiological needs, 70 percent in his safety needs, 50 percent in his love needs, 40 percent in his self-esteem needs, and 10 percent in his self-actualization needs.

As for the concept of emergence of a new need after satisfaction of the prepotent need, this emergence is not a sudden, saltatory phenomenon but rather a gradual emergence by slow degrees from nothingness. For instance, if prepotent need A is satisfied only 10 percent, then need B may not be visible at all. However, as this need A becomes satisfied 25 percent, need B may emerge 5 percent; as need A becomes satisfied 75 percent, need B may emerge 90 percent, and so on.

Unconscious Character of Needs

These needs are neither necessarily conscious nor unconscious. On the whole, however, in the average person, they are more often unconscious rather than conscious. It is not necessary at this point to overhaul the tremendous mass of evidence which indicates the crucial importance of unconscious motivation. It would by now be expected, on a priori grounds alone, that unconscious motivations would on the whole be rather more important than the conscious motivations. What we have called the basic needs are very often largely unconscious although they may, with suitable techniques, and with sophisticated people become conscious.

Cultural Specificity and Generality of Needs

This classification of basic needs makes some attempt to take account of the relative unity behind the superficial differences in specific desires from one culture to another. Certainly in any particular culture an individual's conscious motivational content will usually be extremely different from the conscious motivational content of an individual in another society. However, it is the common experience of anthropologists that people, even in different societies, are much more alike than we would think from our first contact with them, and that as we know them better we seem to find more and more of this commonness, We then recognize the most startling differences to be superficial rather than basic, e.g., differences in style of hairdress, clothes, tastes in food, etc. Our classification of basic needs is in part an attempt to account for this unity behind the apparent diversity from culture to culture. No claim is made that it is ultimate or universal for all cultures. The claim is made only that it is relatively *more* ultimate, more universal, more basic, than the superficial conscious desires from culture to culture, and makes a somewhat closer approach to common human characteristics, Basic needs are *more* common human than superficial desires or behaviors.

Multiple Motivations of Behavior

These needs must be understood *not* to be *exclusive* or single determiners of certain kinds of behavior. An example may be found in any behavior that seems to be physiologically motivated, such as eating, or sexual play or the like. The clinical psychologists have long since found that any behavior may be a channel through which flow various determinants. Or to say it in another way, most behavior is multimotivated. Within the sphere of motivational determinants any behavior tends to be determined by several or *all* of the basic needs simultaneously rather than by only one of them. The latter would be more an exception than the former. Eating may be partially for the sake of filling the stomach, and partially for the sake of comfort and amelioration of other needs. One may make love not only for pure sexual release, but also to convince one's self of one's masculinity, or to make a conquest, to feel powerful, or to win more basic affection. As an illustration, I may point out that it would be possible (theoretically if not practically) to analyze a single act of an individual and see in it the expression of his physiological needs, his safety needs, his love needs, his esteem needs and self-actualization. This contrasts sharply with the more naive brand of trait psychology in which one trait or one motive accounts for a certain kind of act, i.e., an aggressive act is traced solely to a trait of aggressiveness.

Multiple Determinants of Behavior

Not all behavior is determined by the basic needs. We might even say that not all behavior is motivated. There are many determinants of behavior other than motives.[9] For instance, one other important class of determinants is the so-called "field" determinants. Theoretically, at least, behavior may be determined completely by the field, or even by specific isolated external stimuli, as in association of ideas, or certain conditioned reflexes. If in response to the stimulus word "table," I immediately perceive a memory image of a table, this response certainly has nothing to do with my basic needs.

Secondly, we may call attention again to the concept of 'degree of closeness to the basic needs' or 'degree of motivation.' Some behavior is highly motivated, other behavior is only weakly motivated. Some is not motivated at all (but all behavior is determined).

Another important point [10] is that there is a basic difference between expressive behavior and coping behavior (functional striving, purposive goal seeking). An expressive behavior does not try to do anything; it is simply a reflection of the personality. A stupid man behaves stupidly, not because he wants to, or tries to, or is motivated to, but simply because he *is* what he is. The same is true when I speak in a bass voice rather than tenor or soprano. The random movements of a healthy child, the smile on the face of a happy man even when he is alone, the springiness of the healthy man's walk, and the erectness of his carriage are other examples of expressive, nonfunctional behavior. Also the *style* in which a man carries out almost all his behavior, motivated as well as unmotivated, is often expressive.

We may then ask, is *all* behavior expressive or reflective of the character structure? The answer is no. Rote, habitual, automatized, or conventional behavior may or may not be expressive. The same is true for most 'stimulus-bound' behaviors.

It is finally necessary to stress that expressiveness of behavior, and goal-directedness of behavior are not mutually exclusive categories. Average behavior is usually both.

Goals as Centering Principle in Motivation Theory

It will be observed that the basic principle in our classification has been neither the instigation nor the motivated behavior but rather the functions, effects, purposes, or goals of the behavior. It has been proven sufficiently by various people that this is the most suitable point for centering in any motivation theory.[11]

Animal- and Human-Centering

This theory starts with the human being rather than any lower and presumably 'simpler' animal. Too many of the findings that have been made in animals have been proven to be true for animals but not for the human being. There is no reason whatsoever why we should start with animals in order to study human motivation. The logic or rather illogic behind this general fallacy of 'pseudosimplicity' has been exposed often enough by philosophers and logicians as well as by scientists in each of the various fields. It is no more necessary to study animals before one can study man than it is to study mathematics before one can study geology or psychology or biology.

We may also reject the old, naive, behaviorism which assumed that it was somehow necessary, or at least more 'scientific' to judge human beings by animal standards. One consequence of this belief was that the whole notion of purpose and goal was excluded from motivational psychology simply because one could not ask a white rat about his purposes. Tolman (18) has long since proven in animal studies themselves that this exclusion was not necessary.

Motivation and the Theory of Psychopathogenesis

The conscious motivational content of everyday life has, according to the foregoing, been conceived to be relatively important or unimportant accordingly as it is more or less closely related to the basic goals. A desire for an ice cream cone might actually be an indirect expression of a desire for love. If it is, then this desire for the ice cream cone becomes extremely important motivation. If however the ice cream is simply something to cool the mouth with, or a casual appetitive reaction, then the desire is relatively unimportant. Everyday conscious desires are to be regarded as symptoms, as surface indicators of more basic needs. If we were to take these superficial desires at their face value me would find ourselves in a state of complete confusion which could never be resolved, since we would be dealing seriously with symptoms rather than with what lay behind the symptoms.

Thwarting of unimportant desires produces no psychopathological results; thwarting of a basically important need does produce such results. Any theory of psychopathogenesis must then be based on a sound theory of motivation. A conflict or a frustration is not necessarily pathogenic. It becomes so only when it threatens or thwarts the basic needs, or partial needs that are closely related to the basic needs (10).

The Role of Gratified Needs

It has been pointed out above several times that our needs usually emerge only when more prepotent needs have been gratified. Thus gratification has an important role in motivation theory. Apart from this, however, needs cease to play an active determining or organizing role as soon as they are gratified.

What this means is that, e.g., a basically satisfied person no longer has the needs for esteem, love, safety, etc. The only sense in which he might be said to have them is in the almost metaphysical sense that a sated man has hunger, or a filled bottle has emptiness. If we are interested in what *actually* motivates us, and not in what has, will, or might motivate us, then a satisfied need is not a motivator. It must be considered for all practical purposes simply not to exist, to have disappeared. This point should be emphasized because it has been either overlooked or contradicted in every theory of motivation I know.[12] The perfectly healthy, normal, fortunate man has no sex needs or hunger needs, or needs for safety, or for love, or for prestige, or self-esteem, except in stray moments of quickly passing threat. If we were to say otherwise, we should also have to aver that every man had all the pathological reflexes, e.g., Babinski, etc., because if his nervous system were damaged, these would appear.

It is such considerations as these that suggest the bold postulation that a man who is thwarted in any of his basic needs may fairly be envisaged simply as a sick man. This is a fair parallel to our designation as 'sick' of the man who lacks vitamins or minerals. Who is to say that a lack of love is less important than a lack of vitamins? Since we know the pathogenic effects of love starvation, who is to say that we are invoking value-questions in an unscientific or illegitimate way, any more than the physician does who diagnoses and treats pellagra or scurvy? If I were permitted this usage, I should then say simply that a healthy man is primarily motivated by his needs to develop and actualize his fullest potentialities and capacities. If a man has any other basic needs in any active, chronic sense, then he is simply an unhealthy man. He is as surely sick as if he had suddenly developed a strong salt hunger or calcium hunger.[13]

If this statement seems unusual or paradoxical the reader may be assured that this is only one among many such paradoxes that will appear as we revise our ways of looking at man's deeper motivations. When we ask what man wants of life, we deal with his very essence.

SUMMARY

1. There are at least five sets of goals, which we may call basic needs. These are briefly physiological, safety, love, esteem, and self-actualization. In addition, we are motivated by the desire to achieve or maintain the various conditions upon which these basic satisfactions rest and by certain more intellectual desires.

2. These basic goals are related to each other, being arranged in a hierarchy of prepotency. This means that the most prepotent goal will monopolize consciousness and will tend of itself to organize the recruitment of the various capacities of the organism. The less prepotent needs are minimized, even forgotten or denied. But when a need is fairly well satisfied, the next prepotent ("higher") need emerges, in turn to dominate the conscious life and to serve as the center of organization of behavior, since gratified needs are not active motivators.

Thus man is a perpetually wanting animal. Ordinarily the satisfaction of these wants is not altogether mutually exclusive, but only tends to be. The average member of our society is most often partially satisfied and partially unsatisfied in all of his wants. The hierarchy principle is usually empirically observed in terms of increasing percentages of nonsatisfaction as we go up the hierarchy. Reversals of the average order of the hierarchy are sometimes observed. Also it has been observed that an individual may permanently lose the higher wants in the hierarchy under special conditions. There are not only ordinarily multiple motivations for usual behavior, but in addition many determinants other than motives.

3. Any thwarting or possibility of thwarting of these basic human goals, or danger to the defenses which protect them, or to the conditions upon which they rest, is considered to be a psychological threat. With a few exceptions, all psychopathology may be partially traced to such threats. A basically thwarted man may actually be defined as a 'sick' man, if we wish.

4. It is such basic threats which bring about the general emergency reactions.

5. Certain other basic problems have not been dealt with because of limitations of space. Among these are *(a)* the problem of values in any definitive motivation theory, *(b)* the relation between appetites, desires, needs and what is 'good' for the organism, *(c)* the etiology of the basic needs and their possible derivation in early childhood, *(d)* redefinition of motivational concepts, i.e., drive, desire, wish, need, goal, *(e)* implication of our theory for hedonistic theory, *(f)* the nature of the uncompleted act, of success and failure, and of aspiration level, *(g)* the role of association, habit and conditioning, *(h)* relation to the theory of interpersonal relations, *(i)* implications for psychotherapy, *(j)* implication for theory of society, *(k)* the theory of selfishness, *(l)* the relation between needs and cultural patterns, *(m)* the relation between this theory and Alport's theory of functional autonomy. These as well as certain other less important questions must be considered as motivation theory attempts to become definitive.

Notes

1. As the child grows up, sheer knowledge and familiarity as well as better motor development make these "dangers" less and less dangerous and more and more manageable. Throughout life it may be said that one of the main conative functions of education is this neutralizing of apparent dangers through knowledge, e.g., I am not afraid of thunder because I know something about it.
2. A "test batter" for safety might be confronting the child with a small exploding firecracker, or with a bewhiskered face, having the mother leave the room, putting him upon a high ladder, a hypodermic injection, having a mouse crawl up to him, etc. Of course I cannot seriously recommend the deliberate use of such "tests" for they might very well harm the child being tested. But these and similar situations come up by the score in the child's ordinary day-to-day living and may be observed. There is no reason why those stimuli should not be used with, for example, young chimpanzees.
3. Not all neurotic individuals feel unsafe. Neurosis may have at its core a thwarting of the affection and esteem needs in a person who is generally safe.
4. For further details see (12) and (16, Ch. 5).
5. Whether or not this particular desire is universal we do not know. The crucial question, especially important today, is "Will men who are enslaved and dominated inevitably feel dissatisfied and rebellious?" We may assume on the basis of commonly known clinical data that a man who has known true freedom (not paid for by giving up safety and security but rather built on the basis of adequate safety and security) will not willingly or easily allow his freedom to be taken away from him. But we do not know that this is true for the person born into slavery. The events of the next decade should give us our answer. See discussion of this problem in (5).
6. Perhaps the desire for prestige and respect from others is subsidiary to the desire for self-esteem or confidence in oneself. Observation of children seems to indicate that this is so, but clinical data give no clear support for such a conclusion.

7. For more extensive discussion of normal self-esteem, as well as for reports of various researches, see (11).
8. Clearly creative behavior, like painting, is like any other behavior in having multiple, determinants. It may be seen in "innately creative" people whether they are satisfied or not, happy or unhappy, hungry or sated. Also it is clear that creative activity may be compensatory, ameliorative or purely economic. It is my impression (as yet unconfirmed) that it is possible to distinguish the artistic and intellectual products of basically satisfied people from those of basically unsatisfied people by inspection alone. In any case, here too we must distinguish, in a dynamic fashion, the overt behavior itself from its various motivations or purposes.
9. I am aware that many psychologists and psychoanalysts use the term "motivated" and "determined" synonymously, e.g., Freud. But I consider this an obfuscating usage. Sharp distinctions are necessary for clarity of thought, and precision in experimentation.
10. To be discussed fully in a subsequent publication.
11. The interested reader is referred to the very excellent discussion of this point in Murray's *Explorations in Personality* (15).
12. Note that acceptance of this theory necessitates basic revision of the Freudian theory.
13. If we were to use the word "sick" in this way, we should then also have to face squarely the relations of man to his society. One clear implication of our definition would be that (1) since a man is to be called sick who is basically thwarted, and (2) since such basic thwarting is made possible ultimately only by forces outside the individual, then (3) sickness in the individual must come ultimately from sickness in the society. The "good" or healthy society would then be defined as one that permitted man's highest purposes to emerge by satisfying all his prepotent basic needs.

Abraham H. Maslow was born in 1908. He attended the University of Wisconsin, receiving a B.A. in 1930, an M.A. in 1931, and a Ph.D. in 1934. Maslow joined the faculty of Brandeis University in 1951, where he was professor and department chairman. While at Brandeis he completed his best known book, *Motivation and Personality* (1954) in which he developed his famous hierarchy theory of needs. Maslow died on June 8, 1970.

References

(1). A. Adler, *Social Interest* (London: Faber & Faber, 1938).
(2). W. B. Cannon, *Wisdom of the Body* (New York: Norton, 1932).
(3). A. Freud, *The Ego and the Mechanisms of Defense.* (London: Hogarth, 1937).
(4). S. Freud, *New Introductory Lectures on Psychoanalysis* (New York: Norton, 1933).
(5). E. Fromm, *Escape from Freedom* (New York: Farrar and Rinehart, 1941).
(6). K. Goldstein, *The Organism* (New York: American Book Co., 1939).
(7). K. Horney, *The Neurotic Personality of Our Time* (New York: Norton, 1937).
(8). A. Kardiner, *The Traumatic Neuroses of War* (New York: Hoeber, 1941).
(9). D. M. Levy, "Primary Affect Hunger," *American Journal Psychiatry*, 94 (1937), pp. 643-652.
(10). A. H. Maslow, "Conflict, Frustration, and the Theory of Threat," *Journal of Abnormal (Social) Psychology*, 38 (1943), pp. 81-86.
(11). A. H. Maslow, "Dominance, Personality and Social Behavior in Women," *Journal of Social Psychology*, 10 (1939), pp. 3-39.
(12). A. H. Maslow, "The Dynamics of Psychological Security-Insecurity," *Character and Personality*, 10 (1942), pp. 331-344.
(13). A. H. Maslow, "A Preface to Motivation Theory," *Psychosomatic Medicine*, 5 (1943), pp. 85-92.

From MANAGEMENT CLASSICS, edited by Michael T. Matteson and John M. Ivancevich, Goodyear Publishing Co., 1977. Original to *Psychological Review*, Vol. 50, No. 4, 1943, pp. 370–396.

The True Measure of a CEO

Aristotle has something to say about that.

James O'Toole

In 400 B.C., Aristotle argued that a leader's task is to create conditions under which all followers can realize their full human potential. In this view, leadership is not about the leader's needs for wealth, power, and prestige—rather, it is about the leader's responsibility to create an environment in which followers can develop the capabilities with which they were born.

Today, given the nature of 24/7 work conditions, and the commitment to long hours that American corporations demand of employees, the only place where most people have the opportunity to develop their capacities is at work. Hence, if corporations and their CEOs do not provide the opportunity for their employees to grow, they effectually deny them their basic humanity. That is why creating a culture in which the true and basic needs of employees are addressed is the core ethical issue in corporate leadership today.

Aristotle provides us with a set of ethical questions to determine the extent to which an organization provides an environment conducive to human growth and fulfillment. And, he would say, not only does an ethical leader create that environment—he does so consciously, and not coincidentally. Motivation is important in ethics. Miami hoteliers cannot claim credit for sunny days, and leaders in Silicon Valley get no ethical credit for providing jobs that are accidentally developmental. Just because working with computers may be inherently a developmental task, one is not necessarily a marvelous employer for providing people with that opportunity.

Aristotle also asks the extent to which we as leaders observe decent limits on our own power in order to allow others to lead and develop. He says that too many leaders turn their people into passive recipients of their moral feats. In practice, celebrity CEOs such as Citigroup's Sandy Weill and Sun's Scott McNealy have behaved as if there were only one leader in each of their respective organizations—themselves—and not only have garnered credit for all good decisions made in their companies but have amassed for themselves the best opportunities to learn through leading. Worse, they have dismissed and discouraged executives who have challenged their authority, particularly upcoming stars who shined too brightly and thus threatened the CEO's status as the sole source of organizational enlightenment.

In essence, here are the questions that Aristotle asks CEOs and other leaders to ask themselves:

- To what extent do I consciously make an effort to provide learning opportunities to everyone who works for me?
- To what extent do I encourage full participation by all my people in the decisions affecting their own work?
- To what extent do I allow them to lead in order to grow?
- To what extent do I measure my own performance as a manager or leader both in terms of realizing economic goals and, equally, creating conditions in which my people can fulfill their own potential in the workplace?

I do not pretend that it is easy for leaders to create ethical cultures. Tough sacrifices and trade-offs are demanded. For starters, leaders must behave courageously and consistently to meet their ethical responsibilities to employees. For example, during the extended 2001-04 recession, when hundreds of thousands of American workers were losing their jobs, most corporate leaders assumed they had no other choice but to lay off workers. But out in Silicon Valley, the CEO of Xilinx Inc., Wim Roelandts, believed that there had to be other alternatives, even when his company's profits plummeted by 50 percent in 2001. His own board and some of his top executives argued that the only way he could stem the flow of red ink was to lay off workers. But driven by his stated communitarian values of respect

moral responsibility to address the needs of workers; instead, the assumption is that if workers do not like the conditions being offered, they are free to quit and look for employment elsewhere.

Certainly, Aristotle would have something to say about that.

***JAMES O'TOOLE** is research professor at the Center for Effective Organizations at the University of Southern California's Marshall School of Business, Mortimer J. Adler Senior Fellow at the Aspen Institute, and author of, most recently,* Creating the Good Life: Aristotle's Guide to Getting It Right, *from which this article is adapted.*

The Myth of Charismatic Leaders

It can be foolish, futile, and even dangerous to follow leaders just because they're charismatic. Be careful of hero worship, and step forward.

By Joseph A. Raelin

Perhaps no subject has captivated the American business audience more than leadership. Within the practice of leadership, charisma is thought to be the quality that, though often considered metaphysical, represents the hallmark of inspirational leadership.

If leadership has something to do with inspiring a cadre of followers to do things in their own interest but also for the greater good, then we certainly need individuals who have a special talent to recruit others to work together towards a common cause.

Often, such individuals have heroic qualities because they're thought to persist in spite of the odds against them. They're also thought to possess particular heroic characteristics, such as courage and persistence, to face and prevail against those who would resist their noble efforts.

Many social critics have begun to challenge that heroic view of leadership. Should leadership rest upon the shoulders of one individual? We're beginning to see that many of the tasks that we need to perform in order to achieve our missions cannot be accomplished awaiting orders from just one person. All of us need to act and take a leadership role within our own domains.

Is it possible, then, that leadership may be as much a collective as an individual property? Do we need a savior to steer us out of trouble, or can we rely upon each other to find our way in the world?

If leadership is something other than being in charge of others—if it belongs not to the hero (without whom the followers will surely founder) but to the collective urged to face their own problems, then there may be a need to revise the ancient, obdurate concept of charisma.

The sway of charisma

Charisma comes from the Greek word meaning "gift," suggesting that leaders have special gifts to distribute. Their gifts aren't necessarily physical; they're more likely to be social. In fact, it's commonly thought that the pleasing personality of a charismatic person is his or her greatest gift. So, by definition, charismatics sway people and shape the future by their sheer presence and personality.

Charismatic leaders are thought to differ from mere mortal leaders by their ability to formulate and articulate an inspirational vision, as well as by actions that foster the impression that they *are* extraordinary people. Some observers go as far as to suggest that divine qualities exist in charismatic leaders—following Max Weber, who in *Economy and Society* asserted that these people are "set apart from ordinary [people] and treated as endowed with supernatural, superhuman, or at least exceptional powers and qualities... [that] are not accessible to the ordinary person but are regarded as divine or as exemplary."

Unfortunately, even if we were to decide on what are the ingredients of a charismatic personality, I doubt we would ever find that charismatics are persuasive in all environments and for all times. The post-war demise of Winston Churchill is a sufficient case. Except for exceptional circumstances when a community is in dire straits and genuinely asks for the direction of an outspoken member, there are severe problems in allowing a given individual—particularly a charismatic—to control a community.

As soon as one attempts to identify the particular characteristics that make up a charismatic personality, one begins to exclude a host of candidates for leadership. Here's how perennial CEO Lawrence Bossidy, formerly of Allied-Signal and Honeywell, unwittingly characterizes leaders in his chapter, "Reality-Based Leadership: Changes in the Workplace," in *The Book of Leadership Wisdom* (John Wiley & Sons, 1998):

> *You all know the maxim, "Leaders are born, not made." That's only half true. Some people are, indeed, born leaders, and you can spot them a mile away. The trouble is, there simply aren't enough of them to go around So, we need to find individuals with innate intelligence, an eagerness to learn, and a desire to work with others, and give them the tools and encouragement they need to become effective leaders, too. They may never run the company, but they can make enormous contributions to the success of your organization.*

Bossidy's comments show that he identified in advance the also-rans because of a notion of what it takes to be a leader.

Using the Freudian term *narcissist*, Michael Maccoby and Roy Lubit point out in separate articles (Maccoby: "Narcissistic Leaders," *Harvard Business Review*; Lubit: "The Long-Term Organizational Impact of Destructively Narcissistic Managers," *Academy of Management Executive*) that though charismatics can charm the masses with their rhetoric and can draw the big picture, they tend to be grandiose and distrustful. Narcissists tend to keep themselves emotionally distant from others and generally don't tolerate dissent. They're also poor listeners, show little empathy, can be brutally exploitative, seldom mentor, and aren't restrained by conscience. Their excessive promotion of self and lack of concern for others can become utterly destructive to their organizations because they're prone to make reckless business decisions, divert people's energies away from their real work, and ultimately drive away the community's most talented people.

In what strikes me as a stark contrast to democratic practice, followers working under narcissists are advised to find out what their bosses think before presenting their own views. That way, they can keep any dissent to a minimum. People are advised to generally let the narcissistic boss take credit for the followers' ideas and contributions.

In addition to claiming to have a unique vision and compelling language, a charismatic leader might also attempt to acquire the symbolic accouterments of the role of savior. Depending on the society in question, this might be represented by a certain look or stature, by particular vestments or possessions, or by a relationship or lineage to prior historical figures. It was reported that during the Taliban control of Afghanistan, the spiritual leader, Mullah Mohammad Omar, rose to power by acquiring the very cloak of the Prophet Mohammed, which had been folded and padlocked in a series of chests in a crypt in the royal mausoleum at Kandahar. Myth had it that the padlocks to the crypt could be opened only when touched by a true *amir-ul-momineen*, a king of the Muslims. After the collapse of the Taliban regime, the people of Afghanistan came to know of Omar's brutality and how he duped them into obedience through the Taliban's rigid interpretations of the Koran. In the words of a young Kandahari: "We trusted men we thought were holy and educated in the Koran, and because many of us did not know Arabic, we could not study the Koran carefully ourselves. When we saw Omar in the cloak, all of Afghanistan hoped that… the rains would begin. But, in truth, we did not know what he was saying. We only followed." (*Boston Globe*)

The charisma-followership connection

Charisma is increasingly being seen as a condition interconnected with followership. The qualities of charisma need to be appreciated by followers or by a following community. Often, a charismatic emerges within the community as it faces some level of psychic distress. Distress occurs when people are unable to understand the direction in which the surrounding environment might be changing, what the potential impact of those changes on the organization might be, and whether particular responses by management might or might not be successful. Further, people might perceive that any erroneous decision on the part of management could risk the survival of the organization. In that instance, people may look to a leader for psychological comfort in order to reduce their stress and anxiety. Such leaders might be able to turn the uncertainty of their followers into a vision of opportunity and success.

Yet, it's precisely at that point followers are particularly susceptible to charismatic salvation. They find themselves in a dependent state and look to their leaders to satisfy their needs. Charismatics are all too willing to comply by offering them hope, and usually, paternal direction. That's in contrast to leaders who might choose to work with their followers to face and manage their conflicts.

Some observers have suggested that in the presence of charismatics, followers can experience inspiration, empowerment, and even awe. Those states are created by specific acts undertaken by leaders—behaviors such as dramatizing a mission, assuring followers of their competency, projecting self-assurance, and enhancing their own image. Other accounts of charismatic leaders unabashedly assert that leaders need to engage in impression management, in image building, and in manipulation of meaning in order to bind "subordinates" closely to them and to their vision. It's no wonder, then, that charismatic leaders are granted enormous license to direct an organization—be that in a direction of pro- or anti-social practices.

There's always a chance that followers might learn to manage their affairs on their own, by which time they may no longer need the charismatic. Followers might even feel ashamed for having debased themselves. When that happens, they might develop resentment against the charismatic, especially if they discover that he or she has an underlying weakness—referred to as "feet of clay." That phenomenon is well captured in a story recounted by one of my former students:

> *I will tell a story about meeting a celebrity. This person was a very popular singer in a 1980s band. From age 12 to 18, I was obsessed with this individual. My friends weren't all that impressed with him, and I was made fun of quite a bit, but that didn't dissuade me. Well, the 1980s came and went, and I moved on. But just last year, I found out that a co-worker's husband is my teenage heartthrob's first cousin, and she gave me tickets to a concert with the band, on a comeback tour. I was thrilled; all of the excitement came back. I was, after all, on my way to meet the subject of my awe. I'm sure by now you realize where this is going. Meeting this person was a big disappointment. I went backstage and shook his hand and talked a bit. He was arrogant and conceited, and his behavior made me feel stupid for wanting to meet him. My awe was destroyed by the close encounter.*

Most charismatic leaders are capable of capitalizing on awe, offering their followers a set of idealized goals. The more idealized those goals are, the more likely it is the leaders will be credited with extraordinary vision. An idealized vision further serves to highlight the uniqueness of the charismatic leader, making him or her even more admirable and worthy of identification and imitation. Jay Conger, Rabindra Kanungo, and Sanjay T. Menon say in their article "Charismatic Leadership and Follower Effects" (*Journal of Organizational Behavior*) that it's "this idealized quality of the charismatic leader's goals—supported by appealing rhetoric—that distinguishes him or her from other leaders."

We might note that charismatics need not be narcissistic, egocentric, or hard-driving. More critical is that they're seen as saviors who, through their superb vision, can appeal to the masses and save the day. Indeed, Jim Collins, in his book *Good to Great*, depicts his "level-5 leaders" as humble and shy and as people committed to diverting credit to others. Yet, they're at the same time recognized as having individually turned companies around or having led them in a strategic direction that, though unpopular, resulted in success.

For example, in an article in the *Harvard Business Review*, Collins refers to Alan Wurtzel as a leader "responsible for turning Circuit City from a ramshackle company on the edge of bankruptcy into one of America's most successful electronics retailers." Collins cites Charles R. "Cork" Walgreen II as the iron-willed leader who transformed dowdy Walgreens by proclaiming to his executive staff, "OK, now I am going to draw the line in the sand. We are going to be out of the restaurant business completely in five years." Can you imagine the silence in the room? "Cork" may have had a quiet demeanor, but he was resolute. His followers knew that the leader, their charismatic leader, had spoken. Yet, did he truly act alone?

The contagion of charisma

Views that disentangle leadership from individual action don't coincide with the charismatic mindset because they don't credit control as emanating from a single individual. People don't require salvation from the top; salvation is produced by their own mutual hard work and compassion towards each other. One folds into one's own community. Although we may temporarily focus attention on a speaker, we simultaneously seek connections to ourselves and to others.

James Meindl, author of "On Leadership: An Alternative to the Conventional Wisdom" (*Research in Organizational Behavior*) and a professor of organization and human resources at the State University of New York at Buffalo, goes as far as to suggest that charisma is no more than a romantic notion that people conjure to uplift their spirits. Most of us tend to overemphasize a leader's prowess. As followers interact, they begin to define a social reality of leadership representing special mythical qualities endowed only by very special people. Although those qualities may not, in fact, exist, they're often ascribed to a leader by either an implicit or carefully conceived orchestration by particular members of the follower community. Called "carriers," those members essentially spread the news of the charismatic leader's mythical qualities throughout society. In that way, charisma becomes a contagion. What is spread, though, isn't necessarily real but rather reactions that represent no more than pre-existing shared profiles of what leaders are supposed to be like. And we know what the profile tends to be: the hero who can save us! Meindl suggests that followers are predisposed to look for a cause and a leader for whom they can become true believers.

I see charisma as not necessarily a set of personality or emotional characteristics that define the attributes of leadership. Charisma is more of a social process, often implicitly set up between follower and leader to keep the leader in power. Charismatics rely on that process to sustain their charismatic effect. They enjoy enhancing the romantic images of themselves.

But it's important to deconstruct the romantic view of leadership embedded in the idea of charisma, because its effect can deprive a community of its own power and utility and, left unexamined, can lead to demagogic behavior and deleterious effects on groups not affiliated with the leader. Moreover, the romantic view can lead to carrier abuse among followers, who can exalt a leader's image either without his or her knowledge or after the leader steps aside. In extreme cases, a leader's death may spur martyrdom, a hyper-romantic construct that can be used for practically any purpose. The ultimate end of charismatic practices of that ilk is disempowerment. People no longer control their own destiny, having handed it over to their saviors.

Back down to Earth

We need a leadership that subsists without charismatics, or heroes. It won't be easy. Though we advocate the value of participative leadership and other forms of organizational democratic practice, the drive to have a spiritual leader whom we can love and who can save us sneaks back into our consciousness just as we prepare to assert our own worth and independence. Part of the reason for that is that our culture still seems to value, even revere, individualism while preaching teamwork. Whatever the walk of life—be it a corporate setting, a professional sports team, or an opera—we tend to focus on the star performer, even when he or she may depend entirely on the team or group to achieve prominence.

Another possible explanation for hero worship is a fear of the future, in spire of our era's advances in science and technology. The tragic events of 9/11 heighten our fear. Under that cloud of uncertainty, many people look to heroes, or surrogate parent figures, who can bring us comfort and assurance, who can inspire us and explain the future.

Hero worship is outdated in our age. Indeed, it might have become outdated ever since the common man or woman was thought to be able to go out into the world and make decisions on his or her own. Relying on a single charismatic leader to part the seas for us works as long as the leader can successfully diagnose the environment and make correct decisions. But what happens when this same leader errs? What happens when his or her followers realize that they have the maturity to make their own decisions? What happens when the environment becomes so complex that no single individual could possibly discern all of its elements? What happens when a leader dies and no one is available to take his or her place?

We must graduate from our reliance on charismatics because, sooner or later, they will need us as collaborators in leadership. We no longer need dependent subordinates who are waiting to act on command. We want our colleagues to act on their own initiative, not as loose cannons but as a well-oiled community of members who trust and need their independence and interdependence. Naturally, these initiators will check back with their groups as appropriate. But if we insist that they wait for the proverbial go-ahead, they may lose their chance to act by the time permission is received.

We can no longer afford to be mechanistic in our view of the world. We can't rely on a coterie to await orders from the top, from detached bosses who have sole possession of problem fixes even across the remote corners of the organization. We need organizations that empower anyone who is capable and willing to assume leadership in the moment in his or her relationships with peers, team members, customers, suppliers, and other organizational partners.

Alas, we are in it together. The essence of leadership is collaboration and mutuality.

Joseph A. Raelin *is the Knowles Chair at Northeastern University in Boston, heading up the Center for the Study of Practice-Oriented Education; j.raelin@neu.edu. He's the author of* Creating Leaderful Organizations: How to Bring Out Leadership in Everyone *(Berrett-Koehler, February 2003).*

Can One Man Save GM?

No, but CEO Rick Wagoner is working overtime to make sure his company rises to the life-and-death challenges ahead.

ALEX TAYLOR III

"Are we serious about a coupe and convertible?" demands the chairman of General Motors as he reviews proposed Cadillac body styles. "Or are we just going to talk about it for five years?" The mood at the 7 A.M. Friday product meeting at GM's Design Center, north of Detroit, tenses up a few notches, which is just what Rick Wagoner intends. Everyone here knows that the company is in trouble. But as Wagoner studies the projected images of cars and trucks in development, he wants to be sure his team understands that each arm of GM has to get faster, smarter, sharper—now. Wagoner zeroes in on a new target: A suggested design for Cadillac requires altering the drivetrain. He thinks the idea is a waste of his people's time, and his voice cuts through the room. "We spent $4 billion to shift Cadillac to rear-wheel drive," he declares, "and we need to discuss this." In other words, rethink the project.

The proceedings loosen up once the discussion turns to Hummers. Although the company now acknowledges that high oil prices threaten SUV sales, GM people still love the things. No GM brand enjoys Hummer's consumer awareness—or its profit margins. As drawings of new concepts appear on the three-sided screen, Bob Lutz, GM's renowned product-development chief, takes an optimistic stab at what the future sales might be. Wagoner likes to kid Lutz about his tendency to fall in love with new designs—"Bob's approved 100 programs, and we've done seven of them" he says later—and now he observes that when Lutz predicts the sales volume for a particular model, "you have to take Bob's number and divide by two." Lutz smiles as the room cracks up. But Wagoner, ever the numbers guy in a company that worships car guys, has a serious point to make: He reminds the group that they have to design a Hummer that meets its price target instead of trying to engineer a perfect vehicle that won't be profitable.

Crack-of-dawn meetings and grueling days have become routine for Wagoner, 52, as he tries to save GM from financial meltdown. He has been running fast-forward since April, when he took the dramatic step of assuming direct control over GM's North American operations, moving one level closer to product decisions, marketing strategies, and dealer gripes. The challenges Wagoner faces read like a case study of a company that can't be saved. Losing an average of $1,227 on every vehicle sold during the first six months of 2005 (according to a new study by Harbur Consulting), GM's North American operations piled up $2.5 billion in losses. Wagoner has to figure out how to renegotiate health benefits with a powerful union, generate some effective brand advertising (as opposed to just price-cut advertising), keep the whole company motivated—and come up with some wheels that consumers actually want to buy. If that weren't enough pressure, investor Kirk Kerkorian, who once tried to buy Chrysler, continues to increase his holdings in GM.

> "We've been around too long, and people have heard all our lies. We just have to deliver."

Every week seems to bring a new crisis. The latest is the collapse of Delphi Corp., the big parts supplier spun out of GM in 1999. Delphi has lost more than $5 billion in the past 18 months, and Steve Miller, its new chairman and CEO, wants GM to shoulder some of the burden by taking Delphi's UAW workers back on its payroll. Three-way negotiations among Delphi, GM, and the UAW are underway. Miller put Bethlehem Steel into bankruptcy in 2001, when it was swamped by legacy costs, and says GM might face the same fate.

And so it goes for Wagoner. For several days in August, GM gave FORTUNE the exclusive opportunity to shadow him as he scrambled to rally his troops and save his company. Sitting in on high-level meetings rarely, if ever, attended by outsiders, we got a front-row view of a top executive at a premier American corporation coping with the challenge of a lifetime.

Far from appearing beaten down by the company's problems, Wagoner, a GM man for 28 years, seems energized by them. "There's nothing like a good battle to raise the adrenaline and get everyone focused," he says on the corporate jet taking him from Detroit to Washington. A former college basketball player, he's prone to sports metaphors. Asked if he has second thoughts about casting his lot with the automaker—he has never worked anywhere else—he doesn't hesitate: "If you are in it for the challenge, where else would you want to be than GM? I think it's the biggest game in town."

This may be the big game, but the most persistent rap on Wagoner is that he isn't willing to swing for the fences: make a bold commitment to hybrid cars or fuel cells, pull off a merger, precipitate a showdown with the unions. He prefers a methodical approach, convinced that better execution on all the critical fronts—cost, quality, product development, marketing—is what will save GM. On hybrids, for example, Wagoner insists GM is being prudent. "Do we have an aggressive hybrid program?" he asks. "Yes. Should we bet the company? That would be a big risk, because the economics aren't there and it's still not clear that in 20 years we'll all be driving hybrids."

Critics say such caution will kill the company. "Rick Wagoner has made it clear that he will steer GM through this crisis with a strategy of gradual transition to a 'new' GM," writes Peter DeLorenzo, a former ad executive who specialized in the auto industry and now writes the popular Detroit blog Autoextremist. "I contend that all they're really doing at this point is managing the continued downward spiral of the company while refusing to take the tough actions and make the hard choices needed." Not so, says Wagoner, who insists that GM's biggest issues aren't the result of management errors but structural problems, like rising health-care costs, that are damn near unsolvable. "We are down to a handful of critical issues that we really need to move the needle on," he says. "And the reason that we haven't advanced as quickly on those, frankly, is not because they weren't identified, it is because they are challenging issues."

"This is war," Wagoner is telling representatives of some 50 dealers from the Washington, D.C., area, who are gathered in a suburban Virginia hotel conference room. "The battle lines are being drawn tighter and tighter, and we need to push out." Every two months Wagoner hits the road to talk with GM dealers, who are on the front lines of that war. Dealers are nothing if not blunt, and Wagoner understands the value of their close-to-the-customer view of the business. Wagoner has made sales and marketing one of the targets of his turnaround effort, and he promoted Mark LaNeve, 46, to the top marketing job in March with a mandate to shake things up. Wagoner believes unimaginative marketing has speeded the decline of GM's brands. One example: GM used the same mix of media to promote both Chevy and Buick, even though low-volume Buick cried out for a more targeted approach than highway billboards and network television. After Wagoner challenged him to come up with something "different and fresh," LaNeve created GM's successful clearance-sale promotion, "Employee pricing for everyone." Now LaNeve, who made the trip to Washington with Wagoner, has to figure out how to wean customers from special deals with newly lowered sticker prices that GM calls "value pricing." The automaker is bracing for several months of sharply lower sales while buyers adjust.

As they prepared for the session, Wagoner warned LaNeve to expect some harsh words from the D.C.-area dealers. They are considered a tough bunch; they've been making money, but their margins have shrunk and they're concerned about GM's falling market share. And true to form, the Washingtonians aren't shy with their opinions. One challenges Wagoner to convince buyers that GM products are competitive with Toyota's and Honda's. Another criticizes "value pricing," saying, "If your message is value, you don't have a message. It's weak, it's lame, and Toyota and Honda have a more intelligent message." A third dealer adds, "One of the things we lack at GM is credibility, and that's why we are not perceived as a value."

Wagoner, sitting on a stool in the front of the room, seems unfazed. He explains that GM is "trying to build cars that are richer and more upscale before we can get a price for them. It is hurting our profitability, but it's important for the future." In the end, Wagoner is forced to concede that GM has a credibility problem that it can't erase until its cars start selling again. In the past it has made too many promises—about quality, performance, and durability—that it hasn't lived up to. "We've been around way too long, and people have heard all our lies," he says in a strikingly candid admission. "We just have to deliver."

Workers in and around Detroit also get face time with the chief. Wagoner schedules 90-minute sessions, known as "diagonal slice" meetings, once a month to talk with ten or so salaried employees from all corners of the corporation. (He holds similar meetings during plant visits.) The meetings have taken on an extra urgency lately, as is obvious the second Wagoner walks into the conference room on the 37th floor of one of GM's towers. Immediately the attendees stiffen. Wagoner tells the group that North America "feels a little better than it did three or four months ago," but his message is mixed. Some of GM's new models have gotten good marks from the automotive press. Others, he notes, have been less well received. He calls the market-share declines in major markets "unacceptable,"and reminds them of the magnitude of GM's health-care expenses.

Although Wagoner tries to present an upbeat image, signs of the pressure he is under seep out in a litany of complaints. Among his targets: ill-trained dealership employees ("We've got a lot of initiatives out there, and sometimes the salespeople don't even know") and ineffective advertising ("Part of the reason we don't have strong brands is brand-related advertising"). He's frustrated that GM doesn't get enough credit for technology leadership ("Anybody who lives south of Toledo doesn't have a view of us") or its charitable work. The company tends to "modestly stand in the back of the room," he says, while other corporations spend $100 million bragging about a $10 million contribution. "That's a little cynical," he adds, "but not completely."

When one employee makes a comment about GM moving production to "low-cost countries," Wagoner points out that GM's North American vehicles are built with 85% North American content. Employees are right to be concerned, because GM is actively considering sending production overseas to save money. GM's Korean affiliate already builds one million cars a year that are badged as Chevrolets and sold all over the world, including in the U.S. As Wagoner has said, GM can't grow fast enough to lower its average cost of building cars in the U.S., so it has to find cheaper assembly and parts capacity overseas.

And that brings him to the primacy of the health-care cost issue. "If we don't fix health care," he tells the group, "we can't fix the North American business." While GM employees have lots to complain about—skinnier benefits, smaller 401(k) contributions, no bonuses—they don't air many gripes at this session. On the contrary, they're thrilled to have an audience with the chairman. After the meeting, Britta Gross, an engineer in GM's fuel-cell program, says, "Rick is a guy trying to do the right thing. A lot of us feel a lot of pressure to do all the right things right now."

Thanks in part to his outreach efforts, Wagoner remains a popular figure within the company. Subordinates give him points for stretching GM's capabilities but staying short of the breaking point. "He's kept the angry barbarians at the gate, and his understanding of the culture is invaluable," says one. "He's pushed it as hard as it can be pushed." Critics, though, say that he hasn't pushed nearly hard enough—Wagoner needs to trim the blue-collar workforce by more than the 25,000 already announced and do much more to reform GM's ponderous bureaucracy.

What Wagoner really needs is a megahit—a Chrysler 300C, a Ford Mustang, or even a 1955 Chevy from GM's distant past—something that will produce long waiting lists and fat margins and help lift the cloud of inexorable decline that hangs over the company. Recent efforts have been mixed. There's the Pontiac Solstice, a two-seat roadster that looks snappy but will lose money, at least at first, because of its small volumes. The Chevrolet HHR is a retro-looking minivan/passenger car crossover that more than slightly resembles Chrysler's PT Cruiser. In fact, the auto press is already calling it the "MeToo Cruiser."

The crucial test will come over the next six months, when GM launches its highly touted new models, including the horsepower-heavy 2006 Cadillac STS-V. All of them must succeed, and one or two need to make a breakthrough in customer awareness, to lift GM's image and wean car shoppers off incentive deals. Advance buzz has been favorable on the most critical ones—new full-sized sport-utility vehicles like the 2007 Cadillac Escalade, which makes its debut in January.

"I think we have a chance to continue to be a major force in the industry."

But even a fleet of smash-hit cars won't be enough if Wagoner can't win concessions from the UAW on health-care benefits. Providing coverage for all of GM's 1.1 million active and retired workers and their dependents is slowly strangling the company. GM expects payments to jump $400 million this year, to a total of $5.6 billion, and to go up sharply again in 2006. Wagoner says he's hopeful—"The issue of a shared destiny I think is clearer than ever"—but it's not obvious how he's going to do it. The union certainly doesn't sound particularly amenable to a deal—UAW president Ron Gettelfinger has been publicly calling for Wagoner himself to take a pay cut. (Wagoner made $4.8 million in salary and bonuses last year.)

Fifty years ago, FORTUNE wrote that GM CEO Harlowe Curtice "runs his company with all the urgency of some desperately worried, embattled executive...whose competitors are breathing fire in his face, and who is in imminent danger...of seeing his customers desert him in droves." That attitude didn't survive long after Curtice's retirement, but it permeates GM today. And the conditions described in the passage are no longer imaginary.

If Wagoner makes progress with the unions and GM's new crop of cars produces at least a couple of hits, time will start to be on his side. GM's operations are continuing to improve, and demographics will begin to run in the company's favor. Mortality will shrink the number of UAW workers who retired in the early 1990s as part of GM's last big downsizing, taking a bite out of legacy costs. "If we succeed in addressing some of these tough longer-term issues," says Wagoner, "I think we have a chance to continue to be a major force in the industry." For Wagoner and GM, the stakes couldn't be higher. If he can't fix the North American operations, he will probably be out of a job. And General Motors, American icon, could begin a slow, steady slide to extinction. Can he do it? Wagoner's outlook is hopeful but sober. "This is crunch time," he says. "I'm encouraged by the movement that I see on a number of issues. But I would have to say we don't have a lot of time."

REPORTER ASSOCIATES *Susan M. Kaufman, Oliver Ryan*

Disaster's Future

The prospects for corporate crisis management and communication

Simon Moore

A seismic but dangerously neglected shift in the world of crisis is under way. It's called "information technology." Constant enhancements in the ability of IT to merge rapid information exchange, opinion formation, and decisive stakeholder action will force crisis-hit companies to rethink response strategies. This will have broader consequences for corporate culture, particularly the role of communication. Business will not be able to pick and choose the parts of the information revolution it most likes. Denial and failure to embrace these transformations will put firms at risk from the accompanying changes to global public opinion and its hostile expression.

The revolution in information technology is likely to persist through economic fluctuations, corporate scandals, terrorist uncertainties, and the like. Because of this revolution, business crises and the issues and risks that ignite them are going to occur and unfold very differently in the future. Companies fighting crisis, or containing those issues and risks, must radically adjust their techniques—and perhaps their internal cultures.

IT's strengths are well known and widely touted. Customers around the world are turning to e-commerce, enjoying access to more product choices and finding out more about them. Executives are liberating organizations from expensive non-core functions through increased outsourcing. The management of global operations is being facilitated, including the marketing of international brands and corporate identities. Almost wholly ignored in the forward-looking ferment, though, is the double-edged character of IT's impact in these areas and its deployment by stakeholders as a tool to foment and drive crises. IT is, in short, making firms more vulnerable in more places, much farther away, to sudden calamity.

When considering the part technology plays in crisis, the public, the media, and corporations alike usually focus on its ability to trigger disaster through accidental or malicious system failure. Much is heard about the threats posed by hackers, worms, viruses, or accidental breaches of privacy and security. But technology's role in a crisis is bigger and subtler than that. IT is profoundly affecting all causes of crises—from terrorism to corruption, health scares to product recall. The fight against these forces in the Information Age must continue to address how information is crafted and used, but information will neither be used nor deployed properly in the future unless business understands the changing communication environment. Technology is fusing information with action—a convergence filled with implications for executives and officials confronted by unexpected disaster or charged with identifying and planning for potential crises. The costs of failing to understand will be far more dramatic than in the past.

Two changes must be understood if future crises are to be managed effectively: Internet globalization and outsourcing.

There is no doubt that the current crisis-fighting model can be a highly sophisticated instrument. At its best, it follows a tradition enunciated by American PR pioneer Ivy Ledbetter Lee, whose agency represented mine owners during a bitter coal strike in 1906. In a "Declaration of Principles" sent to newspaper editors, Lee sought to improve media relations for his harassed clients by making a then-revolutionary promise of openness. "This is not a secret press bureau," he announced. "Our plan is, frankly and openly, in behalf of business concerns and public institutions, to supply the press and the public of the United States with prompt and accurate information concerning subjects which it is of value and interest to the public to know about" (Wilcox 1986). In the century that followed, "prompt and accurate" communication, managed in the spirit of Lee's idea, has helped companies through disasters. Famous examples include Tylenol's candid and responsible reaction to its cyanide tampering crisis in 1982 and Pepsi's energetic and open public communication during its 1993 scare over hoax allegations of hypodermic needles in bottles.

At the other extreme, perceived hesitation, reluctance, or outright failure to communicate fully with influential audiences put other companies among those who learned the hard way that crisis management hangs on open communication as much as on taking operational action to fix the physical cause of trouble. Included in this category are: Shell, with its failed attempt in 1995 to sink the decommissioned Brent Spar oil rig in the North Sea in the teeth of overwhelming and occasionally violent environmental and political opposition across the EO; and Firestone, with panicky, ill-coordinated reactions and blame-shifting in the heat of its 2000–2001 tire recall.

Personal and corporate reputations, careers, finances, sales, employee commitment and morale, expert opinion, regulator decisions, and stakeholder trust—all these, in a time of 24-hour news cycles and Internet access, continue to be affected during crisis by corporate communications that, to varying degrees, follow Lee's founding principles of frankness, openness, promptness, and accuracy. In the Information Age, however, following these principles also means accepting more active stakeholder participation, more stakeholders, and a concomitant need to persuasively deliver ever-rising volumes of communication. It is a commitment that creates strain, consuming a crisis-hit company's precious time, resources, and professional expertise, and demanding access to senior levels of decision-making. These requirements can precede the crisis stage itself. Corporations often engage with key audiences on matters that might, in future, create attritional issues or spark crises. The levels of transparency; or "managed openness," that all these activities necessarily stimulate have obliged many companies to review or change their entire internal culture to remove communication blockages that might spawn or prolong a crisis.

Wise companies customarily react to a breaking crisis by taking a series of fairly standard steps, fine-tuned for the specific events at hand and designed to separate crisis management as much as possible from the regular business of the company. These include

- personnel allocated to handle basic inquiries and to monitor and analyze coverage
- a crisis management team (ideally of no more than ten people) drawn from different areas of the company to meet at regular periods and craft statements, releases, and operational decisions
- spokesmen to build credible relations with the media
- active CEO participation in public communication
- constant contact with employees, investors, customers, consumers, independent experts, and other audiences to bypass the media filter and directly deliver critical and undiluted messages

More prosaic but vital and sometimes (as several firms discovered in the aftermath of September 11) complicated steps include locating and equipping dedicated physical space to cope with the influx of reporters or concerned relatives of victims.

Aside from the unique twists and turns thrown up by any particular crisis, further refinements are being forced on this model by the globalization of business and the accompanying difficulty of handling crisis information across different time zones. In spite of all this, the recommended structure has broadly survived the huge demands placed on it.

The structure is now subject to new pressures from emerging technology. First, IT is triggering macrocosmic changes to the way business and society interact. These have been recognized by several business disciplines and even by a few far-sighted communication professionals, though their impacts on crises are almost totally ignored. Second, technology will reshape patterns of information sharing, perception-shaping, and opinion-forming in a crisis, using tools that offer speed, content, and the ability to harness opinion to direct action. The changes raise new dilemmas for crisis managers, employees, investors, regulators, and other key publics, who are forced to consider reworking key messages, reshaping relations with key audiences, and reinventing communication strategy.

Under the "macroscope"

Two changes must be understood if future crises are to be managed effectively: Internet globalization and outsourcing. That these changes are widely viewed as good for business is neither here nor there; whether good or bad, as large-scale influences on the business scene they will inevitably shape crises and issues.

The Internet's role as a collaborative platform to drive issues and crises is expanding due to simultaneous expansions in online diversity and e-commerce and, crucially (as we shall see), new kinds of activism and messages made possible by new kinds of technology. The world's spreading online population has obvious commercial value. The ILO's World Employment Report 2001 notes: "Barely 6 percent of the world's people have ever logged onto the Internet and 85 to 90 percent of them are in the industrialized countries." Most users are from the developed Western nations.

Glimpse ahead a few years and a different situation presents itself. Research points consistently to a runaway increase in online users, which will not confine itself to North America, Western Europe, or Japan. Geopolitical diversity will finally catch up with linguistic diversity. The Internet research firm Nua (2002) estimates from multiple surveys that already 70 percent of the online population is outside the United States. The numbers of users from outside North America and Western Europe are indeed rising, with projected 2000–2004 increases as high as 255 percent in Asia (49 million to 173 million) and 167 percent in Latin America. Overall, according to Forrester Research (2001), online commerce is projected to rise from $1 trillion in 2001 to around $12.6 trillion (or 18 percent of global sales) by 2006.

As a first step in crisis planning and issue management, prudent executives will embark on a "deep rethink" of the scope, content, and value of their interaction with localities, regions, communities, organizations, and individuals.

What are these crunched numbers, best "guesstimates," and forecasts for global Internet use and e-commerce growth telling companies, governments, and nonprofits about the future for crisis and risk? Forrester Research (2000) reports that "North America's share of e-commerce will inevitably fall as this boom echoes across other regions of the world." New customers in Asia-Pacific, the Middle East, Africa, and elsewhere, accessing the services of energetic companies, naturally erode Western domination of the Web in step with a declining share of e-commerce. The new e-consumers will have greater access to information about products, and companies will be jostling for their business. Sooner or later (probably sooner) they will cease to consume in neutral space and—just as many US consumers do today—encounter and wrestle with many more ethical challenges, feelings, and opinions presented to them online by friends, activists, and opinion leaders.

More online consumers and opinion leaders from other cultures and belief systems will—as some feel the small Western club of nations is already doing—talk among themselves, rejecting or shutting out other contributors, with more likelihood of crisis-fomenting action on- and offline. New e-consumers from once largely offline regions will be swiftly mobilized, their emotions and beliefs targeted by experienced opinion leaders. Companies with worldwide operations are already exposed to the impact of global issue management, including highly visible US symbols such as McDonald's and Coca-Cola. More American companies will turn to e-commerce to grow or simply survive as the importance of the domestic marketplace declines. They too will confront the consequences of doing more of their business on a bigger and culturally diverse Internet. For example, it will matter to their business and to crisis management that tens of millions more Asian Muslims are going online, and that the online population in the Arab nations of the Middle East, as has been predicted, continues to double every year from an August 2001 estimate of just 2.75 million.

This need not be a formula for confrontation, but it is one for communication. American companies turning to e-commerce will need a new approach. As a first step in crisis planning and issue management, prudent executives will need to embark on a "deep rethink" of the scope, content, and value of their interaction with localities, regions, communities, organizations, and individuals.

Such a rethink, let alone message construction and coordination in the charged environment of an actual crisis, will be made more urgent and more difficult by outsourcing. Charles Handy (1994) has remarked, "The challenge for tomorrow's leaders is to manage an organization that is not there in any sense which we are used to." Outsourcing is creating such a situation, but it is not always viewed as a harbinger of crisis. More often, it is seen as a way to reduce certain risks. The Outsourcing Institute (1998) found risk reduction among the top ten reasons why polled companies outsourced. It reported, " Outsourcing providers make investments on behalf of many clients, not just one. Shared investment spreads risk, and significantly reduces the risk borne by a single company."

Corporate risks and crises are not born in a vacuum. They are the natural progeny of prevailing conditions, and new prevailing conditions create new, sometimes large, but not necessarily irredeemable crisis problems.

Nevertheless, outsourcing also creates many of the new risks confronting corporate crisis management: first, because IT functions are being outsourced, and second, because IT is driving the outsourcing of other corporate functions, including many found in human resources, customer relations, and production. McKinsey Consulting (Daruvala 2003) predicts that IT outsourcing expenditures dominated by America, Europe, and Japan will reach $346 billion by 2008. Many companies and governments now seek to manage the IT needs of other companies and governments. IBM has made this movement part of a broader shift from hardware toward services, software, and consulting. In India, tech company activity reflects a local outsourcing entrepreneur's comment that "at least 50 to 60 percent of the business we do is in services that we did not operate in six or seven years ago" ("Why India..." 2001). In the Philippines, the Department of Trade and Industry promotes the country as a major center for various IT outsourcing companies worldwide, offering call center services, software development, animation, medical transcription, and business process outsourcing.

It is unlikely, at least for now, that there will be much sustained examination of the crisis communication needs IT outsourcing is creating. To say this is not to imply, as with the Millennium Bug scare, that because of outsourcing, Armageddon is nigh. It is simply to reiterate that corporate risks and crises are not born in a vacuum. They are the natural progeny of prevailing conditions, and new prevailing conditions create new, sometimes large, but not necessarily irredeemable crisis problems.

What are those problems? As the head of IBM Malaysia assured reporters in late 2001, outsourcing "will be like taking the IT department of a company and transferring it to IBM where the people and the assets will both belong to IBM" ("Outsourcing can..."). However, as a pharmaceutical journalist pointed out about his industry, "You can transfer risk, but the ultimate responsibility is with the party that owns the product. At the end of the day, it's not the vendor's name that is on the NDA [new drug application] or product marketing application—t's the sponsor's name" (Miller 2001).

Functions may be distributed, but blame tends to be concentrated. Over the coming decade, many of the skilled personnel responsible for handling a company's information systems will be transferred to companies like IBM, or downsized altogether in favor of new staff and facilities working cheaply for distant subcontractors.

These dispersals have consequences for crisis and issue management, regardless of the function being outsourced. In all cases, the outsourcers are exposed to the vulnerabilities of their subcontractor and the regions in which their services were relocated. This may force the outsourcer—the familiar name on the product—to shoulder more responsibility for local issues often raised by local and global activists, as Nike discovered when its subcontractors' labor practices in Vietnam drew global media attention. Meanwhile, the reverse of this will also become more common: the subcontractor inherits the outsourcer's legacy, assumes responsibility for key capabilities, and thereby becomes vulnerable to the outsourcer's crises.

One of the earliest indications of what this means for IT subcontractors appeared at the end of 2002, when a Saudi investor in Ptech Inc., a small US company, appeared on a US government "blocked list" as a suspected terrorist financier. Ptech, located in Quincy, Massachusetts, a town with a significant Middle Eastern population, maintained software for managing the personal and structural assets of several federal entities, including the FBI and the Pentagon. After a high-profile federal search of the firm's offices, four employees had their bank accounts canceled, others received a slew of hate messages, and as business fell away the company shed 17 out of 27 personnel. Ptech is now fighting for its survival in a climate of ruptured trust and damaged perceptions. "I feel like I'm not allowed to dream," CEO and co-founder Oussama Ziade said ("Software company. . ." 2002).

Outsourcing also complicates the already complex process of managing crises across time zones and lengthy supply chains. A part-time or subcontracted workforce makes the task of internal message coordination more challenging, creating problems of loyalty and commitment among people responsible for a company's information systems. These are people who may have, at best, divided allegiances or, at worst, resentment—particularly under lower pay and worse conditions.

Technology's power punch

It is worrisome that these IT-driven trends are starting to pack an IT-powered punch. Technology is joining emotion to communication and action in powerful new ways, with dramatic prospects for future crises.

Whatever the literal shape of future IT, some common threads of development are widely agreed upon. IT will become

- lighter, more portable
- always on
- ubiquitous, not just restricted to computers
- instantaneous, for all practical purposes
- more appealing to more senses-making more use of, at the least, color, voice, sound, and touch
- available to more people
- better able to exploit increased transparency by finding, storing, and packaging complex information according to the user's personal preference
- capable of semi-independent action as well as information exchange on the user's behalf

In a previous book (Seymour and Moore 1999), my coauthor and I used the term "cobra crises" to describe dire events that strike fast and unexpectedly: an explosion, a crash. Now the phrase "cobra technology" can also be used about IT that offers crisis participants the following:

Speed and ease of access. The first moments of a crisis set the pattern of perceptions and opinion, and often the extent of damage to the company. In those moments, anyone with the right IT tools at hand and the ability to use them faster than others is more likely to have an opinion-leading influence on a crisis.

Convergence, reach, and action— the ability to gather together, from all corners of the Earth if necessary, the right "influencers": the people whose opinions and strategy will control the crisis agenda in the public eye.

What kinds of actions will stakeholders be able to take in the first, charged moments of a crisis? New impetus will be given to boycotts and rumors, and to exploiting corporate dependence on linked systems of computer information and communication.

> IT has also increased the sources and spreaders of rumor. More online users in more countries will spawn more news outlets with less time or inclination to check their sources.

"We can't assume that everyone on the planet is going to be socially responsible," Sun Microsystems's chief scientist reminds us ("From 'long boom'..." 2000). The likelihood of system failures or attacks on companies naturally grows with the growing online population and their ability to disrupt the Internet by accident, out of malice (like the hackers posing as Ford employees who stole the credit records, social security numbers, and bank account numbers of 13,000 people from a reporting agency in 2002), or to make a social or political protest. Traditional terrorism has spawned political "cyber-terrorism," and information itself is the victim. Examples include the 25 Israeli organizations targeted by the Palestinian worm "Injustice"; sites in the United Arab Emirates defaced and pasted with a "Zionist flag"; and numerous US and Chinese confrontations. An FBI survey revealed that 186 US companies recorded a total of $377.8 million in financial losses from security breaches in 2001.

From the perspective of crisis communication, such widely known system failures and attacks reflect the power that technology has given unfamiliar or hostile groups, individuals, and countries. But such attacks need not be the prerogative of these entities alone. Every day, online consumers scattered across the planet could join in, coaxed into action by more militant "*e*-fluentials"—a group identified by PR multinational Burson-Marsteller and research firm Roper Starch as people "who shape the opinions and attitudes of the Internet Community." E-fluentials, even the more moderate ones, may be hard to pin down. Follow-up research estimated that 11.1 million adults fit the broad category in the US alone.

The possibilities of boycotts are also being enlarged by technology. The Millennium Poll on corporate social responsibility (MORI 1999) found that of 25,000 people in 23 countries, 23 percent globally—and nearly half of the Americans surveyed—had "avoided" a company or spoken against it to others because it failed to meet social obligations. And among a smaller 5,000-strong group defined as opinion leaders, 39 percent reported taking direct action against a corporation. At present, the Internet is used by boycotters to promote events, as a resource for downloading leaked memos or viewing "action packs" about "guilty" organizations, or as a forum to exchange news and ideas, draw in support, gain subscriptions, and maintain momentum.

The Net will escalate from promoting boycotts to being the boycott by exploiting new technology and e-commerce. British Telecom's resident scientist and futurist Ian Pearson (2000) raises this possibility with a scenario in which future environmentalists e-mail everyone on the Net recommending economic sanctions against the USA because of its CO_2 emission policies. "By pressing the 'I agree' button, the user's e-commerce preferences are automatically set to exclude products and services from the USA," warns Pearson. "The result could be a billion or more of the richest people on the planet excluding the USA from business, within a few minutes. No geographically based power structure can impose such a penalty so quickly."

Posting rumors is already a widespread Internet activity. It is already clear to crisis consultants and many other observers that, as Denton (2001) puts it, "the uncontrolled flow of opinion, comment, and rumor across the Web has reached an epidemic proportion and remains largely unchecked or unmonitored by the vast majority of firms."

IT intensifies the problems rumors create by rapid dissemination. "The average time for information to flow from the bottom to the top of the gossip food chain can be as little as two to three days," says Denton. Faster-moving rumors proliferate in minutes, not days, and the reduction of the average seems likely with more people online to spread gossip down faster connections, particularly in uncertain times or unstable places. Notes one surprised Zimbabwean economist, "My wife received a message on her cell phone that fuel prices would be increasing by 55% that night" (Bloch 2002).

IT has also increased the sources and spreaders of rumor. More online users in more countries will spawn more news outlets with less time or inclination to check their sources. Many will knowingly post a rumor to scoop competitors, serve social or political agendas, or attract a bigger audience.

The shortened time span shrinks the space needed for reflection and perspective. The ability of investors to rapidly dump or purchase shares, and of online customers to instantly shop elsewhere, makes it harder for more rational or relaxed stakeholders to take time to verify a rumor's truth, and pushes them to follow suit in order to preserve their position financially or with their own key constituencies. Unscrupulous companies may contribute to this by the timely deployment of rumors to lift share prices, raise expectations about new products, or prepare markets for a bad quarter.

Up to now, rumormongers have depended on sources external to the targeted company. But the prospect of infiltrating a company's actual communication strategy has also been raised. In its April 2002 "Attack Trends" report, a government-funded Internet security study group at Carnegie Mellon University warned: "Intruders might be able to modify news sites, produce bogus press releases, and conduct other activities, all of which could have economic impact" (CERT 2002). Misinformation placed *inside* a company, if it occurs frequently enough, weakens the concept of transparency and, ultimately, trust in the Internet itself.

The new crisis response

All these changes and trends present a clear set of problems for the crisis discipline. IT will create crises because of technical failure, either by accident or maliciously inspired. It will create issues by forcing new and powerful audiences to confront ethical or social difficulties. And it will influence a crisis or an issue by its use as a communication tool to shape opinion and provoke individuals and key publics to independent action.

As the number and intensity of IT-mediated disruptions grow, companies are having to face tough challenges:

- maintaining the trust of stakeholders when systems are seriously compromised
- developing communication relationships with large numbers of online opinion influencers (the e-fluentials), globally as well as nationally
- increased monitoring of communication activity relating to the company and the issues connected with it
- how best to "own" but not overtly "control" the forum for such communication activity
- how to craft key messages—or the serious task of finding exact forms of words that publicly summarize the corporation's positions on the crisis and its causes. In the time-compressed Information Age crisis, early and spontaneous messages that can complement an emotion-laden, highly participative, and transparent environment will be needed. They must also be controlled carefully enough to contain stakeholder speculation and instant hostile actions of the kind described earlier.

Technology is fusing emotion to communication and action in vivid and constantly improving ways—and doing it very quickly. This squashes together the crisis stages of emergence, spread, ebb, and recovery. In such a high-pressure setting, heavy damage occurs as widespread, intense speculation rapidly escalates. Volatility and uncertainty grow because there is less time to identify and engage with opinion-formers, fend off disruptive cyber protests and attacks, and repair the damage to the corporation. There is less time for a crisis team of PR managers, company lawyers, and other senior executives to calmly discuss, agree, decide, and keep pace with the speed and spread of events.

Technology is fusing emotion to communication and action in vivid and constantly improving ways—and doing it very quickly. This squashes together the crisis stages of emergence, spread, ebb, and recovery.

The emerging interactive crisis environment undercuts executives' ability to coordinate their response with one-way communication, in which the company sends completed messages to audiences and awaits a response. Press statements, interviews, e-mails, and news releases prepared by a single crisis team and its spokesperson will not be sufficient to build enduring relationships in the Information Age. Online customers, activists, investors, subcontractors, part-time employees, and other stakeholders scattered over continents and cultures will, as already noted, access their own circles of influence to help form their opinions. The messages, actions, and priorities of subcontractors of outsourced services and part-time telecommuters around the planet will be harder to harmonize or coordinate than full-time, on-site employees. Outsourced workers and services will, again, be less able or inclined to assist in creating effective messages.

What must companies do to keep some positive influence over the messages and viewpoints exchanged in future crises? There has been little investigation of this subject, although some commentary exists on the related problems of corporate communication and reputation management. Yet companies are approaching a position in which communication activity will not only drive the crisis but often will also be the crisis, because many participants will instantly wed communication to concrete action and compel others to do the same to avoid financial or other damage. Vulnerable or crisis-hit companies, therefore, cannot view emerging IT simply as a new set of communication tools. The changes to stakeholder information gathering, opinion formation, perceptions, and actions oblige company leaders to re-evaluate the role and meaning of communication within their organization. As far as crisis management is concerned, this re-evaluation should be based on specific objectives: tighter integration of communication needs into company activities; more emphasis on anticipating issues with crisis potential; early identification and frank (transparent) engagement with key audiences; more emphasis on intelligence gathering; and greater sensitivity to the practical impact of emotional intangibles such as feelings, perceptions, and trust.

British consultant and academic James Bellini (1999) argues that a new phase is dawning in the marketplace in which "business survival will flow from being liked" and customer service "will be based on developing emotional connections with individual consumers." This reality applies to crises and issues as much as to sales and marketing. Companies must place more stress on the "pre-crisis" stage, integrating crisis and issue management through continuous early monitoring and intervention in escalating issues and by maintaining joint issue management programs with outsourced employees, subcontractors, and local critics. There must also be more changes to message content. The accessibility of alternative points of view and information sources, transparency expectations, and the potential distrust of diverse online audiences means that in the midst of a crisis, companies and their spokespeople must consider a very different approach to language, content, and style—less hedged in by legal caveats or corporate-speak. "We need to provide the client's perspective in a way that is fact-based and that acknowledges other points of view," counsels the CEO of PR giant Edelman Worldwide. "We call it 'modified advocacy'" (Holmes 2001).

One obstacle to such approaches is the corporate fear of "unmanaged" messages and of participating in and even encouraging diverse views in the uncontrolled setting of the Web. "To share our dilemmas and problems before we have worked out a solution requires a great deal of self-confidence," a Shell public affairs manager recently admitted ("Do the right thing" 2001). Another obstacle is natural fear or annoyance at the intense level of emotion generated by a crisis and the reluctance of executives to respond in kind, either for legal reasons or out of professional and personal reserve. Yet technology's conversion of the Net into an arena for commerce makes emotion more important to crisis management. By embracing the one, business accepts the risk of the other. Future crises at Internet speed will force companies to pay more attention to the feelings of once-overlooked audiences and sensitive issues, to engage with countries, peoples, and cultures once unknown or left to overseas subcontractors, and to place more weight on the emotional, perceptual talents of their remaining full-time, directly employed workforce.

These factors, supplemented by the shorter crisis life cycle, may compel a restructuring of the crisis management team to enable swifter decisions. Such reorganization might include adding senior-level expertise in online communication, empowered to protect the company's reputation. These executives would engage in continuous online interaction with third-party experts, the manifold sources of news information, key outsourced workers, and subcontractors to prepare messages, identify major participants and their online haunts, and promote dialogue. They would distribute information and launch online forums to present the firm as a transparent, frank participant in the crisis. They would also monitor, contain, and respond immediately to such diverse problems as instant boycotts, scandal, escalating rumors, rampant speculation, unpopularity, or cyber attacks.

Regardless of particular professional expertise, crisis team members and other company officers will need an active understanding of corporate communication strategy and tactics, a deeper awareness of the cultures or beliefs of their global stakeholders, and a comprehension of IT's capacity to deliver fact, feeling, and a commitment to dialogue. In an environment where damage could be instant and overwhelming, the crisis team will be forced to consider releasing some key messages before the usual battery of legal and hierarchical checks. They will need to find independent allies online who do not necessarily speak their language, hold their beliefs, or subscribe to their company's vision, then work with global networks of e-fluentials to help watch and respond to debate and activity. The dispersed and fragmented audiences will make the task of spokesperson too large to be performed by a single CEO or one or two spokesmen addressing Western media and analysts at a press conference or via a webcast from corporate headquarters. Online spokesmen will be needed to respond online to "local" stakeholders, marshal contributions from elsewhere in the company, direct inquiries to independent and perhaps hostile sources, and provide a credible identity for the company in its various markets.

The subjects explored here may be discomfiting, but business will be unable to pick and choose those pans of the information revolution that it most likes. Denial and failure to embrace the changes to crisis management created by emerging technology puts companies at risk from accompanying changes to global public opinion and its hostile expression.

References and selected bibliography

Bellini, James. 1999. Agenda for a new millennium: Technology horizons and the future for business and work. Unpublished paper, London (9 November).

Bloch, Eric. 2002. If rumours were energy, Bill Gates would be envious. *Zimbabwe Independent.* @ www.theindependent.co.zw (22 March).

CERT. 2002. *Overview of attack trends.* CERT Coordination Center, Pittsburgh, PA: Camegie-Mellon University (April).

Daruvala, Toos. 2003. When, where, how, and other questions on going offshore. McKinsey Consulting. @ www.mckinsey.com/knowledge/articles/going_offshore.asp (3 July).

Denton, Nick. 2001. What can be done to limit damage of internet rumors? *Marketing* (31 May): 12.

Do the right thing. 2001. *BC Business* (Vancouver) (1 October): 30.

Forrester Research. 2000. Worldwide e-commerce growth. *Forrester Findings.* Cambridge, Massachusetts (19 April).

——. 2001. Global online trade will climb to 18% of sales. *TextStrategy* (26 December): 1-5.

From "long boom" to days of doom and gloom. 2000. *Javaworld* (4 June): 1.

Handy, Charles. 1994. *The empty raincoat.* London: Random House.

Holmes, Paul. 2001. PR must embrace "the paradox of transparency": Interview with Richard Edelman. *The Holmes Report* (12 March): 3-5.

ILO. 2001. *World employment report 2001: Life at work in the information economy.* Geneva: The Stationery Office Agencies.

Miller, Jim. 2001. Managing the risks in outsourcing. *Biopharm* 25/6 (June): 82.

MORI (Market Opinion & Research International). 1999. The Millennium Poll on Corporate Social Responsibility. @ www.mori.com/polls/1999/mill-poll.shtml (30 September).

Nua. 2002. How many online? @ www.nua.com/surveys/how_many_online/index.html (September).

Outsourcing can save up to 20%. 2001. *New Straits Times* (Kuala Lumpur, 6 October): Busn. sect., 2.

Outsourcing Institute. 1998. *Survey of current and potential outsourcing end-users.* Jericho, NY: The Outsourcing Institute Membership.

Pearson, Ian. 2000. The power of direct action. *Sphere, BT's innovation and technology e-zine.* @ www.btplc. com/sphere/insights/pearson/powerofdirectaction.htm (29 November).

Seymour, Mike, and Simon Moore. 1999. *Effective crisis management: Worldwide principles and practice.* London: Thomson Learning.

Software company tries to survive terrorism investigation. 2002. *Associated Press* (31 December).

Why India is leading in IT outsourcing. 2001. *Asia Pulse* (December): np.

Wilcox, Dennis, Phillip Ault, and Warren Agee. 1986. *Public relations strategies and tactics.* New York: Harper & Row.

SIMON MOORE is the Associate Professor of Information Design and Corporate Communication, Bentley College, Waltham, Massachusetts (smoore@bentley.edu)

UNIT 5
Controlling

Unit Selections

Key Points to Consider

- Control in any organization takes a variety of forms. Which one do you think is the most important for a profit organization? A not-for-profit organization?
- What role do you think the budget process plays in the control function of the organization?
- What impact do you think technology will have on the way that organizations control their operations in the future? Do you think organizations can achieve a high degree of quality in their operations? How?
- How should organizations respond to violence in the workplace? What can be done to prevent it? What can be done once it has happened?

Student Website

www.mhcls.com/online

Internet References

Further information regarding these websites may be found in this book's preface or online.

Bill Lindsay's Home Page
http://www.nku.edu/~lindsay/

Computer and Network Security
http://www.vtcif.telstra.com.au/info/security.html

Internal Auditing World Wide Web
http://www.bitwise.net/iawww/

Office of Financial Management
http://www.doi.gov/

Total Quality Leadership (TQL) vs. Management by Results
http://deming.eng.clemson.edu/pub/den/files/tql.txt

Workplace Violence
http://www.osha-slc.gov/SLTC/workplaceviolence/

Managers must plan, organize, and direct the organization, but how do they know if they are doing a good job? Controlling is the function of management that evaluates their efforts. Is the plan a good one? Is the firm adequately organized to implement the plan effectively? Is the plan being implemented so as to maximize the desired results? What changes need to be made in the plan, or the organization, or the implementation, or any combination thereof to help the firm better achieve its mission, objectives, and goals?

It is necessary to evaluate the firm's results against some sort of criteria. For most firms, those criteria are often financial, defined in terms of profits. However, it is necessary to define and understand control, and to actively engage in procedures that will lead to effective management and evaluation, as Douglas McGregor wrote in the classic article, "An Uneasy Look at Performance Appraisal."

Profitability is not the only measure of effectiveness. In fact, the entire not-for-profit sector of the economy refuses to use profitability as a measure of success. Measures come in other forms for not-for-profits as exemplified by the unqualified success of the March of Dimes in winning the battle against the deadly, crippling disease of polio. The March of Dimes was a success by any standard, but profitability would not be an appropriate criterion for it or other similar ventures. The key is whether the organization has achieved its goals, which may or may not include profitability.

When managers talk about control in the modern corporate sense, they really are talking about two different levels of control. The first is the traditional approach to controlling the firm's operation. This control is centered around the flow of information to determine what is going on in the organization as a whole. New technologies are making this easier. In this era of hostile takeovers, mergers, and acquisitions, managers are seeking to maintain control of their firms and not lose them to someone else in some new financial arrangement.

Shareholders are also awakening to this realization in terms of profitability and other issues with which management has to deal. Management is discovering that decisions concerning the firm can no longer be made solely on the basis of a good financial return. Decision-makers must consider what is socially and politically acceptable to the stockholders. The decision of many firms to leave South Africa to protest apartheid was just one manifestation of the new awareness of non-financial goals and objectives. With the new government in place in South Africa, many firms have decided to return.

But financial control is important. It is obviously a chief concern of many firms, especially small ones, because it is usually the area where they run into trouble. Financial control is the basis of all the other types of control in the organization, because the people who own it have the final say in what the firm does. Such control makes it possible for management to protect itself from corporate raiders, as well as the ability to direct the organization in a successful manner.

Security has also taken on new importance. With the advent of the computer and the World Wide Web, most information that was once the sole possession of the organization may now become public knowledge. "Corporate Security Management: What's Common? What Works?" is a question of greater concern than it was in the past. Traditional concerns of employee theft as well as high-tech and other potential security matters must also be addressed.

Production control is probably the area where the Japanese have made the most strides in recent years. U.S. and European firms have imported many of the ideas and techniques used in Japan over the past 30 years, including TQM, which is now being applied to many areas in addition to the zero defects approach, discussed in "Quality Is Easy."

The Japanese themselves have set up their own plants in the United States, demonstrating that their techniques are transferable. Many changes have taken place in the area of production, including the introduction of computers and robots. Developments do not just involve machines, they include standards, policies, and most especially people. As organizations strive to become more effective and efficient, it will become necessary to redesign the processes that a company uses.

Cost vs. quality and customer service are now two of the hottest areas in the business world. Supply chain management is bringing all the pieces together, from raw materials to the final customer in the most efficient and economical manner, and customer service has always been an important aspect of every organization's efforts.

Are managers more responsive to human values than personnel people? If so, we had better join them in taking...

An Uneasy Look at Performance Appraisal

By Douglas McGregor

Performance appraisal within management ranks has become standard practice in many companies during the past twenty years, and is currently being adopted by many others, often as an important feature of management development programs. The more the method is used, the more uneasy I grow over the unstated assumptions which lie behind it. Moreover, with some searching, I find that a number of people both in education and in industry share my misgivings. This article, therefore, has two purposes:

- To examine the conventional performance appraisal plan which requires the manager to pass judgment on the personal worth of subordinates.
- To describe an alternative which places on the subordinate the primary responsibility for establishing performance goals and appraising progress toward them.

Current Programs

Formal performance appraisal plans are designed to meet three needs, one for the organization and two for the individual:

1. They provide systematic judgments to back up salary increases, promotions, transfers, and sometimes demotions or terminations.
2. They are a means of telling a subordinate how he is doing, and suggesting needed changes in his behavior, attitudes, skills, or job knowledge; they let him know "where he stands" with the boss.
3. They also are being increasingly used as a basis for the coaching and counseling of the individual by the superior.

Problem of Resistance

Personnel administrators are aware that appraisal programs tend to run into resistance from the managers who are expected to administer them. Even managers who admit the necessity of such programs frequently balk at the process—especially the interview part. As a result, some companies do not communicate appraisal results to the individual, despite the general conviction that the subordinate has a right to know his superior's opinion so he can correct his weaknesses.

The boss's resistance is usually attributed to the following causes:

- A normal dislike of criticizing a subordinate (and perhaps having to argue about it).
- Lack of skill needed to handle the interviews.
- Dislike of a new procedure with its accompanying changes in ways of operating.
- Mistrust of the validity of the appraisal instrument.

To meet this problem, formal controls—scheduling, reminders, and so on—are often instituted. It is common experience that without them fewer than half the appraisal interviews are actually held. But even controls do not necessarily work. Thus:

> In one company with a well-planned and carefully administered appraisal program, an opinion poll included two questions regarding appraisals. More than 90% of those answering the questionnaire approved the idea of appraisals. They wanted to know how they stood. Some 40% went on to say that they had never had the experience of being told—yet the files showed that over four-fifths of them had signed a form testify-

ing that they had been through an appraisal interview, some of them several times!

The respondents had no reason to lie, nor was there the slightest supposition that their superiors had committed forgery. The probable explanation is that the superiors, being basically resistant to the plan, had conducted the interviews in such a perfunctory manner that many subordinates did not recognize what was going on.

Training programs designed to teach the skills of appraising and interviewing do help, but they seldom eliminate managerial resistance entirely. The difficulties connected with "negative appraisals" remain a source of genuine concern. There is always some discomfort involved in telling a subordinate he is not doing well. The individual who is "coasting" during the few years prior to retirement after servicing his company competently for many years presents a special dilemma to the boss who is preparing to interview him.

Nor does a shift to a form of group appraisal solve the problem. Though the group method tends to have greater validity and, properly administered, can equalize varying standards of judgment, it does not ease the difficulty inherent in the interview. In fact, the superior's discomfort is often intensified when he must base his interview on the results of a *group* discussion of the subordinate's worth. Even if the final judgments have been his, he is not free to discuss the things said by others which may have influenced him.

The Underlying Cause

What should we think about a method—however valuable for meeting organizational needs—which produces such results in a wide range of companies with a variety of appraisal plans? The problem is one that cannot be dismissed lightly.

Perhaps this intuitive managerial reaction to conventional performance appraisal plans shows a deep but unrecognized wisdom. In my view, it does not reflect anything so simple as resistance to change, or dislike for personnel technique, or lack of skill, or mistrust for rating scales. Rather, managers seem to be expressing very real misgivings, which they find difficult to put into words. This could be the underlying cause:

> The conventional approach, unless handled with consummate skill and delicacy, constitutes something dangerously close to a violation of the integrity of the personality. Managers are uncomfortable when they are put in the position of "playing God." The respect we hold for the inherent value of the individual leaves us distressed when we must take responsibility for judging the personal worth of a fellow man. Yet the conventional approach to performance appraisal forces us, not only to make such judgments and to see them acted upon, but also to communicate them to those we have judged. Small wonder we resist!

The modern emphasis upon the manager as a leader who strives to *help* his subordinates achieve both their own and the company's objectives is hardly consistent with the judicial role demanded by most appraisal plans. If the manager must put on his judicial hat occasionally, he does it reluctantly and with understandable qualms. Under such conditions it is unlikely that the subordinate will be any happier with the results than will the boss. It will not be surprising, either, if he fails to recognize that he has been told where he stands.

Of course, managers cannot escape making judgments about subordinates. Without such evaluations, salary and promotion policies cannot be administered sensibly. But are subordinates like products on an assembly line, to be accepted or rejected as a result of an inspection process? The inspection process may be made more objective or more accurate through research on the appraisal instrument, through training of the "inspectors," or through introducing group appraisal; the subordinate may be "reworked" by coaching or counseling before the final decision to accept or reject him; but as far as the assumptions of the conventional appraisal process are concerned, we still have what is practically identical with a program for product inspection.

On this interpretation, then, resistance to conventional appraisal programs is eminently sound. It reflect an unwillingness to treat human beings like physical objects. The needs of the organization are obviously important, but when they come into conflict with our convictions about the worth and the dignity of the human personality, one or the other must give.

Indeed, by the fact of their resistance managers are saying that the organization must yield in the face of this fundamental human value. And they are thus being more sensitive than are personnel administrators and social scientists whose business it is to be concerned with the human problems of industry!

A New Approach

If this analysis is correct, the task before us is clear. We must find a new plan—not a compromise to hide the dilemma, but a bold move to resolve the issue.

A number of writers are beginning to approach the whole subject of management from the point of view of basic social values. Peter Drucker's concept of "management by objectives"[1] offers an unusually promising framework within which we can seek a solution. Several companies, notably General Mills, Incorporated, and General Electric Company, have been exploring different methods of appraisal which rest upon assumptions consistent with Drucker's philosophy.

Responsibility on Subordinate

This approach calls on the subordinate to establish short-term performance goals for *himself*. The superior enters the process actively only *after* the subordinate has (a) done a good deal of thinking about his job, (b) made a careful assessment of his own strengths and weaknesses, and (c) formulated some specific plans to accomplish his goals. The superior's role is to help the man relate his self-appraisal, his "targets," and his plans for the ensuing period to the realities of the organization.

The first step in this process is to arrive at a clear statement of the major features of the job. Rather than a formal job description, this is a document drawn up *by the subordinate* after studying the company-approved statement. It defines the broad areas of his responsibility as they actually work out in practice. The boss and employee discuss the draft jointly and modify it as may be necessary until both of them agree that it is adequate.

Working from this statement of responsibilities, the subordinate then establishes his goals on "targets" for a period of, say, six months. These targets are *specific* actions which the man proposes to take, i.e., setting up regular staff meetings to improve communication, reorganizing the office, completing or undertaking a certain study. Thus, they are explicitly stated and accompanied by a detailed account of the actions he proposes to take to reach them. This document is, in turn, discussed with the superior and modified until both are satisfied with it.

At the conclusion of the six-month period, the subordinate makes *his own* appraisal of what he has accomplished relative to the targets he had set earlier. He substantiates it with factual data wherever possible. The "interview" is an examination by superior and subordinate together of the subordinate's self-appraisal, and it culminates in a resetting of targets for the next six months.

Of course, the superior has veto power at each step of this process; in an organizational hierarchy anything else would be unacceptable. However, in practice he rarely needs to exercise it. Most subordinates tend to underestimate both their potentialities and their achievements. Moreover, subordinates normally have an understandable wish to satisfy their boss, and are quite willing to adjust their targets or appraisals if the superior feels they are unrealistic. Actually, a much more common problem is to resist the subordinates' tendency to want the boss to tell them what to write down.

Analysis vs. Appraisal

This approach to performance appraisal differs profoundly from the conventional one, for it shifts the emphasis from *appraisal* to *analysis*. This implies a more positive approach. No longer is the subordinate being examined by the superior so that his weaknesses may be determined; rather, he is examining himself, in order to define not only his weaknesses but also his strengths and potentials. The importance of this shift of emphasis should not be underestimated. It is basic to each of the specific differences which distinguish this approach from the conventional one.

The first of these differences arises from the subordinate's new role in the process. He becomes an active agent, not a passive "object." He is no longer a pawn in a chess game called management development.

Effective development of managers does not include coercing them (no matter how benevolently) into acceptance of the goals of the enterprise, nor does it mean manipulating their behavior to suit organizational needs. Rather, it calls for creating a relationship within which a man can take responsibility for developing his own potentialities, plan for himself, and learn from putting his plans into action. In the process he can gain a genuine sense of satisfaction, for he is utilizing his own capabilities to achieve simultaneously both his objectives and those of the organization. Unless this is the nature of the relationship, "development" becomes a euphemism.

Who Knows Best?

One of the main differences of this approach is that it rests on the assumption that the individual knows—or can learn—more than anyone else about his own capabilities, needs, strengths and weaknesses, and goals. In the end, only he can determine what is best for his development. The conventional approach, on the other hand, makes the assumption that the superior can know enough about the subordinate to decide what is best for him.

No available methods can provide the superior with the knowledge he needs to make such decisions. Ratings, aptitude and personality tests, and the superior's necessarily limited knowledge of the man's performance yield at best an imperfect picture. Even the most extensive psychological counseling (assuming the superior possess the competence for it) would not solve the problem because the product of counseling is self-insight on the part of the *counselee*.

(Psychological tests are not being condemned by this statement. On the contrary, they have genuine value in competent hands. Their use by professionals as part of the process of screening applicants for employment does not raise the same questions as their use to "diagnose" the personal worth of accepted members of a management team. Even in the latter instance the problem we are discussing would not arise if test results and interpretations were given *to the individual himself*, to be shared with superiors at his discretion.)

The proper role for the superior, then, is the one that falls naturally to him under the suggested plan: helping the subordinate relate his career planning to the needs and realities of the organization. In the discussions the boss can use his knowledge of the organization to help the subordinate establish targets and methods for achieving them which will (a) lead to increased knowledge and skill, (b) contribute to organizational objectives, and (c) test the subordinate's appraisal of himself.

This is help which the subordinate wants. He knows well that the rewards and satisfactions he seeks from his career as a manager depend on his contribution to organizational objectives. He is also aware that the superior knows more completely than he what is required for success in this organization and *under this boss*. The superior, then, is the person who can help him test the soundness of his goals and his plans for achieving them. Quite clearly the knowledge and active participation of *both* superior and subordinate are necessary components of this approach.

If the superior accepts this role, he need not become a judge of the subordinate's personal worth. He is not telling, deciding, criticizing, or praising—not "playing God." He finds himself listening, using his own knowledge of the organization as a basis for advising, guiding, encouraging his subordinates to develop their own potentialities. Incidentally, this often leads the superior to important insights about himself and his impact on others.

Looking to the Future

Another significant difference is that the emphasis is on the future rather than the past. The purpose of the plan is to establish realistic targets and to seek the most effective ways of reaching them. Appraisal thus becomes a means to a *constructive* end. The 60-year-old "coaster" can be encouraged to set performance goals for himself and to make a fair appraisal of his progress toward them. Even the subordinate who has failed can be helped to consider what moves will be best for himself. The superior rarely finds himself facing the uncomfortable prospect of denying a subordinate's personal worth. A transfer or even a demotion can be worked out without the connotation of a "sentence by the judge."

Performance vs. Personality

Finally, the accent is on *performance*, on actions relative to goals. There is less tendency for the personality of the subordinate to become an issue. The superior, instead of finding himself in the position of a psychologist or a therapist, can become a coach helping the subordinate to reach his own decisions on the specific steps that will enable him to reach his targets. Such counseling as may be required demands no deep analysis of the personal motivations or basic adjustment of the subordinate. To illustrate:

Consider a subordinate who is hostile, short-tempered, uncooperative, insecure. The superior need not make any psychological diagnosis. The "target setting" approach naturally directs the subordinate's attention to ways and means of obtaining better interdepartmental collaboration, reducing complaints, winning the confidence of the men under him. Rather than facing the troublesome prospect of forcing his own psychological diagnosis on the subordinate, the superior can, for example, help the individual plan ways of getting "feedback" concerning his impact on his associates and subordinates as a basis for self-appraisal and self-improvement.

There is little chance that a man who is involved in a process like this will be in the dark about where he stands, or that he will forget he is the principal participant in his own development and responsible for it.

A New Attitude

As a consequence of these differences we may expect the growth of a different attitude toward appraisal on the part of superior and subordinate alike.

The superior will gain real satisfaction as he learns to help his subordinates integrate their personal goals with the needs of the organization so that both are served. Once the subordinate has worked out a mutually satisfactory plan of action, the superior can delegate to him the responsibility for putting it into effect. He will see himself in a consistent managerial role rather than being forced to adopt the basically incompatible role of either the judge or the psychologist.

Unless there is a basic personal antagonism between the two men (in which case the relationship should be terminated), the superior can conduct these interviews so that both are actively involved in seeking the right basis for constructive action. The organization, the boss, and the subordinate all stand to gain. Under such circumstances the opportunities for learning and for genuine development of both parties are maximal.

The particular mechanics are of secondary importance. The needs of the organization in the administration of salary and promotion policies can easily be met within the framework of the analysis process. The machinery of the program can be adjusted to the situation. No universal list of rating categories is required. The complications of subjective or prejudiced judgment, of varying standards, of attempts to quantify qualitative data, all can be minimized. In fact, *no* formal machinery is required.

Problems of Judgment

I have deliberately slighted the many problems of judgment involved in administering promotions and salaries. These are by no means minor, and this approach will not automatically solve them. However, I believe that if we are prepared to recognize the fundamental problem inherent in the conventional approach, ways can be found to temper our present administrative methods.

And if this approach is accepted, the traditional ingenuity of management will lead to the invention of a variety of methods for its implementation. The mechanics of some conventional plans can be adjusted to be consistent with this point of view. Obviously, a program utilizing ratings of the personal characteristics of subordinates would not be suitable, but one which emphasizes *behavior* might be.

Of course, managerial skill is required. No method will eliminate that. This method can fail as readily as any other in the clumsy hands of insensitive or indifferent or power-seeking managers. But even the limited experience of a few companies with this approach indicates that managerial *resistance* is substantially reduced. As a consequence, it is easier to gain the collaboration of managers in developing the necessary skills.

Cost in Time

There is one unavoidable cost: the manager must spend considerably more time in implementing a program of this kind. It is not unusual to take a couple of days to work through the initial establishment of responsibilities and goals with each individual. And a periodic appraisal may require several hours rather than the typical 20 minutes.

Reaction to this cost will undoubtedly vary. The management that considers the development of its human resources to be the primary means of achieving the economic objectives of the organization will not be disturbed. It will regard the necessary guidance and coaching as among the most important functions of every superior.

Conclusion

I have sought to show that the conventional approach to performance appraisal stands condemned as a personnel method. It places the manager in the untenable position of judging the personal worth of his subordinates, and of acting on these judgments. No manager possesses, nor could he acquire, the skill necessary to carry out this responsibility effectively. Few would even be willing to accept it if they were fully aware of the implications involved.

It is this unrecognized aspect of conventional appraisal programs which produces the widespread uneasiness and even open resistance of management to appraisals and especially to the appraisal interview.

A sounder approach, which places the major responsibility on the subordinate for establishing performance goals and appraising progress toward them, avoids the major weaknesses of the old plan and benefits the organization by stimulating the development of the subordinate. It is true that more managerial skill and the investment of a considerable amount of time are required, but the greater motivation and the more effective development of subordinates can justify these added costs.

Note

1. See Peter Drucker, *The Practice of Management* (New York, Harper & Brothers, 1954).

Zero In on the Numbers

Examine budget reports carefully to fine-tune expenses and prepare for next year.

Susan Ladika

If your company is just beginning its new fiscal year, as many companies are, you may assume that it's far too early to start thinking about budgeting for next year. But many financial experts say you should start paying close attention to budget items in the coming weeks—as soon as the first monthly report lands on your desk.

Keeping track of line items month by month, report by report, throughout 2005 not only can make your work on your 2006 budget less painful, but it can also give you, as an HR professional, a close-up look at how the company is doing. With that perspective, you can decide your spending priorities for next year and even, if necessary, quickly adjust your spending for this year.

Theresa Seagraves, president of the consulting firm Theresa L. Seagraves & Associates in Parker, Colo., says HR managers should review budget reports monthly, or at least quarterly. "Business can change rapidly," she says. "You need to be looking a year in advance to predict what you want to do with your budget."

And keep an eye on every line item related to the HR budget—whether there are four of them or 40, advises Steve Eggers, president of CFO Corporate Services in San Diego. Eggers, who teaches a budgeting course for HR managers at California State University San Marcos, says that by looking at budget reports thoroughly, "you've got a really good idea of what adjustments need to be made" when the 2006 budgeting process begins.

Granted, some think of budgeting "as just an exercise in futility that accounting people do to make other people suffer," says certified management accountant Marion Martelli. When she starts talking about the budgeting process in the classes she teaches for the SHRM Academy—a business education program of the Society for Human Resource Management (SHRM)—the HR managers often groan, she says. "But if it's done right, it's like a road map. It's a tool to manage how much cash you're going to get."

That's especially important in tight economic times, when budgets are squeezed and HR managers need to figure out how to stretch their dollars, says Martelli, an associate with Bradley/ Lambert Inc., a training and consulting firm in Los Angeles.

And having a full understanding of particular budget items can be important too when making a case for an expense that doesn't produce revenue. For example, a safety program can reduce workplace accidents, but it's important to know the budget figures that show such programs also reduce company outlays by reducing workers' compensation claims, Martelli says. "Soft explanations are all well and good, but you need to [provide] some numbers."

'One of the worst things you can do is sit on not-so-great data and surprise people later.'

It's important for HR to "show connections" between its programs and the benefits they provide for a company, says Jack Phillips, chairman of the ROI Institute, an organization in Birmingham, Ala, that provides consulting and research on accountability, primarily in HR. For example, he says, if an HR manager can demonstrate that a new wellness and fitness center is adding value, "it can help us hang on to the budget we have, and maybe increase that."

Find Out Why Numbers Vary

When budget reports land on your desk each month, study each one to find the items with the biggest variances—the biggest discrepancies between what was budgeted and what the actual outlay was. And examine all of the variances—favorable as well as unfavorable—Martelli advises.

Discrepancies can have simple explanations. "Sometimes there's miscommunication about where you planned to have the budget items go and where accounting posted them," Martelli says. Or a discrepancy might be a matter of timing, she says. For example, health insurance premiums might have to be paid in advance for not just one month but for six, so the variance will likely even out over time.

But variances can also reflect judgment errors, and by determining how such errors occurred, an HR manager might prevent them in budgeting for the following year.

Eggers says variances "put up flags that we're starting to run off the road." That means HR managers "need to drill down and take a closer look at that particular line item."

However, just because an item comes in under budget doesn't necessarily mean things are going well. A drop in wage outlays, for example, could mean that employees are being sent home because sales have declined and production isn't going as planned—and that could affect HR's budget in other ways, such as overtime costs.

HR managers should look closely at what they can do to reduce variances, some experts advise. If there is an unexpectedly high amount of overtime, for example, it might suggest a need to hire another person. And to cover a deficit in the short run, Martelli says, an HR manager might want to borrow funds from discretionary spending or postpone a departmental function.

Eggers suggests looking at both the absolute numbers and the percentages of any variances to determine their impact on the company. And to find out why variances are occurring, he adds, HR managers should get out from behind their desks and talk with the managers who can provide answers and insight.

Write Down What You See

In addition to examining variances, experts say, HR managers should make notes of what they observe as they go along. Lisa Auerbach, vice president of finance and human resources at Broad Street Community Newspapers in Philadelphia, suggests keeping a simple Word document in the computer that recaps each month's findings.

If health care costs are up $5,000 in a certain month because six new hires joined the payroll the previous month, she says, make a note of it. If hiring more employees caused drug-test costs to go over budget one month, write it down. Or if the numbers indicate that turnover is increasing, note it, there might be a problem in the company that needs to be addressed immediately.

Keeping track on a monthly basis is much easier than getting six months down the road and trying to remember why there were overages in a particular line item. "Budgeting is tough enough without having to spin your wheels," Auerbach says.

Don't Keep The News a Secret

HR's findings about its own budget trends should be shared with others in the top echelons of an organization, Phillips says. "Lots of costs you incur in the HR budget might be things going on in other areas" of the company, such as sexual harassment complaints tied to a supervisor in a particular department.

Corporate leaders also should be apprised of the costs associated with employee turnover, says consultant Seagraves. "There are a lot of hidden costs that upper-level managers just don't calculate."

Seagraves too recommends that budget results be shared with others in the corporation, which can help HR managers gather allies and manage perceptions. If things aren't going according to the budget plan, the HR manager should be the first to know about it so he or she can develop proposals to address the problem. "Still share the news," Seagraves says. "One of the worst things you can do is sit on not-so-great data and surprise people later."

Consider An Alternative Approach

Phillips of the ROI Institute suggests that HR managers think about budgeting along process lines—looking at the activities they undertake to develop a new program or maintain an existing one.

Before implementing a new program, Phillips says, HR managers should take their time and devote some resources to determine if the new program is necessary.

If it's decided that a new program is needed, the HR manager then should compare the costs of designing and developing the program with the costs of acquiring it. For example, if HR is looking for a way to improve retention, the department might design its own solution or pay a consultant to develop one.

Then the manager should consider the costs of implementing the program and making sure that it works, followed by the costs of maintaining the program to ensure that it functions properly.

The final cost would be for evaluating the program to determine its effectiveness and whether it is beneficial for the company.

Phillips says that sometimes programs are introduced with insufficient advance analysis and carried forward with insufficient spending to evaluate their results. "That gets [HR managers] into trouble for not being able to show the contribution" of the program to the company.

Keep an Eye On the Big Picture

HR managers need to stay abreast not only of changes that directly affect their department but also of changes in their particular industry and in the overall economy.

Auerbach of the Philadelphia newspaper group says HR managers need to be aware of changes in the cost of benefits, for example, and determine how costs should be divided between employer and employees. "This could be a pretty huge impact on your budget," she says.

In addition, Auerbach says, HR managers should stay in close touch with other departments, be aware of any company plans to expand or downsize its workforce, and keep tabs on "any unusual things that happened in the current year that should factor into your baseline budget."

Martelli encourages HR managers to look beyond what is happening within their company. "You really have to understand the market," she says. If the unemployment rate is low, for example, it may be harder to recruit the best employees. Look at what the competition is doing, she says, and if you find your company is paying less than competitors are, be aware that you may be hiring less-qualified new workers.

As you look toward the budgeting process for 2006, don't be intimidated, experts say. And don't be afraid to ask for help, says Auerbach, who recommends that you sit down with someone from your company's finance side to go over the budget.

Seagraves takes a similar approach regarding a common concern of HR managers about budgeting: "Get over that fear of estimating," she says. "Every other area of business is using estimates to a certain extent." To estimate well, she continues, "be consistent, be conservative and be thorough enough that you're credible."

And always keep in mind, Eggers says, that budgeting is a flexible process. "Things are going to change," he says. "That's OK. One thing we know about the budget." "It will not happen exactly that way."

Susan Ladika, *based in Tampa, Fla., has been a journalist for more than 20 years and has worked in both the United States and Europe. Her freelance work has appeared in such publications as* The Wall Street Journal-Europe *and* The Economist.

From *HR Magazine,* January 2005, pp. 79-81. Reprinted with the permission of HR Magazine, published by the Society for Human Resource Management, Alexandria, VA, via the Copyright Clearance Center.

Corporate Security Management: What's Common? What Works?

Security Director's Report

There exists a sharp division between what companies do—and don't do—as part of their security process, according to *SDR's 2005 Security Management and Salary Survey*, which analyzed security operations at hundreds of companies. For example, the survey discovered that about half of companies write security responsibilities into managers' job descriptions, while half don't. A similar split exists among many security strategies, from using a workplace violence prevention team to developing performance metrics.

A lack of regulation is at the heart of this incongruity. Unlike, say, health and safety—where companies operate under specific mandates for training, recordkeeping, and in other program areas—companies can largely choose which security strategies to implement. Although being free from regulatory oversight has clear advantages, it also makes it harder for a company to know if it's doing what it should, which makes evaluating the approach of other companies and understanding what is common practice a critical element in effective security strategic planning. To understand the universality of different security management strategies, see the table, "Prevalence of Select Security Management Strategies, by Company Size, 2005."

What works? To gauge their affect, we analyzed the presence of different security strategies against staff turnover and dismissal rates, security budget trends, and security incident data. Toward the goal of preventing crime, we discovered the best solutions typically include a technical, administrative, *and* human component. As one would expect, the survey suggests there is no magic bullet for preventing different types of security incident.

In the area of department management, the survey data suggest that security departments that actively work to increase the profile of the security function—via conducting new employee orientations, measuring employees on their understanding of security policies and procedures, delivering issue-specific training, or developing performance metrics—realize a benefit for their time and effort. It's impossible to pinpoint exactly which security controls or management strategies deserve the most credit, but the data show a multifaceted, aggressive, and proactive security operation appears to be more successful in reducing security events and more effective at driving superior department performance than security programs that rely more heavily on an incident response model. The survey found specifically strong correlations in the following areas:

Department management:

• **Performance metrics.** Security departments that have in place quantitative performance measures reported a better change to their 2005 budget than security departments that don't use metrics—although the difference was not dramatic. (Of security departments that use performance measures, 12.1% received a 2005 budget increase of 7% or more. Of companies that don't, only 7.3% experienced as significant a budget increase.)

Of course, it's impossible to isolate this single factor as a direct cause of the companies' better budget picture, but the results do support what one might expect—that managers will spend money more freely in areas where they can see progress toward a goal. Security performance measures provide management with just such a picture.

• **ROI reporting.** Security directors, who in 2004 reported to management on the monetary return-on-investment (ROI) of security projects, purchases, and expenditures, were more likely to report a 2005 budget increase. (Over half, 58%, of security departments that reported on ROI said they had a budget increase in 2005. By comparison, only 48% of de-

Prevalence of Select Security Management Strategies, by Company Size, 2005

Security Management Strategy	Number of Employees: 1 to 500	501 to 5,000	5,001 or More	All
Conduct drug screening of job applicants	65%	71%	75%	71%
Conduct drug screening of existing employees	35	45	50	44
Conduct drug screening of all security department staff	47	62	52	55
Combine information and physical security under one department	34	35	29	32
Define quantitative performance metrics for the security department	32	55	70	53
Have a security committee with representatives from several depts.	24	42	45	38
Write security responsibilities into managers job descriptions	49	63	39	51
Include adherence to security standards in manager performance reviews	45	56	38	47
Use a workplace violence prevention team to administer prevention	37	55	63	52
Train all supervisors on how to handle workplace violence	54	66	64	61
Provide workplace violence awareness training to all employees	44	65	59	56
Test employees to measure awareness of proper security procedures	50	46	50	49
Provide theft prevention training to staff with laptops/portable devices	40	51	50	47
Security department speaks at new employee orientations	62	74	64	66
Security department attends board meetings to brief on security issues	40	50	46	45
Conduct internal client surveys to measure security performance	37	43	55	46
Track the speed of response to security incidents	52	49	68	56
Enter all security incidents into a computerized database	53	68	80	67
Require employees to wear identification badges	69	89	91	84
Provide temporary and contract workers with ID badges	79	92	95	89
Use computer-based training (software/online) in security training	46	63	68	60
Have in place a formal mentoring program for security officers	31	48	42	41
Use security officers to perform nonsecurity-related functions	53	63	51	56
Have a formal career development program for guards	16	40	35	31
Have guards with specific, formal counterterrorism training	15	25	20	20

(Source: SDRs 2005 Security Management & Security Salary)

partments that did not report on ROI had an increase, the rest had their budgets cut or kept the same.

Staff management:

• **Training.** The security officer turnover rate is significantly lower (14% vs. 31%) at companies that use computer-based training (either software or online) as a part of their security officer training program.

• **Competency testing.** The percentage of security staff dismissed for cause in the last 12 months is higher at companies that conduct measured competency testing of its security staff (11% vs. 7.9%). This may suggest that measured testing helps companies to identify and rid itself of poor performers who are a detriment to the functioning of the department.

• **Drug testing.** The percentage of security staff dismissed for cause in the last 12 months is lower at companies that drug test security job applicants (6.0% vs. 19.9%). This may indicate that some companies are effectively using pre-employment drug screening to reduce its number of bad security department hires.

• **In-house vs. contract.** Proprietary security officers are significantly more likely to have received specific, formal counterterrorism training than contract guards (51.5% vs. 9.1%). Security departments that have in-house officers are also more likely to have defined quantitative performance metrics for the security department and to track the speed of response to security incidents.

Crime prevention:

- **New employee orientation.** Companies where the security department formally addresses new employees reported fewer employee theft incidents per 100 employees (0.85 vs. 1.4). Such data suggest that this simple strategy may be extremely useful for impressing upon new hires that the company takes security seriously and, setting this tone may lead to fewer violations of company rules and procedures.

- **Drug testing.** Companies that drug test in the pre-hire process and those that screen existing employees reported substantially lower rates of employee theft (0.6 theft incidents per 100 employees vs. 1.3).

Quality is Easy

The secret of zero defects and the seven laws of defect prevention make quality a snap.

David C. Crosby

Thousands and thousands of manufacturers struggle every day trying to guard the back door of their organization to stop defective products and services from reaching the customer. For the most part, it is a thankless and impossible job. Many times there are toe-to-toe, nose-to-nose arguments and even an occasional fistfight.

Actually, it is easy and even fun to produce a quality product or deliver a quality service. If one has the skills, the equipment and the right attitude, why would it not be easy? But the toe-to-toe disagreements do happen, defective products are delivered and shoddy services are performed.

It is only when top management takes charge and sets the correct performance standard, and then backs it with time and money, that a quality product or service is delivered. Then, quality is easy.

Defects, or mistakes, must be prevented, not found and fixed. There are several important elements in preventing defects. The zero defects (ZD) concept and the right quality management and control tools can make it happen. However, if the ZD concept is not understood, the tools will not work. And if the tools are not used, the ZD concept can work against a manufacturer.

CONCEPT OF ZERO DEFECTS

Phil Crosby created the ZD concept, and had a wonderful challenge for those who wanted to argue about it. He simply asked, "What part of zero don't you understand?" Zero means no or none; defects are characteristics that do not meet the specification.

Forgotten by many and unknown by most people under 40, zero defects was probably the simplest and most effective defect prevention tool ever conceived. From about 1960 to the mid-1970s, every major company in the United States conducted a zero defects program: General Electric, General Motors, Ford, RCA, Sylvania, Chrysler, Martin, Lockheed and Boeing, as well as the U.S. Army, Navy and Air Force. They all had a ZD program, as did thousands of their suppliers. There was even an American Society for Zero Defects. Today, few companies have such a program.

Why is the zero defects movement almost extinct? Many companies that had a ZD program did not really understand how it worked; they just put up posters. Now, the same people are off chasing other ideas such as Total Quality Management or Six Sigma. New ideas come along, but the zero defects idea is sound and it always works. For quality to be easy, understand and implement the ZD concept and use the tools of quality management.

DEFINITION

Skeptics seem to equate zero defects with perfection. That is only true if perfection is the quality standard. A defect is a characteristic that does not conform to its quality standard—a mistake or an error. So, zero defects does not mean perfection; it means no mistakes or no errors.

Very few, if any, quality standards call for perfection. There is usually some target requirement and some sort of tolerance limit. If a characteristic exceeds the tolerance limits, it is defective; it is a mistake. Zero defects does not mean that mistakes will never happen—zero defects means that defects are never acceptable. Zero defects is a performance standard. That is as complicated as it gets.

A PERFORMANCE STANDARD

When correctly presented, ZD tells all employees that defects are not acceptable in any part of the company activity. The zero defects performance standard must be applied to all departments including accounting, engineering, human resources, purchasing, production, quality, maintenance, sales and marketing, as well as to suppliers. If defects do occur—and they will—action must be taken to prevent their recurrence. If management does not adopt and make the standard of zero defects clear, employees will search for the performance standard they think will please their leader. If management is inconsistent in its performance standard, the quality of products and services will be inconsistent.

Of course, everything starts with the top executive—the boss. The boss must adopt zero defects in his personal performance standard. He must make it clear that zero defects is the standard for each and every direct report, and those managers must pass it on. The zero defects performance standard must travel all the way down the food chain. If a manager, supervisor or employee cannot accept the zero defects performance standard, get rid of them. Who wants an employee, particularly a manager, who thinks it is okay to make mistakes?

If a manager does not understand the zero defects performance standard, has a problem even saying the words or cannot demand zero defects performance, then there will always be a few defects to manage. Time and creative talent will be spent finding and fixing problems, explaining embarrassing mistakes and ultimately paying the price with lost profit.

SEVEN LAWS OF DEFECT PREVENTION

There are seven natural laws that govern zero defects. These laws apply in commercial and consumer manufacturing and service organizations. These rules apply to government and military operations. They apply to all organizations.

In organizations where the seven laws are understood and followed, products and services are produced that consistently conform to the quality requirements. These are happy companies with happy customers. Where these laws are unknown, or ignored, the reverse is true.

The moral is this: Understand and follow these seven simple laws to reach zero defects.

1 People perform to the standards set, or accepted, by their leader.

Stated another way, the product or service looks like the management. Employees want to know what is expected of them. They spend a good bit of time wondering what their leader wants. If the leader does not make a performance standard clear, people will perform to the standard they think their leader wants.

A manager who does not understand that he is the one who determines the quality of the product or service is easy to spot. If a customer finds a defective product, the manager yells, "How did that get out?"

It got out because it was made incorrectly. It was made incorrectly because that manager made his performance standard clear that a few mistakes are acceptable. The question itself puts the blame on the inspector. No action will be taken to prevent the defect, it will happen again and the manager will scream again. The cycle will continue.

Zero defects does not mean that mistakes will never happen—zero defects means that defects are never acceptable.

2 Quality means conformance to the requirement.

There are many, many definitions of quality. The definition conformance to the requirement lets a manufacturer know if he has a quality product or service, or if he has something else. If the requirement needs to be changed, officially change it.

3 Quality is an absolute.

A product or service either conforms to its requirements or it does not. If it conforms, it is quality. If it does not, it is something else. Consider the field goal kicker in football. The quality requirement is to kick the ball over the crossbar, between the goal posts. If the ball sails anywhere between the posts and over the bar, points are awarded. That is quality. If the ball goes anywhere else in the entire universe, it is something else. Quality is an absolute.

4 All products and services must have clear quality standards.

The quality standards are the specifications—the requirement with which to conform. Such specifications can be found on engineering drawings, photographs, manuals, models and other formal documents. One might think this law would be automatic—of course all manufacturers have clear documented quality standards. Then why are those people arguing about what is correct and what is not? If quality is conformance to the requirement, the requirement must be clear and formal, not subject to unofficial change. If one cannot conform to the requirement, maybe the requirement should be officially changed to what the manufacturer and customer really need.

5 All errors are caused by a combination of three things: poor attitude, lack of ability and built-in problems in the workplace.

Attitudes are thought habits that can be changed. Lack of ability can sometimes be improved with training. Problems in the workplace must be identified and eliminated. A zero defects mentality deals with these error causes.

Sometimes people have a dual attitude. They tend to demand error-flee work in the things they buy or the services they receive, but when it comes to their own work, a few defects are acceptable. After all, they are only human, and "to err is human." Ask that same person how many defects are acceptable in the new car he plans to buy. How many mistakes can his dentist make? Are a few mistakes in his paycheck acceptable? Zero defects attacks the dual standard.

Employees must have the ability to do their work correctly, or they usually will do it wrong. It is common for the human resources department not to feel responsibility for the quality of the product or service. But, they are the ones who select and hire the people who make the mistakes. Hiring is a good place to start quality improvement.

Forgotten by many and unknown by most people under 40, zero defects was probably the simplest and most effective defect prevention tool ever conceived.

6 The boss is responsible for quality.

The boss must set the performance standard and provide the wherewithal to produce a quality product or service. If the product or service does not meet its quality requirements, it is the boss' fault. While the responsibility for quality can be shared, the boss' share never gets smaller. The responsibility for quality cannot be given to the quality department, quality circles, Six Sigma black belts or any other person. The product or service looks like the management.

7 The boss must adopt the performance standard of zero defects and make it known.

The performance standard of zero defects means that no defects are acceptable, and that if they occur, corrective action will be taken to prevent them from recurring. The ZD performance standard also means that quality management will accept and promote the idea of preventing defects, not finding them and fixing them.

QUALITY IS EASY

It can be easy and enjoyable to produce a quality product or service. Wrestling with defective products and placating angry customers is a miserable way to live. Either way, it all starts with the boss.

If an organization is struggling with quality problems, question the performance standard. Is it clear? Does it permit defects? Is the performance standard zero defects? Six Sigma says a few defects are acceptable.

Question the attitude of employees at all levels. Then find out if people have the ability to do mistake-free work. Finally, a manager should ask employees about built-in problems in their workplace that prevent them from doing their work correctly every time. Get rid of those problems.

***David C. Crosby** is founder and president of The Crosby Co. (Wedron, IL). He can be contacted at crosby@qualitynews.com. For more information, visit* www.qualitynews.com.

Mail Preparation Total Quality Management

A candid conversation with John Wargo, U.S. Postal Service vice president, Service & Market Development, regarding the postal service's premier mail quality program.

by Richard W. Pavely, MSE

About 3.5 trillion letters ago, the U.S. Postal Service (USPS) embarked on the longest and most successful automation program in American business history, the Automation Plan for Business Mailers. That program, also known as Work Sharing, elevated the process by which the postal service sorted and distributed mail throughout the postal system by introducing POSTNET bar coding and other automation technology. Without it, it's estimated that a 1-ounce First Class letter would now require well over $2 in postage. Key to the success of that Herculean effort was the enlistment of the cooperation and support of the business mailers by offering deep discounts on postage for preparing and submitting automation-compatible mail.

Now, nearly two decades later, the postal service is again embarking on another arduous journey into deeper reaches of improved customer service by incorporating the best and the brightest features of three internationally recognized quality methodologies: the ISO 9000, the Malcolm Baldrige Performance Excellence criteria, and Total Quality Management.

The Mail Preparation Total Quality Management (MPTQM) program is designed to help businesses prepare letter mailings that meet or exceed postal service processing quality standards. Designed by industry mailers, it's a complete system of realistic quality control measures and standardized assessment procedures. It applies to all aspects of the mail preparation process, from the generation and bar coding of a letter to the final sorting and containerizing that takes place just prior to presenting the mailing to the postal service.

To assess the progress of the program and gain a better understanding of the benefits and requirements for participating, this author traveled to USPS Marketing Headquarters in Alexandria, Va. to interview John Wargo, vice president, Service and Management Development. Here are the highlights of that interview, followed by an assessment of the business consequences for participating in the MPTQM program.

OS: Why did the postal service choose to develop the MPTQM program to assure a quality process when other quality programs, such as the Malcolm Baldrige and ISO 9000 programs, already existed?

Wargo: Our initial action was to form an advisory group of postal service customers to help us define the quality program. We began by reviewing the specifications we require for mail and studying the processes the mailers use to produce it. This naturally drove us to a standards- and process management-based approach to quality. We then reviewed the other international methodologies, such as ISO, and decided our approach was more in depth and focused. We borrowed many ideas from those methodologies to strengthen MPTQM, however.

OS: What does the postal service hope to gain from the MPTQM program?

Wargo: Our goal is customer satisfaction. MPTQM will help ease the entry of business mail into our processing and distribution streams... Error free mail will sail through the mail acceptance process. High-quality mail also ensures timely delivery. The resulting customer satisfaction will drive increased use of the mail.

OS: Does the MPTQM program only apply to presort service bureaus and super high-volume mailers?

Wargo: We began MPTQM with presort service bureaus because of the complexity of their mailings. Many other large-volume mailers also have complicated mailings, and some of those mailers are now in the program. Improving quality first with these mailers is in line with our goals. All business mailers are welcome to participate.

OS: Who are list mailers?

Wargo: This is a term we use in the program for all but presort service bureaus. Most, but not all, of these mailers perform mail sortation from a computerized list versus an automated letter sorter or MLOCR (multi-line optical character reader). That's the origin of the term.

OS: Why would a list mailer benefit from becoming certified under the MPTQM program?

"Our goal is customer satisfaction. MPTQM will help ease the entry of business mail into our processing and distribution streams... Error free mail will sail through the mail acceptance process."

Wargo: Program materials, including a training video and work aids, are free. Audits are free. Mail verifications are to be reduced, and fewer postage adjustments will be applied. There are a number of internal benefits mailers are seeing. Some are less down time on machines, fewer rejections of mail, fewer postage adjustments for poor quality, more employee pride in the company, an improved employee retention rate, reduced training costs.

OS: How long does it normally take to become certified in the program?

Wargo: About 12, months from the point of dedicated implementation.

OS: If a firm already has an existing quality program in place, can all or part of that program be incorporated into the MPTQM process? Or would they have to start from scratch with the MPTQM program?

Wargo: Mailers in this situation should contact Scott Hamel for guidance. He can be reached at 703/292-3824 or via the Internet at shamel@email.usps.gov. Following a telephone discussion and mailer registration, he will provide [them with] an MPTQM guidebook, which gives instructions on getting started and includes a "Gap Analysis" for mailers with existing quality programs to use.

OS: Would MPTQM certification be a useful procurement criterion for those firms who purchase production mail products and services from presort service bureaus or list mailers?

Wargo: Definitely. Our plans, in fact, are to move in that direction.

OS: How is the postal service organized to support the program? Are you using field personnel or contractors to conduct the audits?

Wargo: Scott Hamel, who works in the technical side of our headquarters marketing organization, is the program manager. He has a staff of 30 analysts who conduct mailer audits with the support of our district business mail entry offices. Most of his analysts now are Certified Quality Auditors through the American Society for Quality (ASQ). They lead the audits. A contractor was used to help establish this part of the program.

OS: How successful is the program?

Wargo: We are very excited with the results to date. The involved mailers continue to praise the value the process adds to their companies. Our relationships with these customers have improved. In terms of MPTQM's impact on mail quality, we will be building a performance measurement process this spring.

OS: How many service bureaus are certified?

Wargo: Twenty-eight service bureaus are certified.

OS: How many list mailers are certified?

Wargo: Five list mailers are certified.

OS: Do you have some advice for those who are considering investing in the rigors of certification?

Wargo: Interested mailers should contact Scott Hamel who can answer [their] questions and put them in touch with a few certified mailers who have processes most like theirs. Involved mailers have expressed great willingness to share their experiences with others. They recognize that the more MPTQM players we have, the healthier the entire mailing industry will be.

OS: What are your predictions for the MPTQM program?

Wargo: Within three years, all major-volume, and some lesser-volume, mailers will be installing the program. Large-volume postal customers will require their vendors, particularly lettershops and presort service bureaus, to be MPTQM certified.

OS Summary: From a business standpoint, the MPTQM program makes incredibly good sense. The cost to implement it is easy to justify. For starters, anytime you take an excellent program like Malcolm Baldrige and customize it to your unique situation, you raise the likelihood that the end result will be significantly improved. In addition to protecting the discounts that a mailer already enjoys, which can be measured in millions of dollars per year for a production mailer, certification under this program will result in less frequent verifications on the receiving dock, faster insertion into the system, and fewer of the new and nasty postage adjustments.

Furthermore, the routine application of quality standards within a production process will shorten the time for instituting corrective actions and reduce the cost of imbedded systemic problems, which would otherwise remain hidden in the turmoil of production activity.

Obviously, the postal service can't check everything it receives. By qualifying for MPTQM, the mailer positions his or her firm's mail as highly reliable and, therefore, not requiring further attention. That way, the postal service can concentrate its inspection efforts where serious problems are more likely to exist.

Richard W. Pavely, MSE, is president of Corporate Management & Marketing Consultants Inc. of Randolph, N.J. He's an active member of ASO, AQP, MSMA, and several Postal Customer Councils. He can be reached at 973/989-0229 or via the Internet at rpavely@cmmcinc.com.

UNIT 6

Staffing and Human Resources

Unit Selections

Key Points to Consider

- What do you think of the idea of a "Mommy Track?" What do you think of the idea of a "Daddy Track?" What do you think this does to people's careers in highly competitive organizations?
- What do you think about the health-care situation in the United States? Should everyone have health care? Should it be tied to employment?
- Outsourcing of jobs has become a very controversial issue in the United States and other developed countries. Do you think this trend will continue? Do you think your job might ever be outsourced? What do you think you could do to prevent it from being outsourced?
- There is likely to be a shortage of labor in the United States in the next ten to twenty years. Where do you think additional workers may come from? Where is there likely to be an untapped supply?

Student Website

www.mhcls.com/online

Internet References

Further information regarding these websites may be found in this book's preface or online.

Electronic Frontier Foundation "Privacy" Archive
http://www.eff.org

School of Labor and Industrial Relations Hot Links
http://www.lir.msu.edu/hotlinks

U.S. Equal Employment Opportunity Commission
http://www.eeoc.gov

Managers of organizations get things done through people. Managers can plan, organize, direct, and control, but the central focus of all their efforts is people. People determine whether an organization is going to succeed, and the way that people perceive their treatment by management is often the key to that success. In today's world, it is necessary to recognize that people have different needs, wants, and desires. Women have different needs than men that the organization will have to address if it wants to hold on to top performers. Some of these differences are discussed by Felice Schwartz in "Management Women and the New Facts of Life," the article that started the talk about the "Mommy Track," which soon led to talk about the "Daddy Track."

Since human resources are a key to the success of any organization, firms need to hire the very best people they can find because it is people who make the plans, organize the operation, direct the processes to accomplish the organizational goals, and evaluate the results. But while people contribute directly to a firm's success, they also represent a significant cost to the organization. Not only salaries, but also the costs of benefits are rising at an alarming rate. Benefits cost more today than just a few years ago, and workers not only want to keep the benefits they have but seek to add others. Some of their demands include dental and eye care plans, child care, and senior care for their relatives. The Americans with Disabilities Act has also established new criteria for employees with disabilities.

The workforce is changing. It includes more minorities, women, and other groups with different needs and if a corporation wants to hire these people, many of whom are outstanding, they are going to have to meet their needs. Otherwise, these potential employees will go elsewhere, frequently to the competition. No organization can afford to turn its back on such a large pool of potential talent. In the future, that pool of potential talent is likely to include retirees as discussed in "Turning Boomers Into Boomerangs." However, because of the increasing demand for qualified employees, organizations will have to do everything possible to retain good workers, but, they need to be careful in who they are hiring.

Firms are responding to changes in the workforce in a variety of ways. To meet the needs of the future, management must recognize that people, organizations, and the environment will continue to evolve, and that what motivates workers will change in the future. Outsourcing will become a real option for many organizations as professional and white-collar jobs are sent in increasing numbers to other countries. This movement of jobs outside of the developed world will not be without problems, however. There is certain to be a shakeout of these organizations in the developing countries as this industry matures, as discussed in "The Next Bubble?"

Maintaining an effective workforce will be an overarching goal for all organizations in the future. However, organizations in the United States are faced with a dilemma. The workforce in the United States will probably decrease in number over the next several decades as more baby boomers leave, either through retirement or death and fewer younger workers enter the workforce. This demand for workers will be addressed in one of several ways:

(1) people will work longer and retire later, which is already being done;
(2) more immigrants will be allowed into the country; and/or
(3) American workers will put in more hours on the job, something they are already doing.

Management Women and the New Facts of Life

Felice N. Schwartz

The cost of employing women in management is greater than the cost of employing men. This is a jarring statement, partly because it is true, but mostly because it is something people are reluctant to talk about. A new study by one multinational corporation shows that the rate of turnover in management positions is 2 ½ times higher among top-performing women than it is among men. A large producer of consumer goods reports that one half of the women who take maternity leave return to their jobs late or not at all. And we know that women also have a greater tendency to plateau or to interrupt their careers in ways that limit their growth and development. But we have become so sensitive to charges of sexism and so afraid of confrontation, even litigation, that we rarely say what we know to be true. Unfortunately, our bottled-up awareness leaks out in misleading metaphors ("glass ceiling" is one notable example), veiled hostility, lowered expectations, distrust and reluctant adherence to Equal Employment Opportunity requirements.

Career interruptions, plateauing, and turnover are expensive. The money corporations invest in recruitment, training, and development is less likely to produce top executives among women than among men, and the invaluable company experience that developing executives acquire at every level as they move up through management ranks is more often lost.

The studies just mentioned are only the first of many, I'm quite sure. Demographic realities are going to force corporations all across the country to analyze the cost of employing women in managerial positions, and what they will discover is that women cost more.

But here is another startling truth: The greater cost of employing women is not a function of inescapable gender differences. Women *are* different from men, but what increases their cost to the corporation is principally the clash of their perceptions, attitudes, and behavior with those of men, which is to say, with the policies and practices of male-led corporations.

It is terribly important that employers draw the right conclusions from the studies now being done. The studies will be useless—or worse, harmful—if all they teach us is that women are expensive to employ. What we need to learn is how to reduce that expense, how to stop throwing away the investments we make in talented women, how to become more responsive to the needs of the women that corporations *must* employ if they are to have the best and the brightest of all those now entering the work force.

Two facts matter to business: only women have babies and only men make rules.

The gender differences relevant to business fall into two categories: those related to maternity and those related to the differing traditions and expectations of the sexes. Maternity is biological rather than cultural. We can't alter it but we can dramatically reduce its impact on the workplace and in many cases eliminate its negative effect on employee development. We can accomplish this by addressing the second set of differences, those between male and female socialization. Today, these differences exaggerate the real costs of maternity and can turn a relatively slight disruption in work schedule into a serious business problem and a career derailment for individual women. If we are to overcome the cost differential between male and female employees, we need to address the issues that arise when female socialization meets the male corporate culture and masculine rules of career development—issues of behavior and style, of expectation, of stereotypes and preconceptions, of sexual tension and harassment, of female mentoring, lateral mobility relocation, compensation, and early identification of top performers.

The one immutable, enduring difference between men and women is maternity. Maternity is not simply childbirth but a continuum that begins with an awareness of the ticking of the biological clock, proceeds to the anticipation of motherhood, includes pregnancy, childbirth, physical recuperation, psychological adjustment, and continues on to nursing, bonding, and child rearing. Not all women choose to become mothers, of course, and among those who do, the process varies from case to case depending on the health of the mother and baby, the values of the parents, and the availability, cost, and quality of child care.

In past centuries, the biological fact of maternity shaped the traditional roles of the sexes. Women performed the home-centered functions that related to the bearing and nurturing of children. Men did the work that required great physical strength. Over time, however, family size contracted, the community assumed greater responsibility for the care and education of children, packaged foods and household technology reduced the work load in the home, and technology eliminated much of the need for muscle power at the workplace. Today, in the developed world, the only role still uniquely gender related is childbearing. Yet men and women are still socialized to perform their traditional roles.

Men and women may or may not have some innate psychological disposition toward these traditional roles—men to be aggressive, competitive, self-reliant, risk taking; women to be supportive, nurturing, intuitive, sensitive, communicative—but certainly both men and women are capable of the full range of behavior. Indeed, the male and female roles have already begun to expand and merge. In the decades ahead, as the socialization of boys and girls and the experience and expectations of young men and women grow steadily more androgynous, the differences in workplace behavior will continue to fade. At the moment, however, we are still plagued by disparities in perception and behavior that make the integration of men and women in the workplace unnecessarily difficult and expensive.

Let me illustrate with a few broadbrush generalizations. Of course, these are only stereotypes, but I think they help to exemplify the kinds of preconceptions that muddy the corporate waters.

Women who compete like men are considered unfeminine. Women who emphasize family are considered uncommitted.

Men continue to perceive women as the rearers of their children, so they find it understandable, indeed appropriate, that women should renounce their careers to raise families. Edmund Pratt, CEO of Pfizer, once asked me in all sincerity, "Why would any woman choose to be a chief financial officer rather than a full-time mother?" By condoning and taking pleasure in women's traditional behavior, men reinforce it. Not only do they see parenting as fundamentally female, they see a career as fundamentally male—either an unbroken series of promotions and advancements toward CEOdom or stagnation and disappointment. This attitude serves to legitimize a woman's choice to extend maternity leave and even, for those who can afford it, to leave employment altogether for several years. By the same token, men who might want to take a leave after the birth of a child know that management will see such behavior as a lack of career commitment, even when company policy permits parental leave for men.

Women also bring counterproductive expectations and perceptions to the workplace. Ironically, although the feminist movement was an expression of women's quest for freedom from their home-based lives, most women were remarkably free already. They had many responsibilities, but they were autonomous and could be entrepreneurial in how and when they carried them out. And once their children grew up and left home, they were essentially free to do what they wanted with their lives. Women's traditional role also included freedom from responsibility for the financial support of their families. Many of us were socialized from girlhood to expect our husbands to take care of us, while our brothers were socialized from an equally early age to complete their educations, pursue careers, climb the ladder of success, and provide dependable financial support for their families. To the extent that this tradition of freedom lingers subliminally, women tend to bring to their employment a sense that they can choose to change jobs or careers at will, take time off, or reduce their hours.

Finally, women's traditional role encouraged particular attention to the quality and substance of what they did, specifically to the physical, psychological, and intellectual development of their children. This traditional focus may explain women's continuing tendency to search for more than monetary reward—intrinsic significance, social importance, meaning—in what they do. This too makes them more likely than men to leave the corporation in search of other values.

The misleading metaphor of the glass ceiling suggests an invisible barrier constructed by corporate leaders to impede the upward mobility of women beyond the middle levels. A more appropriate metaphor, I believe, is the kind of cross-sectional diagram used in geology. The barriers to women's leadership occur when potentially counterproductive layers of influence on women—maternity, tradition, socialization—meet management strata pervaded by the largely unconscious preconceptions, stereotypes, and expectations of men. Such interfaces do not exist for men and tend to be impermeable for women.

One result of these gender differences has been to convince some executives that women are simply not suited to top management. Other executives feel helpless. If they see even a few of their valued female employees fail to return to work from maternity leave on schedule or see one of their most promising women plateau in her career after the birth of a child, they begin to fear there is nothing they can do to infuse women with new energy and enthusiasm and persuade them to stay. At the same time, they know there is nothing they can do to stem the tide of women into management ranks.

Another result is to place every working woman on a continuum that runs from total dedication to career at one end to a balance between career and family at the other. What women discover is that the male corporate culture sees both extremes as unacceptable. Women who want the flexibility to balance their families and their careers are not adequately committed to the organization. Women who perform as aggressively and competitively as men are abrasive and unfeminine. But the fact is, business needs all the talented women it can get. Moreover, as I will explain, the women I call career-primary and those I call career-and-family each have particular value to the corporation.

With too few men to go around, women have moved from a buyer's to a seller's market.

Women in the corporation are about to move from a buyer's to a seller's market. The sudden, startling recognition that 80% of new entrants in the work force over the next decade will be women, minorities, and immigrants has stimulated a mushrooming incentive to "value diversity."

Women are no longer simply an enticing pool of occasional creative talent, a thorn in the side of the EEO officer, or a source of frustration to corporate leaders truly puzzled by the slowness of their upward trickle into executive positions. A real demographic change is taking place. The era of sudden population growth of the 1950s and 1960s is over. The birth rate has dropped about 40%, from a high of 25.3 live births per 1,000 population in 1957, at the peak of the baby boom, to a stable low of a little more than 15 per 1,000 over the last 16 years, and there is no indication of a return to a higher rate. The tidal wave of baby boomers that swelled the recruitment pool to overflowing seems to have been a one-time phenomenon. For 20 years, employers had the pick of a very large crop and were able to choose males almost exclusively for the executive track. But if future population remains fairly stable while the economy continues to expand, and if the new information society simultaneously creates a greater need for creative, educated managers, then the gap between supply and demand will grow dramatically and, with it, the competition for managerial talent.

The decrease in numbers has even greater implications if we look at the traditional source of corporate recruitment for leadership positions—white males from the top 10% of the country's best universities. Over the past decade, the increase in the number of women graduating from leading universities has been much greater than the increase in the total number of graduates, and these women are well represented in the top 10% of their classes.

The trend extends into business and professional programs as well. In the old days, virtually all MBAs were male. I remember addressing a meeting at the Harvard Business School as recently as the mid-1970s and looking out at a sea of exclusively male faces. Today, about 25% of that audience would be women. The pool of male MBAs from which corporations have traditionally drawn their leaders has shrunk significantly.

Of course, this reduction does not have to mean a shortage of talent. The top 10% is at least as smart as it always was—smarter, probably, since it's now drawn from a broader segment of the population. But it now consists increasingly of women. Companies that are determined to recruit the same number of men as before will have to dig much deeper into the male pool, while their competitors will have the opportunity to pick the best people from both the male and female graduates.

Under these circumstances, there is no question that the management ranks of business will include increasing numbers of women. There remains, however, the question of how these women will succeed—how long they will stay, how high they will climb, how completely they will fulfill their promise and potential, and what kind of return the corporation will realize on its investment in their training and development.

There is ample business reason for finding ways to make sure that as many of these women as possible will succeed. The first step in this process is to recognize that women are not all alike. Like men, they are individuals with differing talents, priorities, and motivations. For the sake of simplicity, let me focus on the two women I referred to earlier, on what I call the career-primary woman and the career-and-family woman.

It is absurd to put women down for having the very qualities that would send a man to the top.

Like many men, some women put their careers first. They are ready to make the same trade-offs traditionally made by the men who seek leadership positions. They make a career decision to put in extra hours, to make sacrifices in their personal lives, to make the most of every opportunity for professional development. For women, of course, this decision also requires that they remain single or at least childless or, if they do have children, that they be satisfied to have others raise them. Some 90% of executive men but only 35% of executive women have children by the age of 40. The *automatic* association of all women with babies is clearly unjustified.

The secret to dealing with such women is to recognize them early, accept them, and clear artificial barriers from their path to the top. After all, the best of these women are among the best managerial talent you will ever see. And career-primary women have another important value to the company that men and other women lack. They can act as role models and mentors to younger women who put their careers first. Since upwardly mobile career-primary women still have few role models to motivate and inspire them, a company with women in its top echelon has a significant advantage in the competition for executive talent.

Men at the top of the organization—most of them over 55, with wives who tend to be traditional—often find career women "masculine" and difficult to accept as colleagues. Such men miss the point, which is not that these women are just like men but that they are just like the *best* men in the organization. And there is such a shortage of the best people that gender cannot be allowed to matter. It is clearly counterproductive to disparage in a woman with executive talent the very qualities that are most critical to the business and that might carry a man to the CEO's office.

Clearing a path to the top for career-primary women has four requirements:

1. Identify them early.
2. Give them the same opportunity you give to talented men to grow and develop and contribute to company profitability. Give them client and customer responsibility. Expect them to travel and relocate, to make the same commitment to the company as men aspiring to leadership positions.
3. Accept them as valued members of your management team. Include them in every kind of communication. Listen to them.
4. Recognize that the business environment is more difficult and stressful for them than for their male peers. They are always a minority, often the only woman. The male perception of talented, ambitious women is at best ambivalent, a mixture of admiration, resentment, confusion, competitiveness, attraction, skepticism, anxiety, pride, and animosity. Women can never feel secure about how they should dress and act, whether they should speak out or grin and bear it when they encounter discrimination, stereotyping, sexual harassment, and paternalism. Social interaction and travel with male colleagues and with male clients can be charged. As they move up, the normal increase in pressure and responsibility is compounded for women because they are women.

Stereotypical language and sexist day-to-day behavior do take their toll on women's career development. Few male executives realize how common it is to call women by their first names while men in the same group are greeted with surnames, how frequently female executives are assumed by men to be secretaries, how often women are excluded from all-male social events where business is being transacted. With notable exceptions, men are still generally more comfortable with other men, and as a result women miss many of the career and business opportunities that arise over lunch, on the golf course, or in the locker room.

The majority of women, however, are what I call career-and-family women, women who want to pursue serious careers while participating actively in the rearing of children. These women are a precious resource that has yet to be mined. Many of them are talented and creative. Most of them are willing to trade some career growth and compensation for freedom from the constant pressure to work long hours and weekends.

A policy that forces women to choose between family and career cuts hugely into profits and competitive advantage.

Most companies today are ambivalent at best about the career-and-family women in their management ranks. They would prefer that all employees were willing to give their all to the company. They believe it is in their best interests for all managers to compete for the top positions so the company will have the largest possible pool from which to draw its leaders.

"If you have both talent and motivation," many employers seem to say "we want to move you up. If you haven't got that motivation, if you want less pressure and greater flexibility, then you can leave and make room for a new generation." These companies lose on two counts. First, they fail to amortize the investment made in the early training and experience of management women who find themselves committed to family as well as to career. Second, they fail to recognize what these women could do for their middle management.

The ranks of middle managers are filled with people on their way up and people who have stalled. Many of them have simply reached their limits, achieved career growth commensurate with or exceeding their capabilities, and they cause problems because their performance is mediocre but they still want to move ahead. The career-and-family woman is willing to trade off the pressures and demands that go with promotion for the freedom to spend more time with her children. She's very smart, she's talented, she's committed to her career, and she's satisfied to stay at the middle level, at least during the early child-rearing years. Compare her with some of the people you have there now.

Consider a typical example, a woman who decides in college on a business career and enters management at age 22. For nine years, the company invests in her career as she gains experience and skills and steadily improves her performance. But at 31, just as the investment begins pay off in earnest, she decides to have a baby. Can the company afford to let her go home, take another job, or go into business for herself? The common perception now is yes, the corporation can afford to lose her unless, after six or eight weeks or even three months of disability and maternity leave, she returns to work on a full-time schedule with the same vigor, commitment, and ambition that she showed before.

But what if she doesn't? What if she wants or needs to go on leave for six months or a year or, heaven forbid, five years? In this worst-case scenario, she works full-time from age 22 to 31 and from 36 to 65—a total of 38 years as opposed to the typical male's 43 years. That's not a huge difference. Moreover, my typical example is willing to work part-time while her children are young, if only her employer will give her the opportunity. There are two rewards for companies responsive to this need: higher retention of their best people and greatly improved performance and satisfaction in their middle management.

The high-performing career-and-family woman can be a major player in your company. She can give you a significant business advantage as the competition for able people escalates. Sometimes too, if you can hold on to her, she will switch gears in mid-life and reenter the competition for the top. The price you must pay to retain these women is threefold: you must plea for and manage maternity, you must provide the flexibility that will allow them to be maximally productive, and you must take an active role in helping to make family supports and high-quality affordable child care available to all women.

The key to managing maternity is to recognize the value of high-performing women and the urgent need to retain them and keep them productive. The first step must be a genuine partnership between the woman and her boss. I know this partnership can seem difficult to forge. One of my own senior executives came to me recently to discuss plans for her maternity leave and subsequent return to work. She knew she wanted to come back. I wanted to make certain that she would. Still, we had a somewhat awkward conversation, because I knew that no woman can predict with certainty when she will be able to return to work or under what conditions. Physical problems can lengthen her leave. So can a demanding infant, a difficult family or personal adjustment, or problems with child care.

I still don't know when this valuable executive will be back on the job full-time, and her absence creates some genuine problems for our organization. But I do know that I can't simply replace her years of experience with a new recruit. Since our conversation, I also know that she wants to come back, and that she *will* come back—part-time at first—unless I make it impossible for her by, for example, setting an arbitrary date for her full-time return or resignation. In turn, she knows that the organization wants and needs her and, more to the point, that it will be responsive to her needs in terms of working hours and child-care arrangements.

In having this kind of conversation it's important to ask concrete questions that will help to move the discussion from uncertainty and anxiety to some level of predictability. Questions can touch on everything from family income and energy level to child care arrangements and career commitment. Of course you want your star manager to return to work as soon as possible but you want her to return permanently and productively. Her downtime on the job is a drain on her energies and a waste of your money.

For all the women who want to combine career and family—the women who want to participate actively in the rearing of their children and who also want to pursue their careers seriously—the key to retention is to provide the flexibility and family supports they need in order to function effectively.

Time spent in the office increases productivity if it is time well spent, but the fact that most women continue to take the primary responsibility for child care is a cause of distraction, diversion, anxiety, and absenteeism—to say nothing of the persistent guilt experienced by all working mothers. A great many women, perhaps most of all women who have always performed at the highest levels, are also frustrated by a sense that while their children are babies they cannot function at their best either at home or at work.

In its simplest form, flexibility is the freedom to take time off—a couple of hours, a day, a week—or to do some work at home and some at the office, an arrangement that communication technology makes increasingly feasible. At the complex end of the spectrum are alternative work schedules that permit the woman to work less than full-time and her employer to reap the benefits of her experience and, with careful planning, the top level of her abilities.

> Incredibly, very few companies have ever studied the costs and statistics of maternity leave.

Part-time employment is the single greatest inducement to getting women back on the job expeditiously and the provision women themselves most desire. A part-time return to work enables them to maintain responsibility for critical aspects of their jobs, keeps them in touch with the changes constantly occurring at the workplace and in the job itself, reduces stress and fatigue, often eliminates the need for paid maternity leave by permitting a return to the office as soon as disability leave is over, and, not least, can greatly enhance company loyalty. The part-time solution works particularly well when a work load can be reduced for one individual in a department or when a full-time job can be broken down by skill levels and apportioned to two individuals at different levels of skill and pay.

I believe, however, that shared employment is the most promising and will be the most widespread form of flexible scheduling in the future. It is feasible at every level of the corporation except at the pinnacle, for both the short and the long term. It involves two people taking responsibility for one job.

Two red lights flash on as soon as most executives hear the words "job sharing": continuity and client-customer contact. The answer to the continuity question is to place responsibility entirely on the two individuals sharing the job to discuss everything that transpires—thoroughly, daily, and on their own time. The answer to the problem of client-customer contact is yes, job sharing requires re-education and a period of adjustment. But as both client and supervisor will quickly come to appreciate, two contacts means that the customer has continuous access to the company's representative, without interruptions for vacation, travel, or sick leave. The two people holding the job can simply cover for each other, and the uninterrupted, full-time coverage they provide together can be a stipulation of their arrangement.

Flexibility is costly in numerous ways. It requires more supervisory time to coordinate and manage, more office space, and somewhat greater benefits costs (though these can be contained with flexible benefits plans, prorated benefits, and, in two-paycheck families, elimination of duplicate benefits). But the advantages of reduced turnover and the greater productivity that results from higher energy levels and greater focus can outweigh the costs.

A few hints:

- Provide flexibility selectively. I'm not suggesting private arrangements subject to the suspicion of favoritism but rather a policy that makes flexible work schedules available only to high performers.
- Make it clear that in most instances (but not all) the rates of advancement and pay will be appropriately lower for those who take time off or who work part-time than for those who work full-time. Most career-and-family women are entirely willing to make that trade-off.
- Discuss costs as well as benefits. Be willing to risk accusations of bias. Insist, for example, that half time is half of whatever time it takes to do the job, not merely half of 35 or 40 hours.

The woman who is eager to get home to her child has a powerful incentive to use her time effectively at the office and to carry with her reading and other work that can be done at home. The talented professional who wants to have it all can be a high performer by carefully ordering her priorities and by focusing on objectives rather than on the legendary 15-hour day. By the time professional women have their first babies—at an average age of 32—they have already had nine years to work long hours at a desk, to travel and to relocate. In the case of high performers, the need for flexibility coincides with what has gradually become the goal-oriented nature of responsibility.

Family supports—in addition to maternity leave and flexibility—include the provision of parental leave for men, support for two-career and single-parent families during relocation, and flexible benefits. But the primary ingredient is child care. The capacity of working mothers to function effectively and without interruption depends on the availability of good, affordable child care. Now that women make up almost half the work force and the growing percentage of managers, the decision to become involved in the personal lives of employees is no longer a philosophical question but a practical one. To make matters worse, the quality of child care has almost no relation to technology, inventiveness, or profitability but is more or less a pure function of the quality of child care personnel and the ratio of adults to children. These costs are irreducible. Only by joining hands with government and the public sector can corporations hope to create the vast quantity and variety of child care that their employees need.

Until quite recently, the response of corporations to women has been largely symbolic and cosmetic, motivated in large part by the will to avoid litigation and legal penalties. In some cases, companies were also moved by a genuine sense of fairness and a vague discomfort and frustration at the absence of women above the middle of the corporate pyramid. The actions they took were mostly quick, easy, and highly visible—child care information services, a three-month parental leave available to men as well as women, a woman appointed to the board of directors.

When I first began to discuss these issues 26 years ago, I was sometimes able to get an appointment with the assistant to the assistant in personnel, but it was only a courtesy. Over the past decade, I have met with the CEOs of many large corporations and I've watched them become involved with ideas they had never previously thought much about. Until recently, however, the shelf life of that enhanced awareness was always short. Given pressing, short-term concerns, women were not a front-burner issue. In the past few months, I have seen yet another change. Some CEOs and top management groups now take the initiative. They call and ask us to show them how to shift gears from a responsive to a proactive approach to recruiting, developing, and retaining women.

I think this change is more probably a response to business needs—to concern for the quality of future profits and managerial talent—than to uneasiness about legal requirements, sympathy with the demands of women and minorities, or the desire to do what is right and fair. The nature of such business motivation varies. Some companies want to move women to their positions as role models for those below them and as beacons for talented young recruits. Some want to achieve a favorable image with employees, customers, clients, and stockholders. These are all legitimate motives. But I think the companies that stand to gain most are motivated as well by a desire to capture competitive advantage in an era when talent and competence will be in increasingly short supply. These companies are now ready to stop being defensive about their experience with women and to ask incisive questions without preconceptions.

Even so, incredibly, I don't know of more than one or two companies that have looked into their own records to study the absolutely critical issue of maternity leave—how many women took it, when and whether they returned, and how this behavior correlated with their rank, tenure, age, and performance. The unique drawback to the employment of women is the physical reality of maternity and the particular socializing influence maternity has had. Yet to make women equal to men in the workplace we have chosen on the whole not to discuss this single most significant difference between them. Unless we do, we cannot evaluate the cost of recruiting, developing, and moving women up.

Now that interest is replacing indifference, there are four steps every company can take to examine its own experience with women:

1. Gather quantitative data on the company's experience with management-level women regarding turnover rates, occurrence of and return from maternity leave, and organizational level attained in relation to tenure and performance.
2. Correlate this data with factors such as age, marital status, and presence and age of children, and attempt to identify and analyze why women respond the way they do.
3. Gather qualitative data on the experience of women in your company and on how women are perceived by both sexes.
4. Conduct a cost-benefit analysis of the return on your investment in high-performing women. Factor in the cost to the company of women's negative reactions to negative experience, as well as the probable cost of corrective measures and policies. If women's value to your company is greater than the cost to recruit, train, and develop them—and of course I believe it will be—then you will want to do everything you can to retain them.

We have come a tremendous distance since the days when the prevailing male wisdom saw women as lacking the kind of intelligence that would allow them to succeed in business. For decades, even women themselves have harbored an unspoken belief that they couldn't make it because they couldn't be just like men, and nothing else would do. But now that woman have shown themselves the equal of men in every area of organizational activity, now that they have demonstrated that they can be stars in every field of endeavor, now we can all venture to examine the fact that women and men are different.

On balance, employing women is more costly than employing men. Women can acknowledge this fact today because they know that their value to employers exceeds the additional cost and because they know that changing attitudes can reduce the additional cost dramatically. Women in management are no longer an idiosyncrasy of the arts and education. They have always matched men in natural ability. Within a very few years, they will equal men in numbers as well in every area of economic activity.

The demographic motivation to recruit and develop women is compelling. But an older question remains: Is society better for the change? Women's exit from the home and entry into the work force has certainty created problems—an urgent need for good, affordable child care; troubling questions about the kind of parenting children need; the costs and difficulties of diversity in the workplace; the stress and fatigue of combining work and family responsibilities. Wouldn't we all be happier if we could turn back the clock to an age when men were in the workplace and women in the home, when male and female roles were clearly differentiated and complementary?

Nostalgia, anxiety, and discouragement will urge many to say yes, but my answer is emphatically no. Two fundamental benefits that were unattainable in the past are now within our reach. For the individual, freedom of choice—in this case the freedom to choose career, family, or a combination of the two. For the corporation, access to the most gifted individuals in the country. These benefits are neither self-indulgent nor insubstantial. Freedom of choice and self-realization are too deeply American to be cast aside for some wistful vision of the past. And access to our most talented human resources is not a luxury in this age of explosive international competition but rather the barest minimum that prudence and national self-preservation require.

Felice N. Schwartz is president and founder of Catalyst, a not-for-profit research and advisory organization that works with corporations to foster the career and leadership development of women.

The Health-Care Tussle

Colleges and their employees struggle over the growing costs of coverage

DAVID GLENN

Ask John H. Scofield, a professor of physics at Oberlin College, about the college's health-insurance plan, and he will grimace. Then he'll pull out a thick three-ring binder of documents he has amassed since at least 1994.

Mr. Scofield is not a satisfied customer. He is fully aware that health-care costs are skyrocketing nationally, and he concedes that Oberlin's recent increases in premiums, copayments, and deductibles are probably a plausible response to those rising costs. Colleges' health-care premiums increased at an average rate of 11.9 percent from 2002–3 to 2003–4, according to a survey conducted last year by the College and University Professional Association for Human Resources.

He believes, however, that his college's administrators have sometimes been less than candid when discussing its health-insurance woes with faculty and staff members. "I went digging around, trying to find out how much was spent on health care," he says. "The trouble is, the numbers don't seem to stack up. You ask in one venue, you get one answer. Then you compare the numbers with something else, and they don't stack up."

Complaints like Mr. Scofield's have led to a series of stormy faculty meetings at Oberlin during the past three years—and also to a bruising conflict over health benefits last summer, when the college negotiated a new contract with its clerical-staff union. That bumpy ride may hold lessons for other institutions.

From Boston to Berkeley, several consecutive years of double-digit increases in employees' heath-care costs have battered college and university budgets already under assault by the usual suspects: cuts in state appropriations, lackluster fund raising, and only modest investment returns. Colleges have responded, in part, by raising tuition and cutting expenses, measures that have only partially alleviated budget woes. Now employees, too, are being asked to chip in.

That has created strain of another sort. Professors and support-staff members accustomed to high-quality health care at low cost—in some cases at no cost—are now shouldering new burdens, and not always happily. Some would say that a longstanding compact between the rank and file and the institutions where they work has been weakened, if not broken.

Given the unprecedented nature of higher education's health-care crisis, no one knows where that breaking point is.

POSTMILLENNIAL PINCH

Oberlin's recent challenges began in 2001. After several years of comfortable surpluses, the college's health-care plan suddenly began running a steep deficit as a result of a few serious illnesses among those it covered, as well as of medical costs that were already rising steeply. Oberlin is self-insured, which means that it pools its own money rather than buying an off-the-shelf policy from a private insurer. (The college does buy external "stop loss" insurance, which kicks in when expenses for a particular employee exceed $150,000 in a calendar year.)

Self-insuring gives Oberlin flexibility in defining its premium rates—but it also leaves the college vulnerable to sudden shocks, like the spike in illnesses in 2001. The college says it spent $9.2-million on health care that year, a figure that alarmed the Board of Trustees, which instructed the administration to get costs under control.

The college took several steps. It made special withdrawals from its endowment, and, since the beginning of 2003, has required faculty and administrative staff members to pay a share of the self-insured plan's premium costs. (Professors' payments are based on percentages of their salaries: 1.75 percent for individual coverage and 4 percent for family coverage.) Last summer clerical and maintenance employees entered a similar arrangement.

"For a school like Oberlin, which, like most colleges, is labor-intensive, the controlling of health-care costs is an important thing because it can mean large increases in our operating budget," says Ronald R. Watts, associate vice president for finance. "Between 1999 and 2002, we saw dramatic increases of over 30 percent in the claims costs on our health-care plan. And the college was picking up between 80 and 90 percent of the cost of the plan at that time."

The college also sharply increased copayments and deductibles. Employees must now pay for many services, up to an annual out-of-pocket maximum of $500 (for support-staff members) or $3,000 (for faculty members on the family plan). "People who have been here for 25-plus years are really feeling a hit," says Tracy L. Tucker, an administrative assistant in the politics department and a former vice president of the clerical union. "We've been loyal to the college, and now this is what they're showing us."

A professor earning $65,000 who opts for family coverage pays 4 percent of her salary—$2,600 a year—in premiums. On top of that, she is responsible for $15 copayments for almost all doctor visits, and 10 percent of the charges for most hospital procedures, up to the annual out-of-pocket maximum of $3,000. She could conceivably spend $5,600 a year, or about 8.6 percent of her salary, on health care.

Oberlin's Health-Care Plan

	PLAN A (for faculty members and administrators)	PLAN B (for administrative assistants and other service employees)
Premium costs	• Individual: 1.75% of salary • Employee + child: 3% of salary • Employee + spouse or domestic partner: 3.5% of salary • Family: 4% of salary	• Individual: 1.55% of salary • Employee + child: 1.65% of salary • Employee + spouse or domestic partner: 1.75% of salary • Family: 2% of salary
Annual deductible	• $250 (individual) • $500 (family)	None
Office visits	$15 copayment per visit	• No charge for the first 5 visits • $5 copayment for visits 6 through 10 • $10 copayment for the 11th visit and beyond
Inpatient hospital care	10% of charges*	No charge
Outpatient services	10% of charges*	No charge
Prescription drugs	• $10 per 30-day supply (generic) • $20 per 30-day supply (brand-name)	$5 per 30-day supply (must be generic)
Annual out-of-pocket maximum	• $1,500 (individual) • $3,000 (family)	$500

* The participant must pay the annual deductible before the plan pays its 90% share for these services.

SOURCE: OBERLIN COLLEGE

Mr. Watts emphasizes that while the college's health-care plan has grown more expensive for employees, it remains generous relative to that offered by other Ohio employers.

That assessment is echoed by Jeffry A. Peters, president of Health Directions, a Chicago-based health consultancy that has no relationship to Oberlin. "This is one of the richest plans I've seen in years," says Mr. Peters, who reviewed summaries of Oberlin's plan at *The Chronicle's* request. "It really appears that the college is trying to prevent income from affecting people's access to care."

Consumer Consciousness

Oberlin's recent moves are hardly unique. Many colleges are requiring their employees to pay a larger share of their health insurance. No one appears to have collected thorough data about the extent of the trend or its impact on the higher-education work force, although the college-human-resources association may do so this year.

The anecdotal reports, in any case, are very broad. "Any mechanism that a university can use to curtail its costs is obviously something that they need to pursue," says Peter J. Martel, president-elect of the association, who is associate vice president for human resources at Bridgewater State College, in Massachusetts. "But there's obviously a challenge when you're talking about what amounts to, and would be perceived as, a giveback on the part of faculty or staff."

Health care was a central issue in recent strikes at Northeastern Illinois University and the City Colleges of Chicago. "The pressure on health-care costs is one way that the union movement in higher education is growing," says William E. Scheuerman, a vice president of the American Federation of Teachers.

Despite the friction, some observers argue that shifting certain costs to employees is a reasonable and important strategy for minimizing health-cost inflation. Higher copayments and deductibles, they say, can make consumers more conscious of their spending and therefore more rational in their health-care choices.

"Employees tend to be somewhat insulated from this," says Luis F. Fernandez, a professor of economics at Oberlin and chair of the college's benefits committee. "That's one problem with health insurance. It insulates you from thinking about what prices are. People are uncomfortable talking about prices with their doctors. But there's going to have to be more of this if we're going to do anything to hold down costs."

The college was wise, he says, to raise copayments and deductibles rather than raise premiums or reduce salaries. A five-year experiment conducted by the RAND Corporation in the 1970s, he says, demonstrated that consumers are highly sensitive to costs associated with copayments and deductibles. "People do respond to price," he says, noting that subjects in plans with high copayments and high deductibles monitored their health more closely than people in traditional plans did, and fared no worse in the long run.

"At some point, you have to start shifting some costs onto employees," says John B. Oakley, a professor of law at the University of California at Davis and chair of the university system's committee on faculty welfare. "It's perceived as shifting some fixed cost that's been the same since 1970 onto the backs of employees. But what they're actually doing is shifting only a part of this compound annual inflation in health-care costs."

Employees at Oberlin do not deny the reality of the health-cost problem, but some have resisted the steps the college has taken.

Toward the front of Mr. Scofield's binder are some of the annual letters he has received detailing his salary and benefits. In the early 1990s, those statements told him that the college was spending about $5,000 annually on his health care—a number that struck him as improbably high, given that he was in good health and was the only member of his family participating in the plan.

"It appears to me," Mr. Scofield says, "that in these letters to employees they're not telling us how much they spent at all. They're telling us how much they *budgeted* for health care. And for many years, I think they spent a whole lot less than they budgeted. I think the value, if you will, of our health-care benefits had been inflated for years, to make our compensation look high. And then, at the end of the year, when they didn't spend nearly as much as they quote-unquote budgeted, this was used as slush funds to move around and pay off other areas."

Mr. Watts, the associate vice president, says the college is "trying to develop ways to give some transparency and to explain the increases in health care. Everybody's interest is in controlling this."

At faculty meetings in 2002 and 2004, proposals were raised to require future health-care surpluses to be placed in a rainy-day fund rather than returned to the general operating budget. But the administration has so far declined to enact such a plan. "In the best world, we'd have that reserve," says Mr. Watts, who nonetheless holds that it would be irresponsible to build up a rainy-day fund for health-care costs while deficits accumulate in other areas of the budget. "You've got to cover your entire operating budget," he says.

"University employees are a particularly difficult cohort of consumers of health care…who not only think they know more than most people, but probably do."

Oberlin employees have also objected to a recently enacted rule that requires working spouses to participate in their own employers' health plans for their primary coverage. "We know of a significant number of people who are facing large cost increases because their spouses are forced to buy their employers' plan," says Julie E. Weir, a library assistant and president of the college's clerical union. "And many of those people now need to be covered double, with Oberlin as secondary coverage, because some of those employers really only offer minimal coverage." (At the beginning of this year, the college adjusted the rule so that spouses must join their employers' plans only if the employer pays at least 50 percent of the cost of the plan.)

The University of California system has not adopted such a rule, but Mr. Oakley, the law professor, says it has had similar concerns. "We've found that we're actually subsidizing other employers," he says, because university employees' spouses and domestic partners will choose the university's plan instead of the stingier or more expensive plans offered by their own employers. "We're now trying to price our plan so that it's not manifestly cheaper per person," he says.

Caveat Emptor

Some people at Oberlin have suggested that the administration has failed to conduct due diligence in securing the cheapest provider networks offered by Cigna, the insurance company that administers the college's self-insured plan. Those accusations derive from last summer's negotiations between the college and its clerical union.

When bargaining stalled, in June, the union persuaded the college to bring in a new consultant to search for cost-saving measures that would not involve higher premiums and deductibles. "We uncovered several things," Ms. Weir says. Among other things, the consultant discovered that certain contracts were structured so that Cigna, and not the college, received the financial benefit when plan members chose generic rather than brand-name prescription drugs. More important, the consultant discovered that Cigna had begun to offer a new, less expensive network, one that included essentially the same physicians as the college's current network. "That network became available to us, and now the college has moved to that network across the board, not only for clerical employees but also for faculty members," says Ms. Weir. "And again, that's only because we asked."

A similar process has gone on this year at the University of Alaska at Fairbanks, where the administration and the faculty union have split the cost of an outside audit of the university's health-care provider. The union insisted on such an audit before it would begin negotiations on the university officials' requests for higher out-of-pocket payments. "They had not audited the Blue Cross plan in 10 years," says Michael L. Jennings, an associate professor of philosophy and the humanities at Fairbanks, who is president of the faculty union. "To their credit, the university has been cooperating with us, trying to make some alternate proposals available."

Administrators at the University of California offer a further warning: As colleges shift certain costs to faculty members and other employees, they must be careful not to push some people off the health plans entirely.

Tiered Premiums

In 2004 the university system adopted a system of "tiered premiums," which, as at Oberlin, are proportional to employees' salaries. "The reasons were not a matter of socialistic thinking, as some have accused," says Harold J. Simon, a professor of medicine on the San Diego campus and a member of the system's committee on faculty welfare. "Rather, we wanted to try to ensure that the university community is as fully insured as is possible."

The faculty-welfare committee was worried, he says, that some of the lowest-paid employees would choose to do without health insurance altogether if their premiums rose too high.

Those employees tend to be young and healthy, he notes—and without them in the pool, the remaining employee group would be relatively unhealthy and thus more expensive to insure. "It is definitely not in our collective interest for people to go uninsured," he says.

Veterans of health-care battles at both Oberlin and Davis say transparency and strong lines of communication between administrators and employees are crucial.

A common misconception among Mr. Oakley's faculty colleagues at Davis, he says, is that the university system's size gives it tremendous leverage when negotiating with health-care providers. "I began with the usual idea that the university must have a lot of purchasing power, and therefore if they weren't fools and scoundrels, my health care would be cheaper," he says. "I began to discover that it's a much more complicated scenario.… University employees are a particularly difficult cohort of consumers of health care, from a provider's perspective. If you have a cohort of people who not only think they know more than most people, but probably do, they're very demanding. I discovered over time that health-care providers are not falling all over themselves to bid for the university's contracts."

One small ray of hope: Both at Oberlin and in the University of California system, employees' premium rates have been frozen for 2005.

Who Are You Really Hiring?

Companies often don't screen executive-level applicants. They should. High echelon crooks and cons can cost you fortunes. But there are ways to safeguard a firm from liars and cheats at the top.

By Shari Caudron

James Baughman was imprisoned for stealing money from student funds while he was a California high school principal. He lied about earning a doctorate at Stanford. He eventually became director of recruitment for Lucent Technologies.

Al Dunlap was fired in 1973 by Max Phillips & Son after just seven weeks of employment. Three years later, he was fired by Nitec Paper Corporation—which soon went broke—over allegations of financial fraud. Twenty years later, he surfaced as chairman and chief executive officer for Sunbeam Corporation.

George O'Leary lied on his résumé about earning a master's degree in education from New York University. He lied about lettering in football for three years at the University of New Hampshire. He later was hired as Notre Dame's football coach.

Lucent, Sunbeam, and Notre Dame were not aware—at the time—that they had hired a felon, an alleged books-cooker, and a liar to fill positions of authority. But these organizations *could* have learned about their employees' tainted backgrounds if they'd taken time to do a routine background check.

Open the help-wanted section of any major metropolitan daily and you'll see ads for front-desk clerks, delivery drivers, and salespeople warning that background checks are required. Drug tests, criminal-record checks, and employment and education verification are de rigueur for the rank and file in many companies. But when it comes to filling upper-level positions, there's a class system at work in corporate America. Instead of sifting through background data for the kind of debris that would prevent a clean hire, companies are all too willing to take executive-level applicants at their word.

"You'd think the logic would be that the higher the position, the more screening companies would do," says Les Rosen, attorney and president of Employment Screening Resources in Novato, California. "But from what we've seen, that's not true. Somehow, there is a sense of impropriety in challenging the credentials of people higher up."

Douglas Hahn, president of HRplus, a background-screening firm based in Evergreen, Colorado, agrees. "At some companies there is definitely a good ol' boy network that prevails," he says. "Executives tend to hire their friends, and they hold the integrity of those friends above that of anybody else in the company. Unfortunately, that sometimes backfires."

And those backfires can be devastating. While a low-level employee might manage to embezzle a few thousand dollars or steal some inventory, a single dishonest executive with the right influence and access to accounts can plunge a company into the depths of bankruptcy, taking scores of jobs and billions of dollars in retirement savings and shareholder investment along with it.

While it might be impossible to safeguard a company against every potential act of dishonesty, HR professionals can minimize the chances for unscrupulous behavior by understanding who it is they really are hiring. This means developing background-checking procedures that are utilized at all levels of the organization, including—and perhaps most especially—those at the very top.

Why checking execs is more important today

Up until two years ago, a go-go economy compelled a lot of companies to hire many employees quickly. The talent war was so brutal that businesses didn't have time to slow down and check every detail of an applicant's background. They had to find candidates, make an offer, and issue a company parking pass before the competition could steal that person away. As a result, corners were cut, guidelines were overlooked, and unscrupulous people slipped through the cracks.

Renee Svec, marketing manager of HireCheck, Inc., an employment-screening firm in St. Petersburg, Florida, tells the story of a *Fortune* 500 company that hired a new executive and decided to forgo the background check. "Not long after he was hired, the executive started coming on to a woman in his department," Svec says. "The woman reported his behavior to the corporate security department, which ran a background check and discovered that the executive had operated under several aliases and served more than one prison term for financial fraud."

Today, there's no reason why someone like this should be offered an executive-level position. The labor market has opened up considerably, and HR professionals now have time to check the background of each potential new hire. Furthermore, there's a lot more motivation to do so. The events of September 11 brought the threat of terrorism to the forefront. The scandals in the Catholic Church heightened awareness of sexual predators. Workplace violence is an ongoing concern, especially when unemployment rises. And the collapse of some of the country's largest corporations has shown the enormous potential for financial fraud at the executive level.

If none of these factors sway you to do more digging into a candidate's past, consider this startling fact: a full 44 percent of all resumes are inaccurate, according to Eric Boden, president and CEO of HireRight, a Web-based employment-screening company based in Irvine, California. The inaccuracies could be little white lies such as listing a volunteer position never held, or major whoppers such as lying about advanced degrees or former jobs. Regardless, with so many people being laid off and looking for work, the temptation to make one's resume more attractive is greater now than it has been in some time. And often, the people who pad their resumes are the people you'd least expect.

Two years ago, HireCheck was introducing its background-screening services to a management team at a hospital. The hospital administrator invited HireCheck to run some test searches on a few employees, and put her staff in charge of selecting the sample employees. Thinking it would be fun to run a check on their boss, the staff members chose the administrator as one of the test cases. In conducting the background search, HireCheck discovered that the administrator had falsified details of her educational background, which was grounds for immediate dismissal.

The administrator's termination—which was unwittingly effected by her own hand— would be laughable if the problem of résumé deception weren't so widespread. But even if lying weren't so commonplace, verifying an employee's background is something that all companies should be doing. After all, it doesn't take a parking lot full of dishonest employees to create havoc for an organization. A single well-placed unethical employee can plunder profits before anyone knows what's under way.

What's that, you say? Conducting extensive background checks on management employees is expensive? Better to save the $2,000 to $10,000 average cost and trust your gut? A Toronto-based trucking company thought it was saving money by not checking the background of a woman hired to manage its accounts department. The woman was impressive, after all, and seemed to have the right credentials. Over the course of two years, the employee siphoned $250,000 from the company's general accounts. Ultimately, she was prosecuted on criminal charges and sentenced to three years in jail. Had the trucking company taken the time to call her previous employer, they would have discovered she'd also defrauded that company to the tune of $100,000.

How to integrate background-checking at all levels

HR professionals have an obvious and important role to play in safeguarding company assets by hiring honest employees. But conducting a thorough background check on every employee is not easy, especially if it's not already an accepted part of the culture to do so. Here are some steps that HR people may want to consider:

1. Lobby for the fact that integrity is important. In many companies, HR gets involved in hiring lower-level workers, but executive recruitment is handled by those at the top, who tap into their own executive network. This is fine, but if the executive team wants to build and maintain a company that holds integrity and honesty in the highest regard, everyone should be subjected to the same level of background-checking once a job offer has been made—and it's HR's job to argue for this.

"HR has got to lobby for the fact that high integrity should be a requirement for every job," says Philip Sullivan, vice president of recruitment and placement at nSight, Inc., a staffing firm in Burlington, Massachusetts. One way to do this is to talk about the potential financial consequences of *not* conducting thorough checks.

For instance, if Sunbeam had done a more thorough background check on Al Dunlap, the company might have discovered the allegations of financial fraud in his background and declined to hire him. It's hard to say for sure, but if Dunlap had not been at the helm, Sunbeam might not have had to endure plummeting stock values, stockholder lawsuits, and eventual bankruptcy.

"If an executive wants to shortcut the process and hire a peer without consenting to a background check," Sullivan says, "HR has to make clear to the executive that, in doing so, he or she is putting his or her own integrity at stake."

2. Treat all employees fairly. All employees should be subject to a standard background-screening that includes a credit check; a review of motor vehicle and criminal records; reference checks; and verification of employment, education, professional licenses, and Social Security number. However, Rosen says, "it is perfectly acceptable to have different levels of screening for different positions as long as everyone is treated *fairly*." Someone on an assembly line, for example, would not necessarily receive the same level of scrutiny as a potential executive. But all assembly-line workers should be treated the same way and all executives should be treated the same way. "What you want to do is conduct the screenings that are appropriate for the position;" he says.

3. Dig deeper with executive candidates. When hiring executives, Rosen suggests going beyond a standard security-screening and conducting something he calls an "integrity check." "The typical pre-employment screening is a low-cost risk-management tool that looks at verifiable, known factors," he says. An integrity check, however, is more investigative and entails looking at such things as involvement in lawsuits, the financial performance of the person's previous firm, and when and why the candidate might have appeared in local or national newspapers.

Detecting Employees Who Steal

Employee fraud is on the rise, soaring from $400 billion in lost revenue for U.S. businesses in 1996 to an estimated $600 billion in 2002. But there are preventive measures that HR executives can take to spot employees who might be stealing.

First, recognize that small businesses are most vulnerable to employee theft, says Dick Stackpool, a consultant with Aon Risk Services in Minneapolis. In a small firm, a single employee has more responsibility, and therefore often has more access to company information and finances than an employee in a large business.

There's also less managerial oversight in small companies and a more familial atmosphere. Many small-business owners refuse to believe that their employees, who have been treated as friends and family, would ever turn on the company, Stackpool says.

Aon and the Association of Certified Fraud Examiners, in Austin, Texas, have identified several trends that can help HR managers detect employees who might steal:

- The majority of employees who steal—68.6 percent, according to ACFE—have no prior criminal record.
- More of them are males—53.5 percent versus 46.5 percent females—who have a high school education or less. "Losses are strongly related to the perpetrator's position, and in many organizations, the vast majority of managerial and executive positions are still held by males' states ACFE's *2002 Report to the Nation.*
- As the employee's education level rises, the incidence of theft declines: 56.9 percent of thieves have a high school education or less, 32.7 percent have a bachelor's degree, and 10.4 percent have a postgraduate education.
- Watch for employees who are struggling financially or suddenly make large purchases far beyond their means. Stackpool poses this question: "Are they going through a difficult time in their lives—possibly a divorce, or their spouse is laid off—or do they have a mountain of debt?" Although most employees undergoing a personal or financial crisis don't steal, he says, "sometimes they find themselves in a situation where they are just taking some cash to get them over the short-term hump, and that short-term hump moves into a long-term hump... and gets out of hand for them."
- Also watch for an increase in fraud prior to, or in the midst of, merger and acquisition activity. "Employees get the 'I'm going to get mine while I can, I don't have a career here' attitude," he says. Most fraud and theft can be prevented with a few simple internal controls:
- Background checks, which could include criminal checks as well as double-checking of references, are a simple preventive measure. "At a minimum, I would think that checking the past employment would be obvious. Many companies never do reference checks or background checks," Stackpool says.
- The duties of employees should be segregated, so that one employee does not have all control and oversight over the finances and/or inventory. "Does the individual who makes bank deposits also reconcile the books, so they can hide the fact that the cash was not deposited?" he asks.
- An internal accounting system, or a system of checks and balances whereby transactions are reviewed and approved by managers, is essential.
- An internal anonymous hotline for employees to report fraud can also be helpful. "Tips from employees led to the highest percentage of cases being discovered (26 percent, according to ACFE)," Stackpool notes.
- Corporate kindness goes a long way "Share the wealth," he adds. Rewards can range from buying pizza for employees to giving them bonus checks. "It makes it more difficult for them to steal in a place where they're valued."

—Christine Blank

4. Don't rely solely on a candidate's former employer. Although a number of states have enacted legislation that protects employers in giving truthful information about a former employee, labor lawyers still counsel HR people to only verify facts of employment. Furthermore, in the age of consolidation and big business, the central HR departments of many companies typically have only sketchy records.

For these reasons, it is not enough to rely on a reference from a former employer. To do an in-depth search, HR people should ask the candidate's supplied references for the names of three other people who might know the candidate.

5. Don't rely solely on search firms. Search firms that don't conduct a thorough background check of candidates can be misled as easily as any employer. In March 1998, Robert Half International Inc. recruited T'Challa Ross as a temporary bookkeeper for Fox Associates Inc., a small advertising agency in Chicago. She performed so well at the job that the company hired her permanently 30 days later. Within months, Ross was taking blank checks from Fox and forging signatures. Within a year, she had embezzled more than $70,000. What makes the case especially disturbing is that the staffing firm had failed to uncover the fact that just two months earlier, Ross had pleaded guilty to stealing $192,873 from another employer and been sentenced to four years' probation and 100 hours of community service.

The problem with relying on staffing services is that they are typically not paid their contingency fee until a job candidate has been placed in the job. Thus, they have a vested interest in placing employees quickly. To ensure that staffing firms take the time to conduct thorough background checks, Eric Archer, president of Spherion Professional Recruiting Group, a professional services staffing firm based in Fort Lauderdale, suggests a pricing mechanism whereby the staffing firm is paid a fee based on two-thirds contingency and one-third retainer. "This shows sincerity on the part of the client who wants to hire someone, and it buys a commitment from the recruiting organization to conduct a more thorough search," he says. This way, if a firm uncovers troubling aspects of a candidate's background that prevent his being hired, the staffing firm still receives some compensation for the work involved.

6. Check everyone, including temps, part-timers, and contract employees. A few years ago, the Los Angeles-based National Academy of Recording Arts and Sciences was preparing for its annual Grammy Awards presentation. To help put together the labor-intensive show, the organization hired several temporary workers. One of them, unbeknownst to the academy's HR people, was a reporter who was posing as a temp in an effort to get inside the academy and gain information on the show's winners. According to HR manager Shonda Grant, the ruse was discovered before the reporter managed to get any privileged information. But ever since then, the academy has required thorough background checks on all employees, including temporary, part-time, and contract workers.

In this era of heightened concern about terrorism and theft, many organizations are choosing to screen the backgrounds of everyone who works for them. In the six months following September 11, for example, Eli Lilly and Company commissioned criminal-background checks of more than 7,000 employees of outside vendors, including construction workers and fast-food staffers.

"There is a clear trend and more genuine concern from companies about checking out all of their employees," Boden says. "Companies are no longer solely concerned with establishing a defense against negligent hiring. They want to be careful about who is being brought in to the business."

7. Don't have interviewers conduct background checks. As a former grocery-store owner and now president of a background-screening firm, Douglas Hahn has interviewed countless people for jobs, and what he's learned is this: you cannot trust your own instincts. "I've been nailed so many times," he says. "At the grocery store, one of my most charismatic, friendly managers was stealing me blind and I had no idea."

Because Hahn has learned to not trust his gut, he always makes it a point to have one person on his staff interview a candidate and another conduct the background check. "People become prejudiced," he says. "You ask questions differently if you've interviewed someone and liked them. For example, instead of asking a reference if there is anything in a person's history that would prevent you from giving him the keys to the vault, you might say, 'There are no problems with this person, right?'"

At HireCheck, Renee Svec confirms that likable and charismatic employees can be particularly challenging. "Recently, we were going to hire a key executive for our office," Svec says. The candidate had been referred by corporate higher-ups who believed she had potential. Svec's team met with the woman and thought she was terrific. The candidate had impressive credentials, an excellent employment history, and professional licensing.

HireCheck offered her the job, contingent on a clean background check. "Basically, everything this woman claimed turned out to be completely false, and we were amazed how she had the nerve to pursue a position with a background-checking company," Svec says. "Prior to that, she'd been our top candidate. She had everybody snookered."

Given the fact that few companies conduct thorough background-screenings on their top-level candidates, chances are good that many more employers are being duped. And sometimes the level of deceit isn't uncovered until it is too late. "We don't often do routine background checks on executives unless it's for a merger or joint venture," says Chris Mathers, vice president of KPMG Forensic, Inc., in Toronto. "But when we do do them, it's typically because a company is about to terminate a person for wrongdoing and they'd never checked that person out in the first place."

Mathers recently worked with an international company that had hired a Harvard graduate with "sterling" credentials. Almost immediately, the company started having problems with the employee, who would stay late at night and engage in bizarre behavior. Eventually, he was caught trying to steal software from the company for his own gain. "Before terminating him, we checked with three previous employers, and all three said the guy was bad news," Mathers says. "He was involved with substance abuse, had assaulted his wife, and had also been terminated at other jobs for stealing.

"Anyone who avoids checking employees does so at their own peril."

Thoroughly checking someone's background doesn't guarantee that you'll prevent the kind of fraud that brought down Enron, WorldCom, and the other corporate disgraces. But in the realm of human behavior, a little safeguarding can go a long way.

workforce.com

For more info on: **Hiring Right** Get 27 steps you can take during hiring to minimize any surprises about the background of one of your employees. workforce.com/02/11/feature1

Contributing editor Shari Caudron lives in Denver. E-mail editors @workforce.com to comment.

The Next *Bubble?*

BY REBECCA FANNIN

How do you know when another bubble is about to burst? The signs of an overinflated tech boom were evident back in the late 1990s but no one paid much attention until it was too late and millions of dollars were sunk in ill-fated ventures.

Now another peak and valley are on the horizon—not in Silicon Valley but far away in India, and not among dot-com startups but among providers of outsourcing services, from call centers to software development houses. As experts and the media hyped offshore outsourcing as the Next Big Thing, the industry ballooned with new and expanding players eager to get their share of business.

The inevitable shakeout in the outsourcing industry could leave your offshore operations stranded.

But CEOs who have outsourced operations in India to save costs during tight economic times should heed the signs of pending consolidation.

Already a shakeout is occurring as some outsourcing competitors go out of business or get gobbled up by bigger rivals in a power play for market share—and survival. CEOs who are not especially clever at picking and managing a good outsourcing provider could find themselves left empty-handed just when their operations have been moved offshore. They may be forced to temporarily halt production, research and development or customer service. Or, if they team up with a provider that suddenly expands to take on new, bigger clients, they could find themselves shoved aside.

Yoshiaki Fujimori, president and CEO of GE Asia in Hong Kong, is thinking ahead about how to mitigate the risks. GE has one of the biggest outsourcing operations in India, which has saved the company millions of dollars, he says. Some 11,000 workers from India handle back-office processing, such as payroll for the company, accounting for annual savings of $300 to $400 million. And its information technology arm in India saves the company another $500 to $600 million each year.

GE is being careful, however, not to place all its orders with any one vendor just in case "one goes away," says Fujimori. GE, like other large firms that outsource IT and business processing, is considering moving other operations to China as an alternative. It has already formed a joint venture there to see if it can achieve more savings in China versus India, he says. The venture, based in Dalian, churns out software in Korean, Chinese and Japanese, "and probably knows Japanese better than I do," quips Fujimori.

With costs for software developers reaching $150 per hour in India, the China option does look attractive. "When you have those kinds of rates, that's not even an advantage over Silicon Valley," points out Harry Sarwari, chairman of outsourcing firm OneBPO in Freemont, Calif.

Companies having new and cheaper options for offshore outsourcing may be just one of the telltale signs that this sector in India is headed toward a correction. Another is the great speed with which the outsourcing market is growing. Indian software and services exports are projected

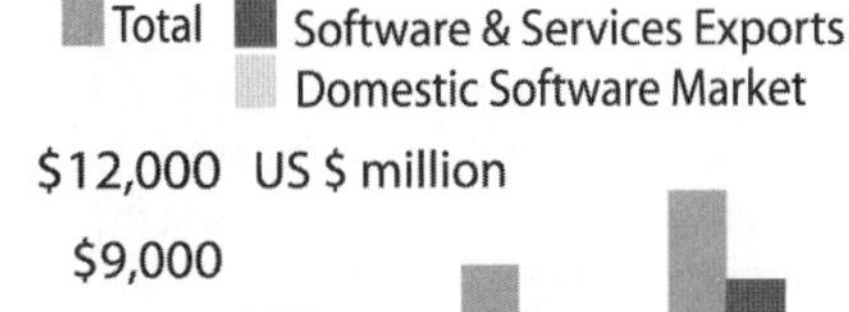

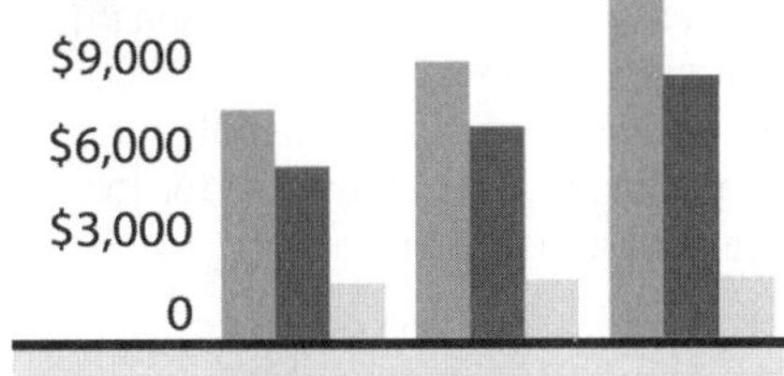

to grow 26 to 28 percent in 2004, weighing in with revenues of more than $12 billion, according to India's National Association of Software and Service Companies. This follows a 26 percent increase in 2003. Broken down by category, information technology products and services are forecast to reach $8.4 billion, or 17 percent growth, on the heels of an 18 percent climb last year, while business process outsourcing will grow by 54 percent to $3.6 billion in 2004, following an increase of 59 percent last year. What's more, NASSCOM is predicting that India's outsourcing sector will employ 1.1 million people by 2008, up from about 650,000 today. It's the kind of growth CEOs dream of, but also the kind that cannot be sustained.

Venture capital to support all this outsourcing continues to pour in. Palo Alto-based Charter Ventures is starting a fund to invest solely in outsourcing companies in India, and Charter is building a facility to house 10 to 12 of these portfolio companies in Bangalore, one of the key cities for outsourcing. Still, Sumir Chadha, founding managing partner of Westbridge Capital Partners, predicts rapid consolidation in the sector, to four or five major players in the next few years. Last summer, his Silicon Valley-based firm put $4 million into Indecomm Global Services, a health care and financial transaction outsourcing player, while another firm in his portfolio, First Ring, was absorbed by ICICI OneSource. Now Indecomm is on the prowl for two more acquisitions, says CEO K.P. Ponnapa, who boasts, "We aim to be a $100 million player in a short time."

Another firm jockeying for competitive advantage, iGate Global Solutions in Freemont, Calif., has acquired three companies that offer specialized services in outsourcing, Bangalore's Quintant Services being its latest. "Outsourcing is becoming more mainstream and companies are saying they can't live without it," says CEO Phaneesh Murthy, also one of the founders of the Indian outsourcing giant Infosys. He points to potential cost savings of 30 to 35 percent from outsourcing as one key driver for the explosion in outsourcing, and predicts that the field will consolidate ever more rapidly, leaving room "over the next few years for 15 to 20 reasonable size companies."

Quality Issues Lead to Failure

MR. Rangaswami, who heads the consultancy Sand Hill Group, agrees, "We are seeing a hyper-market with a lot of consolidations and mergers." He also points to some "quiet failures" among outsourcing providers, which are related to quality service issues rather than excess supply. As one high-profile example of failure due to service issues, he points to a recent decision by Dell to stop routing corporate customers to a technical support call center in Bangalore after it received numerous complaints about thick accents and scripted responses.

"We are starting to see a separation of the tier-one companies from the tier-twos," adds Ananda Mukerji, CEO of ICICI OneSource, a leading outsourcing provider in India. "We have seen a lot of venture capital money coming into this sector, and now many of these portfolio companies are looking for an exit because they realize they are not going to be able to grow and reach critical mass," he says, emphasizing that "scale is important." His own company has grown from 700 to 4,100 employees in the past 18 months, he says. Seven hundred of those new employees came through acquisitions.

So what can CEOs do to make sure their low-cost job centers keep churning out products and services for them? Consultant Rangaswami advises chief executives not to underestimate the time it takes to pick and manage a good partner. The CEO needs to be committed to the project and invest hands-on time, visiting India or China to get the "lay of the land," and becoming involved with the selection process by making final site visits and talking to customers. He says the process should take three to six months and warns against speeding up decision-making "even though some companies are under a lot of pressure to cut costs."

***CEOs also should take precautions* to ensure their most talented software developers are not lured away with better offers and perks.**

CEOs also should take precautions to ensure their most talented software developers aren't lured away with better offers and perks, as they frequently were in the heyday of Silicon Valley. One way to keep the upper hand, advises Rangaswami, is to bring a team of software developers in-house after building up an operation and offer management an ownership stake.

Joe Prang, CEO of Conformia Software in Redwood City, Calif., recommends that companies carefully match their needs with the right size partner. "I wouldn't advise being a small fish in a big pond," says Prang, who has worked with several California-based software developers with information technology operations in India, including his latest company in Saratoga, Calif. He also suggests that executives dole out projects to multiple outsourcing providers as a form of insurance in the impending shakeout.

The most important thing though, he says, is not the company itself but the team working on your business "and the influence and control you have over them." Even if the company gets swallowed up in India, the team may decide to be loyal to an outsourcing customer back in the U.S. provided that company takes steps to create a bond. He advises that multinationals should pick teams that have a "strong affinity with your company." Another way to cement the relationship despite the distances is by setting up a reserve as a bonus pool for the workers, he adds.

One more tactic is to bring the software team in-house, a move Prang has experimented with to prevent high turnover and promote loyalty. When he was head of the enterprise software development firm Aspect Development a few years ago, Prang brought his 75-to-100-member Indian software team in-house and formed a wholly owned subsidiary. That kept the team in place for a few years until the unit was recently acquired by another firm in the outsourcing business, I2 Technologies. Prang had moved on to another software development firm by then, but for him, it was just one more sign that things are just a little overheated.

As the industry rapidly transforms, CEOs too need to be on the watch for telltale signs that their outsourcing partnerships are healthy—and stay that way.

Turning Boomers Into Boomerangs

Older workers want to retire later; companies fear they will soon be short of skills. Why can't the two get together?

The Economist

Last month the first baby-boomers turned 60. The bulky generation born between 1946 and 1964 is heading towards retirement. The looming "demographic cliff" will see vast numbers of skilled workers dispatched from the labour force. In a forthcoming book ("Workforce Crisis" by Ken Dychtwald, Tamara Erickson and Robert Morison) the authors paint a gloomy picture of a shortage of skills and a cut in the supply of labour that are "already threatening the performance of many corporations."

The workforce is ageing across the rich world. Within the EU the number of workers aged between 50 and 64 will increase by 25% over the next two decades, while those aged 20–29 will decrease by 20%. In Japan almost 20% of the population is already over 65, the highest share in the world. And in the United States the number of workers aged 55–64 will have increased by more than half in this decade, at the same time as the 35- to 44-year-olds decline by 10%.

Given that most societies are geared to retirement at around 65, companies have a looming problem of knowledge management, of making sure that the boomers do not leave before they have handed over their expertise along with the office keys and their e-mail address. A survey of human-resources directors by IBM last year concluded: "When the baby-boomer generation retires, many companies will find out too late that a career's worth of experience has walked out the door, leaving insufficient talent to fill the void."

Some also face a shortage of expertise. In aerospace and defence, for example, as much as 40% of the workforce in some companies will be eligible to retire within the next five years. At the same time, the number of engineering graduates in developed countries is in steep decline.

A few companies are so squeezed that they are already taking exceptional measures. Earlier this year the *Los Angeles Times* interviewed an enterprising Australian who was staying in Beverly Hills while he tried to persuade locals to emigrate to Toowoomba, Queensland, to work for his engineering company there. Toowoomba today; the rest of the developed world tomorrow?

If you look hard enough, you can find companies that have begun to adapt the workplace to older workers. The AARP, an American association for the over-50s, produces an annual list of the best employers of its members. Health-care firms invariably come near the top because they are one of the industries most in need of skilled labour. Other sectors similarly affected, says the Conference Board, include oil, gas, energy and government.

Near the top of the AARP's latest list comes Deere & Company, a no-nonsense industrial equipment manufacturer based in Moline, Illinois; about 35% of Deere's 46,000 employees are over 50 and a number of them are in their 70s. Rick McAnally, the company's director of human resources, says that Deere has no overall policy in favour of older workers. It does, however, try to recruit people who will stay with the company for their whole careers, and a number of its employees have more than 40 years' service. The tools it uses to achieve that—flexible working, telecommuting, and so forth—also coincidentally help older workers to extend their working lives. The company spends "a lot of time" on the ergonomics of its factories, making jobs there less tiring, which enables older workers to stay at them for longer.

Likewise, for more than a decade, Toyota, arguably the world's most advanced manufacturer, has adapted its workstations to older workers. The shortage of skilled labour available to the automotive industry (those engineers again) has made it unusually keen to recruit older workers. BMW recently set up a factory in Leipzig that expressly set out to employ people over the age of 45. Needs must when the devil drives.

Other firms are polishing their alumni networks. IBM uses its network to recruit retired people for particular projects. Ernst & Young, a professional-services firm, has about 30,000 registered alumni, and about 25% of its "experienced" new recruits are boomerangs (former employees who return after an absence). Helen Walsh, director of the firm's alumni network (and herself a boomerang), says it is particularly helpful in attracting women back into the workforce.

But such examples are unusual. A survey in America last month by Ernst & Young found that "although corporate America foresees a significant workforce

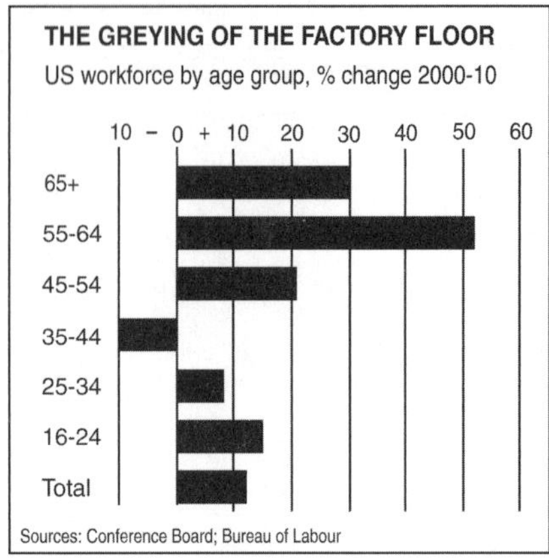

shortage as boomers retire, it is not dealing with the issue." Almost three-quarters of the 1,400 global companies questioned by Deloitte last year said they expected a shortage of salaried staff over the next three to five years. Yet few of them are looking to older workers to fill that shortage; and even fewer are looking to them to fill another gap that has already appeared. Many firms in Europe and America complain that they struggle to find qualified directors for their boards—this when the pool of retired talent from those very same firms is growing by leaps and bounds.

Why are firms not working harder to keep old employees? Part of the reason is that the crunch has been beyond the horizon of most managers. Nor is hanging on to older workers the only way to cope with a falling supply of labour. The participation of developing countries in the world economy has increased the overall supply—whatever the local effect of demographics in the rich countries. A vast amount of work is being sent offshore to such places as China and India and more will go in future. Some countries, such as Australia, are relaxing their immigration policies to allow much needed skills to come in from abroad. Others will avoid the need for workers by spending money on machinery and automation.

Yet older workers are an obvious source of labour, partly because they have good reason to continue working. In a widely quoted article ("Will There Really Be a Labour Shortage?") Peter Cappelli, of the Wharton business school in Philadelphia, argues that "baby-boom workers simply will not be retiring from work in the numbers that many people expect." One reason is that their pensions will not be as generous as they believed—a succession of big firms, such as IBM, General Motors and, in Britain, the Co-operative Society and the Nationwide building society, have announced that they are to trim retirement benefits. A recent Harris/Wall Street Journal survey found that 39% of Americans over 54 now doubt they will have sufficient money for old age. Mr Cappelli concluded that enough of them might stay on to shift the trajectory of the labour force. Using US Bureau of Labour statistics, he predicted that "the labour force will in fact rise from 153m in 2000 to 159m in 2010."

Yet there are plenty of obstacles to overcome if that is to happen. In many European countries, one of the biggest is pay. Adecco, a large global recruitment agency, says that in France and Germany 50- to 65-year-olds earn 60–70% more, on average, than 25- to 30-year-olds. But in Britain they earn more or less the same. That is one reason why more older people are employed in Britain than in Germany. In 1990 the unemployment rate among 55- to 64-year-olds in the two countries was more or less the same—7.2% in Britain and 7.7% in Germany. By 2003, however, the rates were 3.3% and 9.7% respectively.

Companies in continental Europe and Japan are finding it harder to detach age from seniority (and cost) than rivals in America and Britain. At Wal-Mart, a huge American retailer, managers fresh out of college in the southern American states oversee women workers old enough to be their mothers. Ranjit de Sousa, Adecco's director of corporate development, cites one company where the average age of the managers is 35, while that of the employees who report to them is 42. If older workers want to stay in the workforce, they need to accept this topsy-turvy hierarchy.

In some businesses early retirement is institutionalised. At professional-service companies, such as law and accounting firms, partners are encouraged to move out at an early age, often as young as 55, so as to encourage juniors with the promise of becoming a partner. At Deloitte, one of the world's biggest accounting firms, the official retirement age for partners—60—is written into the partnership agreement.

Change the reward system and the age profile changes too. Although British law firms have a "lock-step" reward system, giving partners more or less equal shares of the profits, partners in American firms tend to "eat what they kill." The American system enables older partners to stay on, because they are not an unfair burden. When Jerome Shestack approached the mandatory partners' retirement age (of 68) at his law firm in Philadelphia, he joined another without that condition. He retired from Wolf, Block, Schorr and Solis-Cohen ear-

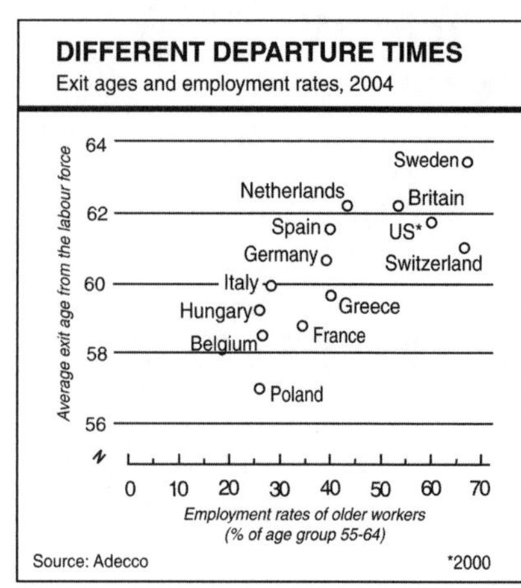

lier this month at 82. At 74 he was president of the American Bar Association.

The government has a big part to play. Switzerland has legislation enabling people who stay at work for up to five years beyond the statutory retirement age to increase their state pension by up to SFr5,000 ($3,825) a year when they eventually draw it. That helps explain why more than 60% of all 55- to 64-year-old Swiss are in work, compared with less than 30% in Italy and Belgium. (For Italy, which has one of the lowest fertility rates in Europe and one of the lowest average retirement ages, the demographic cliff is a precipice looming at its feet.)

In some countries the tax system works against older workers. Britain will not let a taxpayer receive a pension and a salary from the same employer. In America pension schemes will often withhold benefits from a retired person if he is rehired or works for more than 40 hours a month. Companies wishing to hire their pensioners have to find ways round the rules. Japanese companies such as Mazda rehire them on one-year renewable contracts.

Staying on

Legislation designed to help older workers can act against them. In some ways, America's Age Discrimination in Employment Act discourages the rehiring of retired workers, by requiring that all employees receive equal benefits, such as health-care insurance. That is invariably more expensive for older employees, so it acts as a deterrent to hiring them. Similar legislation is due to come into force in Britain in October this year, following an EU directive compelling member states to outlaw discrimination on the grounds of age.

Even if the law changes, older workers must still overcome hostile attitudes at work. Many people assume that older employees are less motivated, take more sick leave and cost more. The evidence is that many people over 65 have plenty to offer even if they are no longer at their peak. Some studies show that the over-40s are less likely to be off sick, and are more highly motivated and productive (except where great physical effort is required).

The best thing managers can do is to make work flexible. Much of this accords with what women and younger workers say they want. IBM believes that one of the reasons people come to work for it "is because we take workplace flexibility seriously." Flexibility appeals to all ages.

The encouragement for older workers to stay is often a by-product of other initiatives. Many companies are cultivating a more diverse workforce, partly because legislation in some countries decrees it, partly because they believe it can help them. Although diversity means chiefly recruiting more women and ethnic minorities, it (almost by default) helps older workers, too. Measures, such as flexible work schedules, designed to encourage mothers to return to the workforce can also encourage older workers to stay.

Oddly enough, older workers stand to gain from efforts to recruit younger workers. Sabri Challah, the head of Deloitte's human-capital practice, says that companies are making great efforts to recruit (and retain) the youngest cohort of workers, the "Generation Y." These 20-somethings (who are entering the workforce later and staying for a shorter time with each employer) have very different attitudes to work, life and careers than their parents did. In trying to design flexible working lives for them, companies may be accommodating grey hair as well.

In the longer run, though, firms need to talk seriously to employers about their plans for retirement. Many have no demographic profile of their workforce and little idea about how much of it is retiring when. Mr Chillah says many are embarrassed to ask senior employees about taking less pay for less work. In America employers are also often afraid to discuss retirement plans for fear of lawsuits under age-discrimination legislation.

That is a pity. A report last year by Merrill Lynch, a large financial-services firm, argued that "baby-boomers fundamentally will reinvent retirement". They will, said the report, "cycle" between periods of work and leisure well beyond the age of 65. While many are focused on making extra money, many more say they will do it for the "mental stimulation and challenge." As the Conference Board, an American association of businessmen, put it last year: "working in retirement, once considered an oxymoron, is the new reality".

Do Americans Work Too Hard?

By Fred Maidment

Americans spend more time on the job than workers in any other industrialized country, with the exceptions of South Koreans and the Czechs. The South Koreans are unique because they are the only industrialized country with a six-day work week, and the Czechs put in 113 hours per year more than Americans (Koreans, Czechs, Americans are hardest workers, 2001). South Koreans spend so much time on the job that many believe it is actually hurting their economy (Prasso, Sheridan, Ihlwan, Moon, "Less Work, More Shopping," *Business Week*, Sept. 9, 2002). They averaged more than 47 hours per week in 2000, as comparred to the American 38, which, in the United States, is an increase of more than 40 minutes per week since 1990.

What is surprising is that the workforce in the United States, the country with easily the largest and most rapidly growing major post-industrialized economy, continues to increase the number of hours on the job while the rest of the developed world adds more leisure time to its schedule. A study sponsored by the Families and Work Institute shows that almost 11 million Americans work more than 60 hours per week ("Americans work longer than Japanese, Germans," *HR Briefing*, Aug. 1, 2002).

That same report stated that the average American male worked 49 hours per week, besting the average South Korean by 1.5 hours per week, as reported by the International Labor Organization. American women worked a reported average of 42 hours per week according to the Families and Work Institute study.

Some of the drawbacks to putting in more hours on the job involve the health and well-being of the workforce, as well as the health of the economy. From a purely economic perspective, it can be overdone, as may be the case in South Korea, where a five-day work week may actually increase economic growth, because the workers will then have time to spend their money.

Work Can Kill

From the perspective of the workers, men working more than 60 hours a week and missing sleep are at twice the risk of having a heart attack as those who work 40 hours per week. Many American workers never take a full lunch break and over half think about work over the weekend ("In Brief," *Personnel Today*, July 16, 2002, p. 8). This can lead to "karoshi" (Hatfield, Peter, "If you think you're overworked, think again," *New Scientist*, Dec. 8, 2001), a Japanese word for "death through overwork." Karoshi has been recognized by the Japanese government since the 1970s as a cause of death and has resulted in some 40 claims for compensation per year since then.

Because karoshi was narrowly defined, most of those cases have been rejected, but now, based on a study sponsored by the Ministry of Health and Welfare, and led by Osamu Wada of the Saitame Medical School, that definition may be broadened.

The study found a strong relationship between karoshi and excessive overtime hours during the three months before death. Workers who put in more than 100 overtime hours in the last four weeks, and more than 80 overtime hours per month in the previous five months had an even higher likelihood of karoshi.

Americans need to remember that they now work longer than the average Japanese citizen, putting in more than 2.5 hours more per week. While some Americans have died on the job (Iococca, Lee, *Iococca: An Autobiography*, New York, Bantam, 1984), or from what the Japanese might call karoshi, these events have been viewed as isolated instances. Such deaths were considered the result of job demands and stress that the deceased individuals were simply unable to handle. No pattern was sought, and, therefore, no pattern was found. They were simply written off as isolated instances.

However, the evidence clearly suggests that karoshi is not an isolated instance. As Americans spend more time on the job, they're certain to experience it.

The battle cries of American industry have been to "do more with less," "downsize," "re-engineer" and "right-size," to name only a few. This has translated to greater productivity for the American worker and American industry, but it has also translated to longer hours, and more stress, frequently resulting in medical problems for the employee, and often greater stress at home.

HR's Role

Human resource executives are on the front lines in addressing to workers the consequences of putting in excessive hours on the job. The problems workers experience have to be addressed by human resource professionals and are likely to involve the programs HR administers.

Proper health care and drug, family and other forms of counseling will help curb the rising cost of health insurance and use of family leave. Additional stress on the job has been shown to make people more susceptible to physical illness and disease.

This is eventually going to mean lost time on the job. An employee may be putting in 60 hours a week now, but, eventually, he or she will be getting at least some of those 60 hours back, at home, sick in bed. Approaches for dealing with this stress need to be developed so as to minimize the impact on the workforce.

As the stress bar continues to move upward and as more is expected from fewer employees, and more time on the job is required to fulfill those expectations, the spector of karoshi becomes a greater possibility. An organization can "re-engineer" or "right-size" up to a point, but the amount of people available to do the work does.

Obtaining greater productivity from the workforce is one thing. Increasing worker productivity to the point where the employees start to approach death by overwork can expose the organizations to legal liability claims, as the government of Japan has recognized for some 30 years.

Fred Maidment is an associate professor at the Ancell School of Business of Western Connecticut State University.

UNIT 7

Perspectives and Trends

Unit Selections

31. **The Discipline of Innovation**, Peter F. Drucker
32. **Thinking Locally, Succeeding Globally**, Elizabeth Esfahani
33. **The Great Wal-Mart of China**, Clay Chandler
34. **American Corporations: The New Sovereigns**, Lawrence E. Mitchell
35. **The Real Reason You're Working So Hard...and What You Can Do About It**, Michael Mandel
36. **For New "Old Boys" Only**, Stewart Crainer and Des Dearlove
37. **The Tone at the Top and Ethical Conduct Connection**, Barbara Lamberton, Paul H. Mihalek, CPA, and Carl S. Smith, CMA, CFM, CPA
38. **The Road to Stronger Corporate Governance**, Linda Zong
39. **Up to the Challenge**, Mark Henricks
40. **Determining the Strategies and Tactics of Ownership Succession**, James Ahern
41. **In Fourth Year of 'War on Terror': Successes, Failures, Blowback from Iraq**, Charles J. Hanley

Key Points to Consider

- In the future, organizations are going to have to take a more proactive role in the affairs of the communities around them. How do you see them being involved in those activities?
- Multinational corporations are growing in power and in influence. How do you see this affecting the economy both in the United States and abroad? Do you think that this will develop greater understanding between cultures?
- Corporate culture is one of the most powerful forces in any organization. Do you see any possible models for corporate organization and culture in the future? How do you think corporate culture affects the way people work in organizations?
- Ethics are a primary concern of any organization. Is it OK to take home a pen, a pencil, or to make personal copies on the office copier? Where do you draw the line? When do people cross it? What role does management play in establishing the ethics and culture of an organization?
- What are some of the ways that a small, successful business can continue to grow and prosper?
- What have been some of the successes and failures of the War on Terror? Do you think this has had an impact on business and industry? In what way?

Student Website

www.mhcls.com/online

Internet References

Further information regarding these websites may be found in this book's preface or online.

Institute for International Economics
http://www.iie.com

Small Business Management
http://management.tqn.com/msubs.htm

Terrorism Research Center
http://www.terrorism.com

World Trade Organization (WTO) Web Site
http://www.wto.org/index.htm

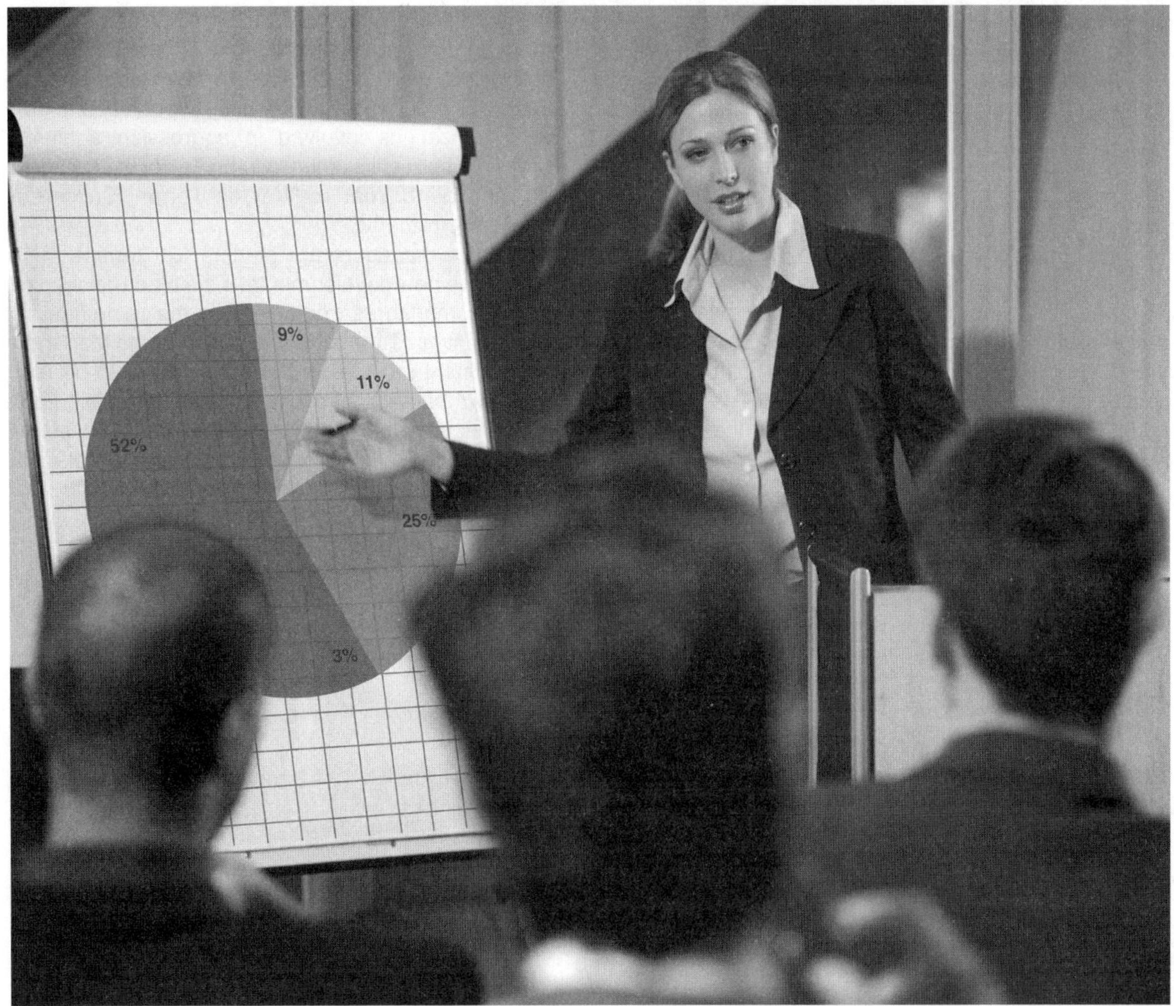

Managers are facing new challenges. While it is never possible to determine exactly what the future will hold, there are certain trends and movements that can be perceived by an aware and thoughtful manager. Innovation is always going to be an important feature for a society that depends on technology to remain ahead of its competition and to maintain its standard of living and competitive edge. In "The Discipline of Innovation," Peter Drucker identifies seven kinds of opportunities that may be used to help develop innovation, which is highly important to a technologically advanced society such as the United States.

The multinational corporation is changing the way people do business. These corporate giants are coming to dominate the global economy in ways that have not been foreseen. Most of these companies started in the United States, but there are also organizations with European and Japanese roots that would fall into this category. These organizations are very powerful, but they must be "Thinking Locally, Succeeding Globally" to survive in a highly competitive global economy. Just being big is not necessarily going to guarantee success. However, working hard to establish a position in a market will generally bring success as seen in "The Great Wal-Mart of China."

Another development in American society has been the rise of the small businessperson. Over the past decade, the number of people employed by Fortune 500 industrial companies has declined, while the size of the workforce has increased. Many of these new workers have entered small firms. Small businesses tend to be family businesses, and it is often difficult to determine where the business ends and the family begins. In addition, these businesses are entrepreneurial in nature. Entrepreneurs serve the highly creative function of creating new jobs and new businesses. They develop and market new products and services and are often on the cutting edge of the new technology of tomorrow, both technical and managerial. One of the major challenges facing these firms is how to continue to grow once they experienced initial success as seen in "Up to the Challenge."

Corporate culture is an aspect of organizations that many people know about but few truly understand. Every organization has a culture, which to a certain degree is a reflection of the values and ethics of senior management, as well as the values and ethics of the society of which the organization is a part. Paying attention to the culture is a key element in developing the organization and achieving success. Organizations that have strong cultures tend to be more successful than organizations that do not, and ensuring the strength of the organizational culture is a primary concern of management because it is from the culture that so many other aspects of the organization flow. But as organizations evolve, the types of culture and forms of organization will need to evolve with them. The demands that the organization puts on managers if they are going to be successful is examined in "The Real Reason You're Working So Hard."

Managers and their organizations have been criticized over the past several years for a lack of ethics and morality. A small—and when they are caught—highly publicized minority has indeed played fast and loose with the law and with ethics. Some continue to do so, especially in the global arena where it has sometimes been difficult to enforce the rules of the corporations themselves concerning illegal acts. These acts have caused all managers to look more closely at their own behavior and to develop ethical guidelines. The courts are starting to take a dimmer view of white-collar crime, to the point of sending some executives, such as Charles Keating and Martha Stewart, to prison. Ethical and principled behavior on the part of executives in organizations will lead to greater competitive strength and profitability as demonstrated in "The Road to Stronger Corporate Governance."

Another interesting development for managers has been the role of business in the War on Terror. Exactly what is the responsibility of American industry in the war against terrorists? With global operations all over the world, and interests in and with many foreign organizations, how should U.S. industry act and respond to other organizations it knows are engaging in activities that either directly or indirectly support countries, individuals, or organizations involved in aggression against the United States? The results of the War on Terror in 2005 are reviewed in "In the Fourth Year of 'War on Terror': Successes, Failures, Blowback from Iraq."

Finally, managers are starting to examine their careers in light of the new developments in the marketplace. In earlier generations, managers would work for the same firm for their entire working lives. That is no longer the case. Managers in today's environment must be flexible. They have to be responsible for their own careers, because the firms they join could go out of business or be purchased, and they could be left without a job. Managers must look after themselves and make career moves independently, if they hope to succeed.

The Discipline of Innovation

In business, innovation rarely springs from a flash of inspiration. It arises from a cold-eyed analysis of seven kinds of opportunities.

by Peter F. Drucker

How much of innovation is inspiration, and how much is hard work? If it's mainly the former, then management's role is limited: Hire the right people, and get out of their way. If it's largely the latter, management must play a more vigorous role: Establish the right roles and processes, set clear goals and relevant measures, and review progress at every step. Peter Drucker, with the masterly subtlety that is his trademark, comes down somewhere in the middle. Yes, he writes in this article, innovation is real work, and it can and should be managed like any other corporate function. But that doesn't mean it's the same as other business activities. Indeed, innovation is the work of *knowing* rather than *doing.*

Drucker argues that most innovative business ideas come from methodically analyzing seven areas of opportunity, some of which lie within particular companies or industries and some of which lie in broader social or demographic trends. Astute managers will ensure that their organizations maintain a clear focus on all seven. But analysis will take you only so far. Once you've identified an attractive opportunity, you still need a leap of imagination to arrive at the right response—call it "functional inspiration."

DESPITE much discussion these days of the "entrepreneurial personality," few of the entrepreneurs with whom I have worked during the past 30 years had such personalities. But I have known many people—salespeople, surgeons, journalists, scholars, even musicians—who did have them without being the least bit entrepreneurial. What all the successful entrepreneurs I have met have in common is not a certain kind of personality but a commitment to the systematic practice of innovation.

Innovation is the specific function of entrepreneurship, whether in an existing business, a public service institution, or a new venture started by a lone individual in the family kitchen. It is the means by which the entrepreneur either creates new wealth-producing resources or endows existing resources with enhanced potential for creating wealth.

Today, much confusion exists about the proper definition of entrepreneurship. Some observers use the term to refer to all small businesses; others, to all new businesses. In practice, however, a great many well-established businesses engage in highly successful entrepreneurship. The term, then, refers not to an enterprise's size or age but to a certain kind of activity. At the heart of that activity is innovation: the effort to create purposeful, focused change in an enterprise's economic or social potential.

Sources of Innovation

There are, of course, innovations that spring from a flash of genius. Most innovations, however, especially the successful ones, result from a conscious, purposeful search for innovation opportunities, which are found only in a few situations. Four such areas of opportunity exist within a company or industry: unexpected occurrences, incongruities, process needs, and industry and market changes.

Three additional sources of opportunity exist outside a company in its social and intellectual environment: demographic changes, changes in perception, and new knowledge.

True, these sources overlap, different as they may be in the nature of their risk, difficulty, and complexity, and the potential for innovation may well lie in more than one area at a time. But together, they account for the great majority of all innovation opportunities.

1 Unexpected Occurrences

Consider, first, the easiest and simplest source of innovation opportunity: the unexpected. In the early 1930s, IBM developed the first modern accounting machine, which was designed for banks. But banks in 1933 did not buy new equipment. What saved the company—according to a story that Thomas Watson, Sr., the company's founder and long-term CEO, often told—was its exploitation of an unexpected success: The New York Public Library wanted to buy a machine. Unlike the banks, libraries in those early New Deal days had money, and Watson sold more than a hundred of his otherwise unsalable machines to libraries.

Fifteen years later, when everyone believed that computers were designed for advanced scientific work, business unexpectedly showed an interest in a machine that could do payroll. Univac, which had the most advanced machine, spurned business applications. But IBM immediately realized it faced a possible unexpected success, redesigned what was basically Univac's machine for such mundane applications as payroll, and within five years became a leader in the computer industry, a position it has maintained to this day.

The unexpected failure may be an equally important source of innovation opportunities. Everyone knows about the Ford Edsel as the biggest new-car failure in automotive history. What very few people seem to know, however, is that the Edsel's failure was the foundation for much of the company's later success. Ford planned the Edsel, the most carefully designed car to that point in American automotive history, to give the company a full product line with which to compete with General Motors. When it bombed, despite all the planning, market research, and design that had gone into it, Ford realized that something was happening in the automobile market that ran counter to the basic assumptions on which GM and everyone else had been designing and marketing cars. No longer was the market segmented primarily by income groups; the new principle of segmentation was what we now call "lifestyles." Ford's response was the Mustang, a car that gave the company a distinct personality and reestablished it as an industry leader.

Unexpected successes and failures are such productive sources of innovation opportunities because most businesses dismiss them, disregard them, and even resent them. The German scientist who around 1905 synthesized novocaine, the first nonaddictive narcotic, had intended it to be used in major surgical procedures like amputation. Surgeons, however, preferred total anesthesia for such procedures; they still do. Instead, novocaine found a ready appeal among dentists. Its inventor spent the remaining years of his life traveling from dental school to dental school making speeches that forbade dentists from "misusing" his noble invention in applications for which he had not intended it.

This is a caricature, to be sure, but it illustrates the attitude managers often take to the unexpected: "It should not have happened." Corporate reporting systems further ingrain this reaction, for they draw attention away from unanticipated possibilities. The typical monthly or quarterly report has on its first page a list of problems—that is, the areas where results fall short of expectations. Such information is needed, of course, to help prevent deterioration of performance. But it also suppresses the recognition of new opportunities. The first acknowledgment of a possible opportunity usually applies to an area in which a company does better than budgeted. Thus genuinely entrepreneurial businesses have two "first pages"—a problem page and an opportunity page—and managers spend equal time on both.

2 Incongruities

Alcon Laboratories was one of the success stories of the 1960s because Bill Conner, the company's cofounder, exploited an incongruity in medical technology. The cataract operation is the world's third or fourth most common surgical procedure. During the past 300 years, doctors systematized it to the point that the only "old-fashioned" step left was the cutting of a ligament. Eye surgeons had learned to cut the ligament with complete success, but it was so different a procedure from the rest of the operation, and so incompatible with it, that they often dreaded it. It was incongruous.

Doctors had known for 50 years about an enzyme that could dissolve the ligament without cutting. All Conner did was to add a preservative to this enzyme that gave it a few months' shelf life. Eye surgeons immediately accepted the new compound, and Alcon found itself with a worldwide monopoly. Fifteen years later, Nestlé bought the company for a fancy price.

Such an incongruity within the logic or rhythm of a process is only one possibility out of which innovation opportunities may arise. Another source is incongruity between economic realities. For instance, whenever an industry has a steadily growing market but falling profit margins—as, say, in the steel industries of developed countries between 1950 and 1970—an incongruity exists. The innovative response: minimills.

An incongruity between expectations and results can also open up possibilities for innovation. For 50 years after the turn of the century, shipbuilders and shipping companies worked hard both to make ships faster and to lower their fuel consumption. Even so, the more successful they were in boosting speed and trimming their fuel needs, the worse the economics of ocean freighters became. By 1950 or so, the ocean freighter was dying, if not already dead.

All that was wrong, however, was an incongruity between the industry's assumptions and its realities. The real costs did not come from doing work (that is, being at sea) but from *not* doing work (that is, sitting idle in port). Once managers understood where costs truly lay, the innovations were obvious: the roll-on and roll-off ship and the container ship. These solutions, which involved old technology, simply applied to the ocean freighter what railroads and truckers had been using for 30 years. A shift in viewpoint, not in technology, totally changed the economics of ocean shipping and turned it into one of the major growth industries of the last 20 to 30 years.

3 Process Needs

Anyone who has ever driven in Japan knows that the country has no modern highway system. Its roads still follow the paths laid down for—or by—oxcarts in the tenth century. What makes the system work for automobiles and trucks is an adaptation of the reflector used on American highways since the early 1930s. The reflector lets each car see which other cars are approaching from any one of a half-dozen directions. This minor invention, which enables traffic to move smoothly and with a minimum of accidents, exploited a process need.

Knowledge-based innovations can be temperamental, capricious, and hard to direct.

What we now call the media had its origin in two innovations developed around 1890 in response to process needs. One was Ottmar Mergenthaler's Linotype, which made it possible to produce newspapers quickly and in large volume. The other was a social innovation, modern advertising, invented by the first true newspaper publishers, Adolph Ochs of the *New York Times,* Joseph Pulitzer of the *New York World,* and William Randolph Hearst. Advertising made it possible for them to distribute news practically free of charge, with the profit coming from marketing.

4 Industry and Market Changes

Managers may believe that industry structures are ordained by the good Lord, but these structures can—and often do—change overnight. Such change creates tremendous opportunity for innovation.

One of American business's great success stories in recent decades is the brokerage firm of Donaldson, Lufkin & Jenrette, recently acquired by the Equitable Life Assurance Society. DL&J was founded in 1960 by three young men, all graduates of the Harvard Business School, who realized that the structure of the financial industry was changing as institutional investors became dominant. These young men had practically no capital and no connections. Still, within a few years, their firm had become a leader in the move to negotiated commissions and one of Wall Street's stellar performers. It was the first to be incorporated and go public.

In a similar fashion, changes in industry structure have created massive innovation opportunities for American health care providers. During the past ten or 15 years, independent surgical and psychiatric clinics, emergency centers, and HMOs have opened throughout the country. Comparable opportunities in telecommunications followed industry upheavals—in transmission (with the emergence of MCI and Sprint in long-distance service) and in equipment (with the emergence of such companies as Rolm in the manufacturing of private branch exchanges).

When an industry grows quickly—the critical figure seems to be in the neighborhood of 40% growth in ten years or less—its structure changes. Established companies, concentrating on defending what they already have, tend not to counterattack when a newcomer challenges them. Indeed, when market or industry structures change, traditional industry leaders again and again neglect the fastest growing market segments. New opportunities rarely fit the way the industry has always approached the market, defined it, or organized to serve it. Innovators therefore have a good chance of being left alone for a long time.

5 Demographic Changes

Of the outside sources of innovation opportunities, demographics are the most reliable. Demographic events have known lead times; for instance, every person who will be in the American labor force by the year 2000 has already been born. Yet because policy makers often neglect demographics, those who watch them and exploit them can reap great rewards.

The Japanese are ahead in robotics because they paid attention to demographics. Everyone in the developed countries around 1970 or so knew that there was both a baby bust and an education explosion going on; about half or more of the young people were staying in school beyond high school. Consequently, the number of people available for traditional blue-collar work in manufacturing was bound to decrease and become inadequate by 1990. Everyone knew this, but only the Japanese acted on it, and they now have a ten-year lead in robotics.

Much the same is true of Club Mediterranee's success in the travel and resort business. By 1970, thoughtful observers could have seen the emergence of large numbers of affluent and educated young adults in Europe and the United States. Not comfortable with the kind of vacations their working-class parents had enjoyed—the summer weeks at Brighton or Atlantic City—these young people were ideal customers for a new and exotic version of the "hangout" of their teen years.

Managers have known for a long time that demographics matter, but they have always believed that population statistics change slowly. In this century, however, they don't. Indeed, the innovation opportunities made possible by changes in the numbers of people—and in their age distribution, education, occupations, and geographic location—are among the most rewarding and least risky of entrepreneurial pursuits.

6 Changes in Perception

"The glass is half full" and "The glass is half empty" are descriptions of the same phenomenon but have vastly different meanings. Changing a manager's perception of a glass from half full to half empty opens up big innovation opportunities.

All factual evidence indicates, for instance, that in the last 20 years, Americans' health has improved with unprecedented speed—whether measured by mortality rates for the newborn, survival rates for the very old, the incidence of cancers (other than lung cancer), cancer cure rates, or other factors. Even so, collective hypochondria grips the nation. Never before has there been so much concern with or fear about health. Suddenly, everything seems to cause cancer or degenerative heart disease or premature loss of memory. The glass is clearly half empty.

Rather than rejoicing in great improvements in health, Americans seem to be emphasizing how far away they still are from immortality. This view of things has created many opportunities for innovations: markets for new health care magazines, for exercise classes and jogging equipment, and for all kinds of health foods. The fastest growing new U.S. business in 1983 was a company that makes indoor exercise equipment.

A change in perception does not alter facts. It changes their meaning, though—and very quickly. It took less than two years for the computer to change from being perceived as a threat and as something only big businesses would use to something one buys for doing income tax. Economics do not necessarily dictate such a change; in fact, they may be irrelevant. What determines whether people see a glass as half full or half empty is mood rather than fact, and a change in mood often defies quantification. But it is not exotic. It is concrete. It can be defined. It can be tested. And it can be exploited for innovation opportunity.

7 New Knowledge

Among history-making innovations, those that are based on new knowledge—whether scientific, technical, or social—rank high. They are the superstars of entrepreneurship; they get the publicity and the money. They are what people usually mean when they talk of innovation, although not all innovations based on knowledge are important.

Knowledge-based innovations differ from all others in the time they take, in their casualty rates, and in their predictability, as well as in the challenges they pose to entrepreneurs. Like most superstars, they can be temperamental, capricious, and hard to direct. They have, for instance, the longest lead time of all innovations. There is a protracted span between the emergence of new knowledge and its distillation into usable technology. Then there is another long period before this new technology appears in the marketplace in products, processes, or services. Overall, the lead time involved is something like 50 years, a figure that has not shortened appreciably throughout history.

To become effective, innovation of this sort usually demands not one kind of knowledge but many. Consider one of the most potent knowledge-based innovations: modern banking. The theory of the entrepreneurial bank—that is, of the purposeful use of capital to generate economic development—was formulated by the Comte de Saint-Simon during the era of Napoleon. Despite Saint-Simon's extraordinary prominence, it was not until 30 years after his death in 1825 that two of his disciples, the brothers Jacob and Isaac Pereire, established the first entrepreneurial bank, the Credit Mobilier, and ushered in what we now call finance capitalism.

The Pereires, however, did not know modern commercial banking, which developed at about the same time across the channel in England. The Credit Mobilier failed ignominiously. A few years later, two young men—one an American, J. P. Morgan, and one a German, Georg Siemens—put together the French theory of entrepreneurial banking and the English theory of commercial banking to create the first successful modern banks: J. P. Morgan & Company in New York, and the Deutsche Bank in Berlin. Ten years later, a young Japanese, Shibusawa Eiichi, adapted Siemens's concept to his country and thereby laid the foundation of Japan's modern economy. This is how knowledge-based innovation always works.

The computer, to cite another example, required no fewer than six separate strands of knowledge:

- binary arithmetic;
- Charles Babbage's conception of a calculating machine, in the first half of the nineteenth century;
- the punch card, invented by Herman Hollerith for the U.S. census of 1890;
- the audion tube, an electronic switch invented in 1906;
- symbolic logic, which was developed between 1910 and 1913 by Bertrand Russell and Alfred North Whitehead;
- and concepts of programming and feedback that came out of abortive attempts during World War I to develop effective antiaircraft guns.

Although all the necessary knowledge was available by 1918, the first operational digital computer did not appear until 1946.

Long lead times and the need for convergence among different kinds of knowledge explain the peculiar rhythm of knowledge-based innovation, its attractions, and its dangers. During a long gestation period, there is a lot of talk and little action. Then, when all the elements suddenly converge, there is tremendous excitement and activity and an enormous amount of speculation. Between 1880 and 1890, for example, almost 1,000 electric-apparatus companies were founded in developed countries. Then, as always, there was a crash and a shakeout. By 1914, only 25 were still alive. In the early 1920s, 300 to 500 automobile companies existed in the United States; by 1960, only four of them remained.

Innovation requires knowledge, ingenuity, and, above all else, focus.

It may be difficult, but knowledge-based innovation can be managed. Success requires careful analysis of the various kinds of knowledge needed to make an innovation possible. Both J. P. Morgan and Georg Siemens did this when they established their banking ventures. The Wright brothers did this when they developed the first operational airplane.

Careful analysis of the needs—and, above all, the capabilities—of the intended user is also essential. It may seem paradoxical, but knowledge-based innovation is more market dependent than any other kind of innovation. De Havilland, a British company, designed and built the first passenger jet, but it did not analyze what the market needed and therefore did not identify two key factors. One was configuration—that is, the right size with the right payload for the routes on which a jet would give an airline the greatest advantage. The other was equally mundane: How could the airlines finance the purchase of such an expensive plane? Because de Havilland failed to do an adequate user analysis, two American companies, Boeing and Douglas, took over the commercial jet-aircraft industry.

Principles of Innovation

Purposeful, systematic innovation begins with the analysis of the sources of new opportunities. Depending on the context, sources will have different importance at different times. Demographics, for instance, may be of little concern to innovators of fundamental industrial processes like steelmaking, although the Linotype machine became successful primarily because there were not enough skilled typesetters available to satisfy a mass market. By the same token, new knowledge may be of little relevance to someone innovating a social instrument to satisfy a need that changing demographics or tax laws have created. But whatever the situation, innovators must analyze all opportunity sources.

Because innovation is both conceptual and perceptual, would-be innovators must also go out and look, ask, and listen. Successful innovators use both the right and left sides of their brains. They work out analytically what the innovation has to be to satisfy an opportunity. Then they go out and look at potential users to study their expectations, their values, and their needs.

To be effective, an innovation has to be simple, and it has to be focused. It should do only one thing; otherwise it confuses people. Indeed, the greatest praise an innovation can receive is for people to say, "This is obvious! Why didn't I think of it? It's so simple!" Even the innovation that creates new users and new markets should be directed toward a specific, clear, and carefully designed application.

Effective innovations start small. They are not grandiose. It may be to enable a moving vehicle to draw electric power while it runs along rails, the innovation that made possible the electric streetcar. Or it may be the elementary idea of putting the same number of matches into a matchbox (it used to be 50). This simple notion made possible the automatic filling of matchboxes and gave the Swedes a world monopoly on matches for half a century. By contrast, grandiose ideas for things that will "revolutionize an industry" are unlikely to work.

In fact, no one can foretell whether a given innovation will end up a big business or a modest achievement. But even if the results are modest, the successful innovation aims from the beginning to become the standard setter, to determine the direction of a new technology or a new industry, to create the business that is—and remains—ahead of the pack. If an innovation does not aim at leadership from the beginning, it is unlikely to be innovative enough.

Above all, innovation is work rather than genius. It requires knowledge. It often requires ingenuity. And it requires focus. There are clearly people who are more talented innovators than others, but their talents lie in well-defined areas. Indeed, innovators rarely work in more than one area. For all his systematic innovative accomplishments, Thomas Edison worked only in the electrical field. An innovator in financial areas, Citibank for example, is not likely to embark on innovations in health care.

In innovation, as in any other endeavor, there is talent, there is ingenuity, and there is knowledge. But when all is said and done, what innovation requires is hard, focused, purposeful work. If diligence, persistence, and commitment are lacking, talent, ingenuity, and knowledge are of no avail.

There is, of course, far more to entrepreneurship than systematic innovation—distinct entrepreneurial strategies, for example, and the principles of entrepreneurial management, which are needed equally in the established enterprise, the public service organization, and the new venture. But the very foundation of entrepreneurship is the practice of systematic innovation.

***Peter F. Drucker** is the Marie Rankin Clarke Professor of Social Science and Management at Claremont Graduate University's Peter F. Drucker Graduate School of Management in Claremont, California. He has written more than two dozen articles for HBR. This article was originally adapted from his book* Innovation and Entrepreneurship: Practice and Principles *(Harper & Row, 1985).*

Thinking Locally, Succeeding Globally

Elizabeth Esfahani

IF YOU'VE GOT KIMCHI IN YOUR FRIDGE, IT'S HARD TO keep it a secret. Kimchi, made from fermented cabbage seasoned with garlic and chili, is served with most meals in Korea, but when it's stored inside a normal refrigerator, its pungent odor taints nearby foods. That's why, two decades ago, South Korean appliance manufacturer LG Electronics introduced the kimchi refrigerator, a product specifically designed to address the odor problem. Featuring a dedicated compartment that isolates smelly kimchi from other foods, the fridge gradually became a must-have in Korean homes, inspiring rivals such as Samsung to offer similar models. Kimchi refrigerators have become a fixture in 65 percent of Korean homes, and after facing down the competition, LG is the country's top-selling manufacturer, according to GfK, an international market research firm.

The kimchi fridge has become a model for the approach LG uses to expand into new global markets. A $38 billion powerhouse in global electronics and appliances. LG says it is the world's top producer of air conditioners and one of the top three players in washing machines, microwaves, and refrigerators. Critical to this success has been LG's focus on in-depth localization—an approach that emphasizes understanding the idiosyncrasies of key local markets by opening in-country research, manufacturing, and marketing facilities. "Localization has been a key element of LG's successful global expansion, especially in non-U.S. markets," says analyst Michael Bertz of WR Hambrecht.

"Gone are the days where you could just roll out one product for the global market," explains Hamad Malik, LG's Middle East marketing director. "We speak to consumers individually."

Nowhere is the success of LG's approach more evident than in India, where GfK says the company is now the clear leader in virtually every appliance and electronics category—from microwaves to televisions—despite having entered the market in 1997, two years after Samsung. LG initially differentiated itself by introducing a line of health-oriented products, like televisions that reduced eyestrain. By 1999, however, it had set up local research and design facilities, manufacturing plants, and a network of service centers. With a population of more than 1 billion that spans several religions and languages, says Sandeep Tiwari, LG's home appliances marketing head in India, the country functions like dozens of smaller regional markets.

To meet the needs of Indian consumers, LG rolled out refrigerators with larger vegetable- and water-storage compartments, surge-resistant power supplies, and brightly colored finishes that reflect local preferences (red in the south, green in Kashmir). Some of LG's Indian microwaves have dark-colored interiors to hide masala stains. In 1999, LG introduced a television for cricket fans that came with a built-in cricket videogame. Its Ballad television was offered with extraloud sound after research showed that many Indians use their TVs to listen to music as well. Over time, these efforts have paid off. LG enjoys unprecedented dominance in India, with sales that are projected to reach $1.8 billion this year. In some categories, such as washing machines, LG says its market share is more than twice that of its nearest competitor.

Localization helps LG gain traction in emerging markets, where consumers have few preexisting brand loyalties. In Iran, LG offers a microwave oven with a preset button for reheating shish kebabs—a favorite dish. LG now claims to command roughly 40 percent of the Iranian microwave market. Meanwhile, LG's Primian refrigerator includes a special compartment for storing dates; the fruit, a Middle Eastern staple, spoils easily.

While not always huge sellers, LG's localized products clearly generate buzz. In September the company made headlines throughout the Middle East by unveiling a gold-plated 71-inch flat-screen television that sells for $80,000—a tribute to the region's famous affinity for gilded opulence. In Russia, LG's research revealed that many people entertain at home during the country's long winters, prompting the company to develop a karaoke phone that can be programmed with the top 100 Russian songs, whose lyrics scroll across the screen when they're played. Introduced in late 2004, the phone has been a hit, selling more than 220,000 handsets, LG says.

All this experience will be put to the test as LG moves to make its presence felt in China, the world's biggest consumer market, where major international brands must compete against domestic rivals such as Haier, the Qingdao-based white-goods manufacturer. Just as it did in India, LG is establishing extensive in-country facilities in China—from manufacturing to product marketing. LG opened an R&D operation in Beijing in 2002 and has since ramped up its staff to more than 1,500. The company also reached out to local consumers by creating an "LG village," a high-profile initiative that transformed a decrepit agricultural community into a showcase for LG technologies. The efforts seem to be paying off: With help from such simple touches as making the exteriors of products red—a lucky color in China—LG raked in sales of $8 billion on the mainland last year.

Elizabeth Esfahani *(eesfahani@business2.com) is a staff writer at Business 2.0.*

From *Business 2.0,* Vol. 6, issue 11, December 2005, pp. 96-97.

The Great Wal-Mart of China

For the world's biggest company, the key to growth lies in the world's biggest country.

Clay Chandler

"THIS WAY, LADIES! Follow me!" It's two weeks before the opening of Wal-Mart's first supercenter in Chongqing, and Baker Jiang, Wal-Mart's manager for western China, has invited a delegation of women on a tour. A small army of red-shirted associates greets the ladies at the door with a rousing Wal-Mart cheer. Inside, Jiang whisks the group around shelves piled with toys, sporting goods, and household appliances, past the new film-processing machines, and down the escalator to the produce department, butcher shop, and bakery where, donning mask and hairnet, he beckons visitors to inspect for cleanliness. Wal-Mart, he says, "will never use tap water to make your bread." By tour's end, it is the women who are cheering. "This blouse is so cheap," says one. "Can I buy it now?" Another gives Jiang a coquettish nudge. "We've waited so many years for this. What took you so long?"

Wal-Mart doesn't get that kind of reception in many parts of the U.S. these days. In its home market the giant retailer is under siege, blamed for evils from squeezing suppliers and crushing the corner grocer to busting unions and driving down wages. But good luck convincing Chinese consumers that the arrival of a supercenter should be cause for public outcry. In Chongqing, a metropolis of 31 million where shopping options have long been limited to dank, state-run stores with surly clerks or open-air markets where the tomatoes may or may not be as fresh as the garbage, the locals say, "Bring it on!"

"So what if they take business from other shopkeepers?" says 51-year-old Sheng Xuehua. "They should, if they can do a better job." Out on the street, construction worker Li Daping agrees. "We can't wait for Wal-Mart to open. We're practically counting the days."

Opening day, when it arrives June 30, brings pandemonium. There's a giddy rush when doors swing wide at 7:30 A.M. Thousands of shoppers scamper from aisle to aisle, heaping carts with spinach, cooking oil, whatever they can grasp. A truckload of roasted ducks sells out in minutes. By 8 A.M. the queue for rotisserie chicken at 85 cents a bird is 50 people long. Shoppers snatch five-kilogram sacks of rice as fast as employees can unload them. At tanks near the entrance, housewives lunge at live grass fish as long as their arms. At 9:30, a cadre of local officials joins Wal-Mart's Asia CEO, Joe Hatfield, for a ceremony on the public square outside. There's a brass band, fire-breathing Sichuan opera dancers, and a traditional lion dance. Hatfield paints the eye of a lion's head to bring good luck. But the gesture seems superfluous: Inside, each of the store's 75 checkout lanes is backed up 15 customers deep. By closing time at 10 P.M., 120,000 customers have trooped through the doors. But there is little time to savor success. Wal-Mart opens its next supercenter in Shanghai in less than a month. In the world's most populous market, the world's biggest retailer is playing catch-up.

Wal-Mart no longer sells snake, but the fare is pretty exotic. **Spicy chicken feet** and stinky tofu are perennial favorites.

WAL-MART PLANS to roll out 15 new stores in China this year, including its first supercenters in Beijing and Shanghai, and it has enticed analysts with talk of increasing floor space by as much as 50% a year. Company executives won't elaborate on expansion plans, but Hatfield, a chain-smoking 30-year Wal-Mart veteran who has run the China operation since 1995, says his orders from Bentonville, Ark., are clear. At last year's annual meeting, held in Shenzhen, members of Wal-Mart's board admonished him to "get a lot more aggressive."

And no wonder. Wal-Mart can't sustain the astronomical U.S. growth rates of the past decade forever. Sooner rather than later, the company will need help from overseas. But the Beast of Bentonville has yet to emerge as a dominant player in any of the foreign markets that account for about 20% of its global sales. In Germany it is still struggling to stanch losses at the two retailers it acquired in the 1990s. In Japan it has yet to articulate a clear strategy for its 38% stake in the troubled Seiyu chain. The company has had better luck in emerging economies, such as Mexico, where there are fewer entrenched incumbents. But executives have long viewed China, with its vast population and booming economy, as their best bet for long-term global growth. In an interview with FORTUNE last year, former Wal-Mart CEO David Glass proclaimed China "the one place in the world where you could replicate Wal-Mart's success in the U.S."

It was slow going at first. The company sent an advance team of executives to China in 1994 and, two years later, opened the first Wal-Mart supercenter in Shenzhen, the gritty boomtown across the border from Hong Kong. Before the first store opened, an alliance with a Thai supermarket chain collapsed, forcing Wal-Mart to surrender planned developments in Shanghai and Shenyang. Beijing checked Wal-Mart's expansion with regulations, limiting foreign retailers to a handful of large cities and obliging them to offer at least 35% of each store to local partners. The Sam's Club format, with its emphasis on membership fees and high-volume sales, left Chinese customers cold. By the end of last year, Wal-Mart could boast just 43 stores in China—a far cry from the 3,719 it operates in the U.S. The company doesn't disclose financial results for China. But China's chamber of commerce reported in its annual retail ranking that Wal-Mart grossed $916 million last year—less than 2% of the company's international sales, and a tiny sliver of its $288 billion total revenue.

Those numbers have nowhere to go but up. The demographics are dazzling: 100 cities with populations of more than a million; 150 million urban families with annual incomes of more than $10,000 within the next ten years; more than $6 trillion in total retail spending this year, and growing at a 15% annual clip. And unlike India, which forbids foreign direct investment in the retail sector, China is opening its doors to outside players. The crucial turning point came last December, when Beijing, in keeping with terms of its admission to the World Trade Organization, granted foreign retailers permission to invest independently in any city they choose.

But many hurdles remain. Hatfield says his biggest challenge is finding qualified managers. Each supercenter, which mixes produce and general merchandise, requires hiring and training 500 employees. Locating sites is just as tricky. In most Chinese cities, municipal governments control prime real estate, giving an edge to state-owned retailers. And then there's the competition. In America, Wal-Mart may be the 800-pound gorilla, but in China, it's still a chimp, jostling with Chinese conglomerates such as the state-run Shanghai Brilliance group, as well as with foreign rivals such as France's Carrefour. Wang Zongnan, president of Brilliance, China's largest retailer with 3,300 stores and sales of $8.1 billion, says he doesn't lose much sleep worrying about Wal-Mart. "Local retailers have the advantage in all large economies," he says. "I see no reason to doubt that will be the case in China too."

WAL-MART HOPES to prove that thinking wrong. By opening in Chongqing, on the upper reaches of the Yangtze River, it is establishing a beachhead for expansion well beyond China's densely populated eastern seaboard. And to get it right, Hatfield and his lieutenants pulled out all the stops, working with development partners from Shenzhen and Singapore to secure a prime location at Nine Dragon Plaza, a public square across from the municipal zoo. The store is surrounded by residential developments and lies at the terminus of a new light-rail line. Store manager Sunny Han estimates that more than a million people live within a four-mile radius. But that same circle includes three stores operated by New Century, a retail group owned by the local government, as well as a lively street market and a gleaming new Carrefour as big as Wal-Mart. To lure customers, Wal-Mart will open an hour and a half earlier and close later, and it will deploy a fleet of free shuttle buses to ferry residents to the store.

At the open-air market on nearby Go Forward Street, peddlers hawking long beans and acorn squash were bracing for the worst a few weeks before the opening. "I'll definitely switch to Wal-Mart," said Liu Bijuan, a stocky housewife picking through baskets of eggplants and cucumbers. In a stall nearby,

"I'm a believer in Sam's philosophy that when it comes to good ideas, you should **steal shamelessly**," Hatfield says.

a butcher scratched himself lazily as flies swarmed over slabs of beef. But at the Carrefour up the road, it was a different story. The space is vast and well stocked. Shoppers thronged the food counter, and prices for many items were comparable to those in Wal-Mart stores.

Carrefour came to China a year after Wal-Mart but has expanded more rapidly. The French retailer's China CEO, Jean Luc Chereau, credits his success to the 12 years he spent building Carrefour's business in Taiwan. "It was in Taiwan that we discovered Chinese culture," he says. "By the time I moved to Shanghai in 1999, I was well prepared." But Carrefour has also demonstrated superior operating savvy and a greater tolerance for risk. By forging alliances with local governments, it circumvented many of Beijing's restrictions, fashioning a network of 60 hypermarkets in 25 cities, with sales last year of nearly $2 billion. This year China's largest foreign retailer vows to match Wal-Mart's China expansion store for store.

STILL, IT'S EARLY DAYS, and Wal-Mart has deep pockets. More important, perhaps, is that Hatfield and his team have become adept at replicating Wal-Mart's corporate culture and figuring out what Chinese consumers want. Headquarters for Wal-Mart's retail operation—a dingy warren tucked behind the first supercenter in Shenzhen—reflect the company's reputation for pinching pennies. But Hatfield spends little time there. Most days you'll find him roaming Wal-Mart stores, scouting the competition, or foraging for products in urban street markets. "I'm a big believer in Sam's philosophy that when it comes to good ideas, you should steal shamelessly," he says. "You have to get out there and ask, 'What are our competitors doing that we're not?' You have to be hungry for new knowledge every day."

Hatfield's pursuit of local knowledge has produced surprising differences in the look and feel of Wal-Mart's stores in China. Chinese customers tend to do their shopping on foot, not by car. They have smaller apartments and smaller refrigerators, so they buy in smaller quantities and are accustomed to going to market every one or two days. So Wal-Mart supercenters in China devote lots of floor space to food. Perishable products get pride of place and come in a mind-boggling assortment of shapes, colors, and flavors. Except for the prices and the smiley faces, a U.S. customer venturing into the produce department at a Chinese Wal-Mart might think he had stumbled into a Whole Foods store in San Francisco.

Wal-Mart's managers have learned a lot about Chinese customers. One early discovery: They want to put their hands on the merchandise, shucking each corncob before putting it in their basket, or demanding that associates not only take a fitted sheet out of the plastic but demonstrate it on an actual bed. Chinese shoppers also have a thing for clamor. Often managers can goose sales simply by dispatching associates to restack an item noisily in the middle of the floor. And at the Chongqing opening, bottles of red wine moved briskly when bundled with free cans of Sprite. (In China they like their cabernet carbonated.)

The fare can get a lot more exotic than that. Since the SARS epidemic two years ago, Wal-Mart's China stores have stopped slaughtering poultry on the premises and no longer offer rabbits or snakes. But spicy chicken feet and stinky tofu are perennial favorites. In Chongqing, those who come too late to catch a grass fish can choose from a selection of lobsters, turtles, and live bullfrogs the size of soccer balls. At most supercenters, the bestselling items are prepared lunches served in Styrofoam containers: two meats, two vegetables, rice, and a cup of hot soup, freshly prepared onsite—all for less than $1. A typical supercenter sells more than 1,000 a day. Hatfield says the sight of truck and taxi drivers retching on the side of the road helped convince him that there was an opportunity for Wal-Mart to boost midday store traffic by luring customers from local street vendors.

Another innovation is what Wal-Mart calls "retail-tainment." Stores provide space for local school groups to perform, and they organize daily activities for the elderly. Residents are welcome to wander in and freeload on air conditioning. It's savvy marketing, of course. But it may have long-term benefit: If Wal-Mart can succeed in weaving itself into the fabric of urban communities, it may head off the image problems that have arisen in other markets.

Unlike the merchandise, Wal-Mart's management practices have required little tinkering for China. If anything, the red shirts, mass cheering, incessant pep rallies, and veneration of a deceased founder seem characteristics far better suited to the People's Republic than the American South. Two hours of buttonholing Chongqing associates as they left work failed to identify anyone who would confess to feeling oppressed. What's striking about all this regimentation, though, is that it's so focused on answering the wants of individuals. At times, Baker and Sunny, with their folksy PR tours and community-outreach projects, seem like old-time Boston ward heelers.

Another constant is the obsession with *tian tian ping jia*—everyday low prices. Hatfield, darting around a supercenter in Shenzhen, ticks off item after item: "Men's dress slacks? Eight

The red shirts and **mass cheering** seem better suited to the People's Republic than the American South.

bucks—and that's including alterations. Those dress shoes? $4.80. They were three times that two years ago." Wal-Mart lured customers to the Chongqing opening by advertising DVD players for $23.97 and in-line skates for $11.93. Often products are displayed with signs declaring the value of the discount wrested from suppliers by Wal-Mart buyers.

Although Wal-Mart's shelves bristle with U.S. consumer brands—from Crest toothpaste and Clairol shampoos to Oreos and Gatorade—almost everything is made in China. And, as in the U.S., suppliers have trouble sorting out whether Wal-Mart's embrace is a bear hug or a death grip. Consider Dong Yongjian, the 33-year-old proprietor of a spicy-chicken-feet factory an hour's drive from the Chongqing store. Wal-Mart buyers stumbled on Dong's product four years ago at a rival retailer in Shenzhen. They sent a team of auditors to inspect his factory and began stocking his chicken feet in stores. Dong's chicken-feet recipe—which he guards as zealously as Colonel Sanders did his "secret blend of 11 herbs and spices"—was an immediate hit. Wal-Mart has become Dong's top customer. But while sales are booming, profits aren't. "They want the lowest prices I can possibly give them," says Dong. "I see this is a long-run relationship, so I'm doing my best to hold down costs." At the headquarters of Yunan Red Wine, a salesman says that to win Wal-Mart's business his company had to knock prices down 15%, undermining its pricing power with other customers.

If the associates on the sales battlefront in Chongqing represent one face of Wal-Mart's operation in China, suppliers waiting in the reception area of Wal-Mart's global procurement headquarters in Shenzhen are another. The room, with a poster of Sam Walton on one wall and Wal-Mart's latest share price on another, is an exporters' purgatory. Supplicants take a number and wait for an audience with Wal-Mart buyers or quality inspectors. Those whose products are deemed worthy of Wal-Mart's U.S. customers can see sales rocket almost overnight. Many come bearing items of whimsy—dancing Christmas trees, Jar Jar Binks action figures, Nerf dart sets. But this is a tense place. On a recent afternoon, there was no mirth in the eyes of Li Xiaolong as he stepped into a tiny conference room, strapped on the target-shaped vest manufactured by his Dongguan employer, and waited for a Wal-Mart buyer to fire Nerf darts into his chest. Last year Wal-Mart spent $18 billion on merchandise from China-based suppliers, most of it toys, footwear, Christmas decorations, and sporting equipment, accounting for 3% of China's total exports. If Wal-Mart were a country, it would be China's sixth-largest export market.

Wal-Mart buys only about 10% of what it sells in U.S. stores from suppliers in China. But at a March meeting for investment analysts in Shenzhen, company executives spoke of raising China purchases significantly—to perhaps double the current amount—over the next five years. Critics say that pits American workers against Chinese, who earn $5 a day. Andrew Tsuei, head of Wal-Mart's overseas procurement office, offers no apologies. "My job is to find the best value for our customers while sourcing in an ethical way," he says. "China gives us competitive products and meets our quality and ethical standards. There's no reason for us not to buy here."

Wal-Mart executives say they hold suppliers to U.S. standards for business ethics as well as product quality, dispatching hundreds of auditors to monitor working conditions, compensation, and safety records—though Tsuei acknowledges that gauging compliance is a challenge. In China, as in the U.S., Wal-Mart has resisted calls for labor unions. Chinese associates, however, aren't up in arms. That's because Chinese unions are creatures of the state, run to collect dues for the party and keep tabs on workers, not represent them. In November, after months of public sniping by the government-controlled All China Trade Federation, Beijing and Bentonville reached a compromise. Wal-Mart pledged to accept a union should workers formally request one. Thus far they have not.

GIVEN THE SCOPE of Wal-Mart's ambitions in China and the enthusiasm of Chinese shoppers at recent store openings, Bentonville's stated expansion plan looks way too timid. Merrill Lynch analyst Daniel Barry calculates that even if Wal-Mart adds stores at a rate faster than this year's pace, its China retail network will include no more than 230 stores by 2009. That's fewer than the number of stores Wal-Mart will add in the U.S. this year.

Maybe Wal-Mart is just playing its China cards close to the vest. In the U.S., the company's pattern has always been to keep its head down and its mouth shut—until it has piled up all the chips. Wal-Mart International spokesman Elizabeth Keck says that, although Wal-Mart doesn't make projections more than a year out, "it is not correct to assume that we only plan to open 15 new stores a year in China." She also hints at the possibility of growth through acquisition. But her boss, Wal-Mart's International CEO, John Menzer, isn't tipping his hand. "We'll take one store at a time," he told reporters in Beijing this spring.

Back in Chongqing, Joe Hatfield has few doubts about the company's success. Walking into the store after the opening ceremony, he is almost run over by a couple wheeling two large shopping carts piled high with sacks of rice. Does it worry him that on opening day customers have loaded up so heavily they won't need to return to the store for months? "Nah," he laughs, waving to the pair. "Those two'll be back tomorrow. They gotta buy vegetables."

American Corporations: the New Sovereigns

By Lawrence E. Mitchell

ONE of the most striking yet overlooked aspects of the current globalization debate is the quiet retreat of sovereign power—including that of the United States—in the face of imperial conquests by modern American corporations. At least until the recent downturns in the stock market—both the general one in 2000 and the sharper one following the attacks of September 11—a number of these companies, including Wal-Mart, Microsoft, Intel, General Electric, and Hewlett-Packard, have had market capitalizations larger than the gross national products of a number of developed and developing countries, including Spain, Kuwait, Argentina, Greece, Poland, and Thailand. The statistics overwhelmingly demonstrate that such corporations and American capital are increasingly dominant throughout the world. At last count, American institutional assets constituted an aggregate 66.8 percent of the total in five major foreign economies, including those of France and Germany.

Modern democracies are built to ensure the restraint of power and the pursuit of public will by forgoing efficiency for patience and consensus. In contrast, the modern American corporation, with its centralized control and absolute power in the board, is brilliantly and devastatingly built for economic efficiency—the ability to amass huge resources and deploy them instantly. No socialist economy has ever had the command-and-control capacities of the American corporation.

The scary thing is that we have come to see these corporations as built for a single purpose, to maximize stockholder wealth, and we have created them in a manner that exempts them from any of the normal moral constraints we expect from governments or individuals.

It has not always been so. Several factors led to the development of this new ethic over the last couple of decades. Among them were deregulation beginning during the Reagan era, together with an increased emphasis on wealth maximization as a social goal; the expectations created in stockholders by the quick money made in hostile takeovers, especially during the 1980s; and the charging bull market of the 1990s. Those phenomena have instilled stockholder expectations of large and immediate returns.

AMERICAN CORPORATIONS and their managers are thus increasingly driven by the faceless, soulless capital markets—markets composed of individuals with consciences but creating a collective that lacks one. Moreover, pressure on corporations to show higher stock prices fast has been increased by the enormous growth in institutional investors, which now own about half of the equity market in the United States.

They also dominate institutional investing in foreign markets like those of Western Europe. Institutional investors compensate their managers on the basis of their ability to raise the values of their portfolios immediately, so those managers have every incentive to push for short-term stock-price maximization over long-term gain and corporate stability.

In addition to the pressure of institutional investors, American investment banks, and consulting companies, markets are driven by nongovernmental organizations like the World Bank and the International Monetary Fund. Those players have implicitly, and sometimes explicitly, conditioned the supply of American capital (and in the case of the nongovernmental organizations, largely Western capital) to overseas markets on those markets' adoption of American-style, stockholder-centered, corporate capitalism.

To be sure, American corporations have brought the world great benefits: increased travel, communication, health, nutrition, and production capabilities. They have also brought Americans a higher material standard of living. But it is, in large part, the stockholder-centered nature of the corporation that leads it to behave in ways that no thoughtful person really wants, ways that most of us would consider to be irresponsible.

Although no legal doctrine requires it, American capitalist culture has adopted the view that maximizing stock price is the purpose of the corporation, its reason for being. Capital markets demand that maximization, and punish those corporations that fail to meet short-term expectations—just look at the stock price of any corporation that reports disappointing quarterly earnings. Corporate structure implies stock-price maximization: Only stockholders vote for directors, only stockholders have the right to sue, and only stockholders have the ability to sell the company out from under the directors.

Coupled with the maximization goal is the limited liability that shields the corporation. While corporations can be sued for causing harm, and sometimes even criminally prosecuted, the extent of their risk is finite. When a chemical plant in Bhopal, India, explodes because corners were cut, or Love Canal is poisoned because it is cheaper to pollute, or asbestos sickens thousands because the product is unsafe, the injured can recover only from the assets of the corporation. Directors and stockholders generally are not liable for its debts, and so many of the costs of maximizing stock price can be externalized onto all of those people and things, other than the stockholders, whom the corporation's behavior affects—workers, consumers, entire communities, the environment.

Layoffs are a fast way to cut costs and raise stock price. Saving a few dollars by placing a gas tank in not necessarily the safest spot, or by paying insufficient attention to tire safety, increases profit margins. Polluting entails limited risk of being caught and penalized, and the benefits, in terms of savings, sometimes exceed that risk. It's cheaper to shut down plants in areas of high labor cost and move them to other regions, no matter how dependent the community may be on the corporation.

Freed from the responsibilities of ownership, with surrogates directed to manage their corporations to maximize their wealth, American stockholders can, and for the most part do, wash their hands of responsibility for their corporations' behavior. Add to this the fact that most Americans tend to invest in corporations through intermediary institutions—mutual funds, pension funds, and the like—and yet another layer is placed between the stockholder and any feeling of responsibility.

WITH THESE CONDITIONS in place, American corporations have exported the dislocations they often cause at home through devices such as the leveraged, hostile takeover, and norms like stock-price maximization. *BusinessWeek* predicted (again, before the current recession) at least a $1-trillion mergers-and-acquisitions business in Europe, a region that has long celebrated its corporate stability. The profits drawn from such disruptions abroad go directly into the pockets of American stockholders, who demonstrate no concern with the effect of corporate behavior on anyone else. Arguments that transnational business helps the world's disadvantaged by raising their standard of living are disproved by the numbers. A recent United Nations report showed that American-style economic dominance has accelerated the widening gap between rich and poor throughout the world.

According to the UN's *Human Development Report 1999*, "the top fifth of the world's people in the richest countries enjoy 82 percent of the expanding export trade and 68 percent of foreign direct investment—the bottom fifth, barely more than 1 percent." That same wealthy population has 86 percent of the world's gross domestic product, and the income of that group was 74 times that of the bottom fifth in 1997, up from 60 times in 1990. And such data reflect only material wealth—not quality of life, leisure, education, or happiness.

Because the goal of the corporation is to maximize stock price, managers use corporations narrowly and amorally as tools to achieve that end.

At least as dangerous as increasing inequality is the standard of behavior American corporate practices create for companies' managers. Because the goal of the corporation is to maximize stock price, managers use corporations narrowly and amorally as tools to achieve that end. When an ordinary human being with ordinary moral constraints walks into a board room or executive suite, he assumes those tunnel-visioned behaviors. That is, after all, his job. His own sensibilities can be left at the door—and even if they need not be, even if there is latitude (as there surely is) for good corporate behavior, he knows that the market will punish him unless his morality is reflected on the bottom line.

Like many social roles (that of a lawyer comes to mind), this one comes with a socially sanctioned set of expectations. But unlike most other roles, which exist and must interact in a wider social system, we so narrowly define the role of corporate actors as to give them a moral anonymity and a moral out. The corporate managerial role not only leads us to exculpate corporations for simply doing what we've created them to do, but it allows managers themselves to avoid feeling responsible, and being accountable, for their behavior. They have no personal contact with the people their decisions affect—those people are only numbers. The managers don't carry out the decisions themselves and witness the consequences, so they avoid the experiences that might help ensure empathy and restraint.

THE PROGRESS of the American corporation has been toward ever greater world dominance, not only in the products it sells and the services it provides, which export American culture throughout the world, but also in its exportation of American-style, stockholder-take-all capitalist practices. Given corporations' efficiency and speed in contrast to those of governments, corporations can establish strongholds and affect entire cultures long before those cultures have time to react. And once in place, corporate wealth and economic dominance allows them to remain firmly entrenched.

The problem is not only one of America against the developing world. American corporations, aided by the investment community, have also largely colonized the various forms of capitalism that used to distinguish Western European business from ours. Corporate behavior in Germany, France, Scandinavia, and Italy, for instance, was designed to provide for full employment, social stability, and social welfare. American companies, and American practices, have eroded those core values.

The European anger directed against President George W. Bush on his first visit there in June (somewhat abated since September 11 by a different anger, sympathy, and fear) is symptomatic of even the developed world's feelings of helplessness in the face of the continued onslaught by American-style corporate capitalism.

The recent terrorist attacks have been directed against sovereign governments. But to the extent that much of the unsettled state of the world derives from the increasing divide between haves and have-nots, to the extent that culture wars in America and abroad are driven at least in part by rear-guard actions against disappearing ways of life, the cause lies less in the behavior of sovereign governments such as our own than it does in the collective behavior of corporate America and the American investment community.

Only government has the power, the resources, and the right to restrain corporate conduct and to demand corporate accountability. For far too long we've taken the attitude that business is business, as if that very mantra exempted corporations from the normal moral and responsible conduct that we expect from individual citizens. At the same time, we have granted our corporations almost all of the rights and freedoms of individual citizens. But unless we control our corporate goals and practices, unless our government regulates markets in a way that restrains our voracious drive for wealth, international strife and discord will only worsen.

Lawrence E. Mitchell, a law professor at George Washington University, is the author of Corporate Irresponsibility: America's Newest Export, *published recently by Yale University Press.*

From *The Chronicle of Higher Education,* January 18, 2002, pp. 18-19.

The real reasons you're working so hard...

...and what you can do about it

Michael Mandel

Honk if this sounds like you: While much of America is watching Jon Stewart, Letterman, or Leno, you're stumbling out the office door into a car-service Town Car or groping for the clicker to the BMW in the company parking lot. Once home, you slug down a beer or the last of a bottle of white wine on the door of the fridge, stuff some leftovers in your mouth, and collapse into bed beside your sleeping spouse. A half-dozen hours later, you crawl to the shower, throw on a clean shirt, pour some coffee down your throat, maybe drop a kid or two at school, and jump back on the frenetic work treadmill that you can't shut off.

The good news—if there is any, time-challenged amigo—is that you are not alone. Over 31% of college-educated male workers are regularly logging 50 or more hours a week at work, up from 22% in 1980. About 40% of American adults get less than seven hours of sleep on weekdays, up from 34% in 2001. Almost 60% of meals are rushed, and 34% of lunches are choked down on the run. To avoid wasting time, we're talking on our cell phones while rushing to work, answering e-mails during conference calls, waking up at 4 a.m. to call Europe, and generally multitasking our brains out.

This epidemic of long hours at the office—whether physically or remotely—defies historical precedent and common sense. Over the past 25 years, the Information Revolution has boosted productivity by almost 70%. So you would think that since we're producing more in fewer hours, such gains would translate into a decrease in the workweek—as they have in the past. But instead of technology being a time-saver, says Warren Bennis, a University of Southern California professor and author of such management classics as *On Becoming a Leader*, "everybody I know is working harder and longer."

And the long-hour marathons aren't a result of demanding corporations exploiting the powerless. Most of the groggy-eyed are the best-educated and best-paid—college grads whose real wages have risen by more than 30% since the 1980s. That's a change from 25 years ago, when it was the lowest-wage workers who were most likely to put in 50 hours or more a week, according to new research by Peter Kuhn of the University of California at Santa Barbara and Fernando A. Lozano of Pomona College.

With so many managers and professionals stuck at work, there is a growing consensus among management gurus that the stuck-at-work epidemic is symptomatic of a serious disorder in the organization of corporations. The problem, in a nutshell-to-go is this: Succeeding in today's economy requires lightning-fast reflexes and the ability to communicate and collaborate across the globe. Coming up with innovative ideas, products, and services means getting people across different divisions and different companies to work together. "More and more value is created through networks," says John Helferich, a top executive and former head of research and development at Masterfoods USA, a division of Mars Inc. and the maker of such products as M&Ms. "The guys who are good at it are winning."

Unfortunately, the communication, coordination, and teamwork so essential for success these days is being superimposed on a corporate structure that has one leg still in its gray flannel suit. Without strict gatekeepers (read secretaries), Tom, Jane, and Harry feel free to plug themselves into your electronic calendar. You and a colleague in another part of the company may dream up a great idea for a new product—but it takes months to get approvals from your boss, his boss, and their boss. Or the corporate bigwigs order you to join a taskforce that is supposed to promote collaboration and innovation—but it ends up taking a big chunk of your time. And no matter how many layers of management were supposed to be taken out, there always seem to be more people on the e-mail distribution lists.

You are not imagining things. Despite years of cutting corporate bloat, managers are a much bigger share of the workforce than they were 15 years ago. "We've added a new set of standards

›› Long-Hours Premium

Over the past 15 years, real pay for a 55-hour workweek rose by about 14%, but pay for a "normal" 40-hour week hardly budged.

Data: Peter Kuhn, University of California at Santa Barbara and Fernando A. Lozano of Pomona College

without fully dropping the old," says Thomas H. Davenport, professor of information technology and management at Babson College and author of the new book *Thinking for a Living*.

That helps explain why time pressures seem to be getting worse. Globalization and the Internet create great new opportunities, but they also ratchet up the intensity of competition and generate more work—especially with the existing corporate structure still hanging on tightly. "Nobody wants to give up their territory or their control," says Shoshana Zuboff, a former professor at Harvard Business School. Adds Lowell Bryan, a McKinsey & Co. director: "Professionals are still being managed as if they were in factories, in organizations designed to keep everybody siloed. At less well-run companies, you're struck by how frustrated people are. They work like dogs and are wasting time."

Make that lots of time. Fully 25% of executives at large companies say their communications—voice mail, e-mail, and meetings—are nearly or completely unmanageable. That's according to a new McKinsey survey of more than 7,800 managers around the world. Nearly 40% spend a half to a full day per week on communications that are not valuable. Other surveys echo similar results. "We're making our people compete with sandbags strapped to their legs," says Zuboff.

Five Ways To Work Smarter

Managers and professionals are running as fast as they can to keep pace with a business world turbocharged by technology. Here's how companies can ease time pressures on their knowledge workers—and boost productivity and innovation at the same time:

- **Manage output rather than hours** Eliminate or reduce low-value activities and meetings. That will allow more time for innovation and creative thinking.
- **Train workers in skills appropriate to a more complex corporate structure** Conduct internal surveys to understand how people really spend their time, and use that information to eliminate the worst bottlenecks.
- **Push decision-making further down the hierarchy** Explicitly broaden the range of decisions that lower-level managers and professionals can make without getting approval.
- **Use new technology to foster collaboration** Develop programs that make it easier to find out what colleagues in other parts of far-flung companies are working on—thus helping to identify resources and avoid duplication. Also, learn from newly developing, nontraditional forms of organization, such as blogs and open-source software.
- **Shift hiring emphasis from supervision to collaboration** Rather than adding more managers, create new positions aimed at facilitating internal and external networks.

A Digital Spine

There is hope, however, and the promise of at least partial liberation from the tyranny of time constraints. Why? Because the long-term interests of individuals and smart companies are aligned. To compete, successful corporations will have to make it easier and less time-consuming for their employees to collaborate. They will learn how to live with fewer time-sapping meetings and unnecessary feedback loops—or find themselves outrun by more nimble competitors. The eventual result: less frustration for knowledge workers.

Moves in this direction are already under way as savvy companies analyze their internal social networks and identify bottlenecks. Intel Corp., for example, sees an opportunity in creating technology that lowers the time cost of teamwork. And others, such as Eli Lilly & Co., are providing more corporate support for both internal and external networks. "It's a new mental model for how you run a company," says McKinsey's Bryan. "The winners will be those who can handle more complexity."

At the same time we may see a rise in new forms of Web-based organizations where people can contribute without having their time eaten up by existing hierarchy. Blogs, collaborative online databases (called wikis) and open-source software development all use the Net to handle much of the coordination among people rather than relying on top-down command and control. Such a shift to a digital spine could eventually lessen bureaucratic time burdens on overworked professionals, especially those in such high-cost industries as health care.

If history is any guide, the stuck-at-work epidemic will turn out to be a transitional phase. Historically, as countries and individuals get richer, they work less. Look at the late 19th century, when the U.S. was still a relatively poor country, with a per capita income about equal to that of China today. Back then the typical male household head had precious little leisure time, perhaps only about 1.8 hours a day, on average, after subtracting time for work, chores, and meals. The average factory worker put in about 60 hours a week, with only one day off. In-

›› Too Many Cooks

Managers make up a much bigger share of the workforce than they did 15 years ago despite years of cutting corporate bloat.
Data: Bureau of Labor Statistics

deed, the first May Day labor demonstrations, in 1886, were driven by the demand for an eight-hour day.

Over time, as U.S. productivity and incomes rose, work hours dropped and leisure time increased. It was no coincidence that the five-day work week was first introduced in 1926 by Henry Ford, a decade after he pioneered high-efficiency, mass-production methods.

By 1970 the 40-hour workweek was the norm. And, at least until recently, European and Asian countries have followed the same trajectory of declining work hours. Since 1991 average annual work hours have dropped by 11% in Japan, 10% in France, 6% in Germany and Britain, and 5% in South Korea. Meanwhile, average monthly work hours in Taiwan are down by 7% over the same stretch. Even work hours in China, while still much higher than in the U.S., may be coming down. "Asians are poorer and still working like crazy," says Alberto Alesina, a Harvard University economics professor who has studied international work hours. "But as they get richer, they are taking more leisure."

The one real exception to the rule has been the U.S. Since 1991 the U.S. has grown substantially faster than Europe and Japan. Nevertheless, average annual work hours are down by less than 2%, and that includes all the low-skilled workers who are in less demand today.

Interestingly, there are signs that global competition is forcing Europeans to start moving away from their tradition of shorter work hours. The number of Germans working more than 40 hours a week rose sharply last year, to 5.3 million from 4.7 million. Siemens, DaimlerChrysler, Deutsche Bahn, and many smaller companies have been able to increase work hours without corresponding increases in pay. French workers seem to be putting in more hours in the past year or two as well.

European executives are sounding more and more like their American counterparts. "Ten years ago, if I was on a business trip, I'd get to my hotel in the evening, and there might be a message or two from my secretary and a couple of faxes," says Philippe Midy, a Paris-based executive at McDonald's Europe who travels extensively around the Continent dealing with supply and logistics issues. Now there's a deluge. "Sometimes I'm answering e-mails at 2 a.m."

At least at the moment, long hours are part of the price to be paid for faster growth, especially if you work for a multinational. "If you are going to be a participant in economic activity that is part of a globalized market," says Stephen S. Roach, chief economist for Morgan Stanley, "you need to be prepared to stretch beyond 9 to 5."

Companies have been willing to pay big bucks for those longer hours. Over the past 15 to 20 years, people working a 40-hour week received virtually no increase in real pay, according to research by Kuhn and Lozano. Yet employees putting in a 55-hour week saw their real pay rise by 14%. The implication: The gains of two decades of growth have mainly gone to ambitious—or fearful—Americans who are working longer hours.

But even high pay can't compensate for unrelenting time pressure. Top managers have to realize that encouraging networks and collaboration demands as much attention and resources as supervising and measuring performance in traditional ways. Most companies have built up large human-resources departments, but few have a department of collaboration. "Most managers don't manage social networks effectively," says Babson's Davenport.

At Intel, the drive to reduce the time spent sharing knowledge and collaborating is an outgrowth of efforts to better coordinate far-flung operations that stretch from Israel to India. One idea being pursued by Luke Koons, director for information and knowledge management, is "dynamic profiling"—technologies that automatically summarize areas on which a researcher or a manager is focusing, based on the subjects of their e-mails and Web searches. Such a regularly updated profile could make it less time-consuming to locate potential collaborators and resources, an especially daunting prospect in a large, innovation-minded company such as Intel. Equally important, dynamic profiling doesn't force individuals to spend hours manually updating their profiles as their focus changes.

The Off Switch

There's plenty of demand for new technologies that more efficiently foster collaboration, such as software that allows virtual meetings, where everyone doesn't need to be present simultaneously. "Our communication tools are woefully inadequate," says Alph Bingham, a top executive at Eli Lilly who is vice-president of e.Lilly. "We are still relying on sticking everyone in a room and hammering it out. It's untenable globally."

Another time-eater: all the meetings and e-mails required to manage details of a collaboration or partnership. "Organizations need to recognize that when you engage in collaboration, there's another level of complexity," says Bingham. Part of the solution is to hire people for a new type of position devoted to facilitating or managing networks and relationships. Lilly, for example, created a new internal group—almost like ombudsmen—to manage communications among Lilly scientists and myriad outside partners. "This allows the scientists to dedicate less of their time to the collaboration," says Bingham.

Adding new software and more people to reduce the cost of collaboration is great—as long as it doesn't create even more work. To really ease the work overload—and, not coincidentally, make corporations more nimble—it's also essential to identify and eliminate unnecessary interactions. "Sometimes people need to remind themselves that there is an off switch—

›› Out Of Control

About 25% of executives at large companies say their communications—voice mail, e-mails, and meetings—are nearly or completely unmanageable.
Data: McKinsey & Co.

and use it," says Paul Saffo, a director at the Institute for the Future, a think tank based in Palo Alto, Calif. "Solitude is the scarce resource in business lives—having that time when you are disconnected and realizing that everything will go along fine without you."

To reduce time pressures—and hike productivity—the number of low-value interactions must be cut. "The usual assumption is that more collaboration is better," says Rob Cross, an assistant professor at the University of Virginia's McIntire School of Commerce who also runs Network Roundtable, a research group whose members include Schlumberger, Microsoft, Intel, Merck, and BP. "But it's important to ask not just where we need to build and connect but where do we need to let go?"

By having workers fill out a 15- to 20-minute online survey, Cross can chart who people communicate with, how much time is spent preparing for which meetings, and where the bottlenecks are. "Then I ask executives: 'What decisions are you making that others can make?'" says Cross. "Are there aspects of your role that you could let go of?"

Masterfoods used this methodology to map out how its product development, packaging, and process-development staff spent their time. The results were surprising. "When we looked at the data, it turned out that it was too hard to do business internally," says Helferich, then head of Masterfoods' R&D. People had to talk to 30 or 40 other people just to get their jobs done, which took away from their time to work on new ideas. Notes Helferich: "We were high-density on task and low-density on innovation." Now Masterfoods is in the process of redesigning the workflow of the packaging group to eliminate a lot of the extraneous steps that took up time.

If you are high enough in your organization, you can simply choose when to make yourself unavailable. Bryan, one of McKinsey's top consultants, says he has given up cell phones and computers, letting others handle his communications. "I never had time to think," says Bryan. "It's amazing how much you can get done if you don't spend all your time interacting."

Many of the most overloaded managers are not yet at a level where they have the luxury of controlling their schedules or dispensing with unproductive e-mails, pesky voice mails, and interminable meetings. But in terms of reducing work overload, perhaps the biggest and most difficult step will be for corporations to give their knowledge workers more freedom over their own time. "The Industrial Age approach to management dies a pretty tough death," says Babson's Davenport. "Even today people end up being evaluated not only on how much they produce but also on how many hours they are in the office."

Of course, there's one shiny new example of where output matters more than process: the Web. Nobody cares how long it took or what time of night it was when someone wrote a blog entry—all that's seen is the final result. Similarly, the success of open-source development projects such as Linux and Apache, the most popular Web server software, rests on the competence of the programmers involved, not on how many hours they log.

Reclaiming Your Life

The web model may give a glimpse of a less overloaded way of life that lets people take charge of their time while still making a decent living and a real contribution to society. Take Ted Husted, a 46-year-old freelance software consultant who lives in a Rochester (N.Y.) suburb. These days he consults 32 hours a week, remotely, for the Oklahoma Environmental Quality Dept., down from 40 as recently as this summer. But he also spends 10 to 15 hours a week as a major contributor to the Apache open-source software project.

Now he has time on weekends to watch his kids play sports. He goes out to lunch with his wife, Barb, every Monday. And he even has time left over to contain the fast-growing maple trees on his corner lot. Meanwhile, his work on the open-source project garners him visibility and respect among his peers. "I think I can keep this pace up indefinitely," says Husted. "But I have to have discipline about it. Now I make sure there's at least one day when I don't even touch a keyboard."

Few people will ever make a living as a blogger or a contributor to an open-source software project. But there is pressure to find new ways of organizing work, from both corporations and overworked individuals. "In terms of hours, I keep thinking we're on the verge of a backlash," says Babson's Davenport.

Hours Drop More Elsewhere

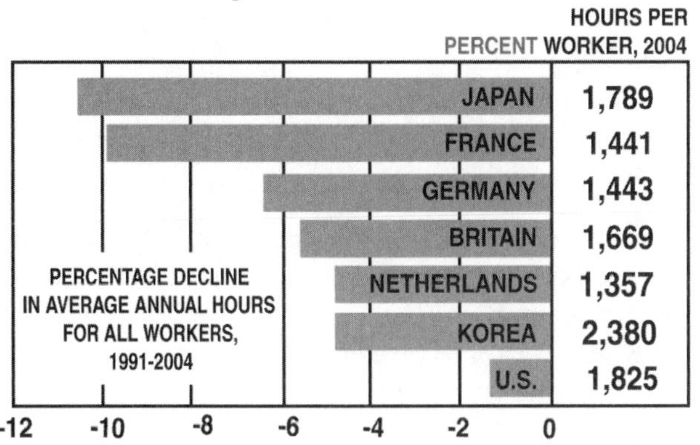

Data: Organization for Economic Cooperation & Development

Try telling that to Ken Middleton, director of convention sales for Houston's Convention & Visitors Bureau. In the aftermath of Hurricane Katrina, he has been putting in grueling 70-hour weeks hustling to find space for meetings that had been scheduled for New Orleans. Even in normal times, though, he works 55 hours a week, including four to six hours on weekends. Does he feel overworked? "Absolutely—but doesn't everyone? My wife says I need to get a hobby and stick to it. There isn't time for that right now." Who has even a moment for a backlash?

For New "Old Boys" Only

The old-fashioned club is being transformed into the new-fashioned network.

By Stuart Crainer and Des Dearlove

The Reform Club on London's prestigious Pall Mall is not a place normally associated with business models. It is, the large doorman informs us, a gentleman's club and one in which gentlemen are expected to wear ties. We are given ties.

Founded in 1836, the Reform Club has no need for a plaque or sign outside. Members know where to find it. Inside, the clubhouse is full of pillars, testament to the classical pretensions of its architects. It has the air of having witnessed better days. From here, Jules Verne's fictional hero Phileas Fogg set off to travel the world in 80 days.

Our well-traveled interviewee appears from behind one of the pillars. He is wearing a garish tie and gestures to our surroundings. "Think of this as the emergent business model: the club," he says. "What could be simpler? Think of the psychology of belonging, the ability to share knowledge with like-minded people, the prestige." The club enthusiast is Leif Edvinsson, a highly networked Swede best known for his championing of the concept of intellectual capital. To Edvinsson, the club is not a leftover from the pages of P.G. Wodehouse but, rather, a vibrant entrepreneurial engine of value and ideas. "The club is part of the emerging new theory of the firm, a model in which everybody is in charge," he says.

Today's network-obsessed business world has spawned a new generation of clubs. The club concept suits the times: Businesses are increasingly seen as communities of people serving client communities. The onus is on relationships rather than processes—and if clubs are about anything, they are about relationships.

A club may be defined as an association of people with shared interests meeting in a specified place (even if the place is now as likely to be cyberspace as Fifth Avenue). In the past, businesspeople typically congregated in groups with social, charitable, political, artistic, or philosophical aims. They met in dining halls, lodges, restaurants, clubhouses. Some of these clubs encouraged business-related networking—how many jobs got filled by the right two people standing next to each other at the bar?—and some went so far the other way that they prohibited members from opening briefcases on the premises.

Now, more and more, people are brought together by and for business. *That's* their shared interest.

Of course, not all clubs, business-focused or otherwise, label themselves as such. Words such as *network* and *institute* are popularly substituted, though the effect and the intent are often the same. The Conference Board, the publisher of *Across the Board*, is in important respects a club: While its conferences are open to all, only corporate members of the Board can belong to councils and receive other benefits. And some organizations that proclaim themselves to be business clubs are little more than management portals attempting to sell every known business service.

Most business clubs are different: They are commercial entities in themselves.

Creating a Membership To Die For

Founded in 1987, the Global Business Network owes much of its appeal to its elite list of individual members—thanks in no small part to co-founder Napier Collyns. Described as a networker extraordinaire, Collyns was a member of the original scenario-planning team at Shell under Pierre Wack in the early 1970s, and he quickly gravitated to his natural role as a network coordinator. When GBN was proposed, he was able to populate its elite membership almost singlehandedly from his personal network. Today, he travels constantly, tirelessly communicating with the network and adding names to his contacts book.

Shaking hands with the former Shell executive, you are met by penetrating eye contact—as if he is taking stock. It is a look you suspect he has perfected in more than 30 years of networking with the world's elite from fields as diverse as rock music, computer science, and management. The link between these people appears elusive but is actually close to hand: Collyns collects interesting people. (One of his many contacts quips that GBN stands for "Global Buddies of Napier.")

His conversation is peppered with, "Do you know him?" Names are dropped with consummate ease; connections are instantly made to individuals, organizations, and institutions that crop up. In Collyns' world, everyone (everyone who matters, that is) is connected; it is just a question of identifying the link. "I don't really have a home," he says. (In fact, he owns homes in London, New York, and Berkeley). "I just travel in the GBN. I personally know all but one of our remarkable people—and they know me. The important thing in a network is: Do you know them, or do they know you?"

Collyns describes GBN as "an intellectual elite in a business context." "We instinctively knew this was going to be a networked world even before the Internet was established," he says. "We happened to invent a model that worked. We never tried to market it. We didn't have to. When anyone heard about GBN, they wanted to join."

Membership, he says, can be rewarding both intellectually and financially. "Like all clubs, it started as a group of friends who then select their own friends. But over time, it attracted a variety of new and intriguing people. We set out with 400 names and selected 60 original members; we now have 120. It's an elite club. It's like being a member of an Oxford or Cambridge college; once you're in, you are always a member."

Collyns and GBN's other co-founders grasped early on that electronic communication would have an important influence on the future of global business. "It is not a coincidence that GBN was born as a network at a time when the networking idea was growing," he says. "GBaN was always an online network—from the mid-1980s on— long before the Internet proper." In those days, members used Shell's internal IT network and the Well, an open-communication channel established by GBN co-founder Stewart Brand. "That gave us—all the members of GBN—instant communication."

GBN quickly became a force to be reckoned with in the global economy. It is an image it has cultivated. A 1994 article about GBN in *Wired,* for example, was headlined "Conspiracy of Heretics." "It's very difficult to have an elite group of people that outsiders don't think is a conspiracy," Collyns says.

Exclusivity, he knows, is a key factor in GBN's success. In return for their corporate membership cards, thrusting executives get the chance to hobnob with each other and GBN's remarkable people at seminars and conferences, picking up fresh ideas and perspectives along the way. "People join GBN to hear ideas about the future and share their own ideas," Collyns says. "Belonging allows them to talk to people they couldn't otherwise get access to."

—Stuart Crainer and Des Dearlove

The expanded definition and varied forms have produced a far broader group of club members. True, many prominent business clubs emphasize the elite; after all, the more exclusive the club, the more cachet for members. "The more time you spend with distinguished people, the more distinguished you become," one club insider observes. But exclusivity isn't the main draw for every club: In a significant twist on the traditional club, networks often base their appeal not on how selective they are but how open—the more members the better.

Even exclusivity is different now than in the old-money days when many clubs were formed as—let's face it—havens for wealthy white men to consort with people just like them. Sure, a few prominent clubs still lock out women or Jews or African-Americans—just look at the recent brouhaha involving the men-only Augusta National Golf Club, home of the Masters Golf Tournament. But business clubs have no room for barriers of race or gender: As any free-marketer knows, discrimination against potential customers or co-workers isn't good business.

And the operation of business clubs themselves reflects their shift in focus. While every organization that provides services or meeting spaces needs to bring in income to cover costs, many traditional clubs—from the Lions and Elks to the Harvard and Commonwealth—are nonprofits. Even those that are technically for-profit generally aren't regarded as a means to a financially rewarding end. Most business clubs are different: They are commercial entities in themselves. The lesson of their rise and success is not only that the club network is a model for attracting tomorrow's customers but that it can be profitable.

While clubs are increasingly business-centered and run like businesses, their attraction remains universal and timeless. Clubs imbue their members with a collective identity, a sense of belonging to something larger than themselves. In a world of ambiguity and alienation, clubs offer certainty and a sense of solidarity.

The Power of Networking

During the new-economy boom, the business club was a natural habitat for networking-obsessed entrepreneurs and venture capitalists, who realized that value increases in correlation with the numbers of connections made. Loose networks became clubs—and then businesses. Consider First Tuesday, a meeting place and market for Internet start-ups, which began life in October 1998 at the Alphabet Bar in London's Soho, funded by passing the hat (a bucket, actually) at its cocktail parties. In less than two years, the club grew to 50,000 members and was sold to an Israeli investment group for a reported $50 million. First Tuesday now calls itself "the world's leading network for innovation and technology" and spans 48 cities in 28 countries.

Purists, of course, insist that a network like First Tuesday isn't the same thing as a club, that exclusivity is central to a club's *modus operandi*. Certainly, every club wants to be the natural home of the new power elite. Networks are one thing, *exclusive* networks quite another, and how much exclusivity can there be with a group of 50,000 people?

In recent years, the idea of privileged access has been taken to new heights, as with the Global Business Network. Founded by scenario-planning guru Peter Schwartz and four friends in 1987, GBN emerged around a pool table in a Berkeley, Calif., basement. The co-founders—Schwartz, Yale professor Jay Ogilvy, futurist Stewart Brand, media executive Lawrence Wilkinson, and former Royal Dutch/Shell executive Napier Collyns—envisioned a worldwide learning community of organizations and individuals.

When the five conceived GBN, they had a definite metaphor in mind, says Schwartz. "It was a British metaphor: the high table at Queens College, Oxford, where we were all sitting not too many years before. The level of conversation of the people seated at the table was what we had in mind with GBN. It was more that than the traditional gentlemen's club you find in St. James in London." Indeed, GBN is based in a former tractor factory, in the unglamorous town of Emeryville, near Berkeley.

GBN's corporate members include the likes of Coca-Cola, IBM, General Motors, Shell, and Unilever, which pay $40,000 annually to belong. The government of Singapore is also a member. But key to GBN's success are its individual network members—the so-called remarkable people. Individual members are invited to join only if they can "contribute remarkable insights, original ideas, and deep experience to our understanding of the forces transforming the present and shaping the future." Originally 60 strong, the number of remarkable people has doubled to 120.

Leading GBN members and advisers include management luminaries Gary Hamel, Esther Dyson, Arie de Geus, and Monitor founder Michael Porter. Sun Microsystems co-founder Bill Joy is another GBN member, as is John Kao, author of *Jamming* and founder of The Idea Factory. Kevin Kelly of *Wired*, musicians Brian Eno and Peter Gabriel, and novelist Douglas Coupland are GBN members or advisory members.

"We made some good choices at the beginning," Schwartz says. "Most fundamentally, we saw the power of networking, that you could really amplify your business model and connection and create much more value through a network model—and it worked. We were among the first to see that." GBN's network serves members well despite remaining tight, and regularly scheduled events introduce them to a variety of outside perspectives.

GBN has three main activities: First, its WorldView membership services include recommended books, regular meetings—including the famed "learning journeys"—and a steady flow of publications and essays on topical issues. Second, it offers training courses, mainly on scenario planning. Third, corporate members can choose to contract GBN's strategic-consulting services.

Schwartz believes that it is a model that suits the times. "Lots of people have tried to create the model where you get people to feel that they belong to your community—whether it is airline miles or the idea that I can go to a grocery store and get a discount because I'm a member of the loyalty program," he says. "So the notion of making people feel they belong to something that delivers value, and then building platforms of service and products on top of that, is a strong model."

Publisher Richard Stagg, of Pearson Education, attended a three-day GBN event in New York and confirms the appeal. "It was one of the most stimulating experiences' I've ever had in business," he says. "At one point, I found myself in a discussion group with the head of a Texas oil company, a filmmaker, a professor, and someone who worked with the CIA."

Exposing members to diverse perspectives is a GBN hallmark. Stagg also experienced a GBN learning journey, involving a tour of New York City. "I spent the afternoon teamed up with a teenager in a public school in the South Bronx. He told me that he used to do all his learning through the Web but he'd just discovered books. As a publisher, that really makes you stop and think. If I was a company, I would definitely join a network like that. I would send along maybe my marketing director and my brightest young thing in the strategy department."

Enough bright young things have shown interest to make GBN financially attractive: The club was bought in December 2000 for a seven-digit figure and is now part of the consulting firm Monitor.

Lucky I Ran Into You

If one of clubs' attractions is that they allow members to rub shoulders with the great and the good, another is that they allow them to do so in an informal way. There's no need to make an appointment when, with a minimum of planning, you can

Positively Churchillian

Silicon Valley's prosperity is built on a heady cocktail of brains and contacts. Among the organizations bringing the two together is the Churchill Club, based in Campbell, Calif. Founded in 1985 as a nonprofit, it now boasts more than 5,000 members and has a staff of seven.

The club, founded by *Forbes* publisher Rich Karlgaard and Anthony Perkins, chairman and editor-in-chief of Red Herring Communications, prides itself on being a place where "important people say important things."

The Churchill Club invites speakers and gives members an opportunity to network and rub shoulders with the digerati and others. Over the years, it has hosted many of the brightest stars in the high-tech firmament, including Marc Andreessen, Steve Ballmer, John Chambers, Jim Clark, Larry Ellison, Andy Grove, Meg Whitman, and a certain William Henry Gates III. Earlier this year, it received a call from the White House; George W. Bush's April 30 visit was the first time that a sitting president had addressed the Churchill Club.

As its name suggests, the Churchill doffs its cap in the general direction of the United Kingdom. "The original mission of the club was more political," explains co-executive director Kim Moeller. "The two founders thought of Jefferson and Lincoln but wanted to be nonpartisan. Winston Churchill was nonpartisan and also had a wealth of other interests apart from politics. Over the years our focus has shifted to business, technology, and entrepreneurialism."

The Churchill's highest membership level—"Prime Minister"—costs $10,000 (members include Cisco Systems, IBM, Intel, and Microsoft), "Cabinet level" membership costs $5,000 (members include McKinsey & Co. and Nortel Networks), membership in the "House of Lords" costs $2,500, and down to $1,000 "House of Commons" and $125 individual memberships.

So why do people join? "First, we present a broad range of topics, so it is a good place to get information on your industry and other industries. People also like to hear from people who started their own companies. In addition, some of our programs give very specific advice—such as a recent one on doing business in Europe," says Moeller. "The second reason is to network." Members appreciate the diversity of people they meet. They're not all from the same industry.

"For corporations, often it's a question of visibility. When companies—big or small—are interested in increasing their visibility in Silicon Valley, they join. Corporations also benefit from the networking opportunities, especially at the higher level of membership."

Moeller believes that the Churchill benefits from having panels of speakers rather than individuals running through their standard speeches. "That way you get people to say things they wouldn't normally say. We want it to be Churchillian in nature—solid information, contrarian thinking, combined with wit."

—Stuart Crainer and Des Dearlove

simply bump into the person with whom you want to speak.

In business, the boundaries of most relationships are clearly defined, circumscribed by a contract, assignment, or transaction. Opportunities to meet with potential clients and suppliers without a formal agenda are rare. Moreover, continuity of relationship depends on an ongoing stream of work.

The club is different. Continuity of relationships is provided by membership; members continue to associate over many years regardless of their formal business ties. The doors are always open—even if they're periodically redecorated.

Dallas-based ClubCorp, which operates 72 private business clubs across the United States and in Beijing and Singapore, has stayed in business by adjusting its mission over the years. At ClubCorp's 30,000-square-foot Tower Club in Dallas, local oil barons used to fly helicopters over for lunch. These days, long after the oil and real-estate booms have gone quiet, the membership mix is more diverse, with executives from law firms and accounting firms as well as tycoons, and the club offers a range of social activities. The core remains the same: a gathering place for top businesspeople who pay for the privilege of gathering.

Others in different fields have discovered the benefits of the steady revenue that a membership organization brings. Consider the Strategos Institute, part of Strategos, the consulting operation founded by Gary Hamel. Catering to both companies and individuals, the Strategos Institute is a club in all but name. The institute develops programs that offer members customized relationships and access to research and managerial tools and events such as executive workshops and summits. "Membership brings your company into an elite circle of leading-edge organizations that truly form a knowledge-creating community," according to Strategos.

Strategos has used the club model to create a new twist on conventional consulting. The beauty of its approach is that customer loyalty is built in. In traditional consulting, lines of communication go cold, and billing ends between assignments. The club model provides a continuous stream of revenue. To its members, it also offers cachet in abundance.

The Way People Will Interact

All clubs are based on common interests. Whether members share a vocation, a hobby, a neighborhood, a philosophy, or simply a desire to be rich and famous, they are bound by common threads. They have a reason to hang out together.

Many, even most, universities host business clubs for undergraduates already looking beyond their entry into the "real world"—and for those who've already spent years in the workforce. B-school students form and join more targeted groups: Harvard Business School has dozens, including the Australia & New Zealand Club, the Hospitality and Travel Industry Club, and the South Asian Business Association.

Hundreds of local business clubs around the country—indeed, around the world—provide opportunities for people to gather and network, making the kind of connections and insights that turn small businesses into midsize businesses. And in plenty of identity-based business clubs—for Gen-Xers, women, Asian-Americans—members get together in spaces they find more comfortable, to work on issues particular to their group.

It is no longer necessary to go to the clubhouse—the club can come to you.

Most of these clubs don't aspire to growth and fame independent of their members; a few aim higher. The Groucho Club, a bar and restaurant that opened its doors to London's literati in 1984, for example, was meant to be a gathering place for non-clubby media and arty types. Some 350 publishers, writers, and celebrities wrote £1,500 checks to become shareholders.

Taking its name from Groucho Marx's famous quip—"I don't want to belong to any club that will accept me as a member"—the Groucho has thrived. Last year, it was bought for £11.7 million by a consortium including PR star Matthew Freud (great-grandson of Sigmund and also Rupert Murdoch's son-in-law), but a perceived shift in the club's direction, toward glitz and commercialism, left some members unhappy and sparked defections to other London watering holes. Freud's interest lasted only a few months—in August 2002 he announced that he was selling his interest in the Groucho to his partner, restaurateur and chocolate heir Joel Cadbury. The 4,000 remaining club members are waiting to see what happens—after all, even media people need *someplace* quiet to hang out and network.

Indeed, many communities of people with mutual interests need meeting places, which presents opportunities for owners and managers of clubs as well as members. The club as marketplace or commercial matchmaking agency becomes an attractive proposition. Companies such as Garage Technology Ventures have built viable businesses out of providing marketplaces for investors and entrepreneurs to come together with a view to pursuing mutual interests. Clubs can fulfill a similar role.

Clubs' reach and potential are growing. Membership can forge new contacts in distant places or help span disparate groups. Today, an increasingly global economy demands increasingly global clubs, and technology makes that possible. Clubs that reach across national borders can provide access and instant introductions around the world.

The Internet is also spawning a new club model: the virtual club. It is no longer necessary to go to the club house—the club can come to you. One man pushing the concept is Eddie Obeng, founder of Pentacle: The Virtual Business School. Obeng, formerly a B-school lecturer, set up Pentacle in 1994. Today, it has two full-time employees, a network of management trainers, and a turnover of over $1.5 million. Obeng's latest venture is a series of cyber-clubs, dubbed New World Pioneer Clubs.

Obeng believes the days of the fusty clubhouse are numbered. "The traditional business club is heading the way of the dinosaurs," he insists. "People can't spare the time to go to meetings, to seek out people with similar backgrounds, and listen to the outdated philosophy of a management spin doctor."

The first of the Pentacle cyber-clubs, allchange.com, was launched in September 2000. The idea is to provide an interactive site to learn, shop, swap ideas, and "play." It now has more than 850 members; the annual cost of membership ranges from $675 to $7,500.

"The great thing about a club is that it has a barrier to entry," Obeng says. "The people inside want to be there, and if the barrier to entry is a particular competency or expertise, this ensures that club members have quality conversations. Once our love affair with massive corporations comes to an end, clubs will be the way in which people interact. In the short term, people are going to have to become smarter about how they market themselves during a downturn. Clubs offer one possible solution of getting to a very targeted audience in a positive environment."

Stuart Crainer and Des Dearlove are the founders of Suntop Media. Their last article was "The Best Way to Best Practices," in the July/August 2002 issue. They are currently between clubs.

THE TONE AT THE TOP and Ethical Conduct Connection

Barbara Lamberton; Paul H. Mihalek; Carl S. Smith

No company aspires to become the next poster firm for its lack of ethics. Although much debate has swirled around the topic of corporate ethics, few studies have focused on how the tone at the top can pressure accountants to materially alter results—or influence them to choose the ethical path.

To take a closer look at this issue, we conducted a study focused mainly on tone at the top and its effects on the accounting function, but we also asked about the audit function and whether the respondents had a written code of ethics. There's been lots of discussion on how these three issues affect corporate ethics. For example, professional accounting organizations, such as IMA, the American Institute of Certified Public Accountants (AICPA), and the Institute of Internal Auditors (IIA), argue that management's attitude plays a major role in reducing the risk of accounting irregularities. And according to the 1987 *Report of the National Commission on Fraudulent Financial Reporting* (Treadway Commission report), a strong internal audit function also reduces the chances of a major fraud.

So does a written code of ethics foster a strong control environment? Even though the Treadway Commission argued that written codes send an important signal to employees and help communicate expectations, a previous study by Ann Rich, Carl Smith, and Paul Mihalek in 1990 titled "Are Corporate Codes of Conduct Effective?" suggests that written codes are less than effective in terms of fostering ethical behavior. Like our study, the Rich, Smith, and Mihalek study also examined the relationship between written codes and certain management accounting practices.

This topic isn't new, and over the years the profession has issued reports and adopted standards (see "A Brief History of Financial Reporting Integrity"). We wanted our study to take the pulse of those out in the trenches today who may or may not be feeling the pressure to materially alter results.

DATA GATHERING

We gathered information from management accountants and financial managers about top management's attitude toward ethics, whether their employer had an internal audit function, and whether it had a written code of ethical conduct. The resulting questionnaire included additional demographic information, such as job title, background, and years of work experience. We also gathered information about each respondent's corporation, such as annual sales, number of employees, and type of business.

To encourage respondents to complete the questionnaire, the data-gathering process was Web based and anonymous. We e-mailed a random sample of 1,500 IMA members, requesting their input, and then gave those individuals who chose to participate a link to a website that featured the questionnaire. Of the 215 respondents, most had more than six years of applicable experience in accounting-related jobs.

While the majority of the companies reported being in business for more than 30 years, 27% reported being in business between 10 and 30 years, and 18% reported being in business less than 10. The sample included corporations of various sizes: 36.8% with annual sales in excess of $250 million, 11% between $100 and $250 million, 15% between $30 and $100 million, 19% between $10 and $30 million, and 17% totaling less than $10 million. Although the random sample included both public and private corporations, the majority were privately held with manufacturing representing the largest type of business at 33% of the sample.

TONE AT THE TOP

So how concerned is top management with ethics? More than 90% of the respondents reported that the corporation's top management was either highly or somewhat highly concerned with ethical behavior, which compares to 80% from the earlier study by Rich, Smith, and Mihalek.

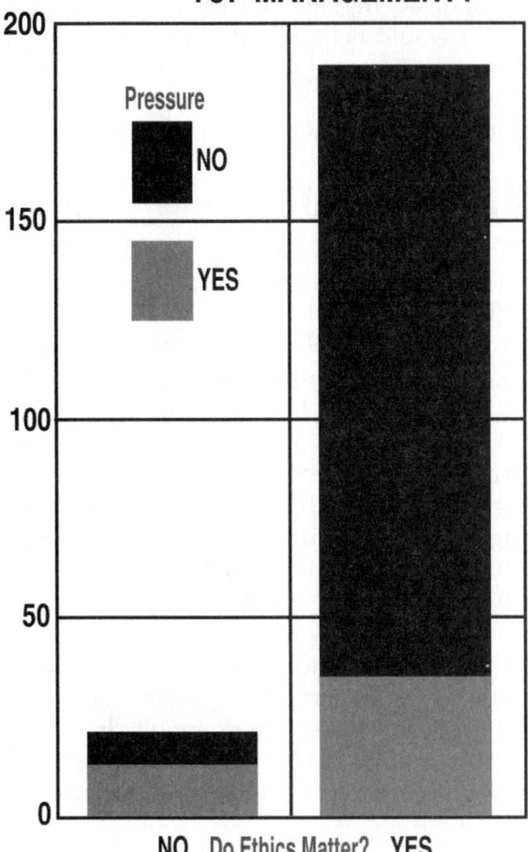

A BRIEF HISTORY OF FINANCIAL REPORTING INTEGRITY

Although recent corporate scandals have raised awareness of ethical standards, concern about the integrity of financial reporting has a long history. For example, the Foreign Corrupt Practices Act in 1977 required that each publicly traded company establish and maintain an effective internal control system to ensure management's responsibilities and actions could be pinpointed. Ten years later, in 1987, the Treadway Commission's *Report of the National Commission on Fraudulent Financial Reporting* concluded that the corporation's tone at the top plays a crucial role in reducing the likelihood of fraudulent financial reporting. This outcome reinforced the fact that corporate management needs to set the right tone by insisting on a strong system of internal controls to mitigate risk. This report also concluded that top management's ethical values pervade the corporation's accounting practices and represent a critical component of its control environment.

More recently, the AICPA's adoption of the Statement on Auditing Standards (SAS) No. 99, "Consideration of Fraud in a Financial Statement Audit," again reinforced these concepts. Within the last five years, several other events have occurred—the demise of Enron, WorldCom, and others—that further emphasized the need for an increased focus on ethics. And in response to the scandals, Congress passed the Sarbanes-Oxley Act of 2002 that dictated massive changes in the practice of accounting and broadened the responsibilities of top management related to the integrity of the financials. Scandals such as Enron and the others and the resulting loss in wealth brought to the forefront the issue of ethics in the workplace while demonstrating the destructive influence of the pursuit of profits at any cost by some top-management teams. The capital market system in the United States is based, in part, on the investing public's trust in reported financial results. By raising concerns about the integrity of financial results, the accounting scandals created a crisis of confidence among users of financial information while focusing unprecedented attention on the role of ethics among top management.

Our results also indicate that ethically concerned management is more likely to be in corporations with written codes of ethical conduct and an internal audit function.

To determine if there were a relationship between valuing ethics at the top and ethical conduct within the corporation, we asked four questions about pressures to alter performance results:

- Was there general pressure to alter results?
- Were there pressures to manipulate earnings?
- Were there pressures to manipulate accounts for calculating return on investment (ROI)?
- Were there pressures to alter the balance sheet?

Our responses (see Figure 1 for the results) indicated that:

- Twenty-two percent (48 out of 210 respondents) reported feeling pressure to alter performance results and that pressure seems to relate to the tone at the top; and
- Nearly 62% of the respondents (13 out of 21) from corporations reporting that ethics don't matter report pressure to alter or "manage" financial results.

In contrast, in corporations where the tone at the top favors ethical conduct, only 19% (35 out of 189) reported pressure to alter results. Similar results were shown with specific financial reporting measures, such as income, balance sheet, and return on investment.

THE INTERNAL AUDIT FUNCTION

More than 50% of the respondents (108 of 215) reported their corporations had internal audit departments compared to 44% in the 1990 Rich, Smith, and Mihalek study. Of the 108 respondents who worked at corporations with internal audit, 76% (82 of 108) interfaced with the company's internal audit staff, and 93% considered the internal auditors to be very knowledgeable or somewhat knowledgeable about their company. There also appeared to be a relationship between perceived knowledge of the internal auditors and the tone at the top. Nearly all respondents (94%) from companies in which top management placed a high regard on ethical conduct rated the knowledge level of their internal auditors favorably.

We also asked about internal audit's effectiveness. More than 82% of these particular respondents felt that it would be difficult to get the internal auditors to agree to questionable accounting practices, and 61% judged it would be difficult to hide negative information from them.

EXTERNAL AUDITORS

About 70% of the respondents (152 of 210) reported that their positions involved interfacing with external auditors, and 88% rated the knowledge level of the external auditors as high or somewhat high. Similar to the results for internal auditors, there appeared to be a relationship between perceived knowledge of external auditors and the tone at the top. Nearly all respondents (91%) from corporations in which top management placed high regard on ethical conduct rated the knowledge level of the external auditors favorably.

In terms of external audit's effectiveness in reducing the risk of fraudulent financial reporting, 79% responded that it would be difficult to get the external auditors to agree to questionable accounting practices, and 58% reported it would be difficult to hide negative information from them.

ETHICAL CONDUCT AND THE INDIVIDUAL

Since the Rich, Smith, and Mihalek research argued that "... ethical standards come from individuals ...," we asked respondents to rate several factors that could help them conduct themselves in an ethical manner given pressure to act otherwise. Almost all mentioned two factors. Both an individual sense of ethics (94%) and a professional code of ethics (90%) were considered important factors that would help an individual resist attempts to materially alter financial results. The results were similar regardless of the tone at the top, the existence of an internal audit function, or a written code of ethics.

ETHICS AT THE TOP MATTER

This study suggests that corporations whose top managers value ethics are less likely to pressure employees to materially alter financial results. Tone at the top plays a critical role in the control environment. And corporations whose top managers value ethics are also somewhat more likely to have their own internal audit department and a written code of ethics.

In spite of the significance of top management's attitude, however, the results also highlight the importance of hiring individuals with a high personal sense of ethics. Virtually all respondents mentioned their individual and professional ethics would play a significant role in helping them resist any attempts to materially alter financial results. Take note, academia. As stated simply in PricewaterhouseCoopers's 2003 "Educating for the Public Trust" report, "To restore the public trust in the accounting profession, the profession also needs to attract students to accounting with a strong personal sense of integrity."

***Barbara Lamberton, Ph.D.; Paul H. Mihalek, Ph.D., CPA; and Carl S. Smith, Ph.D., CMA, CFM, CPA** are professors of accounting in the Department of Accounting and Taxation at the University of Hartford in West Hartford, Conn. You can reach Barbara at lamberton@hartford.edu, Paul at mihalek@hartford.edu, and Carl at casmith@hartford.edu.*

The Road to Stronger Corporate Governance

The past two years have seen such a tidal wave of legal, regulatory and attitude change in corporate governance that it can be difficult to keep up. What key changes should your board be making in how it operates, its membership, and its relationships with management and shareholders?

Linda Zong

The past two years have revealed numerous accounting scandals, embarrassing executive pay practices, and vastly depleted pension funding among some former prominent and well-respected companies. In order to move past this difficult chapter in corporate American business, many companies are rapidly adopting new corporate governance and financial standards. Some companies are even going beyond what is required to demonstrate to investors their solid commitment to good corporate governance.

These changes in corporate governance practices include board independence, board organization, compensation committee charters and responsibilities, board evaluations and director education.

The centerpiece of reform efforts is improved corporate governance, making the board truly independent and effective. The overall aim is to suggest a constructive blueprint for serious reform.

• *Embrace independence.* In November, the Securities and Exchange Commission (SEC) approved new rules proposed and adopted by the New York Stock Exchange and the Nasdaq Stock Market requiring widespread strengthening of corporate governance standards for listed companies. The rules establish a stricter, more detailed definition of *independence* for directors and require the majority of members on listed companies' boards to satisfy that standard. In addition, the rule changes include a number of new provisions on independent director oversight of governance processes, auditing, director nominations, and compensation.

Underlying the independence requirement is the hope that it will empower directors to challenge management on critical business issues and enhance the quality of board decisions. With shareholders and regulators demanding change, directors are exercising their independence from management, raising more questions, probing more information, and spending more time dealing with issues. Corporate directors are responsible to the shareholders of their companies, not to Wall Street. They can fulfill their responsibilities by following good governance practices—beginning with a clear differentiation between the roles of management and the board.

Committee independence from management remains paramount. Committees must be free to render judgments and act upon what they see without undue management influence.

In the Sarbanes-Oxley Act, Congress put even more weight and responsibility on independent directors, or "independent watchdogs," in the words of the Supreme Court. They would supply an independent check on management and represent shareholder interests in investment company affairs. As Harvey J. Goldschmid, commissioner of the SEC said in a speech, as "watchdogs" for the shareholders, independent directors "have the responsibility to guard against abuses that emanate from conflicts of interest and noncompliance with the shareholder protections."

The best management-committee relationships are reciprocal. Committee members need management to help them understand the details of corporate financial performance, reporting processes, and internal controls. The committee, in turn, must support management in creating an environment of sound corporate governance.

Committee independence from management remains paramount. The committee must be free to render a judgment and act upon what it sees, without the undue influence of corporate management. Managers, directors, and advisors face pressures that can cause them to act in their own interests to the detriment of long-term corporate interests. Solutions include more strict standards for director independence.

First, even with an adequate definition of independence, independent directors cannot be expected to carry their monitoring load alone. They are heavily dependent on proper disclosure and the effectiveness of gatekeepers like auditors, lawyers, and compliance officers. Both proper disclosure and the loyalty of gatekeepers to independent directors must be strengthened to help independent directors fulfill their role as "watchdogs."

Second, to strengthen the loyalty of auditors to independent directors (and enhance the effectiveness of committees), audit committees must be directly responsible for the appointment, evaluation, pay, and firing (where appropriate) of the independent auditor or compensation consultant. In addition, the committee has authority to engage independent counsel, accountants, and other advisers. This is a meaningful shift from the past, when external auditors or compensation consultants were ultimately accountable to the committees, yet management was often perceived as the client.

Third, to be consistent with modern corporate governance approaches, it is fair to require the boards to establish effective programs and procedures to assist them in catching fraud or detecting violation of fiduciary duty. For example, the SEC adopted a rule requiring mutual funds and their advisers to adopt policies and procedures designed to prevent securities law violations. These include late trading, abusive market timing, and selective portfolio disclosure.

Another key element of strong corporate governance is the opportunity for outside board members to discuss issues among themselves through executive sessions. The NYSE and Nasdaq pending listing rules would require boards to have executive sessions led by an independent lead director or nonexecutive chairman. This person's responsibilities would typically include oversight of corporate governance procedures as well. According to a Mercer survey, before 2002, only six percent of the 350 large companies in Mercer's database had lead directors. The percentage is expected to increase rapidly.

A board mix of at least 75 percent independent directors seems to be the norm today. Thirty percent of boards polled now evaluate individual directors.

• *Foster transparency*. Corporate governance laws mean more mandated disclosure. There are clear guidelines for board structure, executive and board compensation, financial transparency, regulatory scrutiny, operations, and guidance on shareholder issues. For example, given the fundamental need for directors to scrutinize executive pay and performance of the management team, a board mix of at least 75 percent independent directors now seems to be the norm.

Buck Consultants surveyed Fortune 1000 companies on these issues. The highlights of survey are as follows:

- On board mechanics, the majority of respondents (81 percent) use the full board to designate committee assignments. Executive sessions are most frequently conducted by a lead director (30 percent).
- For director performance evaluation, 30 percent of respondents conduct performance evaluations of individual outside board members. The most frequently cited board performance criteria were overall contribution (95 percent) and board participation (95 percent). Sixty-three percent of respondents conduct committee evaluations in addition to the overall board evaluation.
- On director education, most respondents (78 percent) provide for internal or external director education.

There should be robust discussion on the audit methodology and compensation philosophy, the committee processes, independence and industry experience of the committee members. The general pattern moves toward more frequent meetings to probe deeply into the reasoning of the committee.

A survey conducted by KPMG's Audit Committee Institute last year found that audit committees are meeting more often, with 40 percent expecting to meet eight or more times in 2003, either in person or via conference call. Only six percent expected to meet less than four times. Based on an earlier survey, this represents a significant shift from prior practices when audit committees met, on average, only 4.1 times per year in 2000.

Transparency to shareholders and the public helps committees gain a greater understanding of business models of the companies. The proxy statement is one vehicle for companies to explain their compensation philosophy and actions, describe their governance principles, and respond to proposals from shareholders. It is a particularly important document for compensation committees, who are required to establish a forthright description of pay policies and practices. The proxy also provides a good opportunity for companies to lay out their positions on shareholder proposals, which are becoming both more prevalent and more often detailed than in the past.

• *Encourage accountability*. Raytheon chairman and CEO Dan Burnham believes that being a director is a way to give back to our country. Directors should make their views heard; chairs of board committees should actively determine agendas.

According to a McKinsey report, for the average non-executive director involved in heightened committee work (aside from participation in board meetings) the annual commitment is 20 to 25 days at minimum. Time is not the only issue here, though. The level of financial literacy deemed appropriate for board membership has ratcheted up considerably. Chairing the audit committees in financial institutions is one of the toughest non-executive jobs, demanding a 40 to 50-day commitment per year. Right now, there is a serious shortage of people who are qualified to chair the audit committees.

Independence and skill are the essence of effective board committees. In fact, the two qualities complement each other. Strong and objective independence of the directors is enhanced by deep knowledge of key business issues and qualifications for the monitoring job with full access to timely information.

Not only must members meet the evolving expectations of shareholders and regulators regarding independence and financial literacy, they must also have a thorough understanding of the business of the company. This requires understanding a broad range of issues including the business model, the economic risks and long-term sustainability, the effectiveness of internal controls, as well as the accuracy and transparency of the financial reporting.

Strengthening The Boards Of Directors

Five Basic Steps

Given the central role that independent directors must play in corporate governance and self-regulation, the following five steps should be taken to strengthen the boards of the public corporations:

• *Live with independence, transparency, and accountability.* Never in the SEC's history has aggressive enforcement effort been more central to the commission's role. *Independence, accountability* and *transparency* are the key words at the SEC. Criminal penalties for willful and venal acts are readily available and will be used if necessary. Many companies have already changed the membership of their committees and are searching for independent directors to move towards the improved corporate governance practices.

• *Set parameters for chief executives.* In the future, a board should have freedom to set the parameters within which the chief executive develops the business. Those boundaries should describe the scope of the business, the risk profile, and the enduring values of the corporation. This is a more realistic way of thinking about strategy than the way that it is often characterized by regulators.

• *Focus on performance.* Assessment of the compensation committee and an annual evaluation of the CEO's performance would be required under pending New York Stock Exchange listing requirements. With shareholders increasingly looking at the link between executive pay and performance, directors need to demand more sophisticated analyses of performance to support decisions on executive incentive plan design, target setting, stock options and total compensation levels. CEO evaluation has often been an informal process at best. Now, boards will need to define and measure performance in areas such as leadership, integrity, strategic planning, team building, and succession planning.

• *Conduct board self-assessment.* Boards are evaluating their own performance on a broad array of both quantitative and qualitative metrics, not just shareholder return. Best practices in corporate governance can be monitored through ratings by organizations such as Institutional Shareholder Services (ISS), Governance Metrics International and Standard & Poor's. For instance, corporate governance ratings will appear on the cover of every proxy analysis by ISS. Ratings will look at such factors as board structure, executive pay, financial performance, director education and compensation philosophy statements etc.

• *Adopt governance guidelines.* Companies are required by the NYSE to adopt and disclose their corporate governance guidelines, including rules for an annual performance evaluation of the board and a statement of principles for setting director pay. The guidelines should also cover CEO selection, performance review and succession planning. The compensation committee must also have its own written charter that addresses its purpose, duties, and responsibilities, consistent with the rules of the NYSE, and be subject to an annual performance evaluation by the overall board.

• *Think about revamping the "whole" system.* Paul Coombes, a McKinsey director and an expert in corporate governance, said in an interview that, while new laws and regulations on governance will help reestablish trust, we need to understand how the whole, extended system (including boards, managers, and the financial community) can work better. While boards and auditors and corporate accountability are all important, so, too, are the behavior and workings of the financial community. The whole network needs to be strengthened in the U.S. The legislative and regulatory changes thus far have addressed a series of "symptomatic" failures without articulating a view of the system as a whole and how it should work.

As part of strengthening governance, boards must expand their education and orientation programs. Boards must be able to educate and integrate new directors quickly.

Even if the boards can meet new requirements for independent director membership, they may still lack critical business skills. As part of strengthening governance, boards are implementing or expanding their education and orientation programs. The NYSE has proposed that the audit committee chair have accounting or financial management experience. Such skills may need to be brought in through new director recruitment. Since many boards will be adding new directors, board orientation becomes more important. Effective boards need procedures to educate and integrate new directors quickly.

The board chair sets the tone for much more than board meetings. The chair orchestrates board and self-evaluations, and develops competencies and criteria for future board members and chairpersons. An engaged chair leads to an engaged board, facilitates board recruitment, and substantially improves governance. Your board's chair should always be an independent director. The current scandals highlight the need for a chair who will independently ensure proper disclosure, set sensible board priorities and agendas, and encourage candid, thorough discussions in the boardroom.

To serve the chief executive, the board should be an intelligent, informed and experienced group of people with whom tough decisions can be robustly debated. Some chief executives view disagreement as disloyalty, and fear a factionalized board. They know that discord and lack of direction can result in severe penalties in the marketplace in terms of investor confidence. A truly effective board is an adaptable one, self-critical and good at handling disagreements, with diverse experiences in debating a course of action.

• *Strengthen compensation committees*. The new compensation committee guidelines will no doubt lead some companies to adjust the committee memberships and develop written charters and performance reviews. The board should set up a compensation committee of all external directors. Most importantly, boards must ensure that their committees include members who are qualified to handle compensation and financial issues, and disclose their qualifications in the annual reports.

Compensation committees need to set a pay philosophy for the company addressing principles, linkage to business goals, and the role of each element of the pay mix.

The committee must also establish a compensation philosophy for the company. This is the foundation from which all decisions on executive pay are made. The philosophy statement provides continuity, even when committee members change. To be meaningful, the statement must go beyond a simple expression of competitive positioning. It should also disclose the company's fundamental pay principles, the linkage to business goals, the role of each pay element, and the appropriate mix of compensation elements (for example, cash versus equity, fixed versus variable and short-term versus long-term).

To support this compensation philosophy, the committee must review the state of executive pay in the market on an annual basis to remain current and react to appropriate compensation-related issues. This may be accomplished by ongoing work with an external consultant, or through formal presentations at regular meetings. The committee must also review the entire executive compensation program periodically, to ensure that it remains consistent with the company's business needs, market practices, and pay philosophy. It is important for boards to continue improving the state of affairs in executive pay.

When rising executive pay is examined together with declining corporate profitability and stock prices, shareholders become enraged and demand action from the board leadership responsible. As the board is the instrument for making executive management accountable to providers of capital, one focus of corporate boards is to ensure that there are no inappropriate executive pay arrangements.

The corporate scandals in America have exposed the irrational basis on which executive pay is awarded. To improve corporate governance, pay in the form of stock should be an accurate representation of corporate profit derived from effective executive management. The increase in an executive pay package must be a reward for improved company results, not merely a reflection of a general stock market upswing. Dilution levels from stock option grants should also be monitored and curbed.

A Hewitt report from 2003 reveals that companies are preparing for shifts in director compensation practices as well. The most common types of pay for outside board members include an annual retainer (91 percent), equity compensation (87 percent), committee chair fees (78 percent) and board meeting fees (76 percent).

Within the next year, 38 percent of surveyed companies anticipate increasing the amount of pay for board retainers, and 31 percent expect to increase committee chair fees, particularly for the busy audit committee. Of companies planning to change outside director pay, 78 percent said it was in recognition of the greater demands on directors and 33 percent attributed the competitive market for highlyqualified board members.

• *Impose regulations*. Heightened SEC demands and scrutiny put pressure on board members both in terms of the time they must commit and the skills they must have to be effective. A strong regulatory model has been created together with strong policies for eliminating conflicts of interest in corporate governance.

The main changes in corporate governance laws have come in the area of stock options, such as the requirement that any material changes be approved by shareholders. These changes also include repricing or canceling previous options in lieu of new ones. There is a strong push for convergence in global accounting standards, and the Financial Accounting Standards Board (FASB) is expected to require companies to expense stock options by 2005.

Under NYSE rules released in October 2002, shareholders gained power to review stock-based plans in order to restore investor confidence. The change ends an era in which companies could take advantage of exemptions to issue shares under broadbased stock plans or using treasury stock without shareholder approval. Similar new listing requirements were also issued by Nasdaq for companies traded through that system.

The shareholder approval requirement has a huge impact on broad-based equity awards such as stock options and ad hoc awards, especially those by technology companies. These companies typically used the broad-based plan exemption. Elimination of the treasury stock exemption will also have an impact. For many companies, using treasury stock to satisfy unapproved stock-based awards was a convenient way to meet small or unexpected share requirements for bonus payouts and deferred stock arrangements. Companies will now lose this exemption, and shareholders must approve equity pay even if the shares come from a company's treasury.

New NYSE listing requirements eliminate the broker non-vote rule for stock-based incentive plans. Because shares voted in this manner usually support the plans, companies will lose this cushion of votes.

The NYSE listing requirements also eliminate the broker non-vote rule for stock-based incentive plans. Under current rules, brokers holding shares on behalf of clients are allowed to vote the shares themselves in the absence of specific client instructions, including approval of stock plans utilizing less than five percent of outstanding shares. Since shares voted in this manner usually support stock plans, companies will lose this cushion of votes, especially significant in today's era of close votes on plans.

The regulations also stipulate that compensation committees be comprised of independent directors, diligently conducting matters relating to executive compensation. The Sarbanes-Oxley Act further prohibits grant of loans to directors and senior executives of companies.

No member of the board or management team should have any interest that conflicts or competes with the interests of shareholders.

Board members and managers serve in the interests of the owners of the business, and there should be no tolerance for board members or executives who do not exhibit complete fidelity and devotion to shareholders. No member of the board or management team should have any interest that conflicts or competes with the interests of shareholders. The board, acting as representatives of the shareholders, is responsible for monitoring the management team. Board members should be empowered to thoroughly review decisions proposed by management.

Disclosure of the business' operations and results should lean towards being more complete rather than less complete. Shareholders' interests are best served by simultaneous, widespread disclosure of information about the company. Companies should strictly adhere to generally accepted accounting principles, presenting sound financial data for shareholders to make informed decisions.

Moving forward, companies will need to engage in dialogue with their entire range of stakeholders, not just investors. This is where good governance meets corporate social responsibility. The restoration of trust, integrity, and credibility between public companies and their shareholders is imperative to our capital markets.

Corporate boards and their committees have been entrusted with a major role in corporate governance. Successful committee oversight will require not only compliance with the new laws and regulations, but a process of open communication, devotion to due diligence and independence, and the application of authority to management and the external auditor, attorneys and advisors.

Linda Zong *is a senior compensation analyst with Royal Caribbean Cruise, Ltd. She is a Certified Compensation Professional, Certified Benefits Professional and Global Remuneration Professional.*

UP to the challenge

Are you ready to take the next big step? Meet 3 entrepreneurs who got the chance of a lifetime to push past their problems and make their businesses boom.

Mark Henricks

Entrepreneurs are famous for being loners—committed individualists who seek neither advice nor approval from anyone or anything but their own vision of what their enterprises could one day become. But perhaps that reputation should be revised, because it's easy to find entrepreneurs who are actually ready and willing to accept help in overcoming the obstacles to achieving their goals.

Entrepreneur asked three company founders in three different industries and at three different sales levels to name the primary obstacles preventing them from reaching the next level. Then these problems were posed to panels of experts consisting of business advisors, consultants and experienced entrepreneurs. The problems and some recommended solutions follow.

SmartsCo: Building Better Distribution

In three years, Julie Tucker has grown her startup business to nearly $800,000 in annual sales and two employees, along with a raft of subcontracted designers and others. Last year, SmartsCo was a winner in the Make Mine a $Million women-owned business awards sponsored by American Express and Count Me In, a nonprofit organization supporting female entrepreneurs. Along with recognition, the prize included loans of up to $45,000 and a year of coaching. Now, the San Francisco entrepreneur says the main obstacle standing between her and $1 million in sales is building better channels for distributing the themed trivia games she publishes. Currently, SmartsCo relies on independent sales reps to market its products to bookstores and gift retailers.

"It's like herding cats," Tucker, 37, says of the six sales-rep organizations—fielding a total of 40 reps—that she deals with. "You find them, you sign them up and get them trained in your product, but they're never really working for you." Competition with reps' other product lines, lack of a large product line of her own and failure to land any big national retailer accounts are all problems Tucker cites with her sales-rep distribution approach.

Tucker is focused on the right problem, according to Carol Rehtmeyer, president of Rehtmeyer Inc., an Aurora, Illinois, toy development and manufacturing company. "The most important thing is distribution," she stresses. "You can create the most exciting product, but if you don't get it in front of the public, your product will die."

Rehtmeyer says Tucker will get more attention from reps and retailers if she improves the packaging, reduces the $17 to $25 price range, and considers boosting her product's value by adding samples of or coupons for related products. Co-marketing, such as a tie-in with Starbucks for her coffee-themed game, is another promising area.

SmartsCo needs a full-time employee to manage its network of sales reps, says Salt Lake City small-business consultant Kent Capener. Better yet, major account sales could be done in-house. Capener also recommends finding new retail distribution channels. The food, coffee, wine and beer games should be pitched to specialty store chains to be sold alongside the products the games are about.

SmartsCo's sex trivia game calls for a different approach. "We recommend SmartsCo considers selling this game to the public through direct-response television," Capener says. He suggests test-marketing on a limited scale, followed by a broader rollout if it proves successful.

Richard X. Zawitz, CEO of Tangle Inc., a South San Francisco, California, toymaker, wants Tucker to personally promote the company's products to retailers through industry trade shows. Commissioned sales reps can't be expected to bring an entrepreneur's knowledge and devotion to selling a company's product, he believes. "Sales is the key," he says. "To get sales, you have to go to gift shows."

Zawitz also recommends that Tucker look into new channels of distribution. On his list of possibilities are advertising specialties, business premiums and prizes, international markets and—again—co-marketing tie-ins with established retailers in the niches covered by the games.

Tucker says she already goes to several gift shows and has had some success with business premiums. The company has also hired a part-time person to oversee reps and try to reach national accounts. She resisted any suggestion that packaging or content required tweaking: "That's where our biggest strength is, based on what we hear from our retailers," she says. She hadn't thought of selling the adult-theme game through direct-response TV. The company has begun selling through its website, however, and Tucker speculates that a similar fulfillment mechanism would work with TV.

PoshTots: Attracting Top Talent

Karen Booth Adams has grown online children's furniture retailer PoshTots to $6 million in sales and now faces the challenge of luring top-shelf software developers to Richmond, Virginia, if she is to reach the next rung on her growth ladder: $10 million. "We need people with large e-commerce company expertise, and there aren't a lot of e-commerce companies here to pull resources from," says Adams, 36, who co-founded the company with Andrea Edmunds, 38, in 2000.

PoshTots' talent challenge is especially pressing because Adams plans to expand into web publishing. "There are lots of content-oriented companies in New York City and other [large] cities," she says. "But there aren't a lot of people with experience in online ad sales and e-content here."

Experts and experienced entrepreneurs agree that PoshTots must look beyond Richmond for its talent, and that the keys to doing so effectively are within the company's grasp. Step one is to decide what it is about PoshTots' culture or history that would make a sought-after programmer want to work there, says Jeffrey Davis, chairman and founder of Needham, Massachusetts-based small-business consulting firm Mage LLC.

"All businesses that grow have a story," Davis says. "The more powerful the story, the more it draws people into the organization, because they feel a kinship between themselves and the organization." PoshTots should use its website to express that culture and lure employees as well as customers, he adds, noting that the website lacks information about what it's like to work there and doesn't have a "Careers" page listing employment opportunities.

Mark LeBlanc, a La Jolla, California, small-business consultant, says Adams should try to think about what type of skilled technologist might be lured to her company from a rival in a bigger tech center. In addition to job-related skills, LeBlanc says she should look for people who have attitudes that could make working in an environment such as Richmond highly attractive. For example, a big-city technologist who grew up in a small town might like the idea of a less expensive, slower-paced lifestyle. "When you're creating ads and postings, home in on the attitudes and environmental triggers," LeBlanc says. "That's how you attract the right people."

In the mirror might be the best place to look for PoshTots' assets, says Steven Pribramsky, managing partner at Key West, Florida, accounting and business consulting firm Pribramsky & Zuelch. While he recommends hiring a professional recruiter, he says that whoever does the recruiting should be tasked only with identifying candidates—the rest should be left to Adams.

That's because, in an entrepreneurial company led by a dynamic CEO such as Adams, the co-founder's personality will inevitably put its stamp on the firm's culture. "Whoever comes to work for PoshTots is coming to work for her," Pribramsky says. "She's probably the best marketing piece in the place."

Adding a career page to PoshTots' site is on Adams' to-do list. She likes the idea of looking for new hires who match big-time skills with small-town origins. "A lot of times, if they are willing to move to Richmond, that is their background," she agrees. As for taking a personal hand in hiring, that's a foregone conclusion, given that Adams began her career as a recruiter: "I do all the final interviews with everybody we hire."

Hosted Solutions: Striving for Systematic Growth

Rich Lee, 40, has grown a managed and dedicated website-hosting company to 43 employees and $13 million in revenue in just four years. The Cary, North Carolina, entrepreneur knows that taking Hosted Solutions Inc. to the next level will require different systems, skills and people.

Geographic expansion is imperative. "We are a strong regional player, focused mostly in the Southeast around Carolina and Virginia," Lee says. "Our clients are asking for another facility that is across the mountains or in a different time zone so they can do disaster recovery and data replication [at] a site that is not so close to the three we have now."

He's considering either growing organically or acquiring a smaller regional player, perhaps on the West Coast. But before he does that, he feels he needs to extract and codify the skills and practices his employees have developed so the company can replicate them in a distant location. He also wants to systemize his business so that everything from setting up a new client account to handling trouble tickets is standardized and, as much as possible, automated. "We're coming under a lot more scrutiny from our clients," he says. "They want to come in and see we have best practices in place."

Pribramsky recommends Lee consider assembling focus groups of a half-dozen or so of the best managers and

ASKING FOR HELP

Few people are busier than the founders and heads of growing companies, but if you're an entrepreneur with a question, few people are more likely to take time to give you a well-informed answer. Successful entrepreneurs report that advice from seasoned businesspeople is critical, and these experts are often eager to help.

Any entrepreneur who has overcome the problems you face is a candidate, says Monica Doss, president of the Council for Entrepreneurial Development in Research Triangle Park, North Carolina. The entrepreneur can be in your own industry or a related one, as long as he or she isn't a direct competitor or allied with one as supplier, customer or investor, adds Doss, whose nonprofit organization helps small firms with networking, mentoring and other challenges.

Start with a request for lunch and nothing more, Doss advises. "Most entrepreneurs are not willing to sign on to a long-term mentoring relationship upfront," she says. "Once they've gotten interested, it happens. But they're wary on the front end." It helps if you can get an introduction or referral from a mutual friend or colleague. One entrepreneur Doss knows identifies businesspeople he wants advice from and then arranges to attend a speech or panel discussion they're participating in. He approaches them afterward to request a meeting.

At the first meeting, make sure there are no conflicts of interest. Next, focus on chemistry and whether the person is willing and able to give the advice you need. Should a relationship develop, Doss says, give back by referring job candidates, potential customers and investors to your mentor.

Even if you don't have much to offer your mentor, you'll find other entrepreneurs don't mind helping. Carol Rehtmeyer, president of toy development and manufacturing company Rehtmeyer Inc. in Aurora, Illinois, meets many entrepreneurs through her company, but was so interested in SmartsCo that she called CEO Julie Tucker to talk to her directly about the company's challenges. Says Rehtmeyer, "I just had to touch base with SmartsCo to help them with their pricing and product."

line employees for a particular function, then brainstorm with them to develop rules so that what they do can be repeated across the company. "Those are going to be the gospel going forward," Pribramsky says.

As best practices are identified, a corporate scorecard summarizing important techniques, company values and key metrics will keep Lee and his employees rallied around the new way, says Andrew W. Marcou, director of strategic consulting for CBIZ, a Bethesda, Maryland, national accounting firm. "[The scorecard] will help him communicate with his internal management team and also to external people," says Marcou.

To acquire the expertise necessary to implement the systems, Susan Wilson Solovic, CEO of St. Louis-based online small-business TV network SBTV.com, recommends Lee consider hiring a senior executive with large-company experience. "There is a lot of good human capital available because large companies have downsized, and people with 20 or 25 years' experience doing this kind of work are looking for a job," she says.

The experts' advice resonates with Lee. In fact, he is already studying up on scorecards and preparing to interview a former large-company executive as a candidate for chief technology officer. The focus group was one idea he hadn't thought of, but likes: "That could be a great place to start getting stuff out of people's heads."

MARK HENRICKS is Entrepreneur's *"Staff Smarts" columnist.*

Determining The Strategies And Tactics Of Ownership Succession

By **James Ahern**

Roger Lockwood had two careers; his first was as a professional baseball player in the 1960s. After retiring from baseball, his second career started when he founded his own materials distribution company.

Roger was successful in attracting customers to his new business because of name recognition from his first career and because of his business smarts. His company grew, and by the mid-1990s, revenues approached $20 million.

The deck is stacked against the entrepreneur; only one-third of companies successfully transition to a second generation of ownership

However, Roger had some concerns. His grown children were not interested in the business, and his wife wanted to spend more time with him, pursuing travel and hobbies. Personally, Roger decided he was tired of bearing the responsibility for his company and was at a crossroads—what path of ownership succession should he take?

Roger's situation (his profile has been changed to protect his privacy) parallels that of all successful entrepreneurs. Owners don't live forever, so strategies and tactics must be devised to execute a successful transition. Unfortunately, it seems the deck is stacked against the entrepreneur; it's estimated that only one-third of companies successfully transition to a second generation of ownership.

But, when business owners carefully evaluate the available exit strategies and work with experts in the field (lawyers, business valuators and insurance professionals), a successful transition can be made.

Before determining potential tactics of ownership succession, business owners need to do some soul searching and consider themselves, their family, money, employees, and taxes. These business owners must answer some difficult questions, such as:

1) Do you want out completely? Would you like to stay on as long as possible, but with reduced responsibility?

2) Do you want the company to be a legacy for your children? Are your heirs capable of running the firm, and if not, should they continue to own stock in the firm?

3) How much money do you need from the business to make personal retirement comfortable? Is that amount feasible if you want to walk away from the firm?

4) Is the management team capable of successfully running the firm? Should they be given the opportunity?

5) What will Uncle Sam take from any transaction? What tactics can help minimize the amount paid in taxes?

Business owners have a number of options to execute ownership transition, which we will consider here.

Outright Sale. Probably the most obvious choice is to sell the company, pay taxes on the sale of the business and move on. It should be noted that third-party sales can have some strings attached (usually an employment contract for one to three years, an escrow account for potential liabilities at closing, and potential pay-outs over time through a seller note), but they can represent the simplest exit route for an owner.

But third-party sales may not always be clean. Notes issued to the sellers may not be repaid on a timely basis, and in many instances, an owner can forget about having an enduring legacy when an acquirer takes over the company—it is often barely recognizable a year or two later.

Transition To Children. Another ownership transfer alternative is to transition the company to one's children. Some entrepreneurs have children who are active and want to see the business stay "in the family." This means the company retains all previous customer, employee and vendor relationships, including those with its insurers.

There are, however, roadblocks to this kind of transition, which can include deciding who among the active family members should lead the firm (management by committee is no way to run a business), and how to share the ownership among the second generation. Should the family members who do not work at the firm be eligible for a "free ride" based on the efforts of their sibling(s) leading the company?

And last but not least—the federal government assesses a tax on shares gifted from one generation to the next. Furthermore, in the event of an untimely death, the estate tax liability can be daunting. In this exit strategy, it is essential to look into the variety of insurance products available to ensure a smooth transition and to protect against unforeseen events.

Sale To Management. In a sale to management, the people who have worked closely with the entrepreneur buy out the owner and run the firm. Since they know the business very well, management teams can maintain important customer relationships and continue the prosperity of the company. Unfortunately, management teams also often lack the financial wherewithal to make a cash purchase for 100% of the stock, leaving the owner to take a note or retain an equity stake that would allow the owner a second chance to cash out more stock in future years.

In this kind of transition, sellers can retain a position with the firm. With diminished responsibilities, however, the former owner may lose interest in continuing to work for the company. In addition, unless some provisions have been made, capital gains taxes are payable in each sale, reducing net proceeds to the seller. Banks supporting a sale-to-management strategy will insist on corporate-owned life insurance policies on the buyers to protect against loan repayment problems that could arise due to a premature death.

Sale To Employees. For owners interested in deferring capital gains taxes on the sale of their stock, Employee Stock Ownership Plans, or ESOPs, are worth investigating. ESOPs are defined contribution employee benefit plans designed to hold employer stock. Congress chose to emphasize ESOPs as an ownership transition tool, and as a result, provided a capital gains tax deferral benefit to sellers.

The benefit to the ESOP as buyer is that it can repay the loan it used to acquire the seller's shares—both principal and in—terest-in pretax rather than after-tax dollars. This makes the ESOP exit strategy more favorable to the seller than the management buyout alternative because the principal repayment of the bank or seller note is not tax-deductible in a management buyout.

An owner selling to an ESOP can choose a staggered sale by first selling a minority interest to the ESOP and selling the remaining shares thereafter. This piecemeal approach allows the owner to take some cash off the table and diversify assets. Whether an owner sells all or a partial interest to an ESOP, insurance products once again become important because the bank or seller may require corporate-owned life insurance to support loan repayment in the event a tragedy befalls a key employee.

Close The Doors. Finally, an owner may choose to sell all assets, collect the receivables, pay all liabilities and close the business. Generally this option is exercised by firms that do not have an important role in their markets or are in a market that is rapidly declining. Profitable businesses with a talented workforce, a strong customer list, dedicated suppliers, and product or service proficiency lose all of that value if the business is closed.

An owner should be sure none of the company's intangible assets are salable before proceeding to shut the doors.

Owners planning for succession need to exercise introspection to determine what is important to them before choosing an exit strategy. Each approach to exiting a business has advantages and disadvantages. But, with a carefully structured and executed transition plan, a business owner can truly enjoy a blissful retirement.

James Ahern is a principal at Lakeshore Valuation, L.L.C. in Chicago, Ill. He can be reached at jahern@lakeshore-valuation.com

In fourth year of 'war on terror': successes, failures, blowback from Iraq

CHARLES J. HANLEY

In 2005 the instant terror of exploding bombs and broken bodies gripped central London and teeming New Delhi, Egypt's holiday beaches and Jordan's hilltop hotels. But for the fourth year since the black morning of Sept. 11, the U.S. homeland again was spared a major terror attack.

In the counterterrorist front lines, they're on edge.

"I remain very concerned about what we are not seeing," FBI Director Robert Mueller said early in the year, speaking of possible covert cells in America. Later, as the year waned, FBI analyst Donald Van Duyn told The Associated Press, "I think there's increasing pressure on al-Qaida to do something."

The counterterror campaign scored successes in 2005, killing or capturing key figures around the globe, including a supposed top al-Qaida operative, and sending scores to prison. In midyear, Pakistani President Gen. Pervez Musharraf even ventured that "we have broken their back."

But al-Qaida chief Osama bin Laden and deputy Ayman al-Zawahri remained at large, presumably in the Pakistan-Afghanistan border region. And not long after Musharraf spoke, al-Zawahri spoke, too, declaring in a videotape that America's losses from the Sept. 11, 2001, attacks, when almost 3,000 people died, "are merely the losses from the initial clashes."

In Iraq in particular, terrorism's back was far from broken in 2005.

Hundreds of Iraqis continued to die in a seemingly endless string of suicide and other bombings, from a February car-bomb attack in Hillah that killed 125, mostly police and national guard recruits, to two days of bombings in mid-November that killed a like number of civilians at mosques and a funeral procession north and east of Baghdad.

Iraq is "the central front in the war on terror," U.S. President George W. Bush asserted in a speech Nov. 30 at the U.S. Naval Academy. If so, it became such when the U.S. invasion in 2003 stirred up an insurgent resistance and drew hundreds of Islamic militants from the Arab world to expel the invaders.

Now the Iraq war is producing a new cadre of "professionalized" terrorists who will spread around the globe, the U.S. National Intelligence Council warns.

That blowback seems to have begun.

On Nov. 11 in Morocco, for example, authorities arrested 17 men who allegedly plotted to bomb tourist hotels, led by two European-Arab veterans of the Iraq conflict. The deadliest repercussion from Iraq had come two nights earlier, however, in Jordan's capital, Amman, when three bombers struck three international hotels simultaneously, killing themselves and 59 other people.

The carnage was worst at a wedding party, where the newlyweds' fathers and the bride's mother were among the dead. The three killers were Iraqis, and al-Qaida in Iraq claimed responsibility, denouncing Jordan's ties to Washington. One bomber's wife, who herself failed to detonate an explosives belt that night, had three brothers who were killed by U.S. forces in Iraq, friends said.

Along with newly trained terrorists exported from Iraq, the al-Qaida movement in 2005 seemed to rely more on local "jihadists" who gain video inspiration from the movement, but little else.

Four suicide bombers who struck in London on July 7, killing 52 rush-hour commuters on underground trains and a bus, were British Muslims. In a video that surfaced later, one spoke of being inspired by bin Laden, al-Zawahri and Abu-Musab al-Zarqawi, leader of al-Qaida in Iraq.

"We are at war, and I am a soldier," said one of the bombers, Mohammed Sidique Khan, who had traveled to Pakistan in 2004.

In Egypt's Sinai Peninsula, too, the suicide bombers were believed homegrown.

On July 23, in Sinai's Sharm el-Sheik seaside resort, car bombs and a knapsack bomb tore through a luxury hotel, a market street and the entrance to a beach promenade, killing at least 64 Egyptians and foreign tourists. By October, Egyptian authorities were claiming they had killed the organizer and bombmaker, and had captured others connected with the plot.

A fourth major attack terrorized the people of New Delhi on Oct. 29, eve of a Hindu holiday in the Indian capital, when three bombs went off in markets packed with shoppers and on a bus, killing 60 people. Indian authorities, who quickly made arrests, blamed Muslim militants fighting for Kashmiri secession.

The tactics of terror—of killing innocents, of striking "soft" targets—besieged dozens of countries in 2005. Some like Spain and Sri Lanka have long been bloodied by nationalist insurgencies. In Bangladesh, rocked by a rash of bombings, the terror was relatively new. In Israel, the number of Palestinian suicide bombings fell, as a spotty cease-fire took hold and a 26-foot-high security barrier reached farther along the West Bank border.

Most of the bombings and assassinations occurred in the Islamic world, both on the periphery of Muslim militancy, from southern Russia to Indonesia's island of Bali, and in the Islamic heartland.

In Saudi Arabia, after a series of devastating attacks in 2003-04, authorities aggressively hunted down terror suspects in 2005, killing two identified as leaders of al-Qaida's Saudi branch. Al-Qaida's al-Zawahri, in a tape that surfaced Dec. 11, acknowledged this "defeat."

In Indonesia, in a raid on his hideout on Nov. 9, anti-terrorist forces killed Azahari bin Husin, said to be a key bombmaker for the al-Qaida-linked Jemaah Islamiyah group.

In Pakistan's rugged tribal borderlands, U.S.-Pakistani teamwork led to a missile strike on a mud-walled house Dec. 1 that killed Hamza Rabia, described as a close aide to al-Qaida's al-Zawahri. Six months earlier, U.S. intelligence led Pakistani forces to the capture of Abu Farraj al-Libbi, reputed al-Qaida No. 3. By year's end, however, with al-Libbi in U.S. interrogators' hands, al-Qaida's elusive top two still appeared no closer to capture.

As they have since 2001, governments sought to toughen anti-terrorism laws—in Britain, for example, by allowing police to detain terror suspects for up to three months without charge. Since July's London bombings, the British also have sought to deport 10 Muslim militants, not for any crime, but because they allegedly helped create the "climate" for attacks.

In Spain, France, the Netherlands and elsewhere in 2005, scores of terrorists were convicted and sent away to years in prison. In a U.S. federal court, Zacarias Moussaoui, the only suspect to face U.S. charges in the Sept. 11 attacks, pleaded guilty in April to conspiring to commit terrorism and kill Americans, among other counts, and will be sentenced next year to death or life imprisonment.

But terror prosecutions sometimes faltered.

In the biggest Spanish case, with 17 defendants, suspects allegedly tied to the Sept. 11 attacks were convicted only on lesser charges. The same held true for Indonesia's Abu Bakar Bashir, reputed spiritual leader of the deadly Jemaah Islamiyah, who was sent to prison for only 2 1/2 years.

Later, from his cell, Bashir described the latest Bali bombings, killing 23 people in three tourist restaurants Oct. 1, as a warning from God.

Index

R

S

T

U

V

W

X

Y

Z

Test Your Knowledge Form

We encourage you to photocopy and use this page as a tool to assess how the articles in *Annual Editions* expand on the information in your textbook. By reflecting on the articles you will gain enhanced text information. You can also access this useful form on a product's book support Web site at *http://www.mhcls.com/online/*.

NAME: DATE:

TITLE AND NUMBER OF ARTICLE:

BRIEFLY STATE THE MAIN IDEA OF THIS ARTICLE:

LIST THREE IMPORTANT FACTS THAT THE AUTHOR USES TO SUPPORT THE MAIN IDEA:

WHAT INFORMATION OR IDEAS DISCUSSED IN THIS ARTICLE ARE ALSO DISCUSSED IN YOUR TEXTBOOK OR OTHER READINGS THAT YOU HAVE DONE? LIST THE TEXTBOOK CHAPTERS AND PAGE NUMBERS:

LIST ANY EXAMPLES OF BIAS OR FAULTY REASONING THAT YOU FOUND IN THE ARTICLE:

LIST ANY NEW TERMS/CONCEPTS THAT WERE DISCUSSED IN THE ARTICLE, AND WRITE A SHORT DEFINITION:

We Want Your Advice

ANNUAL EDITIONS revisions depend on two major opinion sources: one is our Advisory Board, listed in the front of this volume, which works with us in scanning the thousands of articles published in the public press each year; the other is you—the person actually using the book. Please help us and the users of the next edition by completing the prepaid article rating form on this page and returning it to us. Thank you for your help!

ANNUAL EDITIONS: Management, 14/e

ARTICLE RATING FORM

Here is an opportunity for you to have direct input into the next revision of this volume. We would like you to rate each of the articles listed below, using the following scale:

1. **Excellent: should definitely be retained**
2. **Above average: should probably be retained**
3. **Below average: should probably be deleted**
4. **Poor: should definitely be deleted**

Your ratings will play a vital part in the next revision. Please mail this prepaid form to us as soon as possible. Thanks for your help!

RATING	ARTICLE
________	1. The Manager's Job: Folklore and Fact
________	2. Success in Management
________	3. The New Organisation
________	4. It's a Flat World, After All
________	5. Globalization and the American Labor Force
________	6. Choose the Right Tools for Internal Control Reporting
________	7. Let's Be Friends
________	8. Embracing Confusion: What Leaders Do When They Don't Know What to Do
________	9. Why Environmental Scanning Works Except When You Need It
________	10. Six Priorities That Make a Great Strategic Decision
________	11. Classifying the Elements of Work
________	12. The Dark Side of Change
________	13. The Change-Capable Organization
________	14. Build Your Own Change Model
________	15. A Theory of Human Motivation
________	16. The True Measure of a CEO
________	17. The Myth of Charismatic Leaders
________	18. Can One Man Save GM?
________	19. Disaster's Future
________	20. An Uneasy Look at Performance Appraisal
________	21. Zero In on the Numbers
________	22. Corporate Security Management: What's Common? What Works?
________	23. Quality Is Easy
________	24. Mail Preparation Total Quality Management
________	25. Management Women and the New Facts of Life
________	26. The Health-Care Tussle
________	27. Who Are You Really Hiring?
________	28. The Next Bubble?
________	29. Turning Boomers Into Boomerangs
________	30. Do Americans Work Too Hard?
________	31. The Discipline of Innovation
________	32. Thinking Locally, Succeeding Globally
________	33. The Great Wal-Mart of China
________	34. American Corporations: The New Sovereigns
________	35. The Real Reason You're Working So Hard...and What You Can Do About It
________	36. For New "Old Boys" Only
________	37. The Tone at the Top and Ethical Conduct Connection
________	38. The Road to Stronger Corporate Governance
________	39. Up to the Challenge
________	40. Determining the Strategies and Tactics of Ownership Succession
________	41. In Fourth Year of 'War on Terror': Successes, Failures, Blowback from Iraq

(Continued on next pa

ANNUAL EDITIONS: MANAGEMENT, 14/e

NO POSTAGE NECESSARY IF MAILED IN THE UNITED STATES

BUSINESS REPLY MAIL
FIRST CLASS MAIL PERMIT NO. 551 DUBUQUE IA

POSTAGE WILL BE PAID BY ADDRESEE

McGraw-Hill Contemporary Learning Series
2460 KERPER BLVD
DUBUQUE, IA 52001-9902

ABOUT YOU

Name Date

Are you a teacher? ❒ A student? ❒
Your school's name

Department

Address City State Zip

School telephone #

YOUR COMMENTS ARE IMPORTANT TO US!

Please fill in the following information:
For which course did you use this book?

Did you use a text with this ANNUAL EDITION? ❒ yes ❒ no
What was the title of the text?

What are your general reactions to the *Annual Editions* concept?

Have you read any pertinent articles recently that you think should be included in the next edition? Explain.

Are there any articles that you feel should be replaced in the next edition? Why?

Are there any World Wide Web sites that you feel should be included in the next edition? Please annotate.

ntact you for editorial input? ❒ yes ❒ no
ote your comments? ❒ yes ❒ no